BLACK PANTHER

THE INTERGALACTIC EMPIRE OF WAKANDA
PART FOUR

Ta-Nehisi Coates
WRITER

Ryan Bodenheim (#19-23), Daniel Acuña (#20, #22-25) & Brian Stelfreeze (#25)
ARTISTS

Michael Garland (#19-20), Daniel Acuña (#20, #22-25), Chris O'Halloran (#21-23) & Laura Martin (#25)
COLOR ARTISTS

VC's Joe Sabino
LETTERER

Meghan Hetrick (#19) & Daniel Acuña (#20-25)
COVER ART

Sarah Brunstad
ASSOCIATE EDITOR

D1244719

BLACK PANTHER CREATED BY **Stan Lee** & **Jack Kirby**

COLLECTION EDITOR JENNIFER GRÜNWALD
ASSISTANT EDITOR DANIEL KIRCHHOFFER
ASSISTANT MANAGING EDITOR MAIA LOY
ASSISTANT MANAGING EDITOR LISA MONTALBANO

VP PRODUCTION & SPECIAL PROJECTS JEFF YOUNGQUIST
BOOK DESIGNER JAY BOWEN WITH ADAM DEL RE
SVP PRINT, SALES & MARKETING DAVID GABRIEL
EDITOR IN CHIEF C.B. CEBULSKI

BLACK PANTHER BOOK 9: THE INTERGALACTIC EMPIRE OF WAKANDA PART FOUR. Contains material originally published in magazine form as BLACK PANTHER (2018) #19-25. First printing 2021. ISBN 978-1-302-92110-1. Published by MARVEL WORLDWIDE, INC., a subsidiary of MARVEL ENTERTAINMENT, LLC. OFFICE OF PUBLICATION: 1290 Avenue of the Americas, New York, NY 10104. © 2021 MARVEL. No similarity between any of the names, characters, persons, and/or institutions in this magazine with those of any living or dead person or institution is intended, and any such similarity which may exist is purely coincidental. Printed in Canada. KEVIN FEIGE, Chief Creative Officer; DAN BUCKLEY, President, Marvel Entertainment; JOE QUESADA, EVP & Creative Director; DAVID BOGART, Associate Publisher & SVP of Talent Affairs; TOM BREVOORT, VP, Executive Editor; NICK LOWE, Executive Editor, VP of Content, Digital Publishing; DAVID GABRIEL, VP of Print & Digital Publishing; JEFF YOUNGQUIST

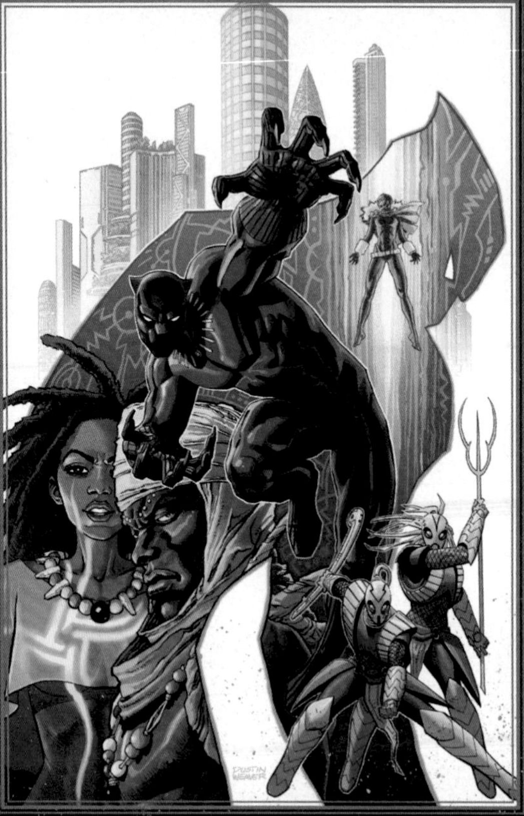
DUSTIN WEAVER

Dustin Weaver
19 VARIANT

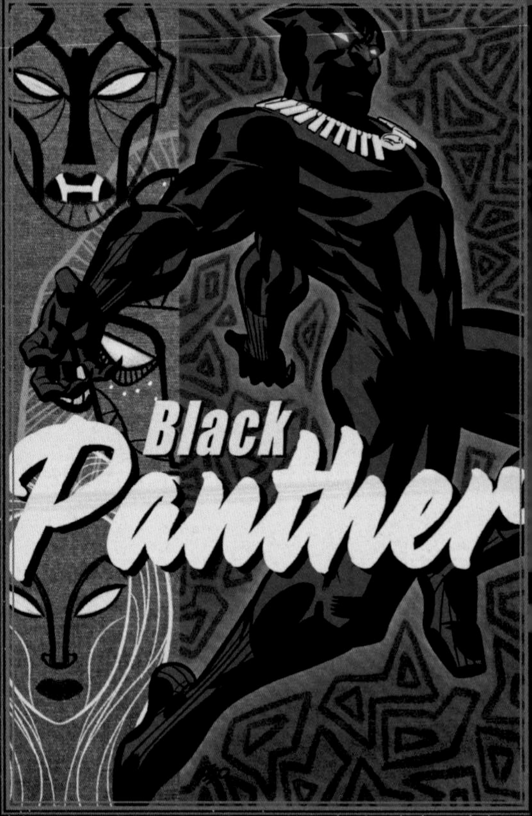
Black
Panther

Michael Cho
20 VARIANT

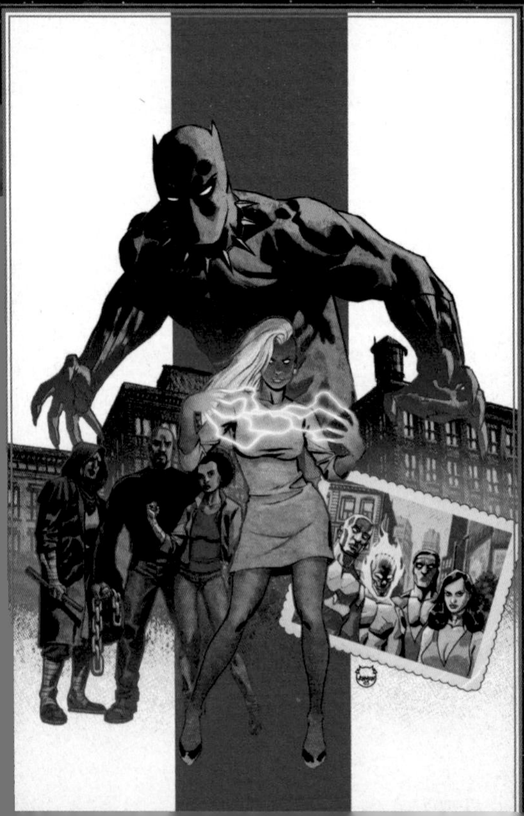

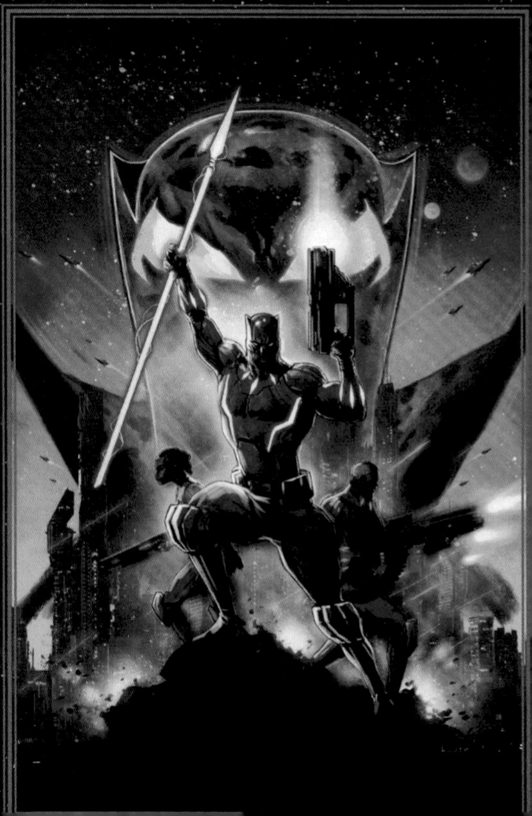

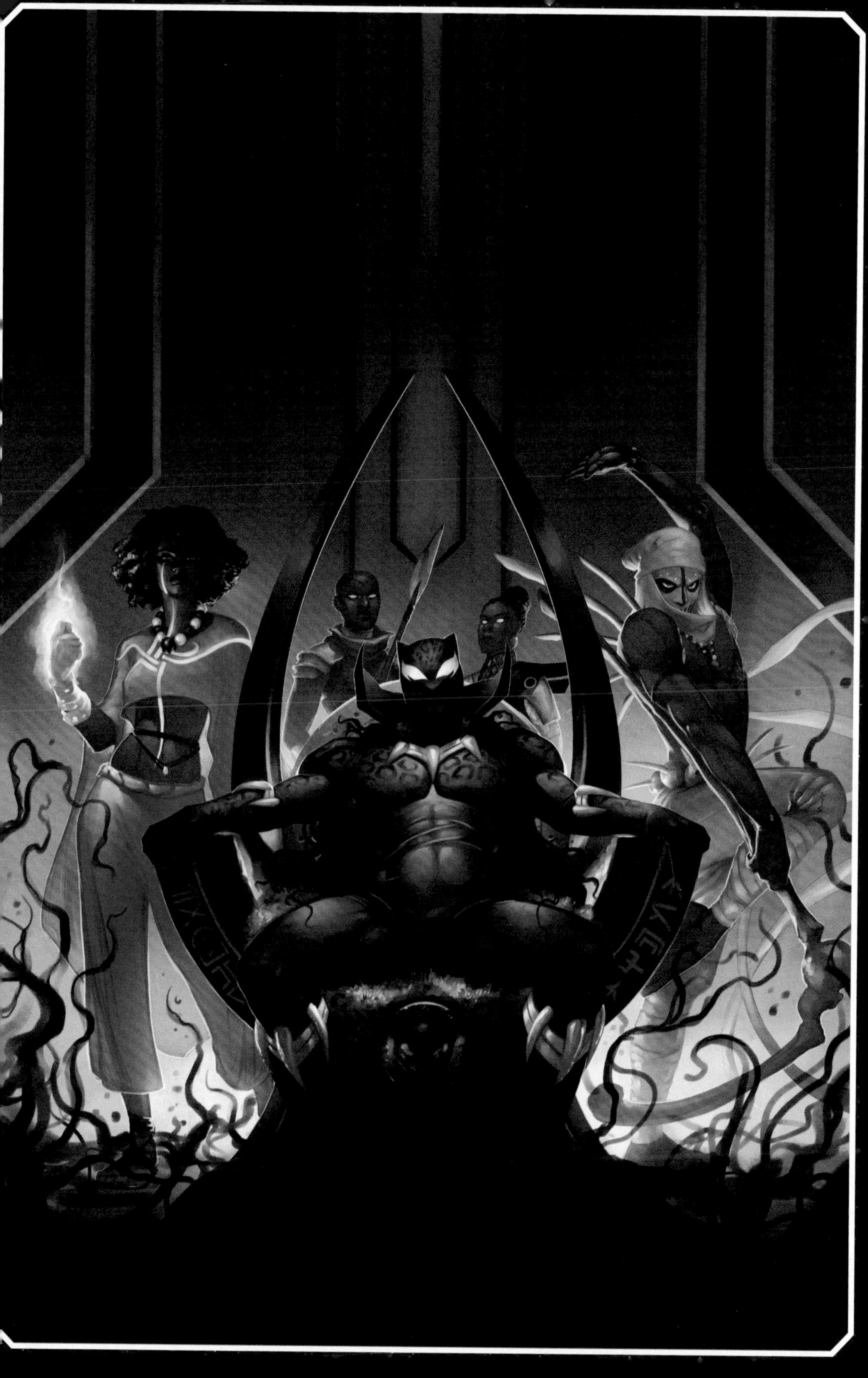

THE INTERGALACTIC EMPIRE OF WAKANDA

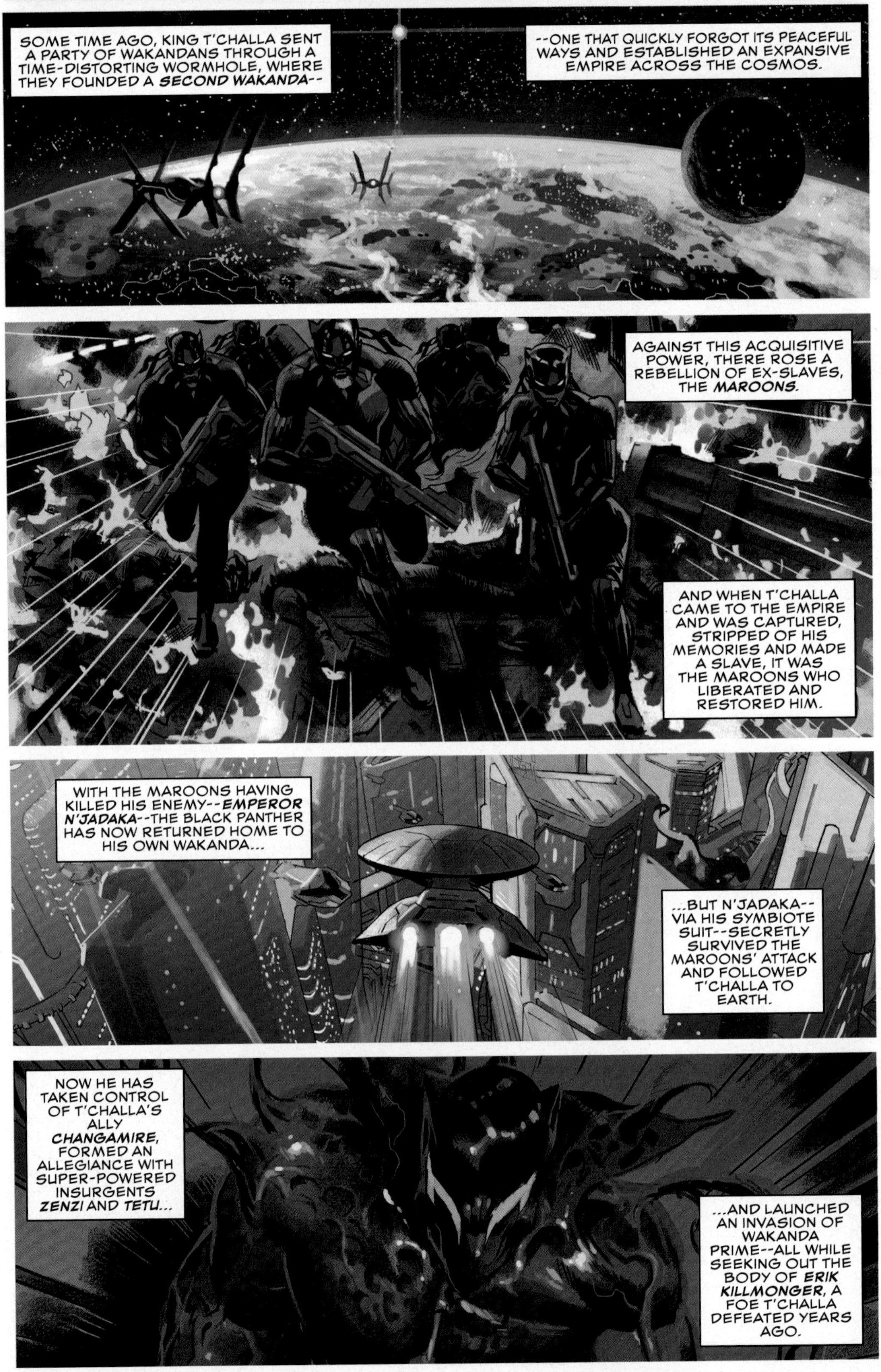

SOME TIME AGO, KING T'CHALLA SENT A PARTY OF WAKANDANS THROUGH A TIME-DISTORTING WORMHOLE, WHERE THEY FOUNDED A *SECOND WAKANDA*--
--ONE THAT QUICKLY FORGOT ITS PEACEFUL WAYS AND ESTABLISHED AN EXPANSIVE EMPIRE ACROSS THE COSMOS.
AGAINST THIS ACQUISITIVE POWER, THERE ROSE A REBELLION OF EX-SLAVES, THE *MAROONS*.
AND WHEN T'CHALLA CAME TO THE EMPIRE AND WAS CAPTURED, STRIPPED OF HIS MEMORIES AND MADE A SLAVE, IT WAS THE MAROONS WHO LIBERATED AND RESTORED HIM.
WITH THE MAROONS HAVING KILLED HIS ENEMY--*EMPEROR N'JADAKA*--THE BLACK PANTHER HAS NOW RETURNED HOME TO HIS OWN WAKANDA...
...BUT N'JADAKA--VIA HIS SYMBIOTE SUIT--SECRETLY SURVIVED THE MAROONS' ATTACK AND FOLLOWED T'CHALLA TO EARTH.
NOW HE HAS TAKEN CONTROL OF T'CHALLA'S ALLY *CHANGAMIRE*, FORMED AN ALLEGIANCE WITH SUPER-POWERED INSURGENTS *ZENZI* AND *TETU*...
...AND LAUNCHED AN INVASION OF WAKANDA PRIME--ALL WHILE SEEKING OUT THE BODY OF *ERIK KILLMONGER*, A FOE T'CHALLA DEFEATED YEARS AGO.

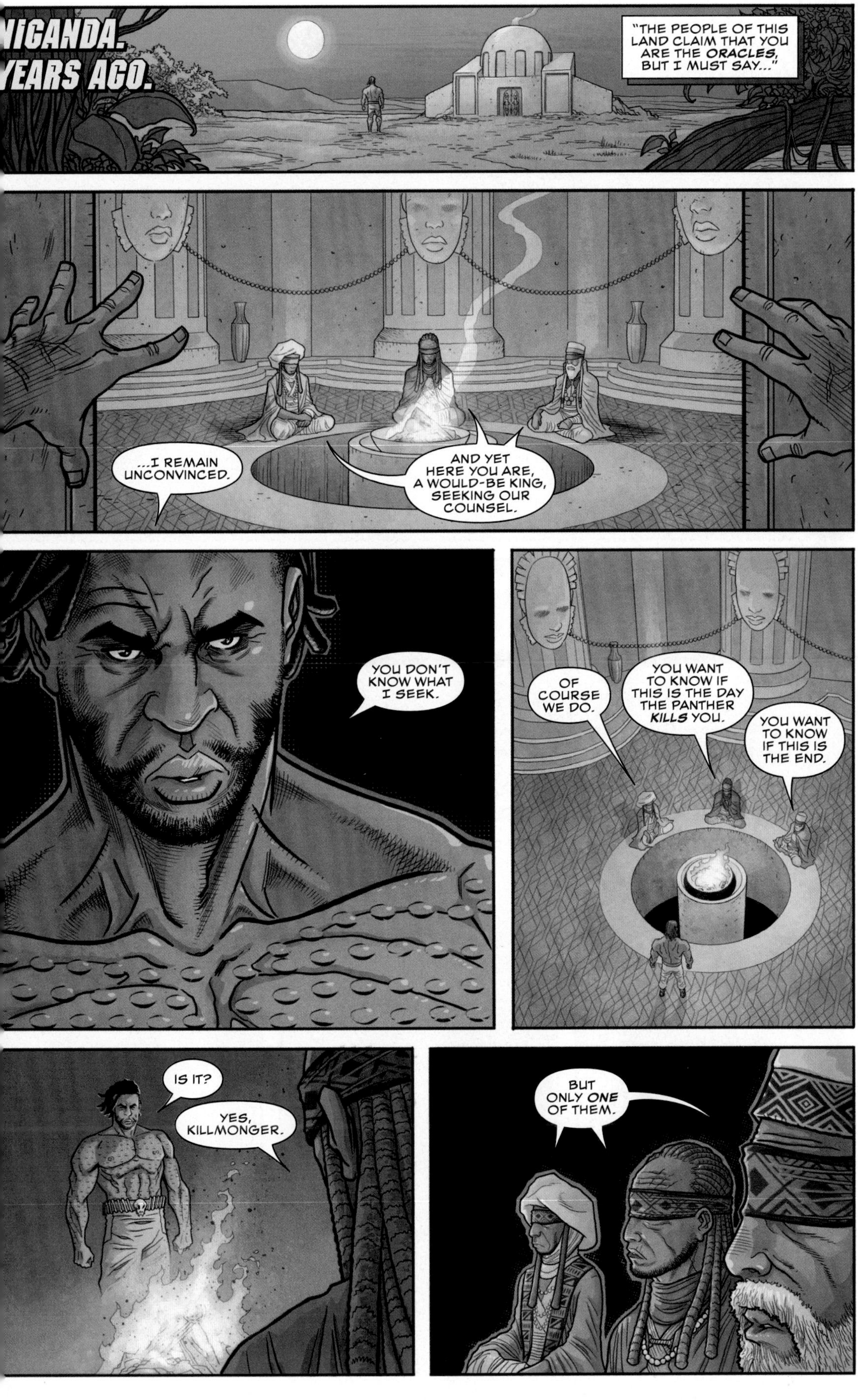
NIGANDA.
YEARS AGO.
"THE PEOPLE OF THIS LAND CLAIM THAT YOU ARE THE ORACLES, BUT I MUST SAY..."
...I REMAIN UNCONVINCED.
AND YET HERE YOU ARE, A WOULD-BE KING, SEEKING OUR COUNSEL.
YOU DON'T KNOW WHAT I SEEK.
OF COURSE WE DO.
YOU WANT TO KNOW IF THIS IS THE DAY THE PANTHER KILLS YOU.
YOU WANT TO KNOW IF THIS IS THE END.
IS IT?
YES, KILLMONGER.
BUT ONLY ONE OF THEM.

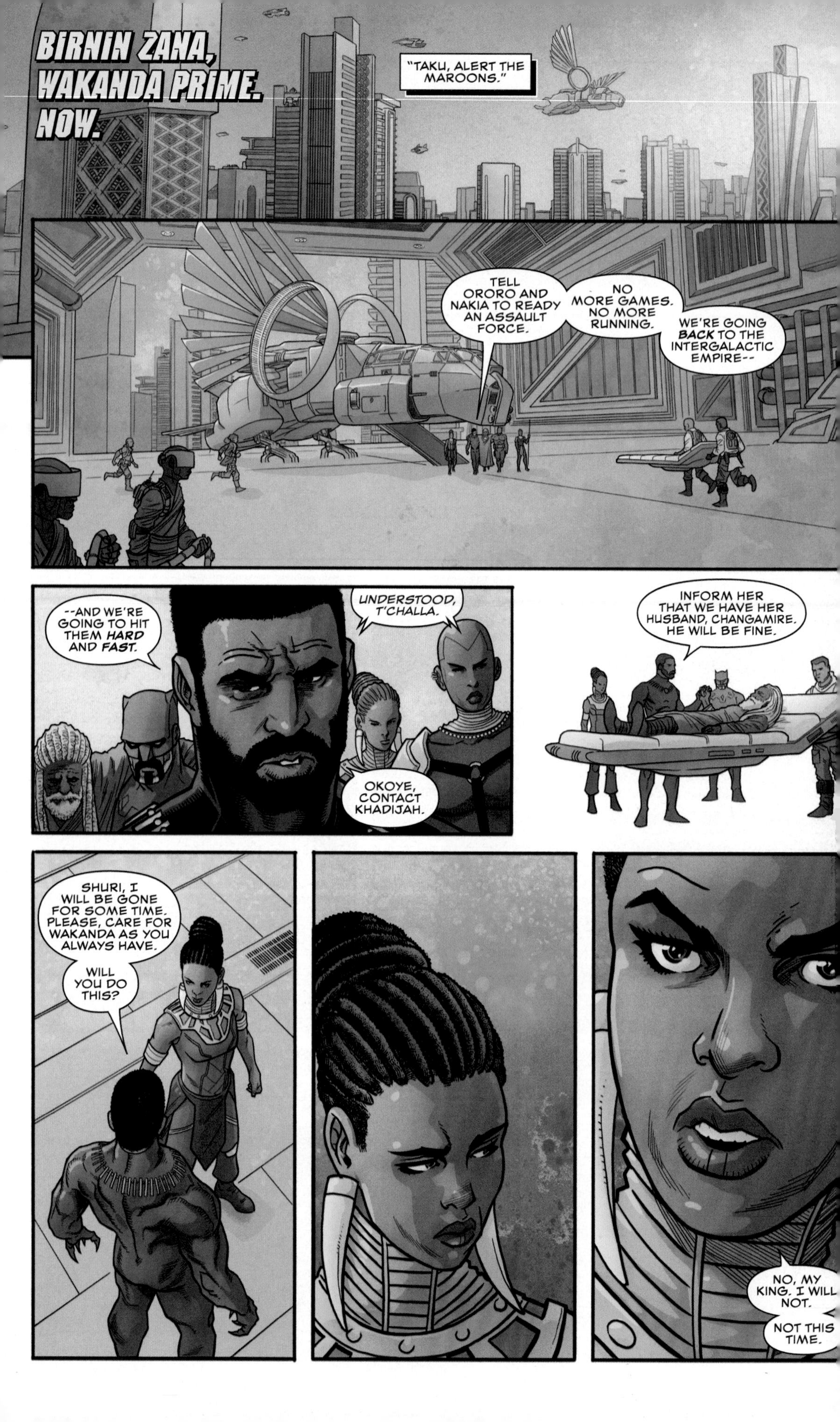
BIRNIN ZANA, WAKANDA PRIME. NOW.
"TAKU, ALERT THE MAROONS."
TELL ORORO AND NAKIA TO READY AN ASSAULT FORCE.
NO MORE GAMES. NO MORE RUNNING.
WE'RE GOING BACK TO THE INTERGALACTIC EMPIRE--
--AND WE'RE GOING TO HIT THEM HARD AND FAST.
UNDERSTOOD, T'CHALLA.
OKOYE, CONTACT KHADIJAH.
INFORM HER THAT WE HAVE HER HUSBAND, CHANGAMIRE. HE WILL BE FINE.
SHURI, I WILL BE GONE FOR SOME TIME. PLEASE, CARE FOR WAKANDA AS YOU ALWAYS HAVE.
WILL YOU DO THIS?
NO, MY KING. I WILL NOT.
NOT THIS TIME.

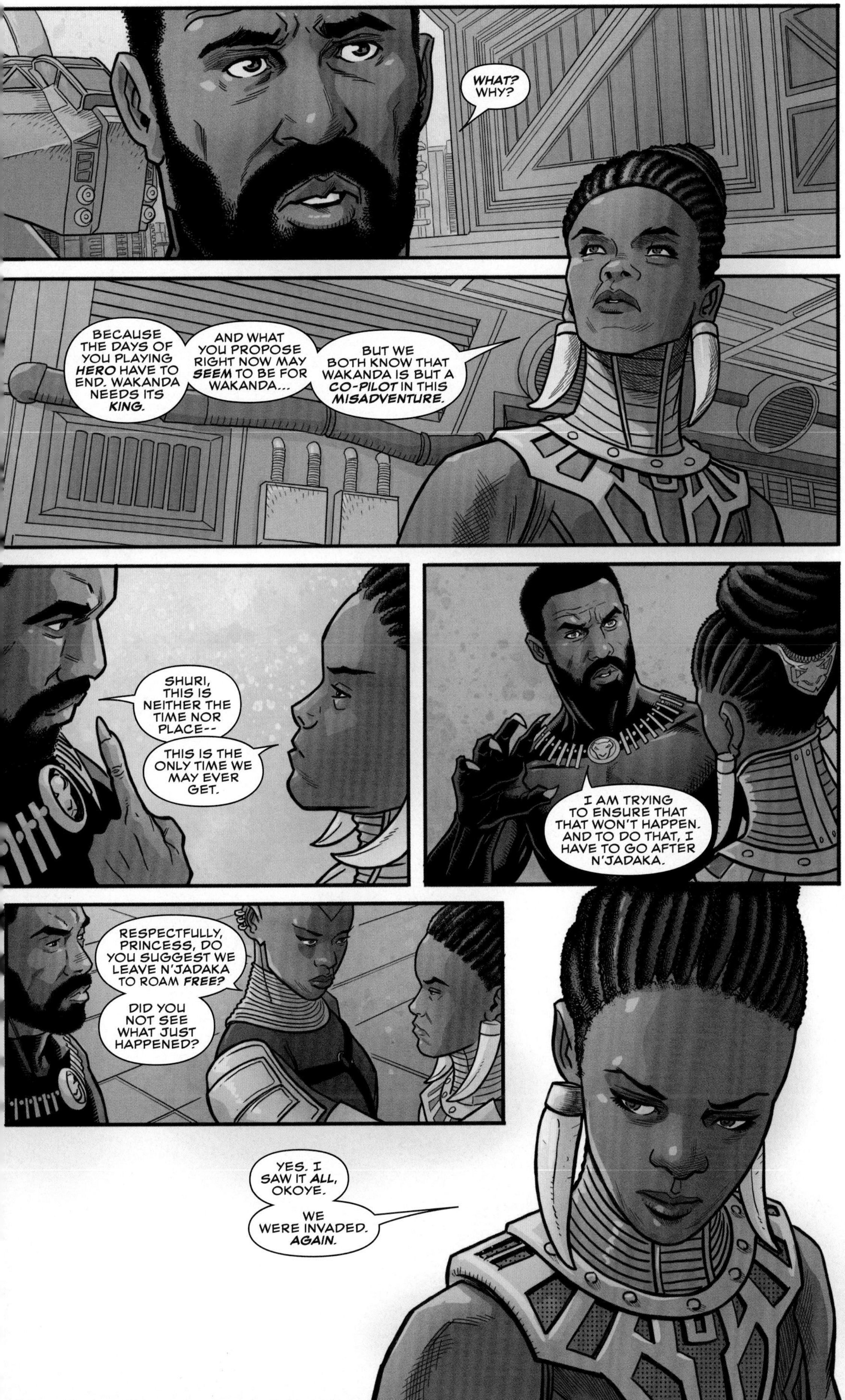
WHAT? WHY?
BECAUSE THE DAYS OF YOU PLAYING HERO HAVE TO END. WAKANDA NEEDS ITS KING.
AND WHAT YOU PROPOSE RIGHT NOW MAY SEEM TO BE FOR WAKANDA...
BUT WE BOTH KNOW THAT WAKANDA IS BUT A CO-PILOT IN THIS MISADVENTURE.
SHURI, THIS IS NEITHER THE TIME NOR PLACE--
THIS IS THE ONLY TIME WE MAY EVER GET.
I AM TRYING TO ENSURE THAT THAT WON'T HAPPEN. AND TO DO THAT, I HAVE TO GO AFTER N'JADAKA.
RESPECTFULLY, PRINCESS, DO YOU SUGGEST WE LEAVE N'JADAKA TO ROAM FREE?
DID YOU NOT SEE WHAT JUST HAPPENED?
YES. I SAW IT ALL, OKOYE.
WE WERE INVADED. AGAIN.

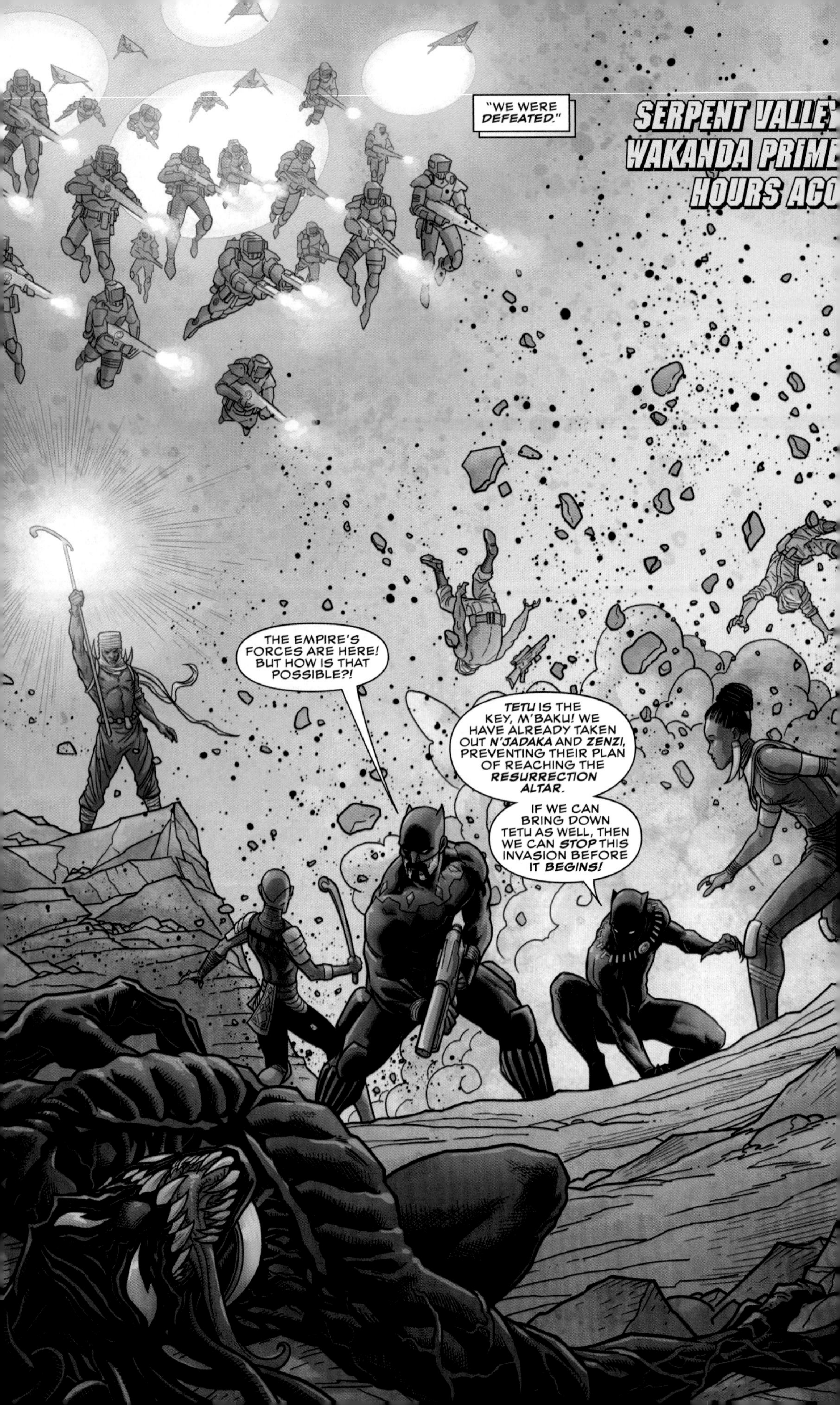
"WE WERE DEFEATED."
SERPENT VALLEY
WAKANDA PRIME
HOURS AGO
THE EMPIRE'S FORCES ARE HERE! BUT HOW IS THAT POSSIBLE?!
TETU IS THE KEY, M'BAKU! WE HAVE ALREADY TAKEN OUT N'JADAKA AND ZENZI, PREVENTING THEIR PLAN OF REACHING THE RESURRECTION ALTAR.
IF WE CAN BRING DOWN TETU AS WELL, THEN WE CAN STOP THIS INVASION BEFORE IT BEGINS!

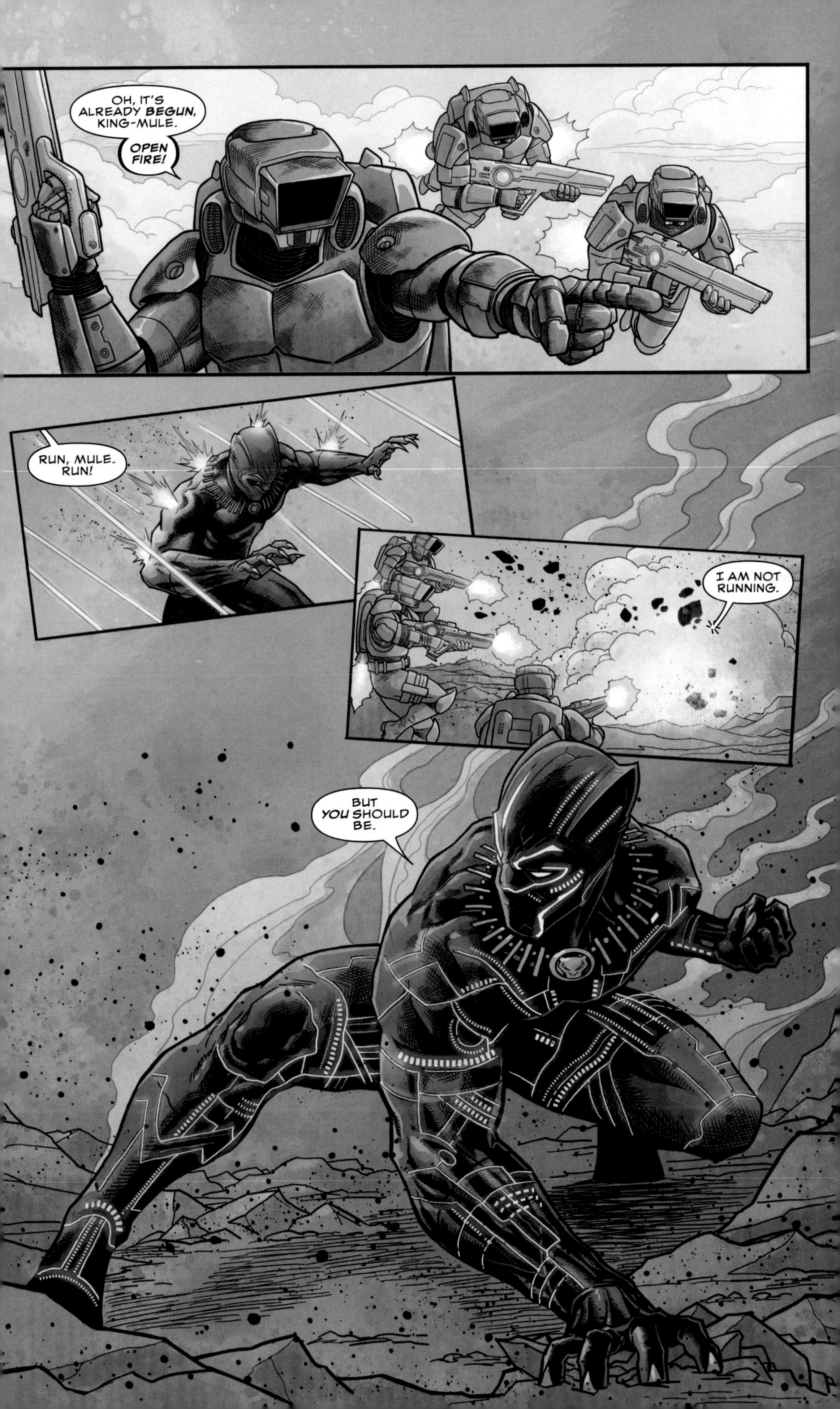
OH, IT'S ALREADY BEGUN, KING-MULE.
OPEN FIRE!
RUN, MULE. RUN!
I AM NOT RUNNING.
BUT YOU SHOULD BE.

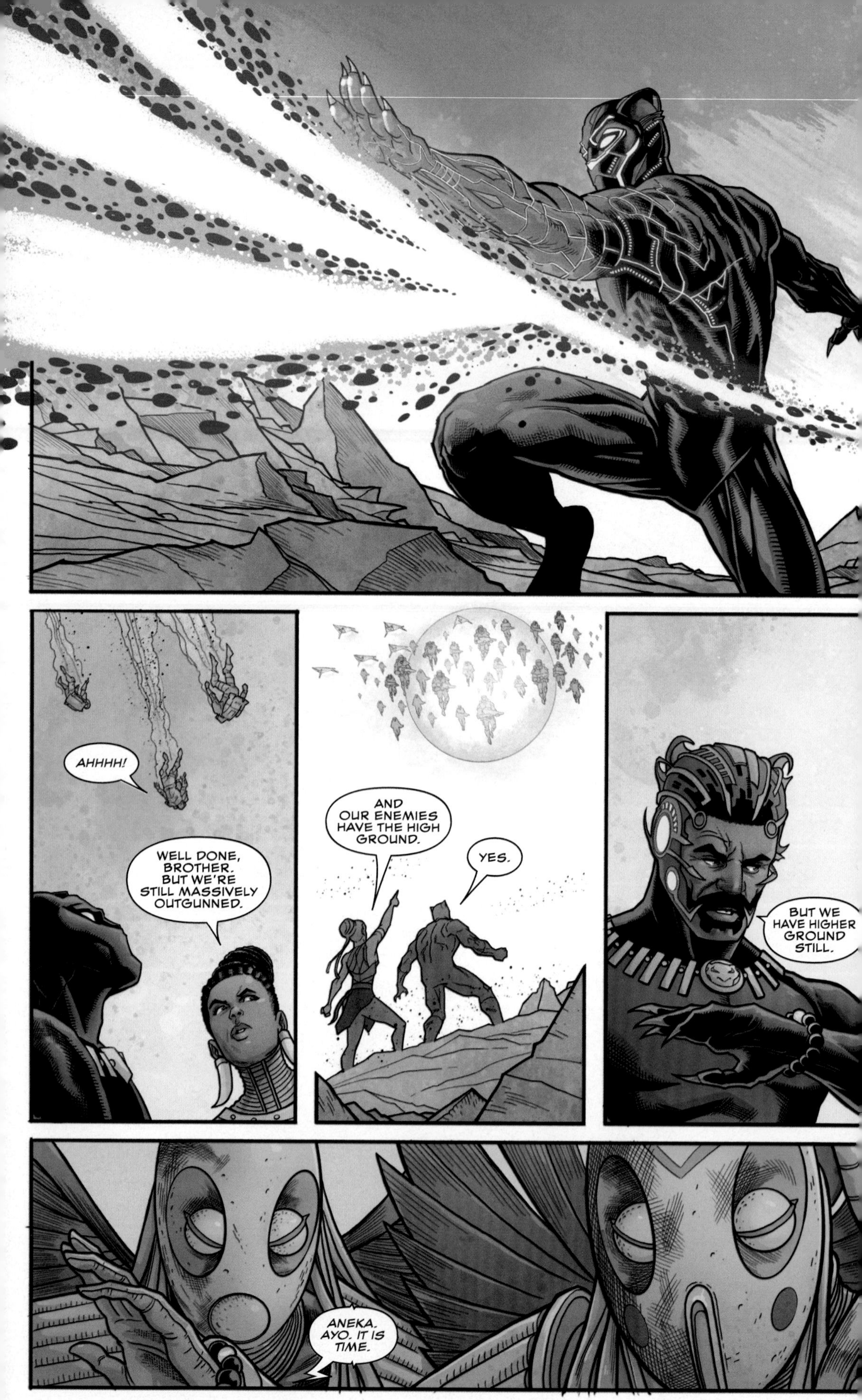
AHHHH!
WELL DONE, BROTHER. BUT WE'RE STILL MASSIVELY OUTGUNNED.
AND OUR ENEMIES HAVE THE HIGH GROUND.
YES.
BUT WE HAVE HIGHER GROUND STILL.
ANEKA. AYO. IT IS TIME.

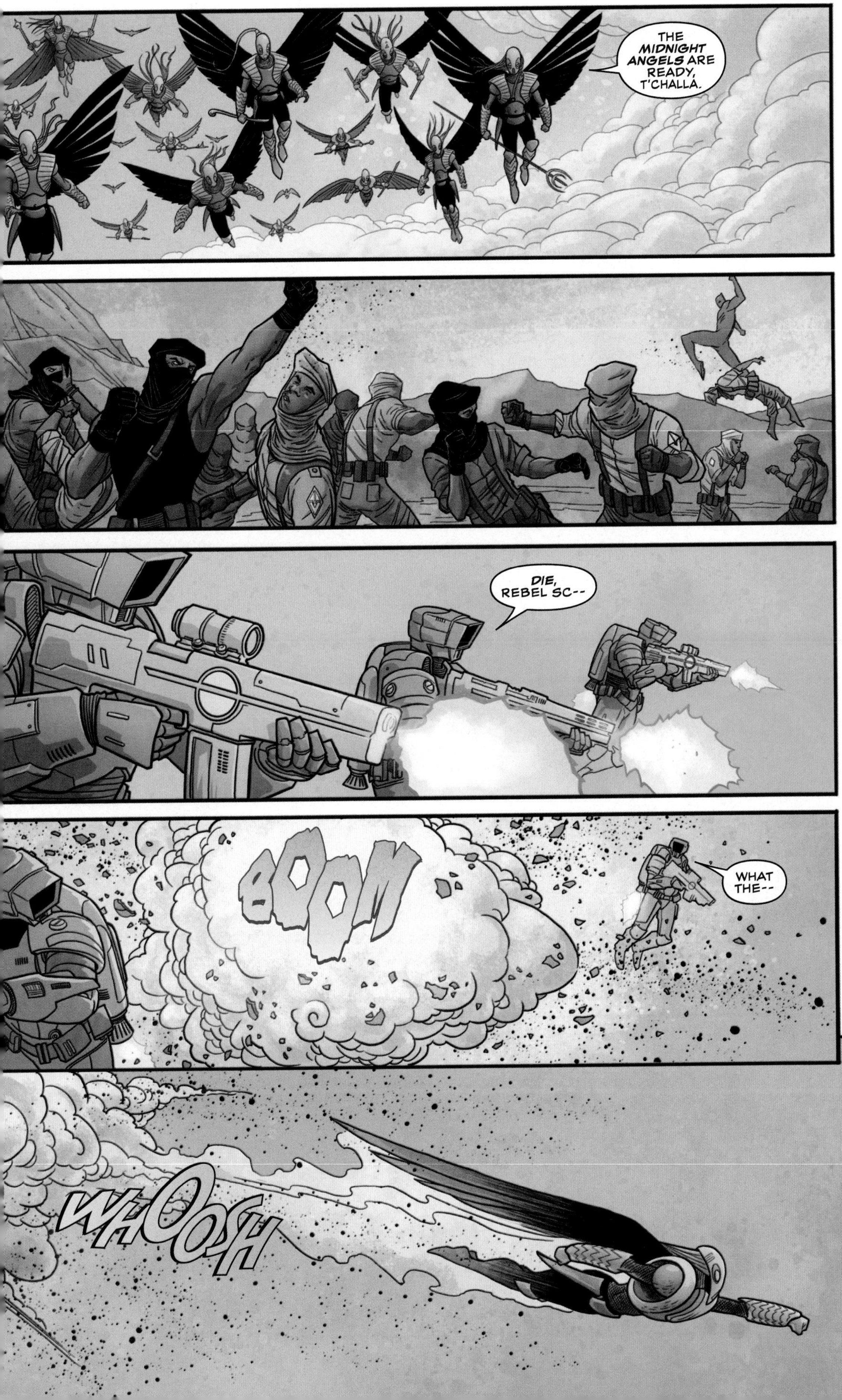
THE MIDNIGHT ANGELS ARE READY, T'CHALLA.
DIE, REBEL SC--
BOOM
WHAT THE--
WHOOSH

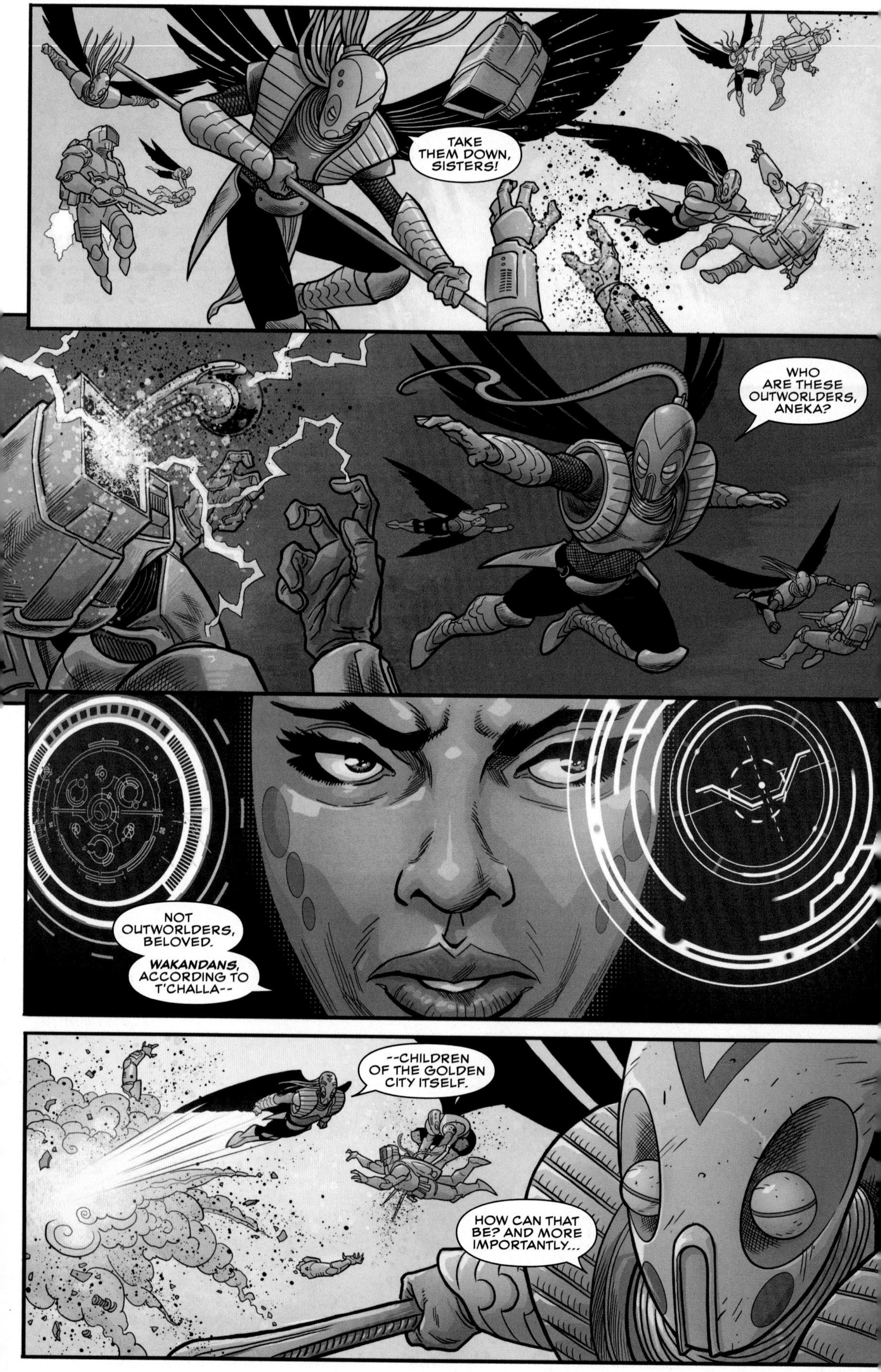
TAKE THEM DOWN, SISTERS!
WHO ARE THESE OUTWORLDERS, ANEKA?
NOT OUTWORLDERS, BELOVED.
WAKANDANS, ACCORDING TO T'CHALLA--
--CHILDREN OF THE GOLDEN CITY ITSELF.
HOW CAN THAT BE? AND MORE IMPORTANTLY...

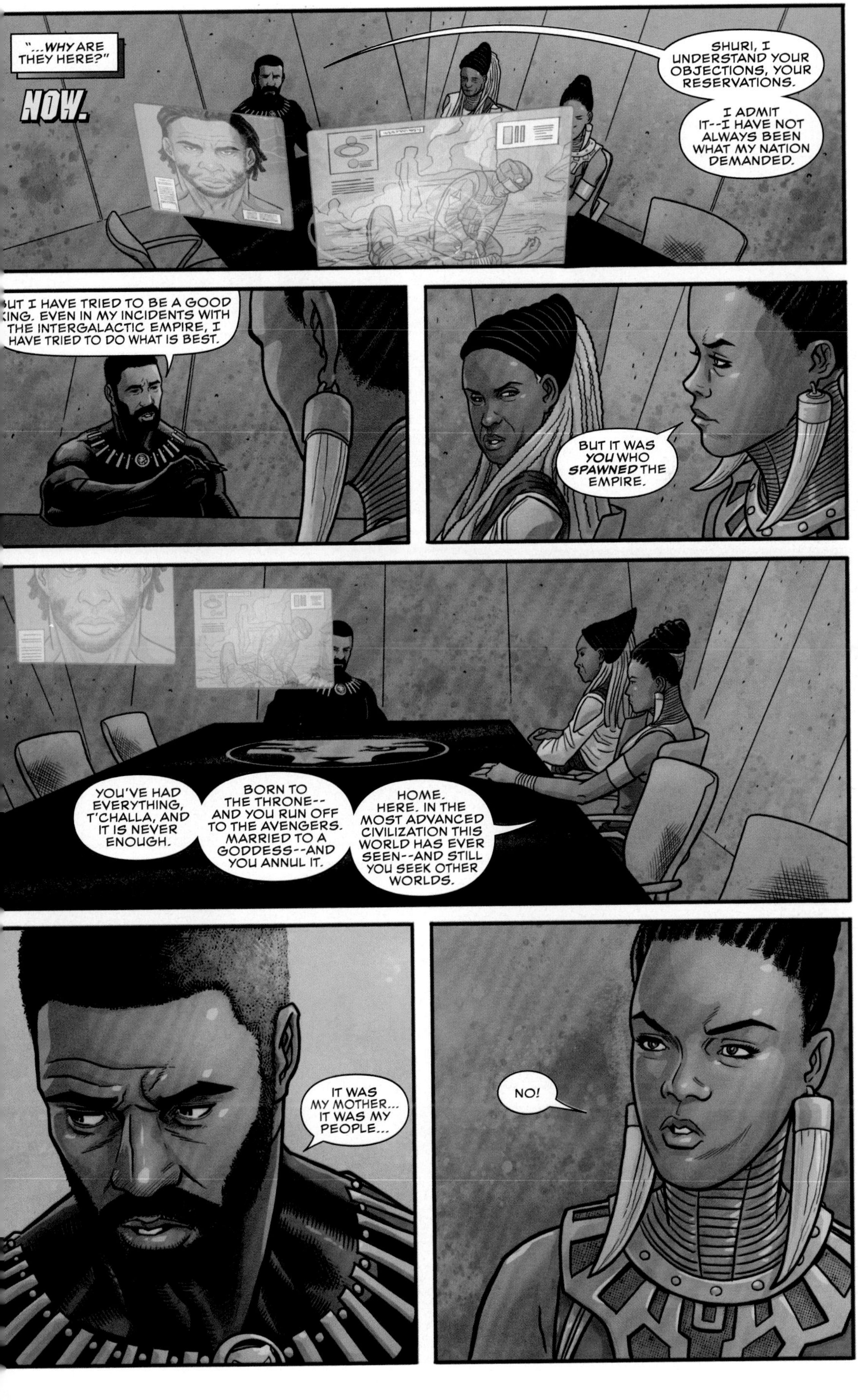
"...WHY ARE THEY HERE?"
NOW.
SHURI, I UNDERSTAND YOUR OBJECTIONS, YOUR RESERVATIONS.
I ADMIT IT--I HAVE NOT ALWAYS BEEN WHAT MY NATION DEMANDED.
BUT I HAVE TRIED TO BE A GOOD KING. EVEN IN MY INCIDENTS WITH THE INTERGALACTIC EMPIRE, I HAVE TRIED TO DO WHAT IS BEST.
BUT IT WAS YOU WHO SPAWNED THE EMPIRE.
YOU'VE HAD EVERYTHING, T'CHALLA, AND IT IS NEVER ENOUGH.
BORN TO THE THRONE--AND YOU RUN OFF TO THE AVENGERS. MARRIED TO A GODDESS--AND YOU ANNUL IT.
HOME. HERE. IN THE MOST ADVANCED CIVILIZATION THIS WORLD HAS EVER SEEN--AND STILL YOU SEEK OTHER WORLDS.
IT WAS MY MOTHER... IT WAS MY PEOPLE...
NO!

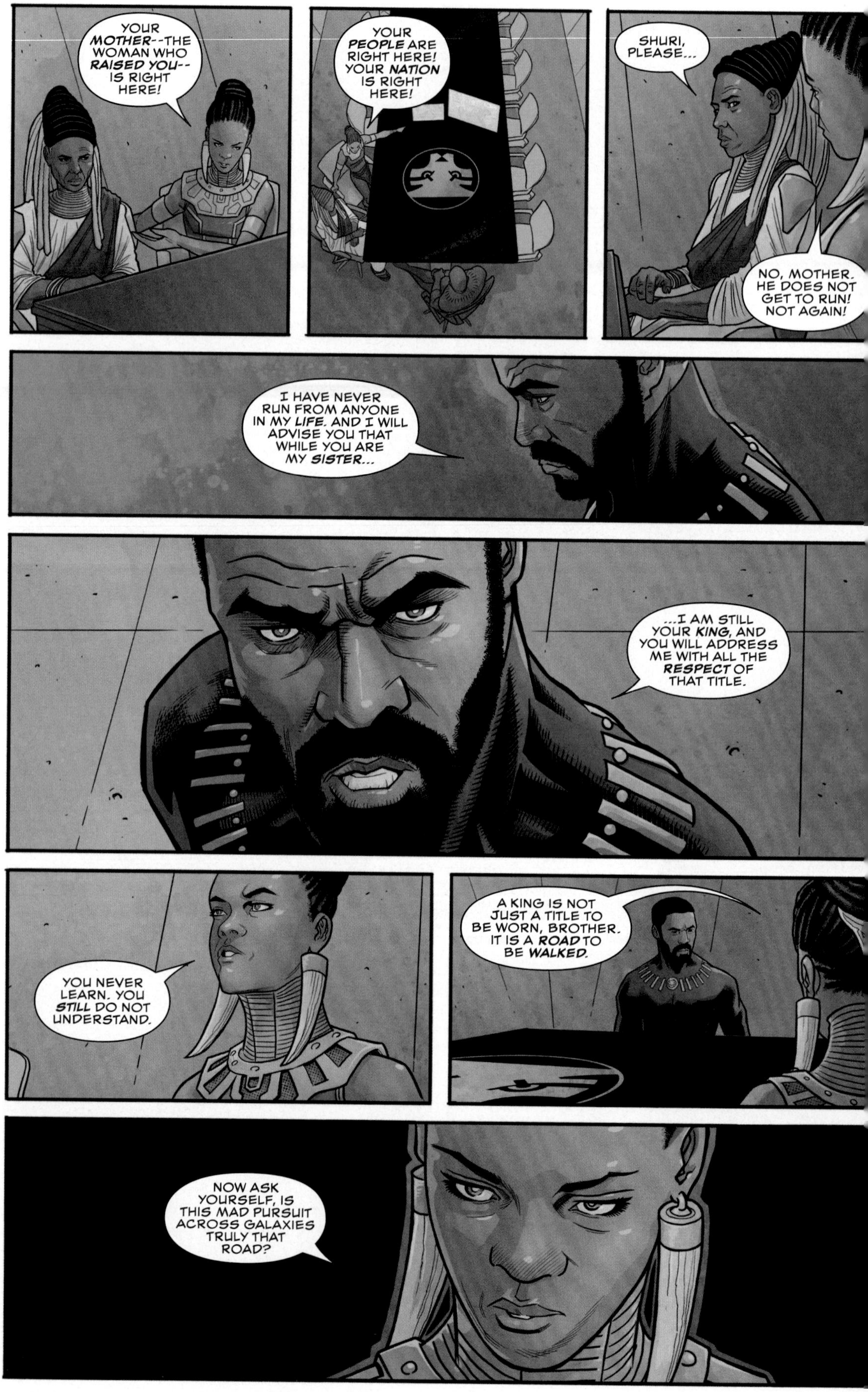
YOUR MOTHER--THE WOMAN WHO RAISED YOU--IS RIGHT HERE!
YOUR PEOPLE ARE RIGHT HERE! YOUR NATION IS RIGHT HERE!
SHURI, PLEASE...
NO, MOTHER. HE DOES NOT GET TO RUN! NOT AGAIN!
I HAVE NEVER RUN FROM ANYONE IN MY LIFE. AND I WILL ADVISE YOU THAT WHILE YOU ARE MY SISTER...
...I AM STILL YOUR KING, AND YOU WILL ADDRESS ME WITH ALL THE RESPECT OF THAT TITLE.
YOU NEVER LEARN. YOU STILL DO NOT UNDERSTAND.
A KING IS NOT JUST A TITLE TO BE WORN, BROTHER. IT IS A ROAD TO BE WALKED.
NOW ASK YOURSELF, IS THIS MAD PURSUIT ACROSS GALAXIES TRULY THAT ROAD?

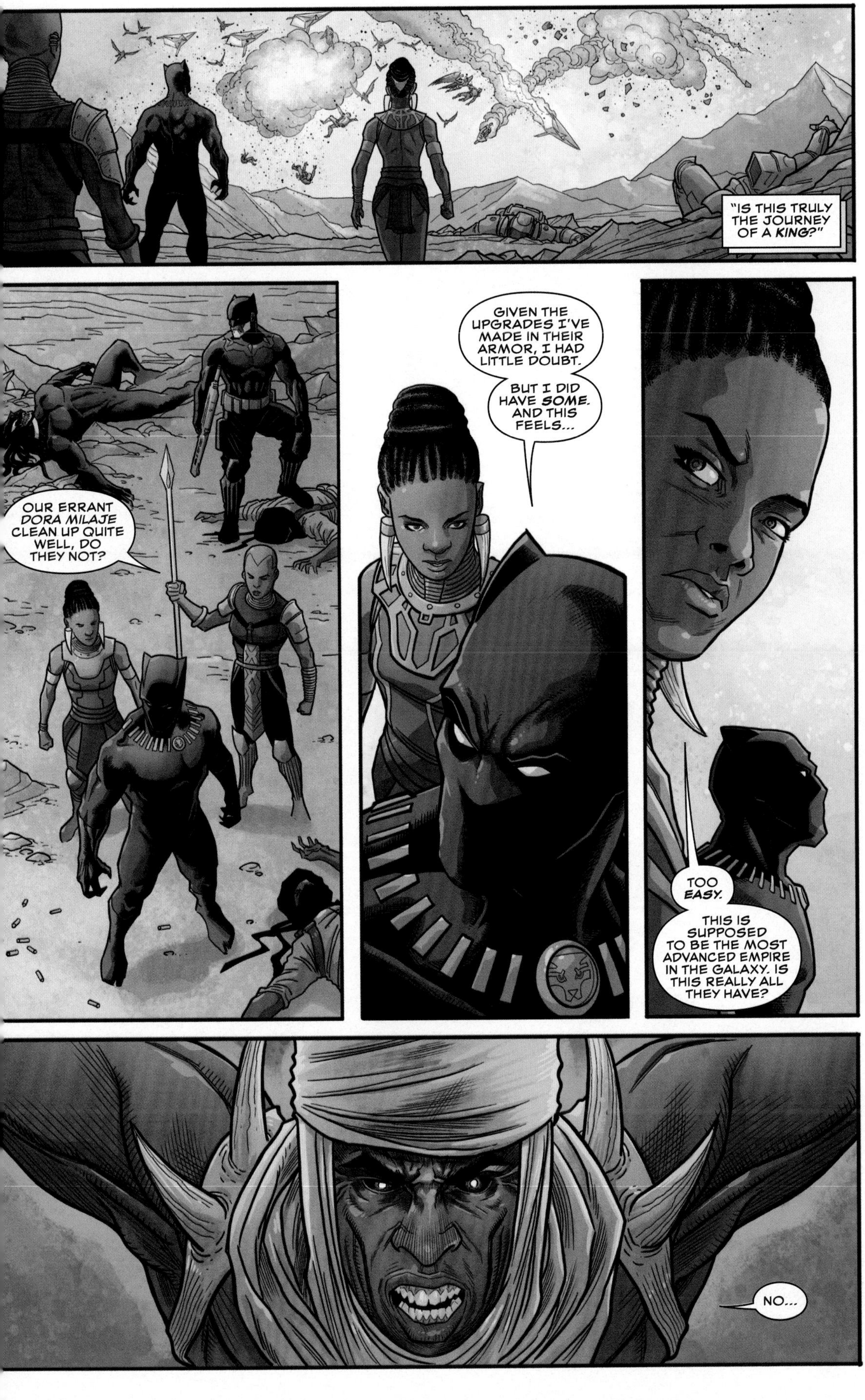

"IS THIS TRULY THE JOURNEY OF A *KING?*"
OUR ERRANT *DORA MILAJE* CLEAN UP QUITE WELL, DO THEY NOT?
GIVEN THE UPGRADES I'VE MADE IN THEIR ARMOR, I HAD LITTLE DOUBT.
BUT I DID HAVE ***SOME.*** AND THIS FEELS...
TOO *EASY.*
THIS IS SUPPOSED TO BE THE MOST ADVANCED EMPIRE IN THE GALAXY. IS THIS REALLY ALL THEY HAVE?
NO...

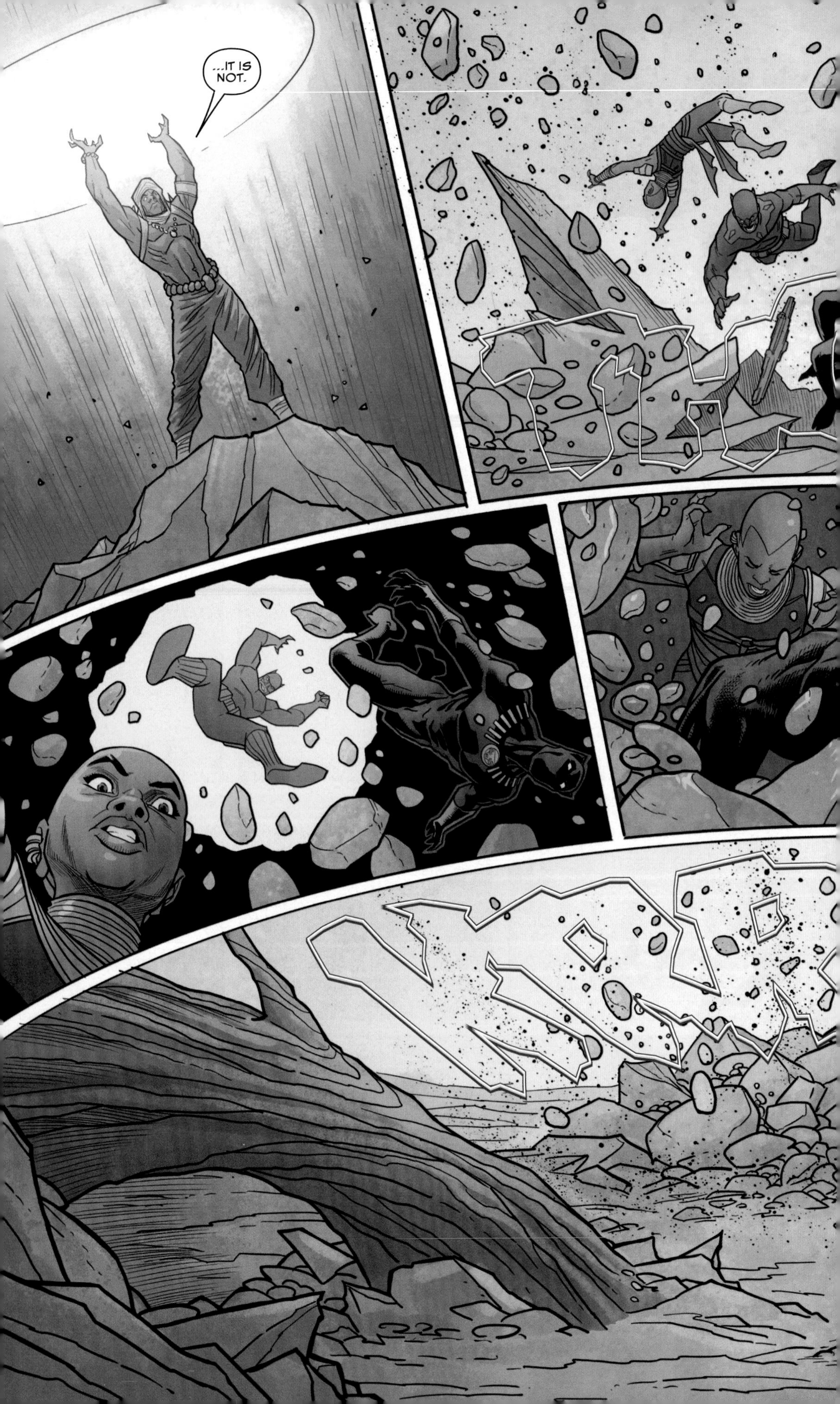
...IT IS NOT.

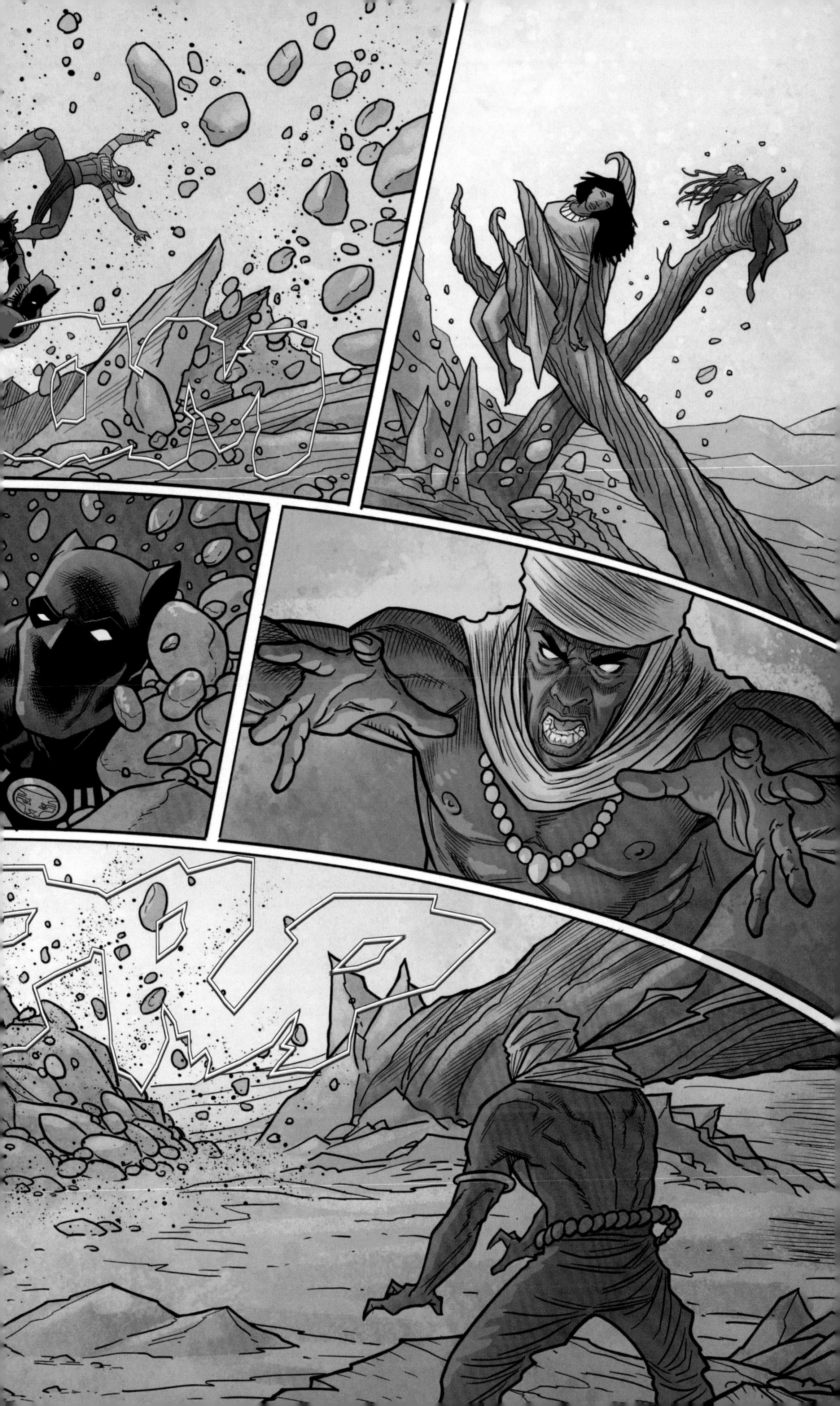

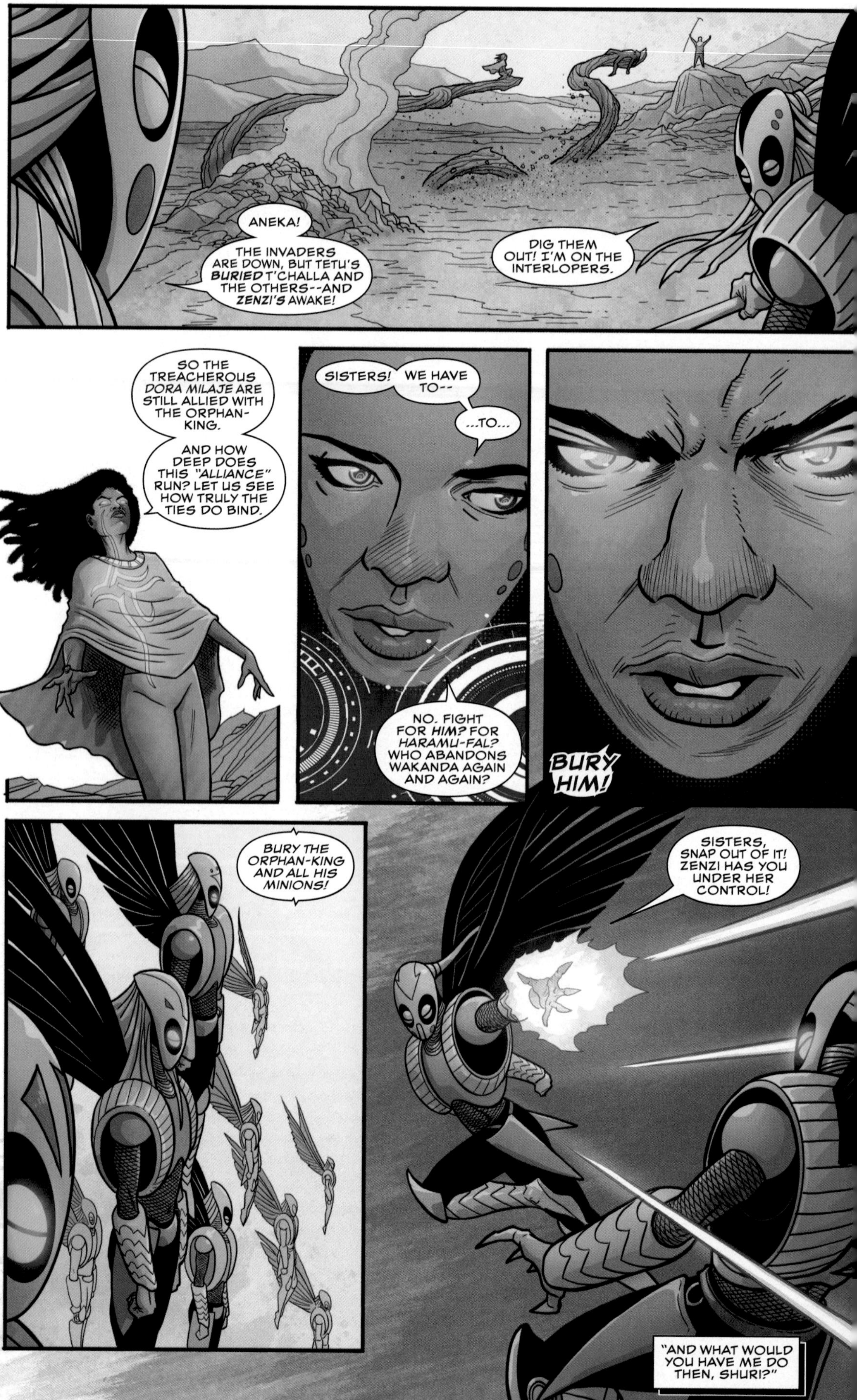
ANEKA!
THE INVADERS ARE DOWN, BUT TETU'S BURIED T'CHALLA AND THE OTHERS--AND ZENZI'S AWAKE!
DIG THEM OUT! I'M ON THE INTERLOPERS.
SO THE TREACHEROUS DORA MILAJE ARE STILL ALLIED WITH THE ORPHAN-KING.
AND HOW DEEP DOES THIS "ALLIANCE" RUN? LET US SEE HOW TRULY THE TIES DO BIND.
SISTERS!
WE HAVE TO--
...TO...
NO. FIGHT FOR HIM? FOR HARAMU-FAL? WHO ABANDONS WAKANDA AGAIN AND AGAIN?
BURY HIM!
BURY THE ORPHAN-KING AND ALL HIS MINIONS!
SISTERS, SNAP OUT OF IT! ZENZI HAS YOU UNDER HER CONTROL!
"AND WHAT WOULD YOU HAVE ME DO THEN, SHURI?"

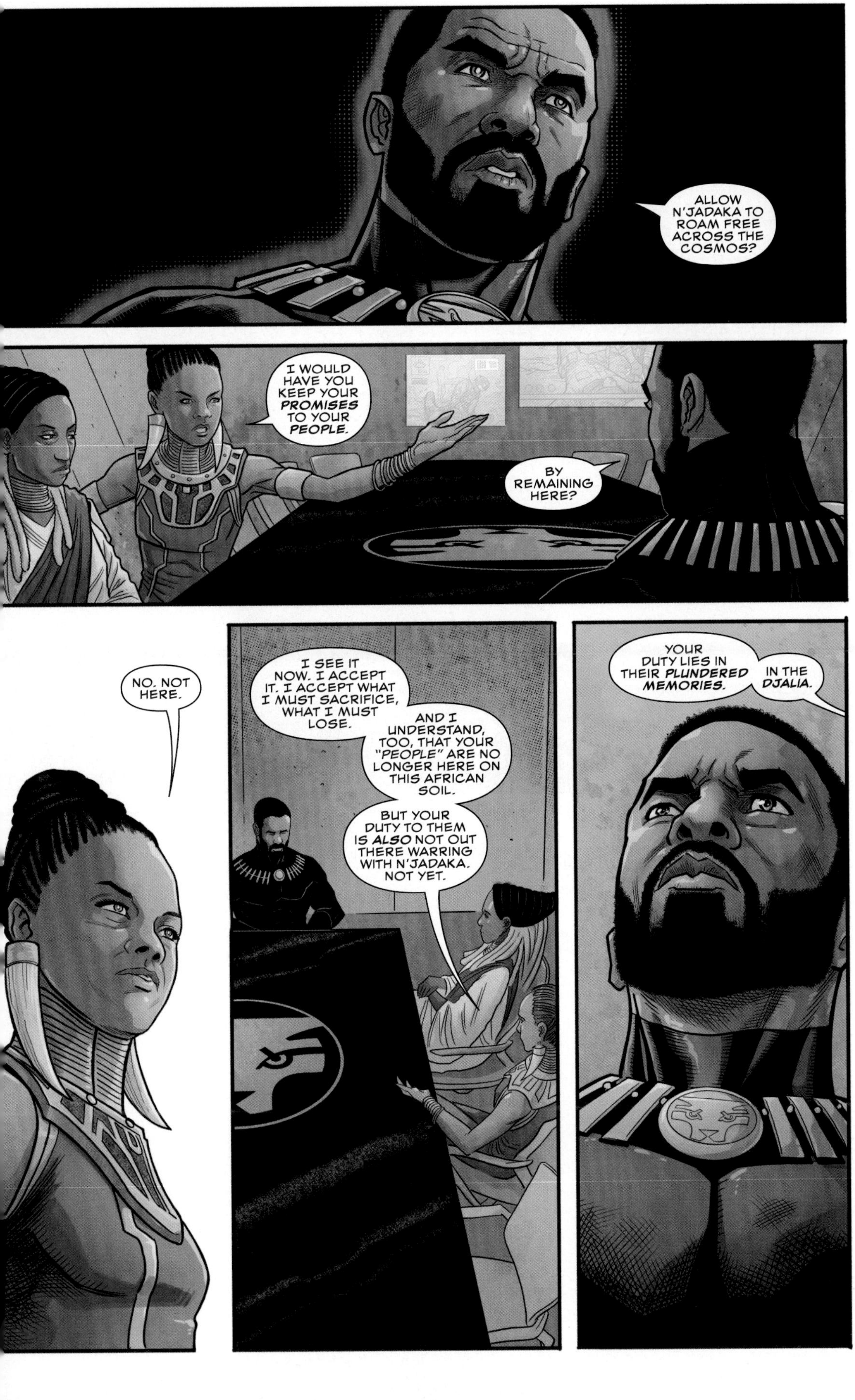
ALLOW N'JADAKA TO ROAM FREE ACROSS THE COSMOS?
I WOULD HAVE YOU KEEP YOUR PROMISES TO YOUR PEOPLE.
BY REMAINING HERE?
NO. NOT HERE.
I SEE IT NOW. I ACCEPT IT. I ACCEPT WHAT I MUST SACRIFICE, WHAT I MUST LOSE.
AND I UNDERSTAND, TOO, THAT YOUR "PEOPLE" ARE NO LONGER HERE ON THIS AFRICAN SOIL.
BUT YOUR DUTY TO THEM IS ALSO NOT OUT THERE WARRING WITH N'JADAKA. NOT YET.
YOUR DUTY LIES IN THEIR PLUNDERED MEMORIES.
IN THE DJALIA.

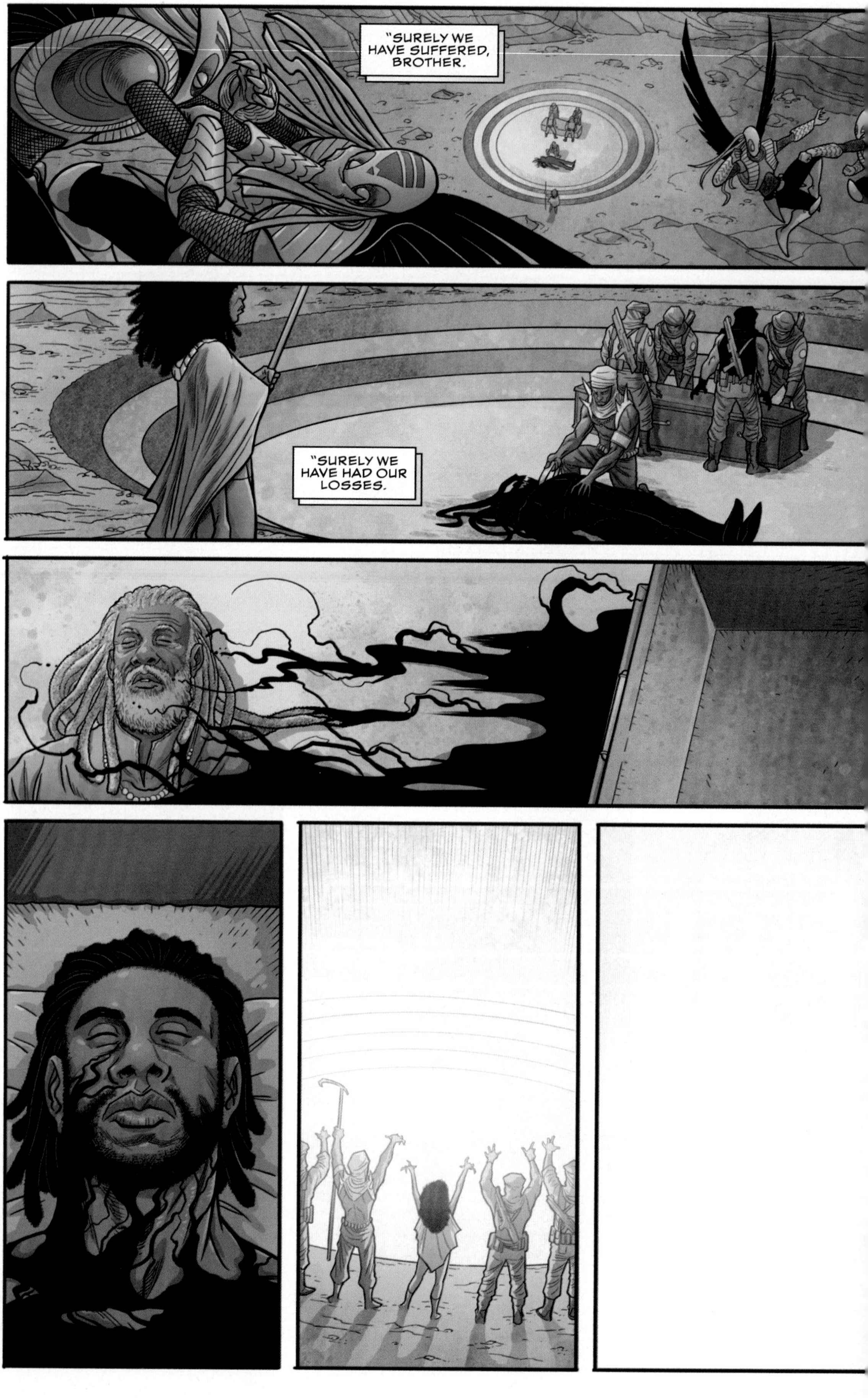
"SURELY WE HAVE SUFFERED, BROTHER.
"SURELY WE HAVE HAD OUR LOSSES.

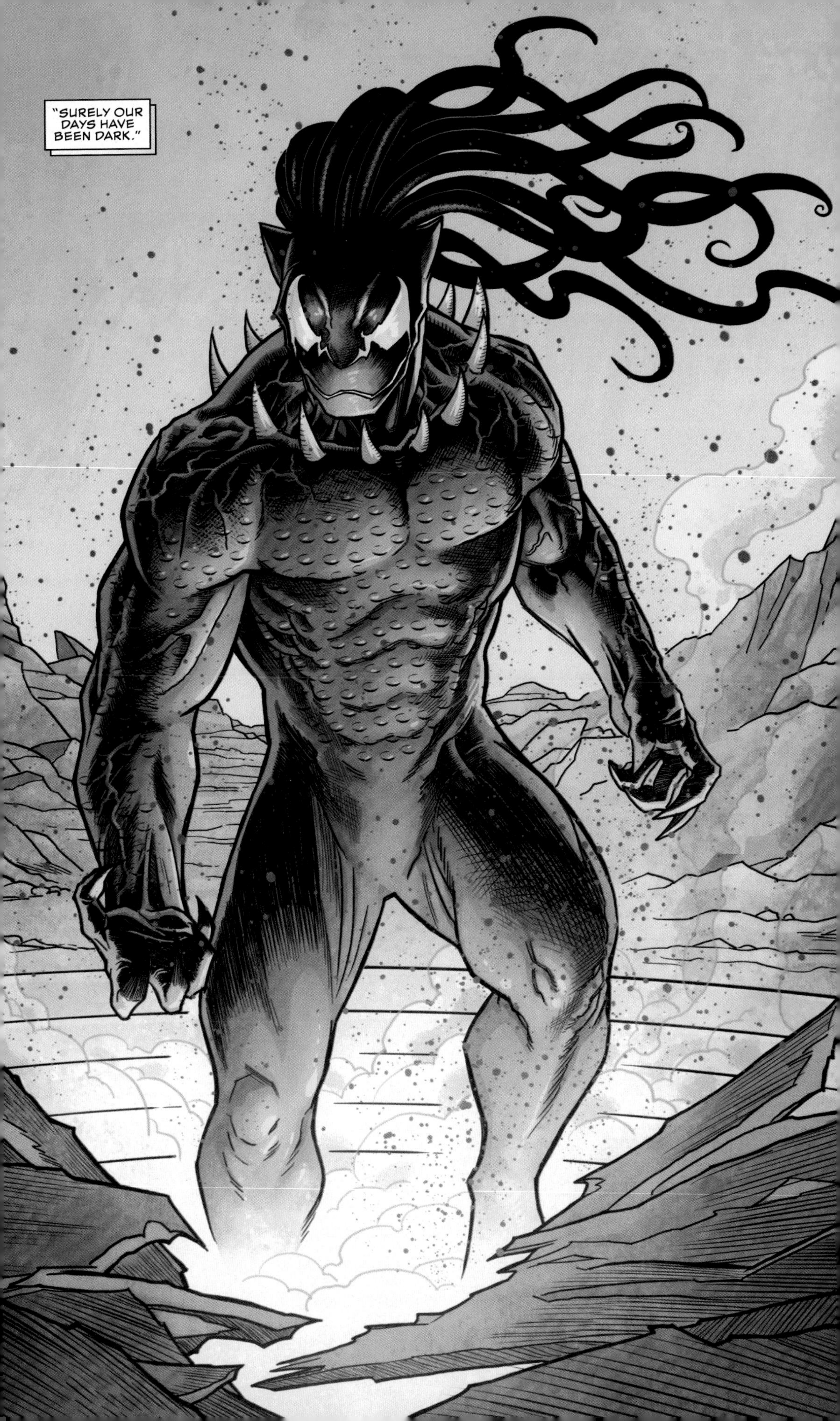
"SURELY OUR DAYS HAVE BEEN DARK."

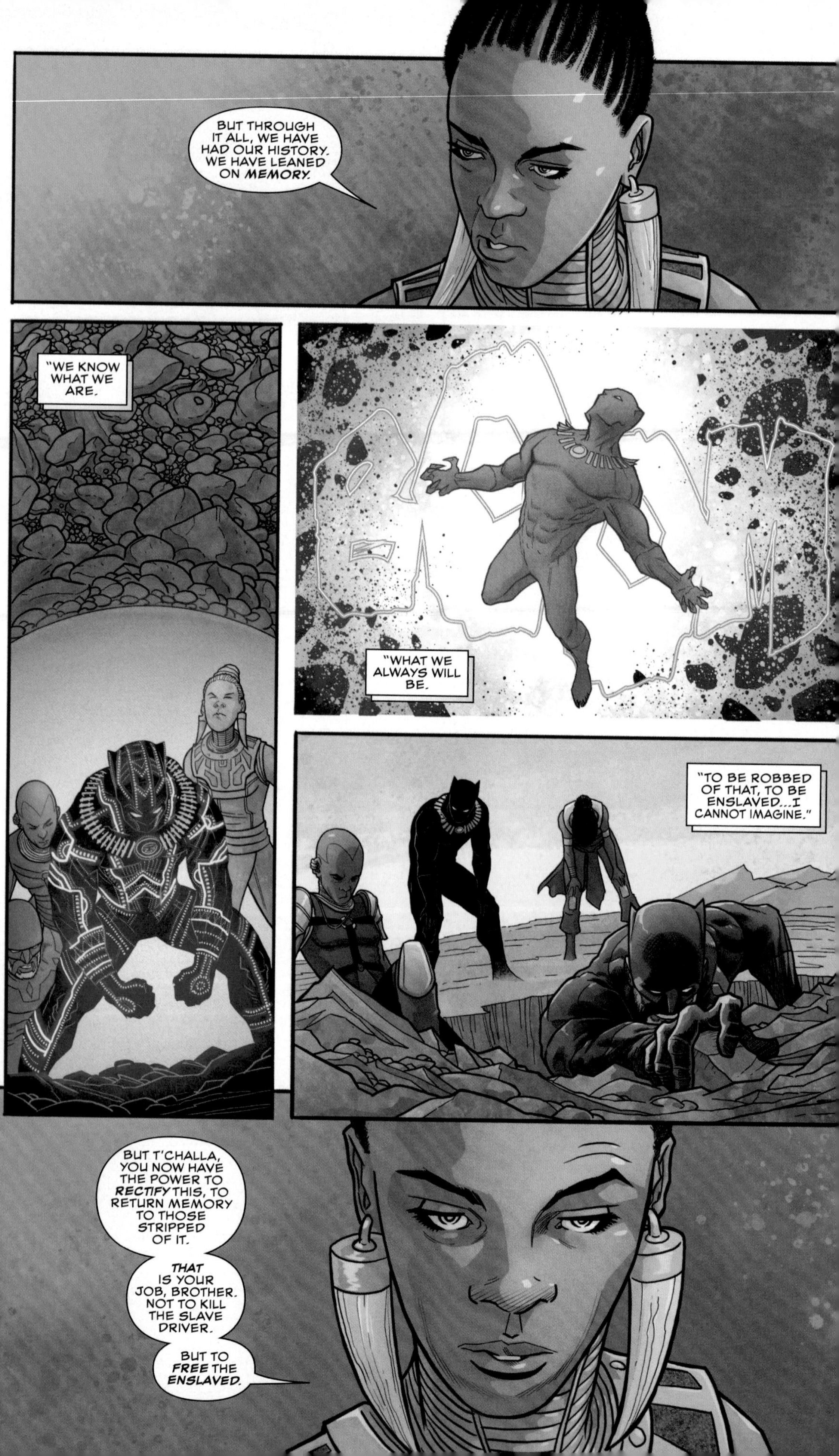
BUT THROUGH IT ALL, WE HAVE HAD OUR HISTORY. WE HAVE LEANED ON MEMORY.
"WE KNOW WHAT WE ARE.
"WHAT WE ALWAYS WILL BE.
"TO BE ROBBED OF THAT, TO BE ENSLAVED...I CANNOT IMAGINE."
BUT T'CHALLA, YOU NOW HAVE THE POWER TO RECTIFY THIS, TO RETURN MEMORY TO THOSE STRIPPED OF IT.
THAT IS YOUR JOB, BROTHER. NOT TO KILL THE SLAVE DRIVER.
BUT TO FREE THE ENSLAVED.

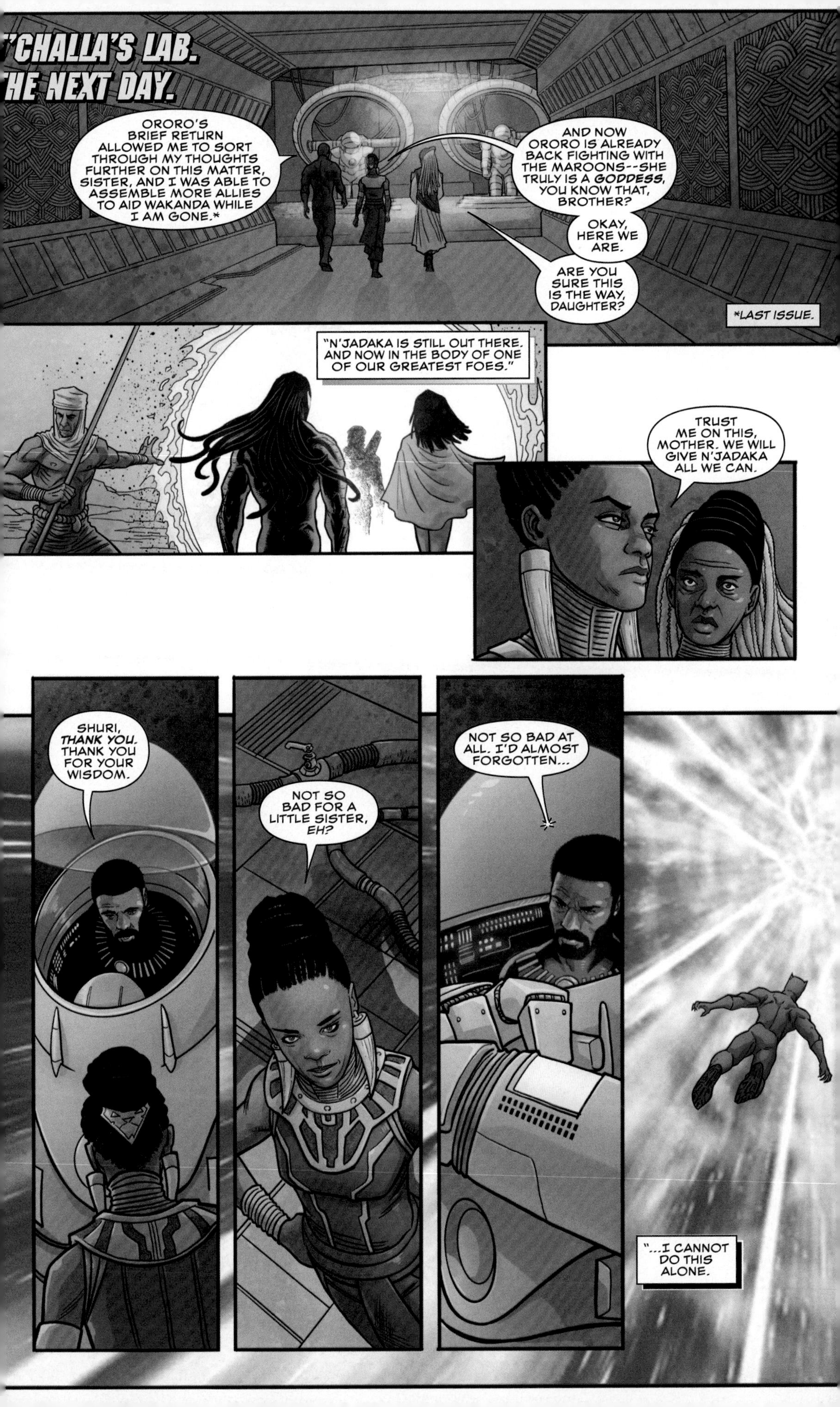

'CHALLA'S LAB.
HE NEXT DAY.
ORORO'S BRIEF RETURN ALLOWED ME TO SORT THROUGH MY THOUGHTS FURTHER ON THIS MATTER, SISTER, AND I WAS ABLE TO ASSEMBLE MORE ALLIES TO AID WAKANDA WHILE I AM GONE.*
AND NOW ORORO IS ALREADY BACK FIGHTING WITH THE MAROONS--SHE TRULY IS A GODDESS, YOU KNOW THAT, BROTHER?
OKAY, HERE WE ARE.
ARE YOU SURE THIS IS THE WAY, DAUGHTER?
*LAST ISSUE.
"N'JADAKA IS STILL OUT THERE. AND NOW IN THE BODY OF ONE OF OUR GREATEST FOES."
TRUST ME ON THIS, MOTHER. WE WILL GIVE N'JADAKA ALL WE CAN.
SHURI, THANK YOU. THANK YOU FOR YOUR WISDOM.
NOT SO BAD FOR A LITTLE SISTER, EH?
NOT SO BAD AT ALL. I'D ALMOST FORGOTTEN...
"...I CANNOT DO THIS ALONE.

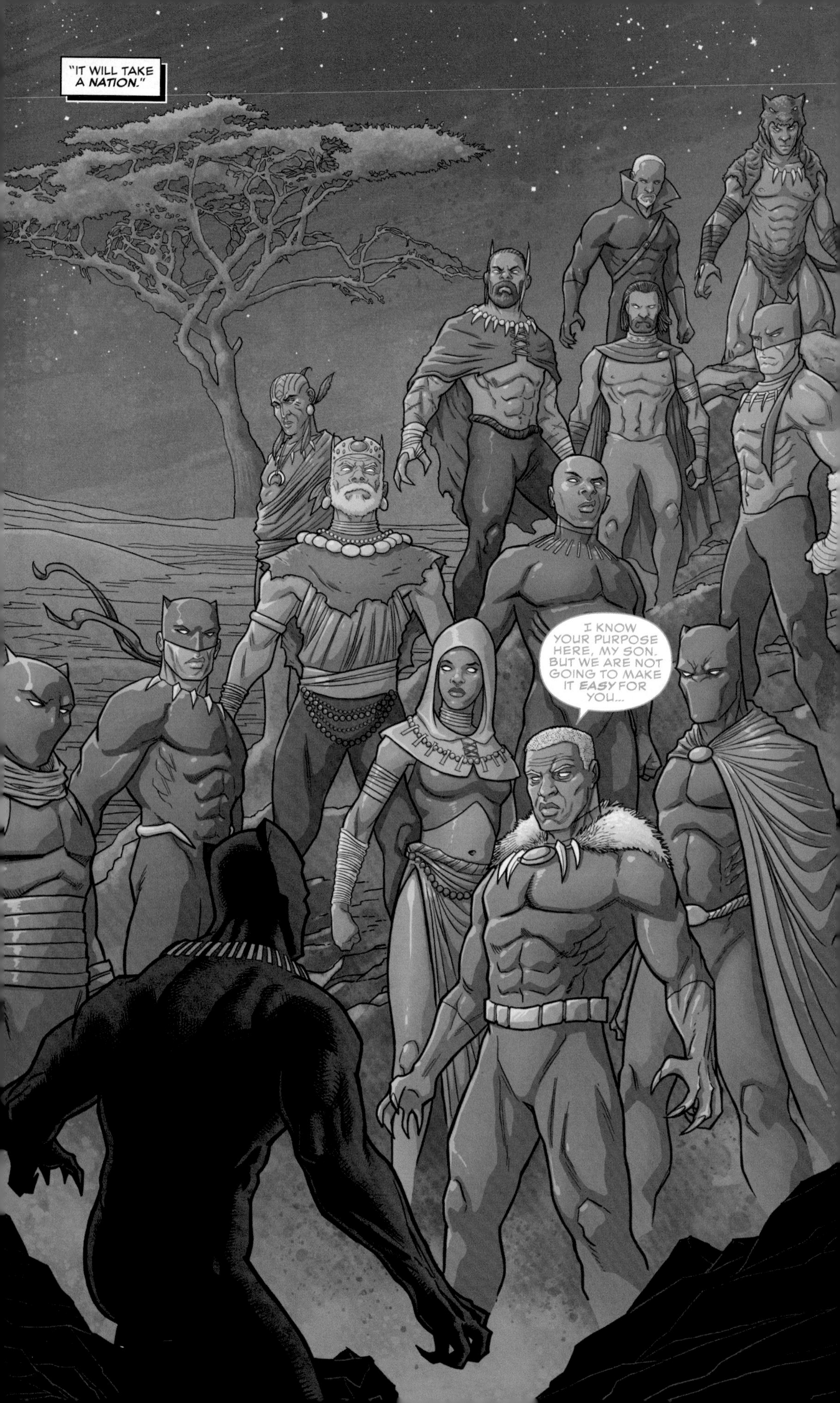
"IT WILL TAKE A NATION."
I KNOW YOUR PURPOSE HERE, MY SON. BUT WE ARE NOT GOING TO MAKE IT EASY FOR YOU...

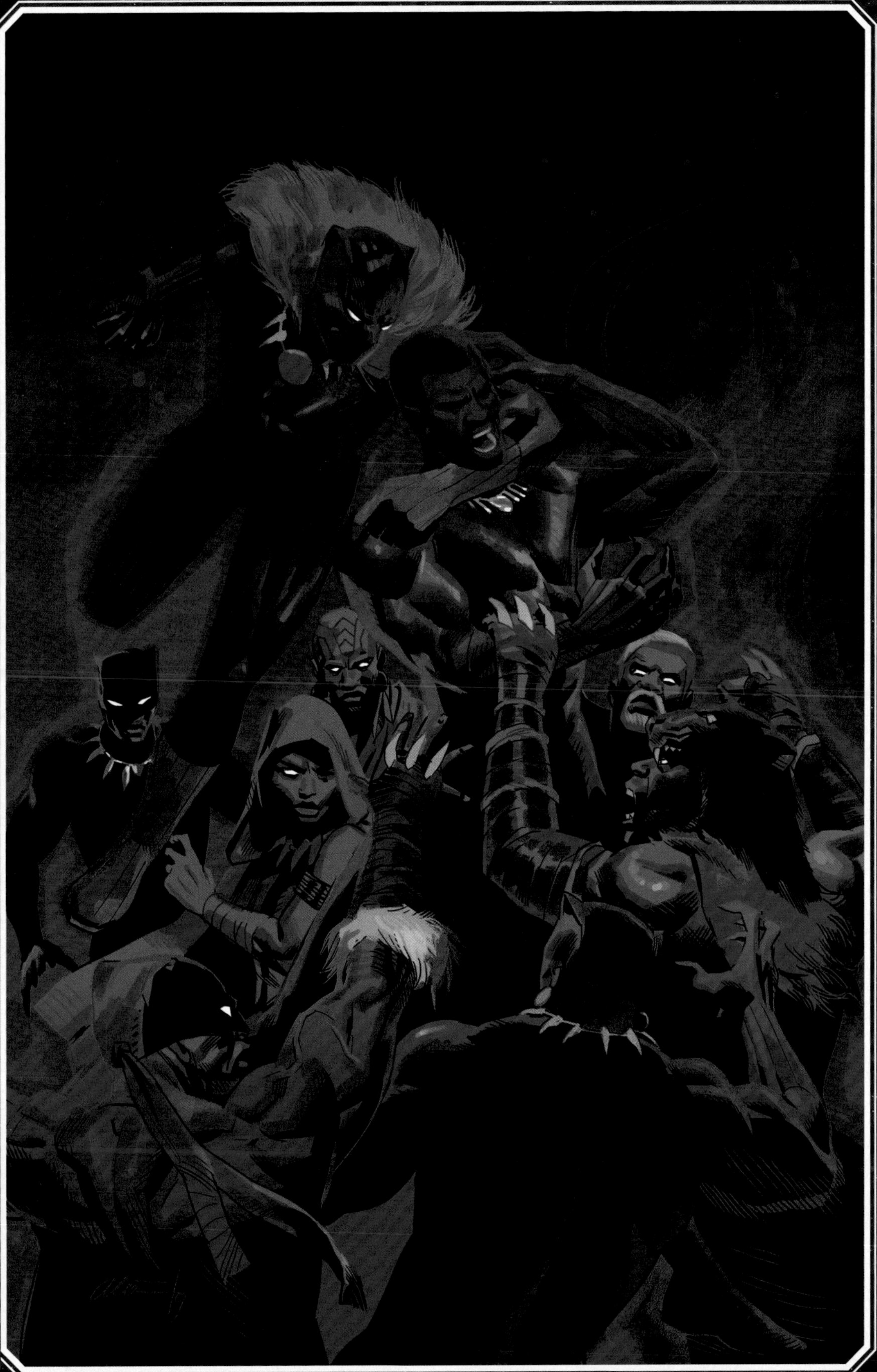

20

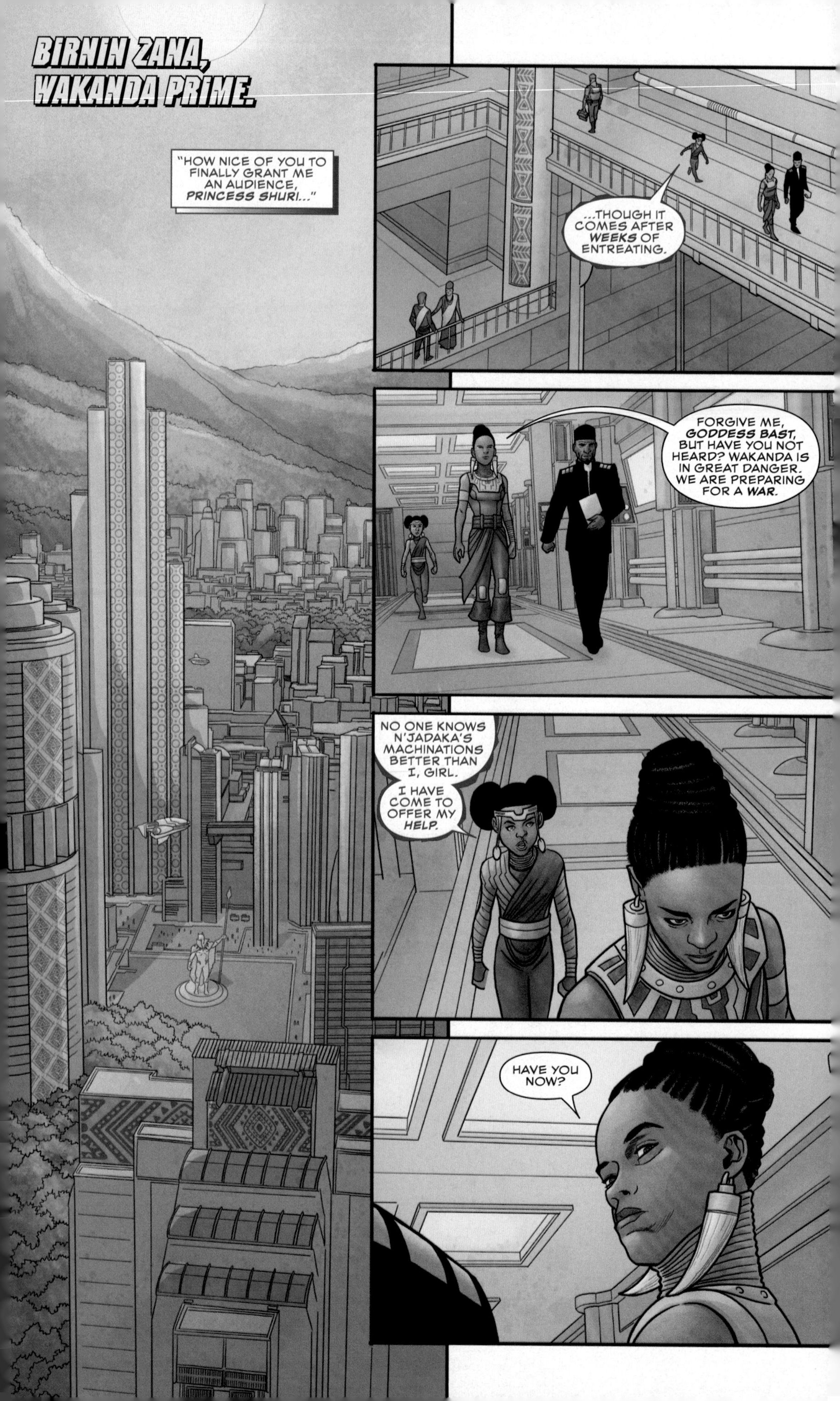
BIRNIN ZANA, WAKANDA PRIME.
"HOW NICE OF YOU TO FINALLY GRANT ME AN AUDIENCE, PRINCESS SHURI..."
...THOUGH IT COMES AFTER WEEKS OF ENTREATING.
FORGIVE ME, GODDESS BAST, BUT HAVE YOU NOT HEARD? WAKANDA IS IN GREAT DANGER. WE ARE PREPARING FOR A WAR.
NO ONE KNOWS N'JADAKA'S MACHINATIONS BETTER THAN I, GIRL.
I HAVE COME TO OFFER MY HELP.
HAVE YOU NOW?

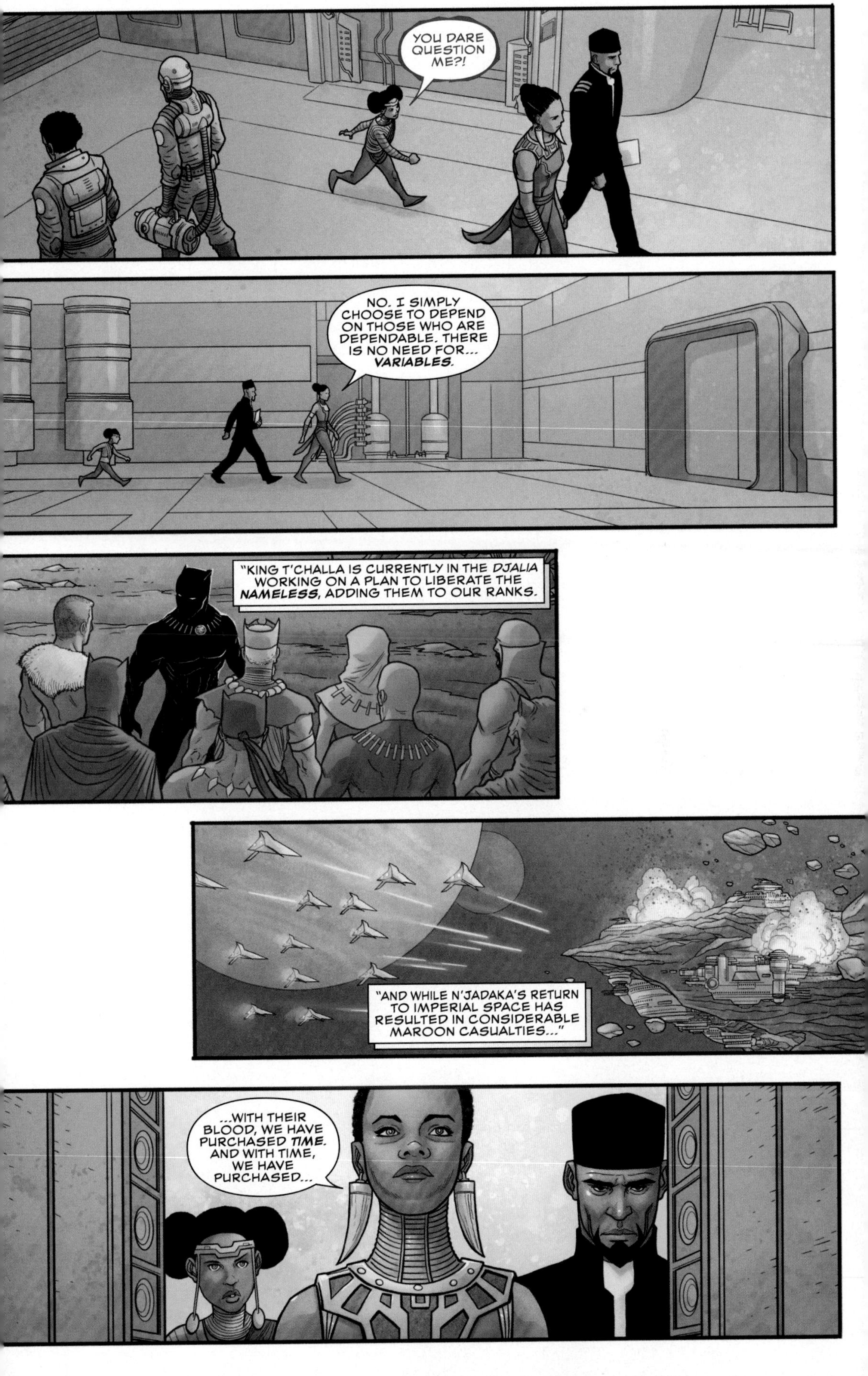
YOU DARE QUESTION ME?!
NO. I SIMPLY CHOOSE TO DEPEND ON THOSE WHO ARE DEPENDABLE. THERE IS NO NEED FOR... VARIABLES.
"KING T'CHALLA IS CURRENTLY IN THE DJALIA WORKING ON A PLAN TO LIBERATE THE NAMELESS, ADDING THEM TO OUR RANKS.
"AND WHILE N'JADAKA'S RETURN TO IMPERIAL SPACE HAS RESULTED IN CONSIDERABLE MAROON CASUALTIES..."
...WITH THEIR BLOOD, WE HAVE PURCHASED TIME. AND WITH TIME, WE HAVE PURCHASED...

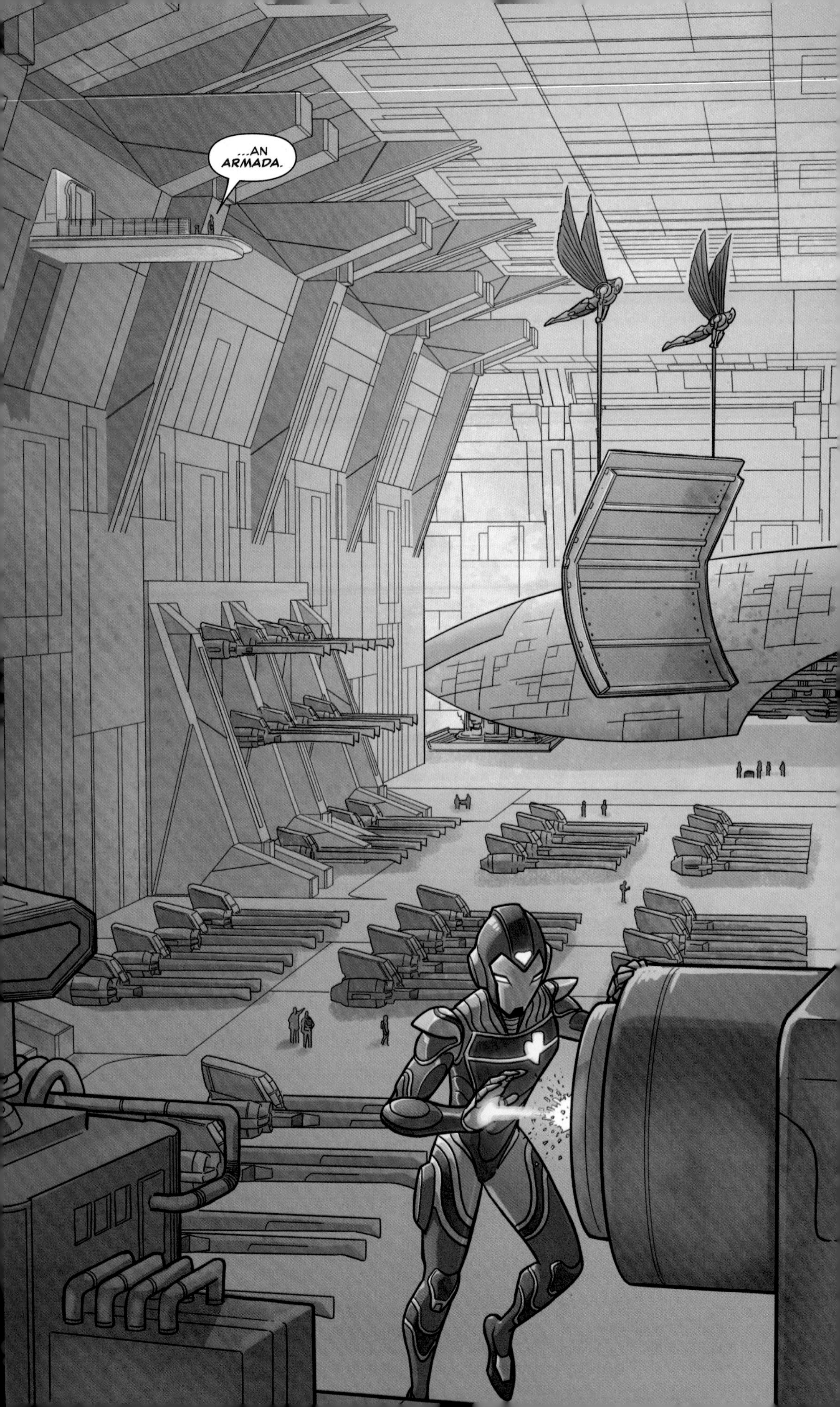
...AN ARMADA.

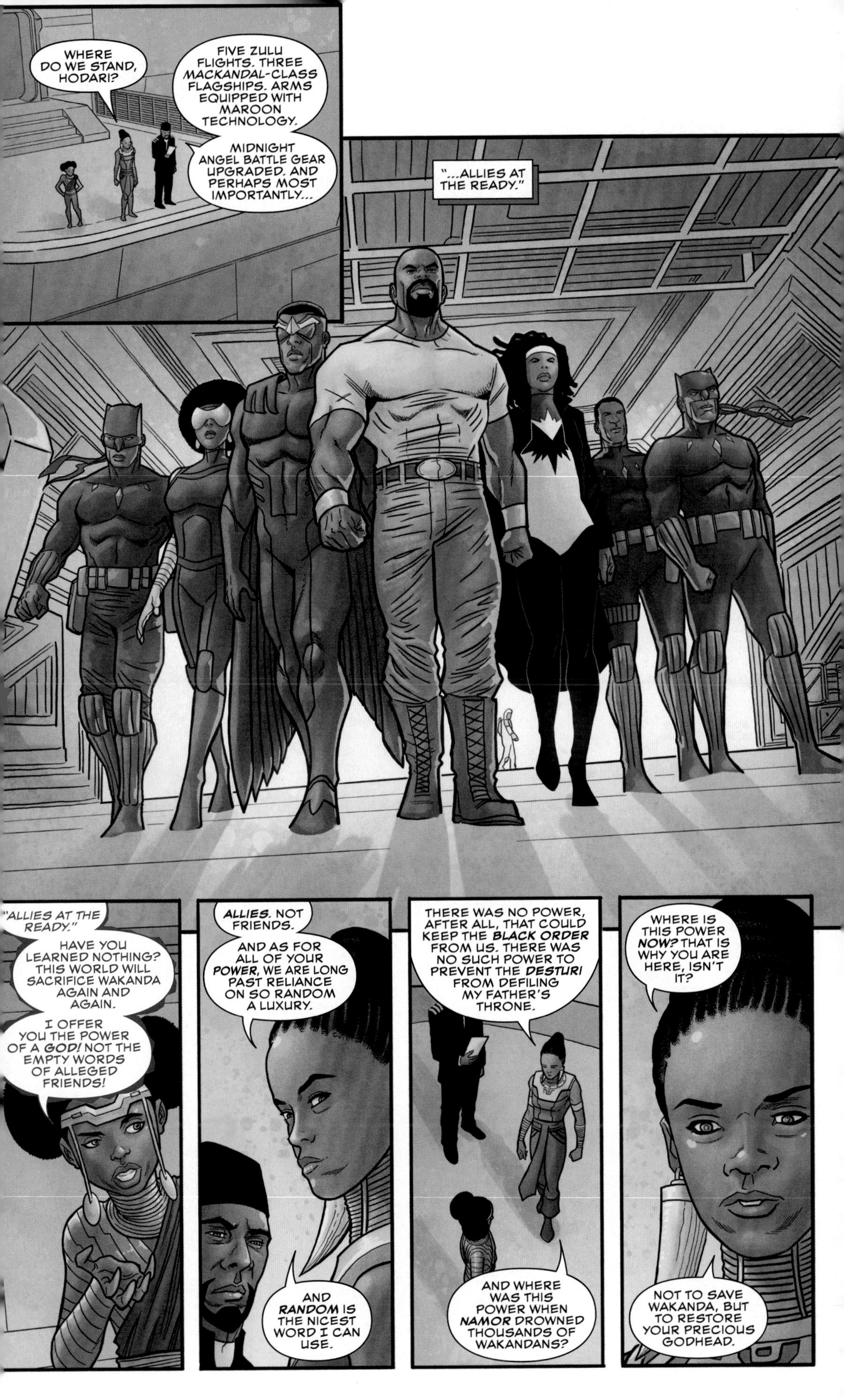
WHERE DO WE STAND, HODARI?
FIVE ZULU FLIGHTS. THREE MACKANDAL-CLASS FLAGSHIPS. ARMS EQUIPPED WITH MAROON TECHNOLOGY.
MIDNIGHT ANGEL BATTLE GEAR UPGRADED. AND PERHAPS MOST IMPORTANTLY...
"...ALLIES AT THE READY."
"ALLIES AT THE READY."
HAVE YOU LEARNED NOTHING? THIS WORLD WILL SACRIFICE WAKANDA AGAIN AND AGAIN.
I OFFER YOU THE POWER OF A GOD! NOT THE EMPTY WORDS OF ALLEGED FRIENDS!
ALLIES. NOT FRIENDS.
AND AS FOR ALL OF YOUR POWER, WE ARE LONG PAST RELIANCE ON SO RANDOM A LUXURY.
AND RANDOM IS THE NICEST WORD I CAN USE.
THERE WAS NO POWER, AFTER ALL, THAT COULD KEEP THE BLACK ORDER FROM US. THERE WAS NO SUCH POWER TO PREVENT THE DESTURI FROM DEFILING MY FATHER'S THRONE.
AND WHERE WAS THIS POWER WHEN NAMOR DROWNED THOUSANDS OF WAKANDANS?
WHERE IS THIS POWER NOW? THAT IS WHY YOU ARE HERE, ISN'T IT?
NOT TO SAVE WAKANDA, BUT TO RESTORE YOUR PRECIOUS GODHEAD.

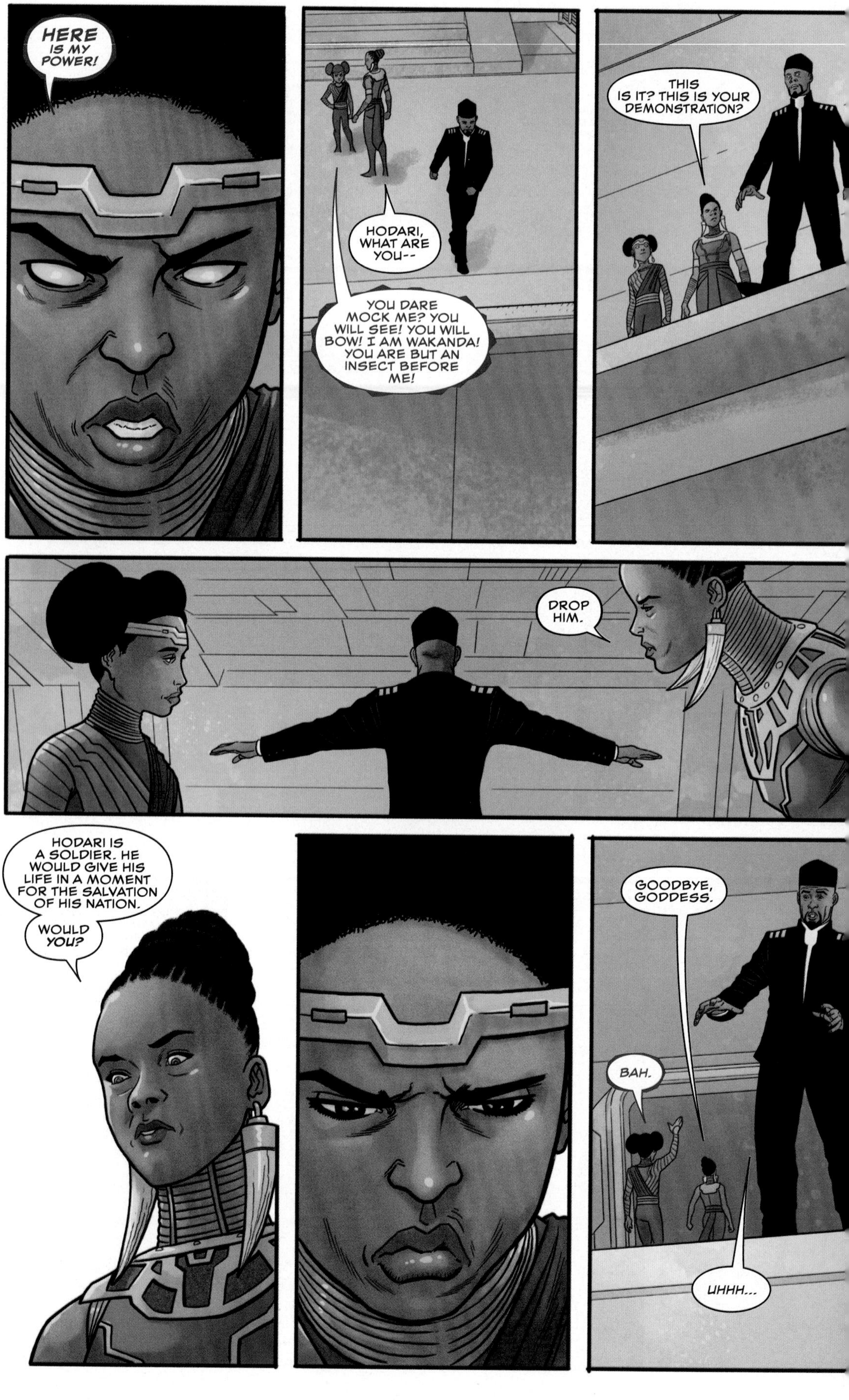
HERE IS MY POWER!
HODARI, WHAT ARE YOU--
YOU DARE MOCK ME? YOU WILL SEE! YOU WILL BOW! I AM WAKANDA! YOU ARE BUT AN INSECT BEFORE ME!
THIS IS IT? THIS IS YOUR DEMONSTRATION?
DROP HIM.
HODARI IS A SOLDIER. HE WOULD GIVE HIS LIFE IN A MOMENT FOR THE SALVATION OF HIS NATION.
WOULD YOU?
GOODBYE, GODDESS.
BAH.
UHHH...

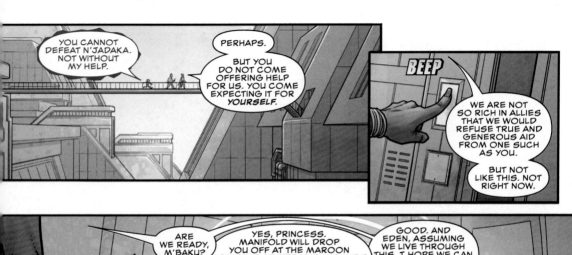

YOU CANNOT DEFEAT N'JADAKA. NOT WITHOUT MY HELP.

PERHAPS.

BUT YOU DO NOT COME OFFERING HELP FOR US. YOU COME EXPECTING IT FOR *YOURSELF*.

BEEP

WE ARE NOT SO RICH IN ALLIES THAT WE WOULD REFUSE TRUE AND GENEROUS AID FROM ONE SUCH AS YOU.

BUT NOT LIKE THIS. NOT RIGHT NOW.

ARE WE READY, M'BAKU?

YES, PRINCESS. MANIFOLD WILL DROP YOU OFF AT THE MAROON COMMAND CENTER, THEN HE AND I WILL GO MAN THE CONTROLS OF THE GALACTIC GATE SO THAT OUR NEW ARMADA CAN BE SENT THROUGH.

GOOD. AND EDEN, ASSUMING WE LIVE THROUGH THIS, I HOPE WE CAN GRAB A MOMENT TOGETHER TO RECONNECT.

OKAY, WELL NOW WE *HAVE* TO LIVE THROUGH THIS.

IF YOU'LL EXCUSE US, BAST, WE HAVE A WAR TO FIGHT.

WHEN YOU ARE PREPARED TO JOIN US, WE WILL BE READY.

BUT WE WILL NOT BE WAITING. NOT ON YOU.

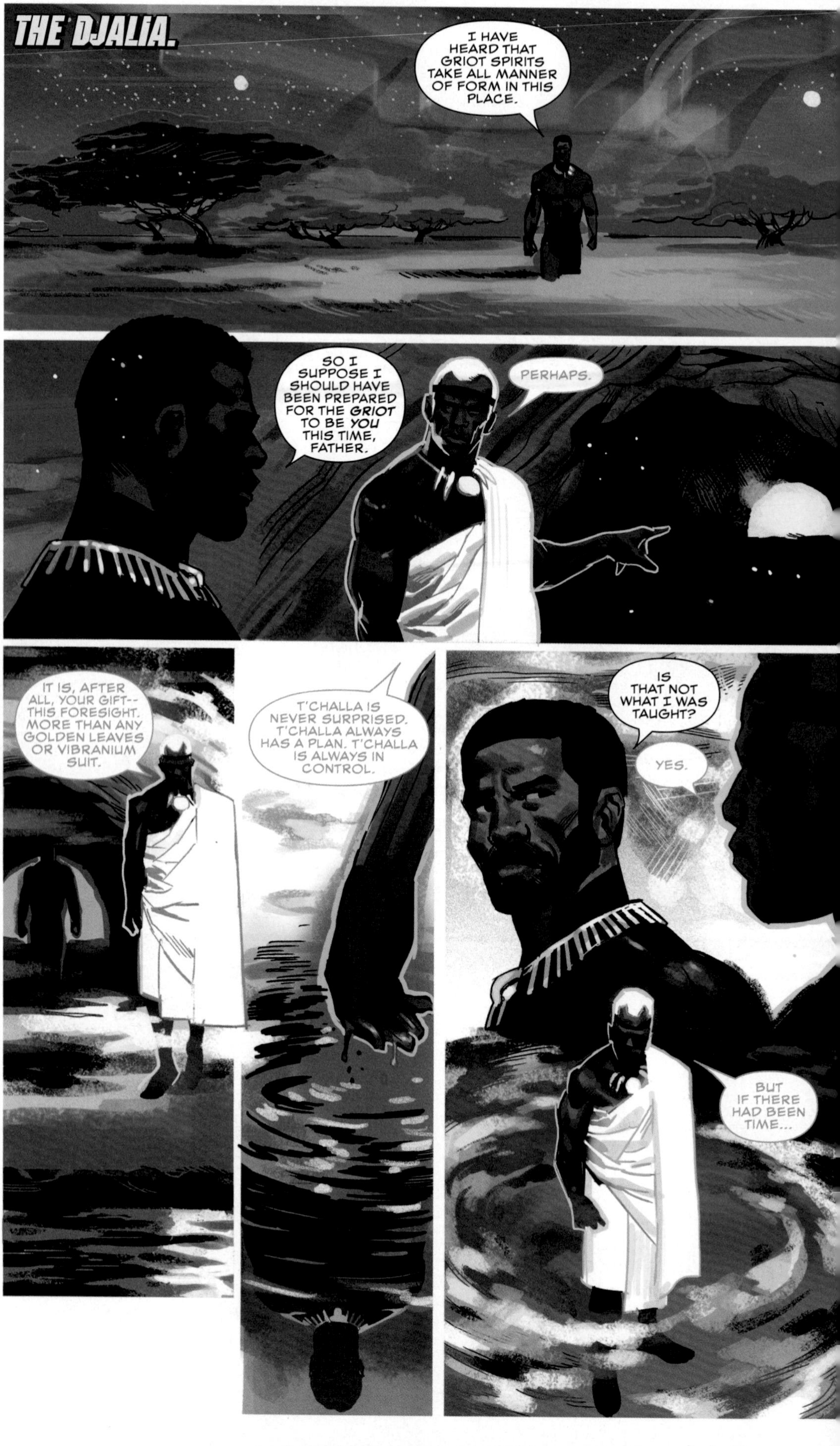
THE DJALIA.
I HAVE HEARD THAT GRIOT SPIRITS TAKE ALL MANNER OF FORM IN THIS PLACE.
SO I SUPPOSE I SHOULD HAVE BEEN PREPARED FOR THE *GRIOT* TO BE *YOU* THIS TIME, FATHER.
PERHAPS.
IT IS, AFTER ALL, YOUR GIFT-- THIS FORESIGHT. MORE THAN ANY GOLDEN LEAVES OR VIBRANIUM SUIT.
T'CHALLA IS NEVER SURPRISED. T'CHALLA ALWAYS HAS A PLAN. T'CHALLA IS ALWAYS IN CONTROL.
IS THAT NOT WHAT I WAS TAUGHT?
YES.
BUT IF THERE HAD BEEN TIME...

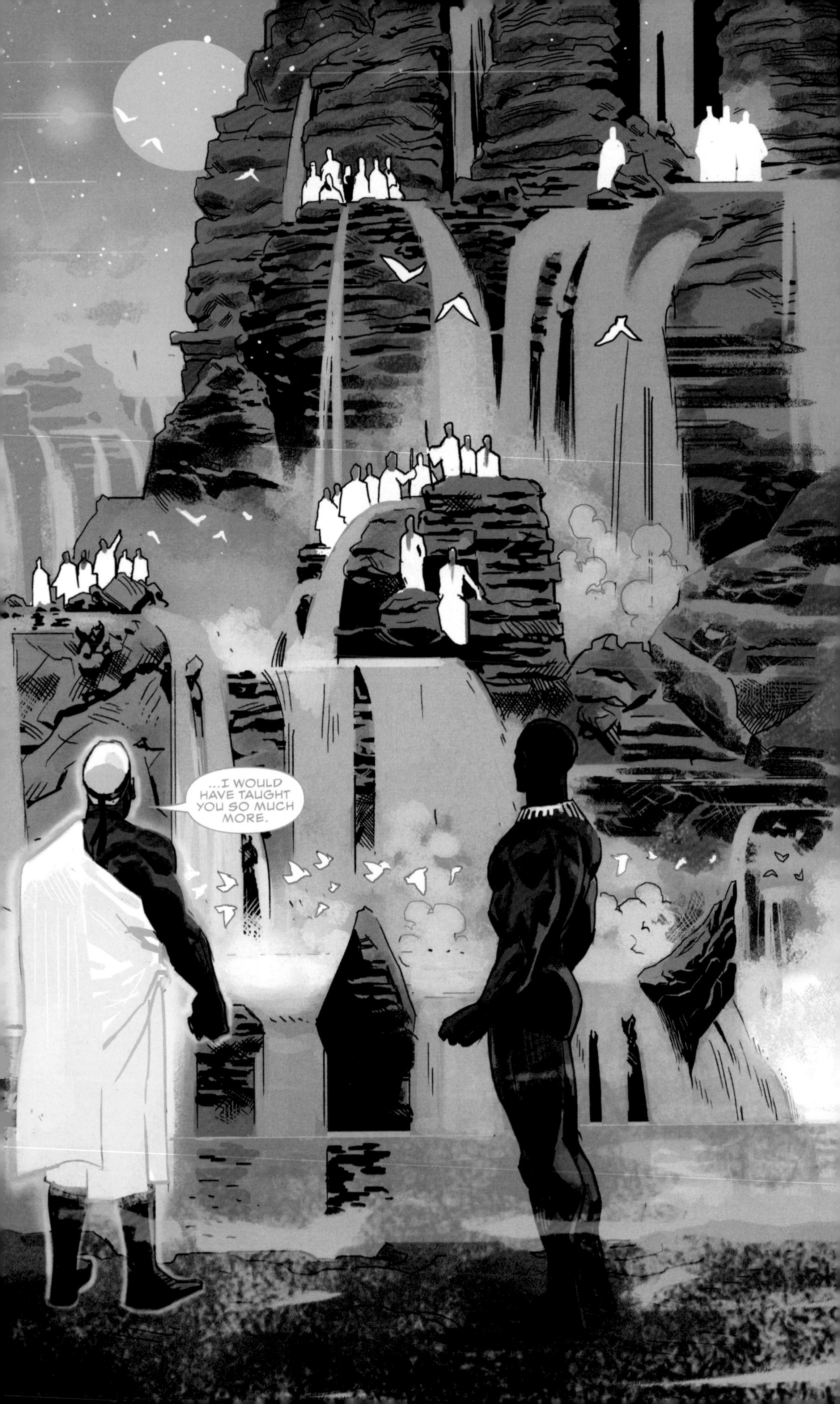
...I WOULD HAVE TAUGHT YOU SO MUCH MORE.

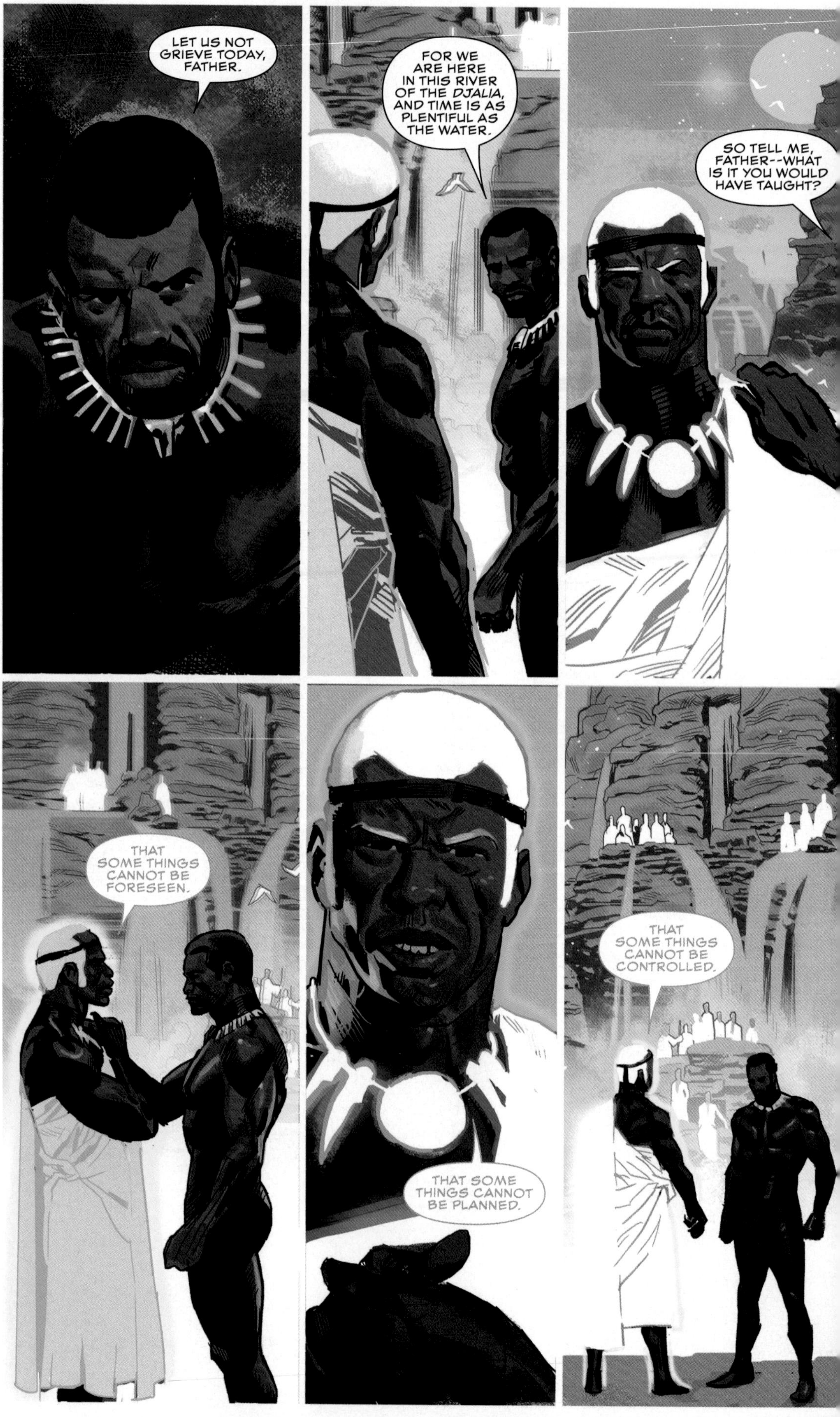
LET US NOT GRIEVE TODAY, FATHER.
FOR WE ARE HERE IN THIS RIVER OF THE *DJALIA*, AND TIME IS AS PLENTIFUL AS THE WATER.
SO TELL ME, FATHER--WHAT IS IT YOU WOULD HAVE TAUGHT?
THAT SOME THINGS CANNOT BE FORESEEN.
THAT SOME THINGS CANNOT BE PLANNED.
THAT SOME THINGS CANNOT BE CONTROLLED.

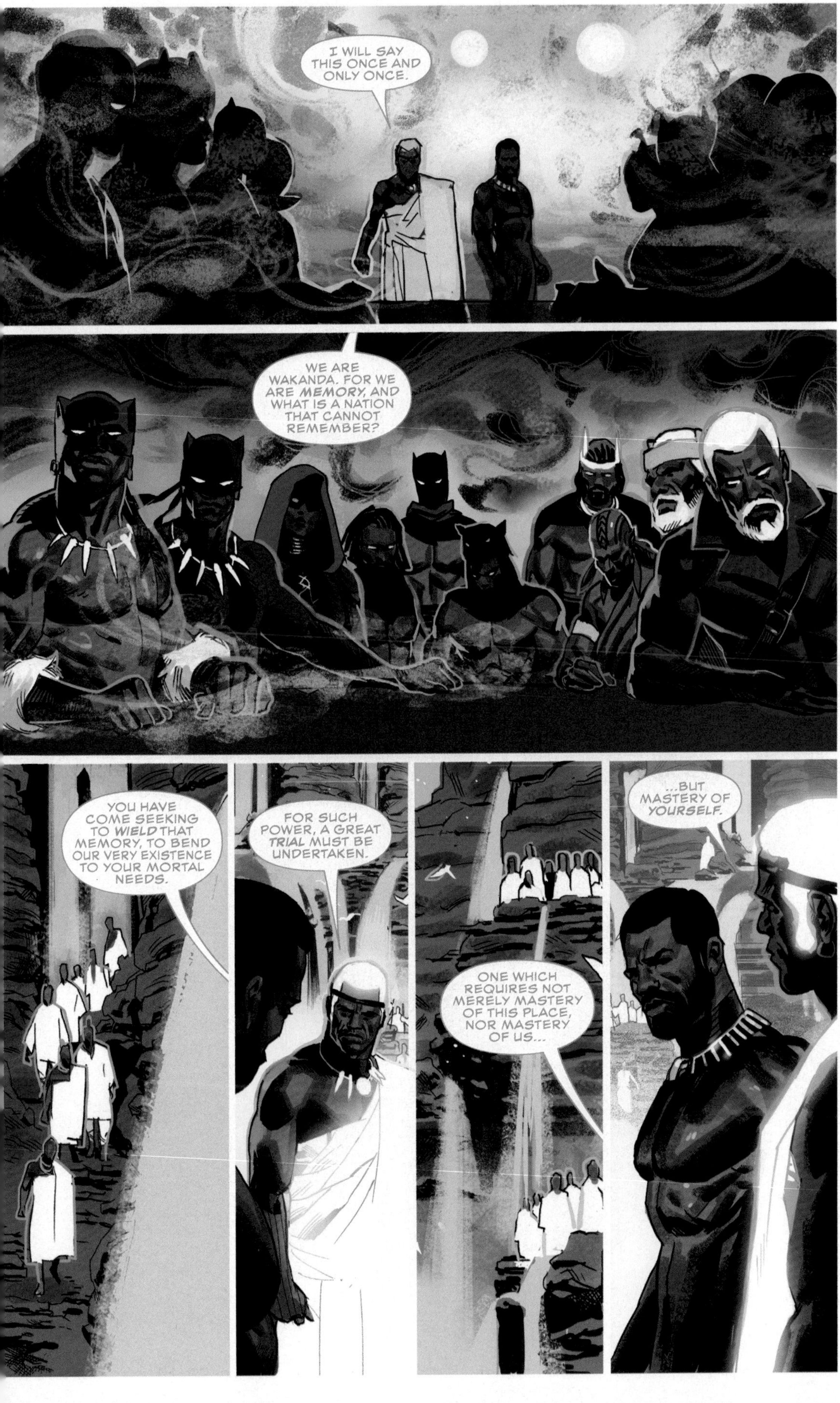

I WILL SAY THIS ONCE AND ONLY ONCE.
WE ARE WAKANDA. FOR WE ARE MEMORY, AND WHAT IS A NATION THAT CANNOT REMEMBER?
YOU HAVE COME SEEKING TO WIELD THAT MEMORY, TO BEND OUR VERY EXISTENCE TO YOUR MORTAL NEEDS.
FOR SUCH POWER, A GREAT TRIAL MUST BE UNDERTAKEN.
ONE WHICH REQUIRES NOT MERELY MASTERY OF THIS PLACE, NOR MASTERY OF US...
...BUT MASTERY OF YOURSELF.

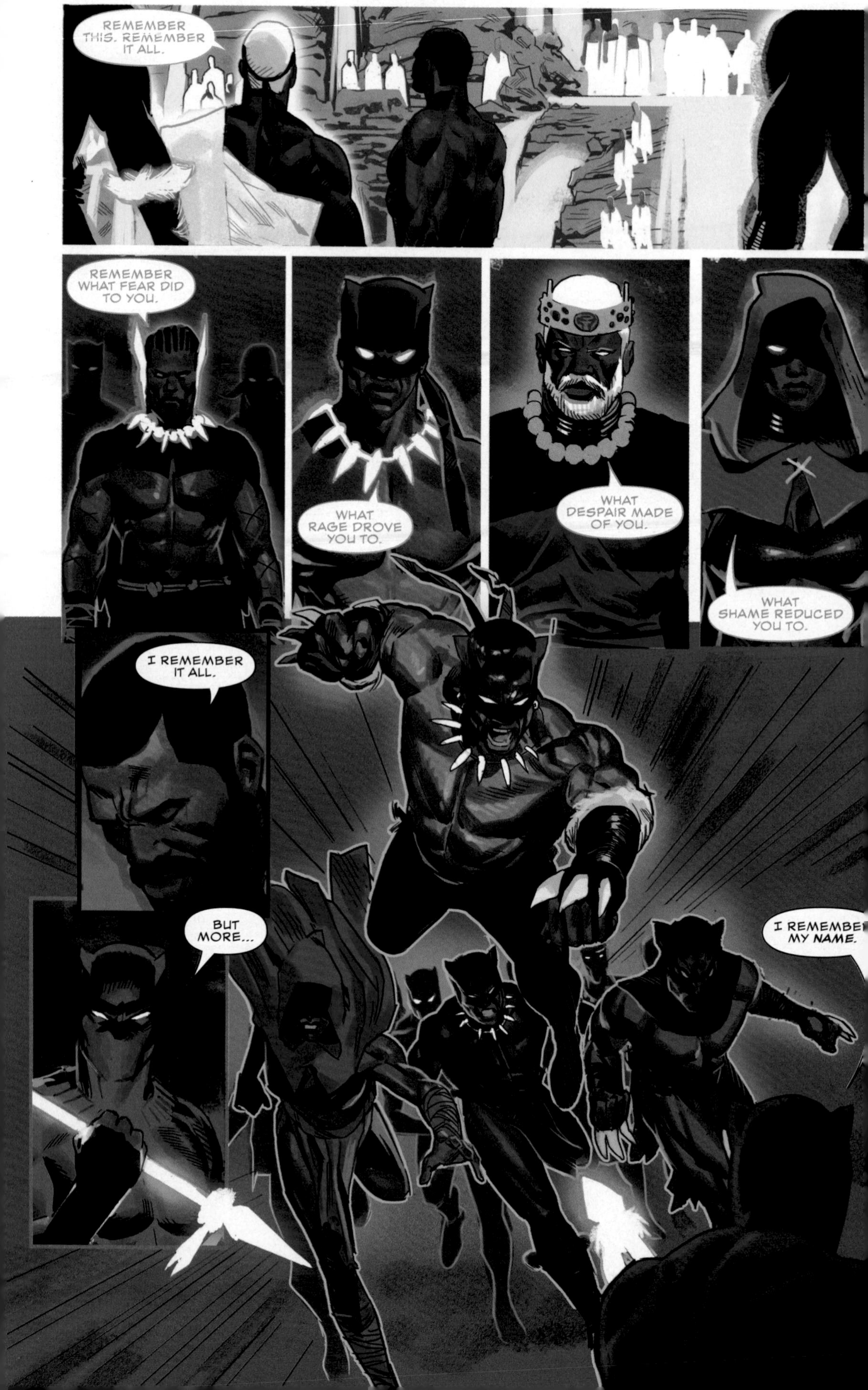
REMEMBER THIS. REMEMBER IT ALL.
REMEMBER WHAT FEAR DID TO YOU.
WHAT RAGE DROVE YOU TO.
WHAT DESPAIR MADE OF YOU.
WHAT SHAME REDUCED YOU TO.
I REMEMBER IT ALL.
BUT MORE...
I REMEMBE MY NAME.

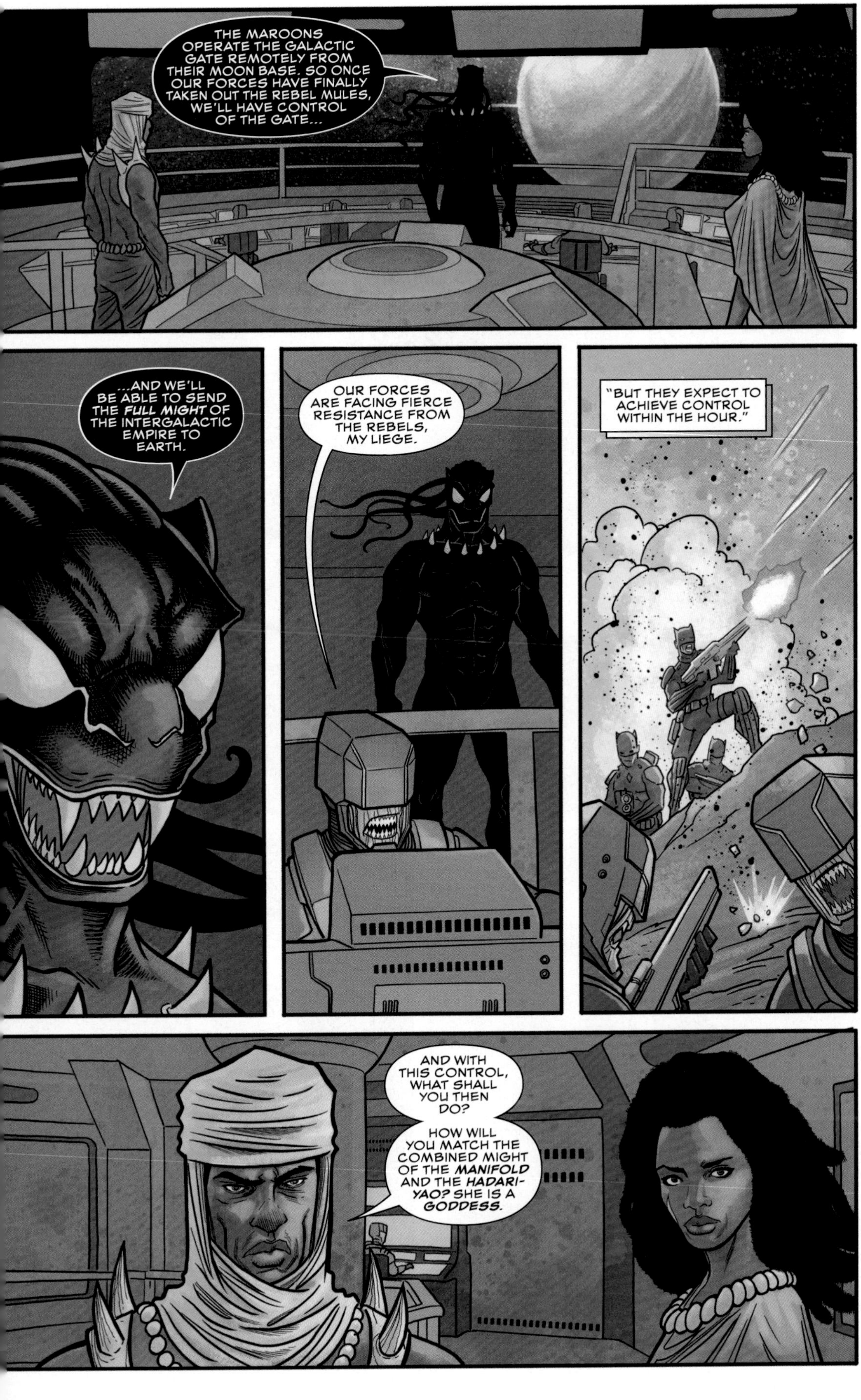
THE MAROONS OPERATE THE GALACTIC GATE REMOTELY FROM THEIR MOON BASE. SO ONCE OUR FORCES HAVE FINALLY TAKEN OUT THE REBEL MULES, WE'LL HAVE CONTROL OF THE GATE...
...AND WE'LL BE ABLE TO SEND THE FULL MIGHT OF THE INTERGALACTIC EMPIRE TO EARTH.
OUR FORCES ARE FACING FIERCE RESISTANCE FROM THE REBELS, MY LIEGE.
"BUT THEY EXPECT TO ACHIEVE CONTROL WITHIN THE HOUR."
AND WITH THIS CONTROL, WHAT SHALL YOU THEN DO?
HOW WILL YOU MATCH THE COMBINED MIGHT OF THE MANIFOLD AND THE HADARI-YAO? SHE IS A GODDESS.

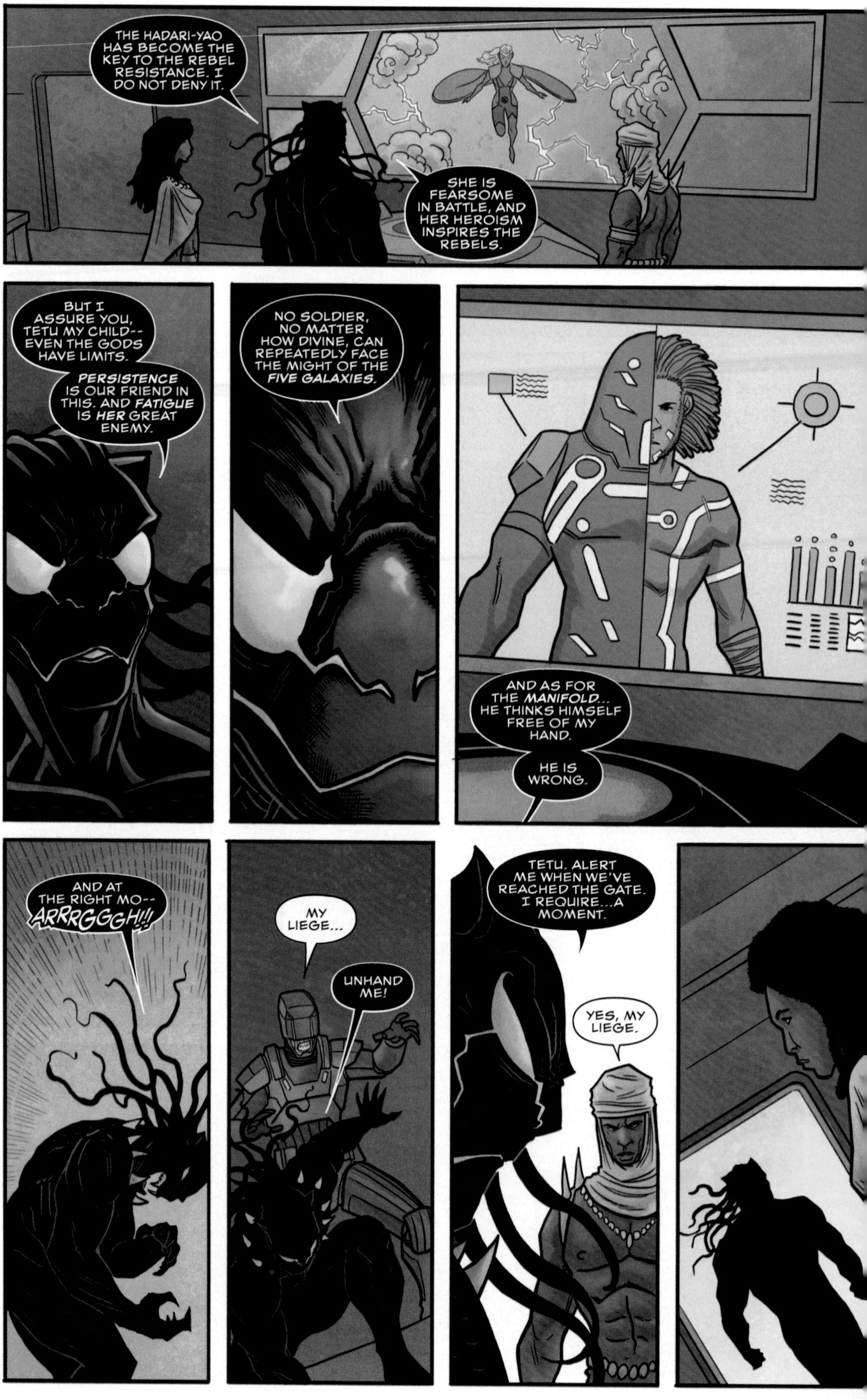
THE HADARI-YAO HAS BECOME THE KEY TO THE REBEL RESISTANCE. I DO NOT DENY IT.
SHE IS FEARSOME IN BATTLE, AND HER HEROISM INSPIRES THE REBELS.
BUT I ASSURE YOU, TETU MY CHILD-- EVEN THE GODS HAVE LIMITS.
PERSISTENCE IS OUR FRIEND IN THIS. AND *FATIGUE* IS *HER* GREAT ENEMY.
NO SOLDIER, NO MATTER HOW DIVINE, CAN REPEATEDLY FACE THE MIGHT OF THE *FIVE GALAXIES*.
AND AS FOR THE *MANIFOLD*... HE THINKS HIMSELF FREE OF MY HAND.
HE IS WRONG.
AND AT THE RIGHT MO-- ARRRGGGH!!!
MY LIEGE...
UNHAND ME!
TETU. ALERT ME WHEN WE'VE REACHED THE GATE. I REQUIRE...A MOMENT.
YES, MY LIEGE.

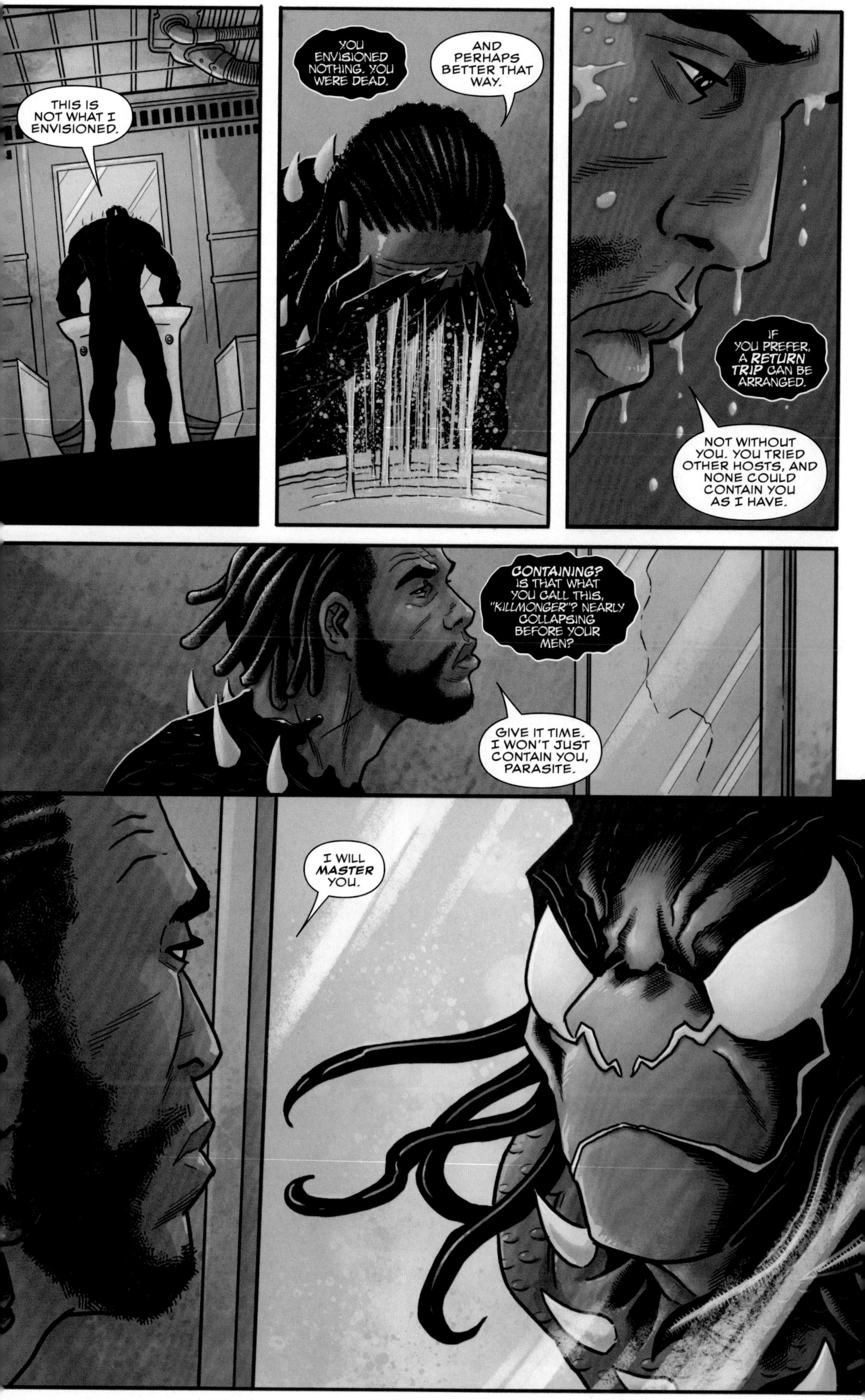
THIS IS NOT WHAT I ENVISIONED.
YOU ENVISIONED NOTHING. YOU WERE DEAD.
AND PERHAPS BETTER THAT WAY.
IF YOU PREFER, A RETURN TRIP CAN BE ARRANGED.
NOT WITHOUT YOU. YOU TRIED OTHER HOSTS, AND NONE COULD CONTAIN YOU AS I HAVE.
CONTAINING? IS THAT WHAT YOU CALL THIS, "KILLMONGER"? NEARLY COLLAPSING BEFORE YOUR MEN?
GIVE IT TIME. I WON'T JUST CONTAIN YOU, PARASITE.
I WILL MASTER YOU.

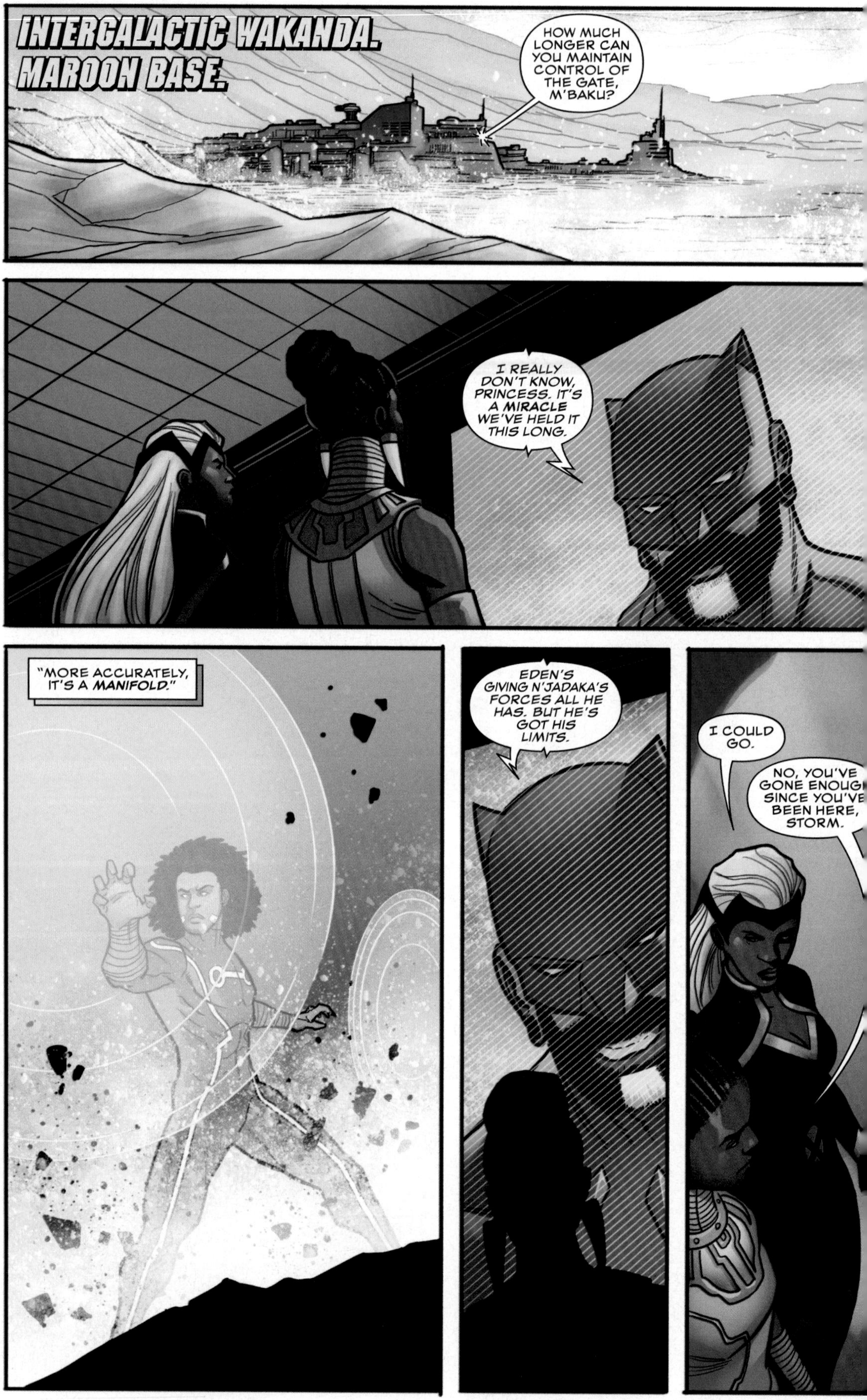
INTERGALACTIC WAKANDA. MAROON BASE.
HOW MUCH LONGER CAN YOU MAINTAIN CONTROL OF THE GATE, M'BAKU?
I REALLY DON'T KNOW, PRINCESS. IT'S A MIRACLE WE'VE HELD IT THIS LONG.
"MORE ACCURATELY, IT'S A MANIFOLD."
EDEN'S GIVING N'JADAKA'S FORCES ALL HE HAS. BUT HE'S GOT HIS LIMITS.
I COULD GO.
NO, YOU'VE GONE ENOUG SINCE YOU'VE BEEN HERE, STORM.

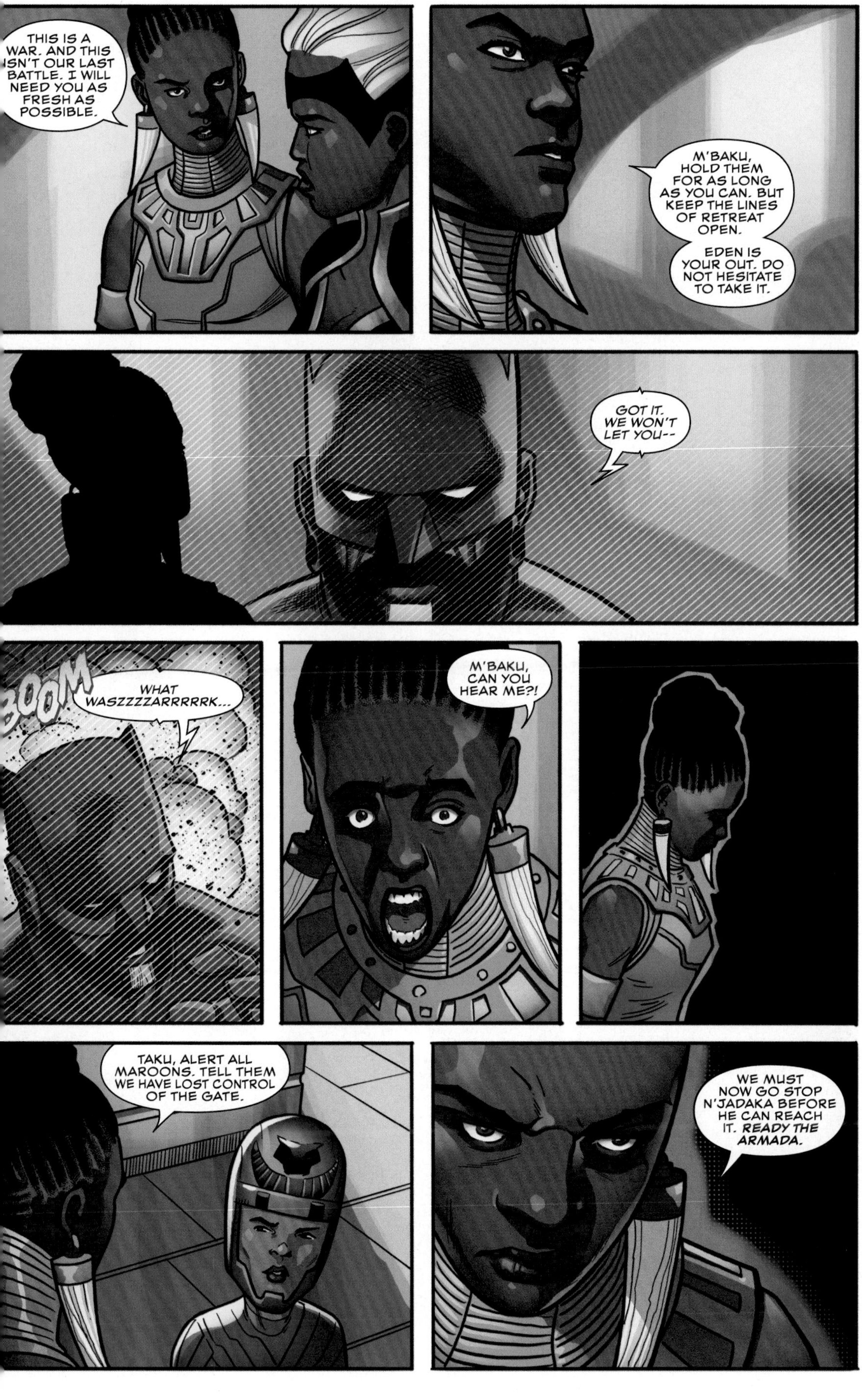
THIS IS A WAR. AND THIS ISN'T OUR LAST BATTLE. I WILL NEED YOU AS FRESH AS POSSIBLE.
M'BAKU, HOLD THEM FOR AS LONG AS YOU CAN. BUT KEEP THE LINES OF RETREAT OPEN.
EDEN IS YOUR OUT. DO NOT HESITATE TO TAKE IT.
GOT IT. WE WON'T LET YOU--
BOOM
WHAT WASZZZZARRRRRK...
M'BAKU, CAN YOU HEAR ME?!
TAKU, ALERT ALL MAROONS. TELL THEM WE HAVE LOST CONTROL OF THE GATE.
WE MUST NOW GO STOP N'JADAKA BEFORE HE CAN REACH IT. *READY THE ARMADA.*

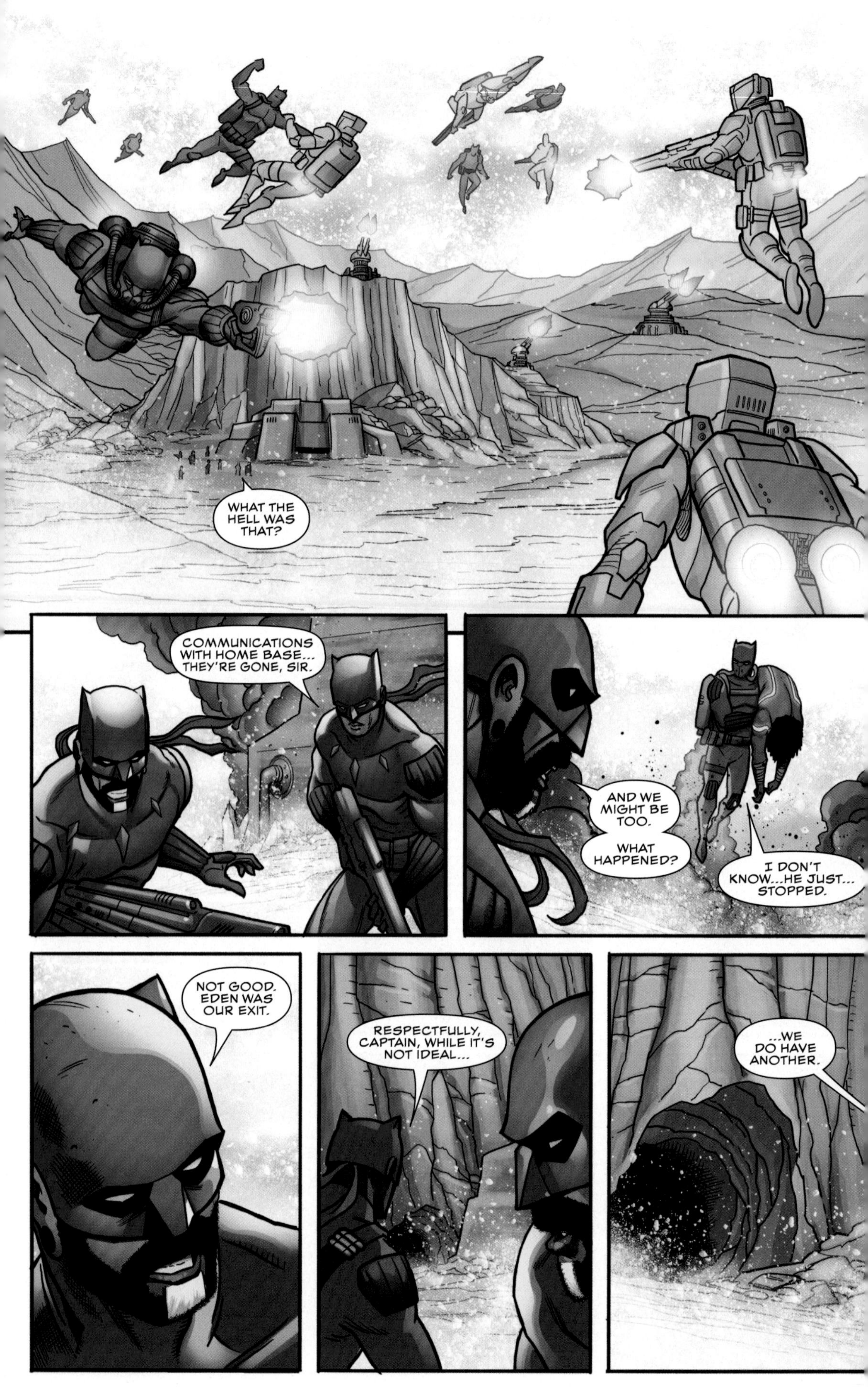
WHAT THE HELL WAS THAT?
COMMUNICATIONS WITH HOME BASE... THEY'RE GONE, SIR.
AND WE MIGHT BE TOO.
WHAT HAPPENED?
I DON'T KNOW...HE JUST... STOPPED.
NOT GOOD. EDEN WAS OUR EXIT.
RESPECTFULLY, CAPTAIN, WHILE IT'S NOT IDEAL...
...WE DO HAVE ANOTHER.

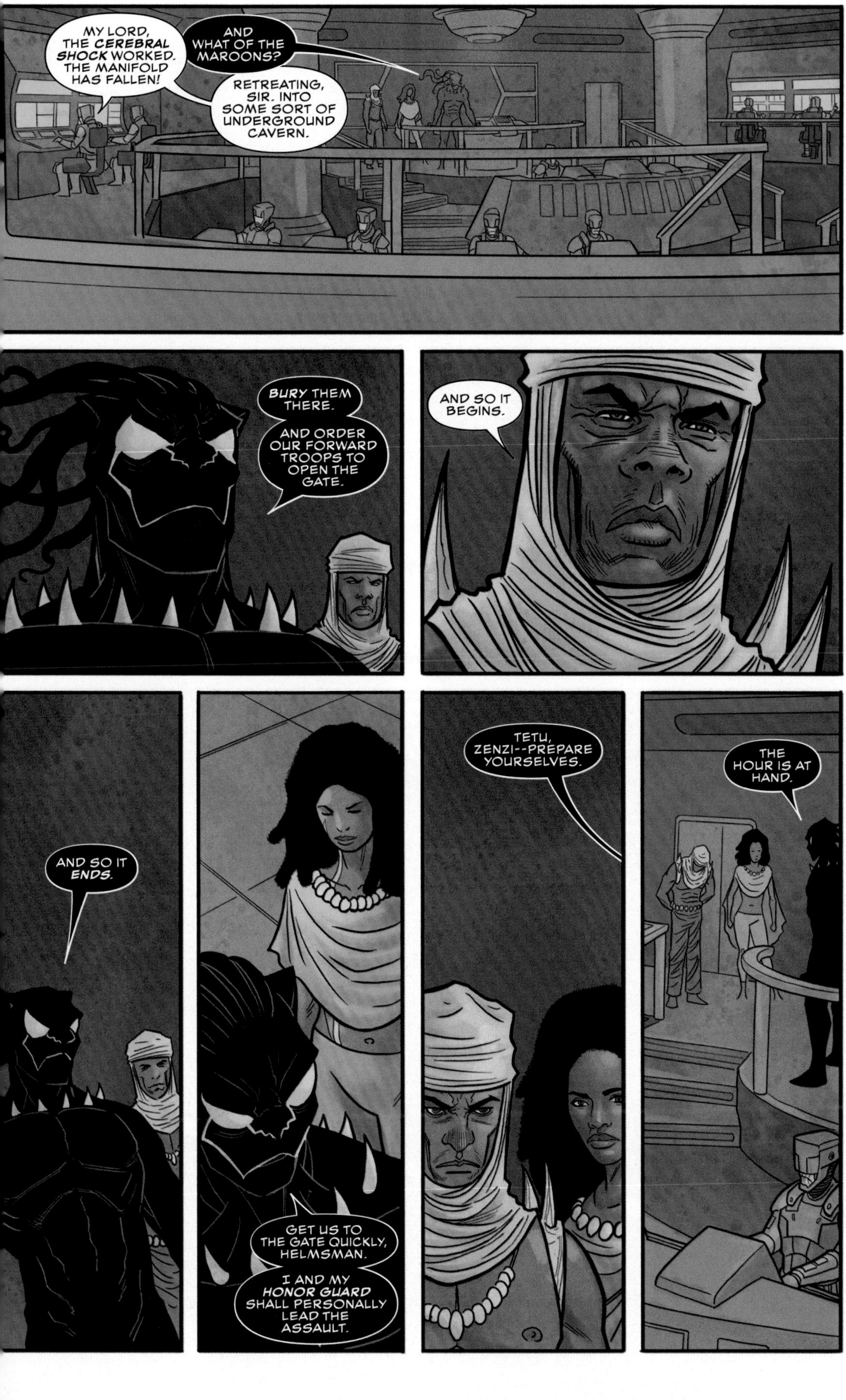
MY LORD, THE CEREBRAL SHOCK WORKED. THE MANIFOLD HAS FALLEN!
AND WHAT OF THE MAROONS?
RETREATING, SIR. INTO SOME SORT OF UNDERGROUND CAVERN.
BURY THEM THERE.
AND ORDER OUR FORWARD TROOPS TO OPEN THE GATE.
AND SO IT BEGINS.
AND SO IT ENDS.
GET US TO THE GATE QUICKLY, HELMSMAN.
I AND MY HONOR GUARD SHALL PERSONALLY LEAD THE ASSAULT.
TETU, ZENZI--PREPARE YOURSELVES.
THE HOUR IS AT HAND.

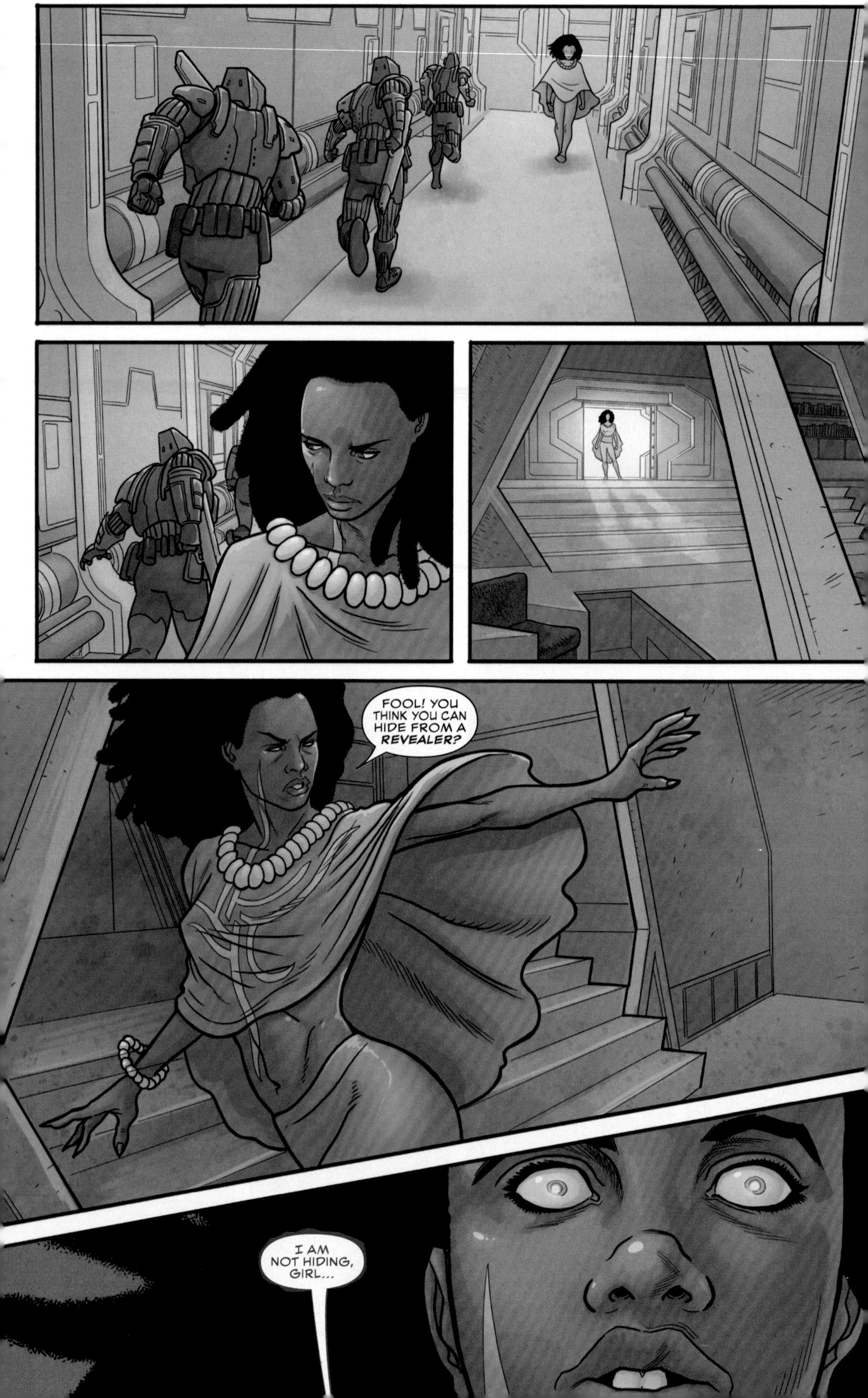
FOOL! YOU THINK YOU CAN HIDE FROM A REVEALER?
I AM NOT HIDING, GIRL...

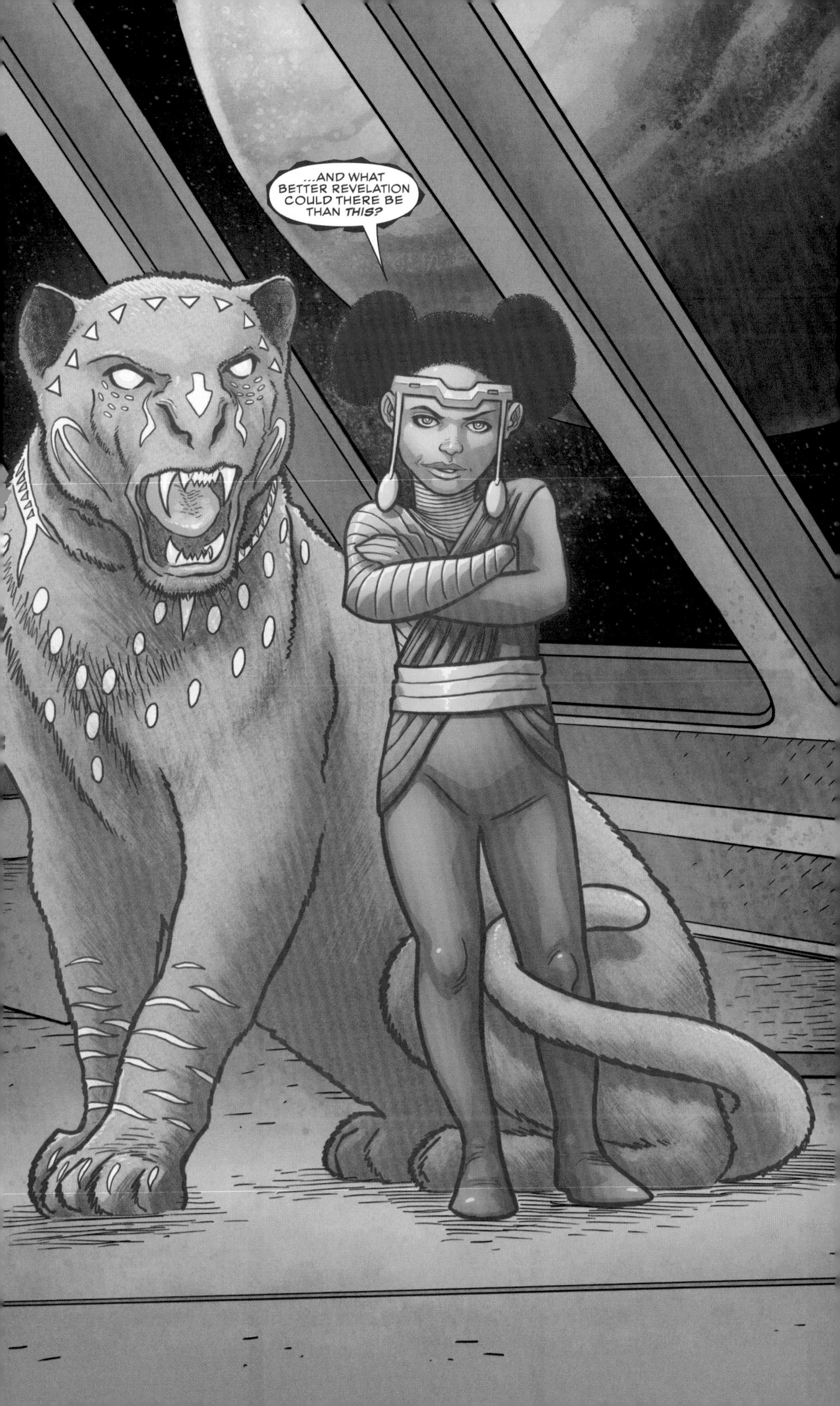
...AND WHAT BETTER REVELATION COULD THERE BE THAN *THIS?*

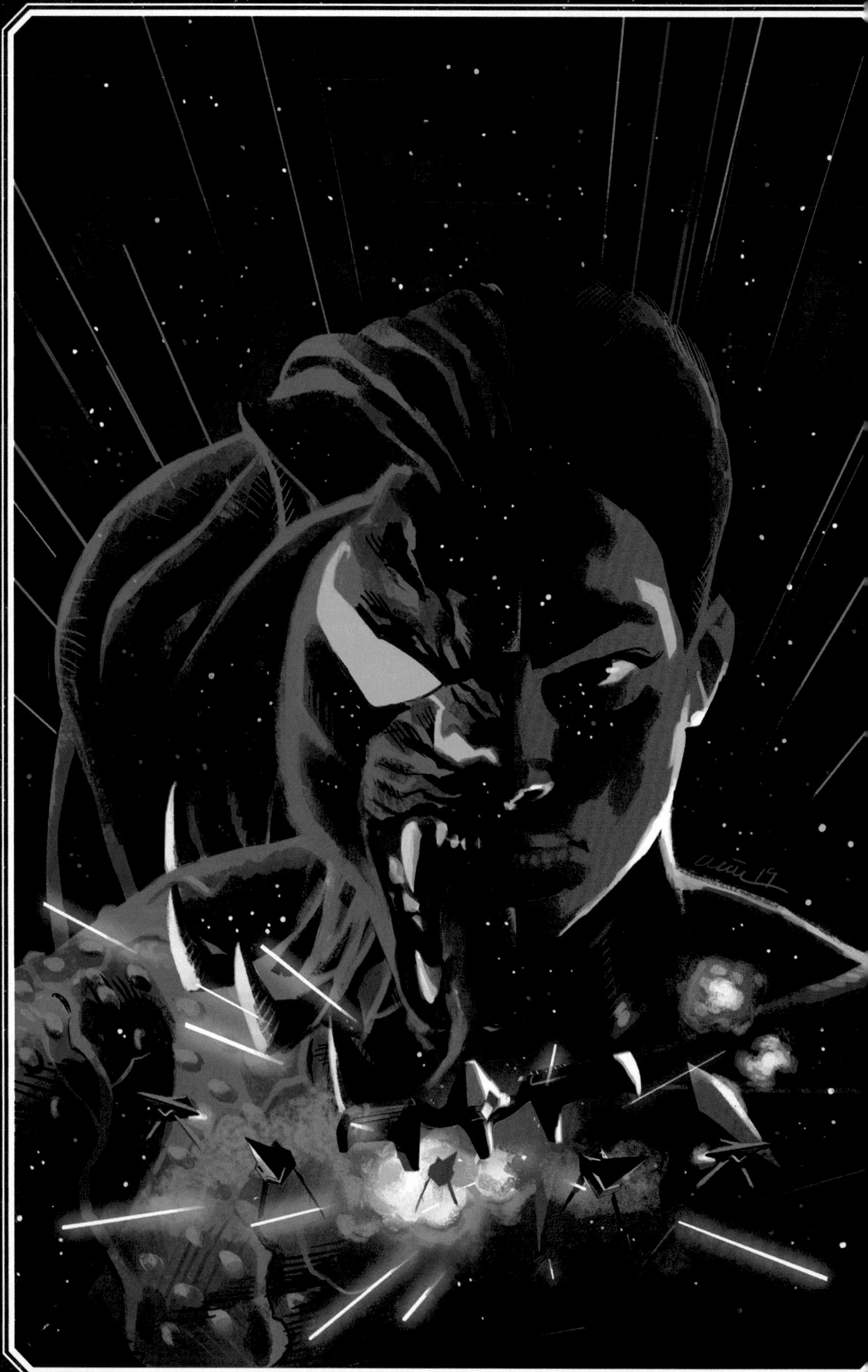

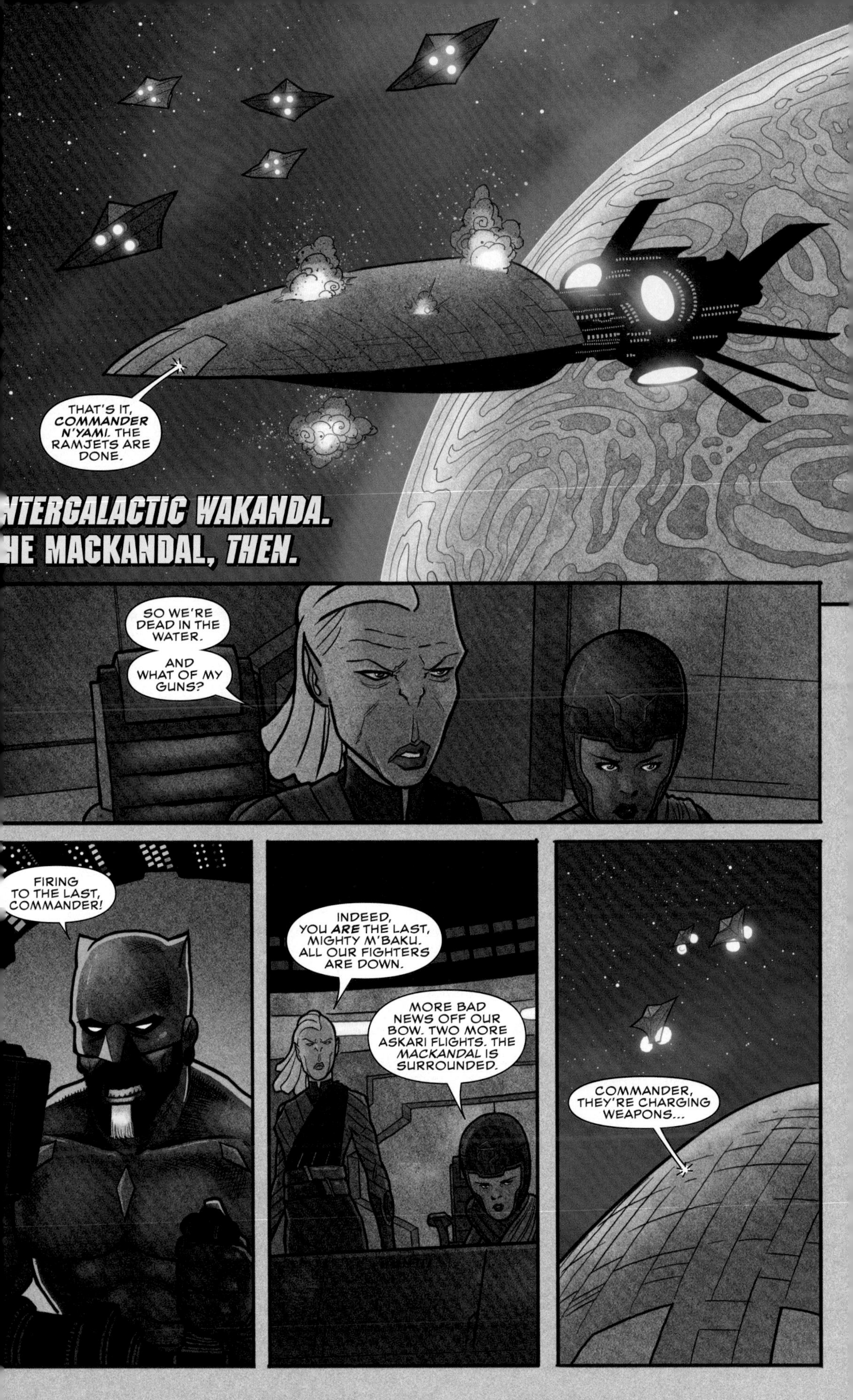
THAT'S IT, COMMANDER N'YAMI. THE RAMJETS ARE DONE.
NTERGALACTIC WAKANDA.
HE MACKANDAL, THEN.
SO WE'RE DEAD IN THE WATER.
AND WHAT OF MY GUNS?
FIRING TO THE LAST, COMMANDER!
INDEED, YOU ARE THE LAST, MIGHTY M'BAKU. ALL OUR FIGHTERS ARE DOWN.
MORE BAD NEWS OFF OUR BOW. TWO MORE ASKARI FLIGHTS. THE MACKANDAL IS SURROUNDED.
COMMANDER, THEY'RE CHARGING WEAPONS...

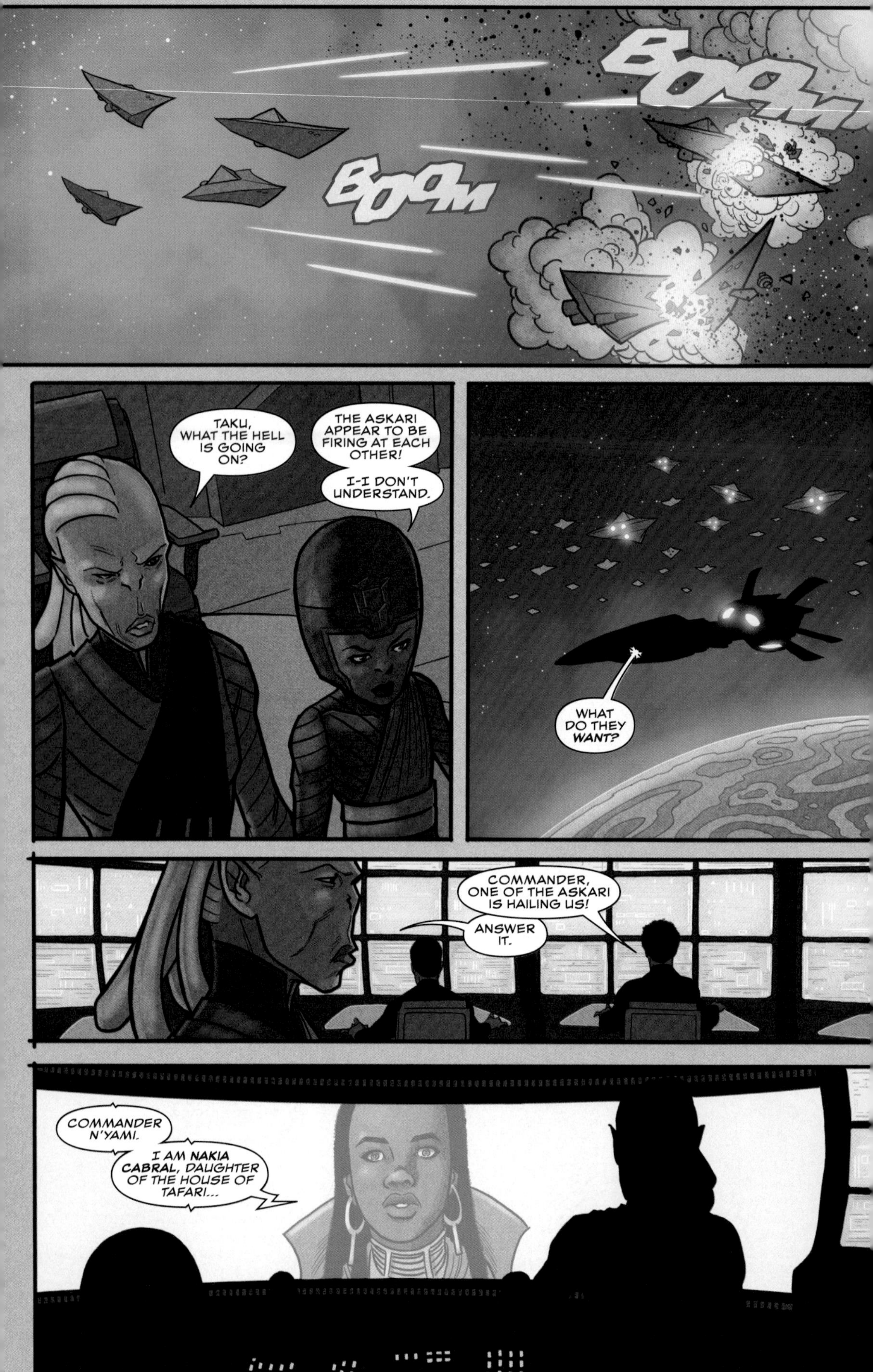
BOOM
BOOM
TAKU, WHAT THE HELL IS GOING ON?
THE ASKARI APPEAR TO BE FIRING AT EACH OTHER!
I-I DON'T UNDERSTAND.
WHAT DO THEY *WANT?*
COMMANDER, ONE OF THE ASKARI IS HAILING US!
ANSWER IT.
COMMANDER N'YAMI.
I AM **NAKIA CABRAL**, DAUGHTER OF THE HOUSE OF TAFARI...

"...AND I COME BEARING GIFTS."

STILL NO COMMUNICATION WITH *SHURI* AND HER FORCES, HELMSMAN?

NO, CAPTAIN NAKIA. THE IMPERIALS ARE LIKELY JAMMING EVERYTHING LONG-RANGE.

BUT WE KNOW THEY LOST CONTROL OF THE *GATE.* SO N'JADAKA IS SURELY ON HIS WAY HERE.

THEN WE KNOW WHAT WE MUST DO. NO ONE GOES THROUGH THIS GATE, MAROONS. GET READY.

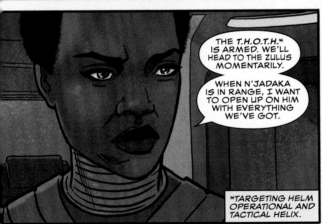

THE *T.H.O.T.H.** IS ARMED. WE'LL HEAD TO THE ZULUS MOMENTARILY.

WHEN N'JADAKA IS IN RANGE, I WANT TO OPEN UP ON HIM WITH EVERYTHING WE'VE GOT.

*TARGETING HELM OPERATIONAL AND TACTICAL HELIX.

THE *COLLECTOR* TOO?

NO, NOT YET.

AND LET'S PRAY NOT EVER.

RESPECTFULLY, CAPTAIN, THE FREEDOM OF THE FIVE GALAXIES-- AND NOW POSSIBLY A *SIXTH*--HANGS IN THE BALANCE.

WE MAY NOT HAVE A CHOICE...

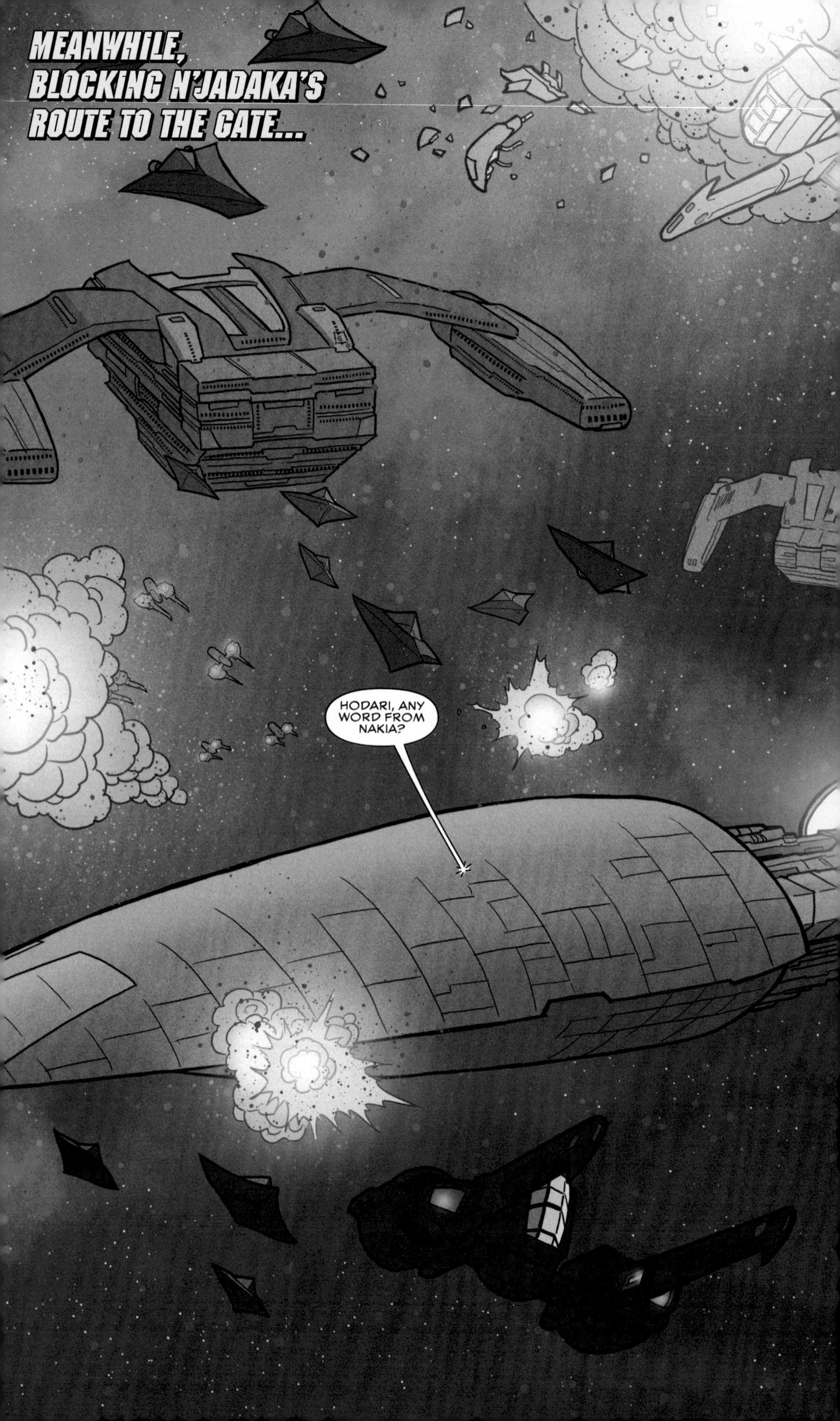
MEANWHILE, BLOCKING N'JADAKA'S ROUTE TO THE GATE...
HODARI, ANY WORD FROM NAKIA?

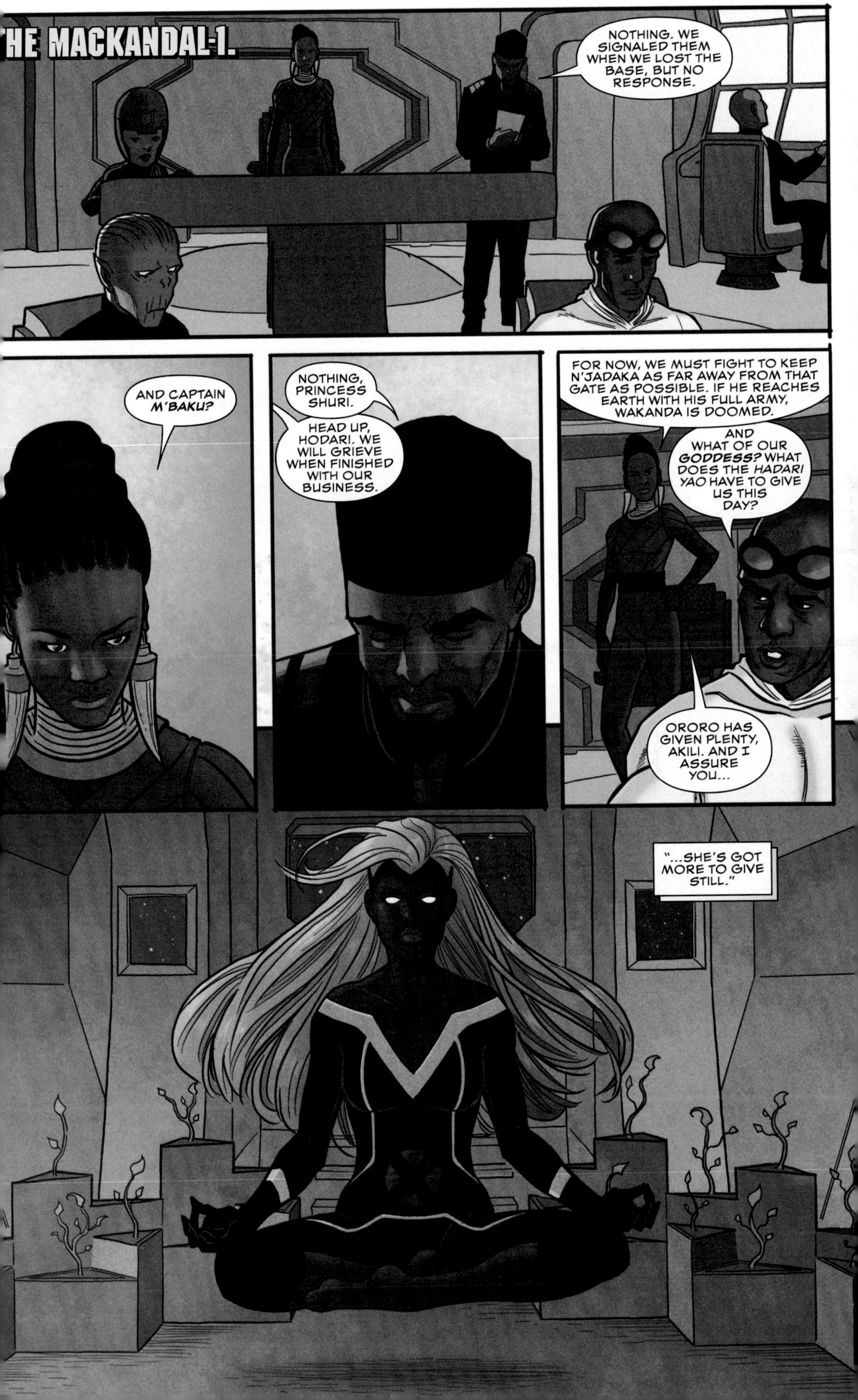
THE MACKANDAL-1.
NOTHING. WE SIGNALED THEM WHEN WE LOST THE BASE, BUT NO RESPONSE.
AND CAPTAIN M'BAKU?
NOTHING, PRINCESS SHURI.
HEAD UP, HODARI. WE WILL GRIEVE WHEN FINISHED WITH OUR BUSINESS.
FOR NOW, WE MUST FIGHT TO KEEP N'JADAKA AS FAR AWAY FROM THAT GATE AS POSSIBLE. IF HE REACHES EARTH WITH HIS FULL ARMY, WAKANDA IS DOOMED.
AND WHAT OF OUR GODDESS? WHAT DOES THE HADARI YAO HAVE TO GIVE US THIS DAY?
ORORO HAS GIVEN PLENTY, AKILI. AND I ASSURE YOU...
"...SHE'S GOT MORE TO GIVE STILL."

HOW MUCH LONGER BEFORE WE TAKE THE REBEL SHIP AND CAN PROCEED TO THE GATE?

WE CAN'T BE SURE, EMPEROR N'JADAKA, BUT THEIR DEFENSES ARE WITHERING AS WE SPEAK.

MY LORD... THIS WOULD BE MUCH EASIER IF WE JUST BLEW THEM OUT OF THE SKY.

BUT WE'RE NOT *GOING* TO BLOW THEM OUT OF THE SKY. WE ARE HERE TO DO THIS *RIGHT*. NOT DO IT *EASY*.

YES, MY LIEGE. WE WILL INFORM YOU THE MOMENT WE ARE READY TO BOARD.

SEE THAT YOU DO.

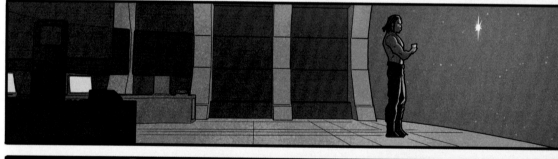

IS IT GETTING *WARM* IN HERE, OR IS IT JUST ME?

IT'S JUST YOU.

IT'S ALWAYS JUST YOU.

WHY SO TOUCHY? IT'S ALL GOING ACCORDING TO PLAN, IS IT NOT?

INDEED IT IS. AND THE END POINT OF THAT PLAN IS *YOUR* PERMANENT *SILENCE.*

PERHAPS. OR MAYBE THE SILENCE WILL BE *YOURS.* BUT I CONFESS THAT THIS IS ALL VERY NEW TO ME. I EXPECTED ONE COHERENT CONSCIOUSNESS.

AND YET HERE WE ARE. THE *TWO* OF US IN THIS *ONE* VESSEL. I'M NOT SURE WHAT WENT WRONG.

WHAT WENT WRONG IS YOU GOT *GREEDY.*

"THE PSYCHIC GRAFT IS COMPLICATED ENOUGH. BUT TO THAT SMALL MIRACLE, YOU ADDED RESURRECTION."

THERE WERE BOUND TO BE... EFFECTS.

YES. BUT THIS IS MORE. YOU ARE THE PSYCHIC RESIDUE OF CERTAIN UNPLEASANT REALITIES.

IT WILL TAKE SOME TIME. BUT THOSE REALTIES ARE PRESENTLY BEING *ALTERED.*

AS YOU SAID, EVERYTHING IS GOING ACCORDING TO PLAN. *MY* PLAN.

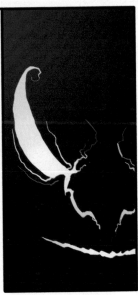

YOU KNOW, I REALLY DO THINK IT'S GETTING WARM IN HERE.

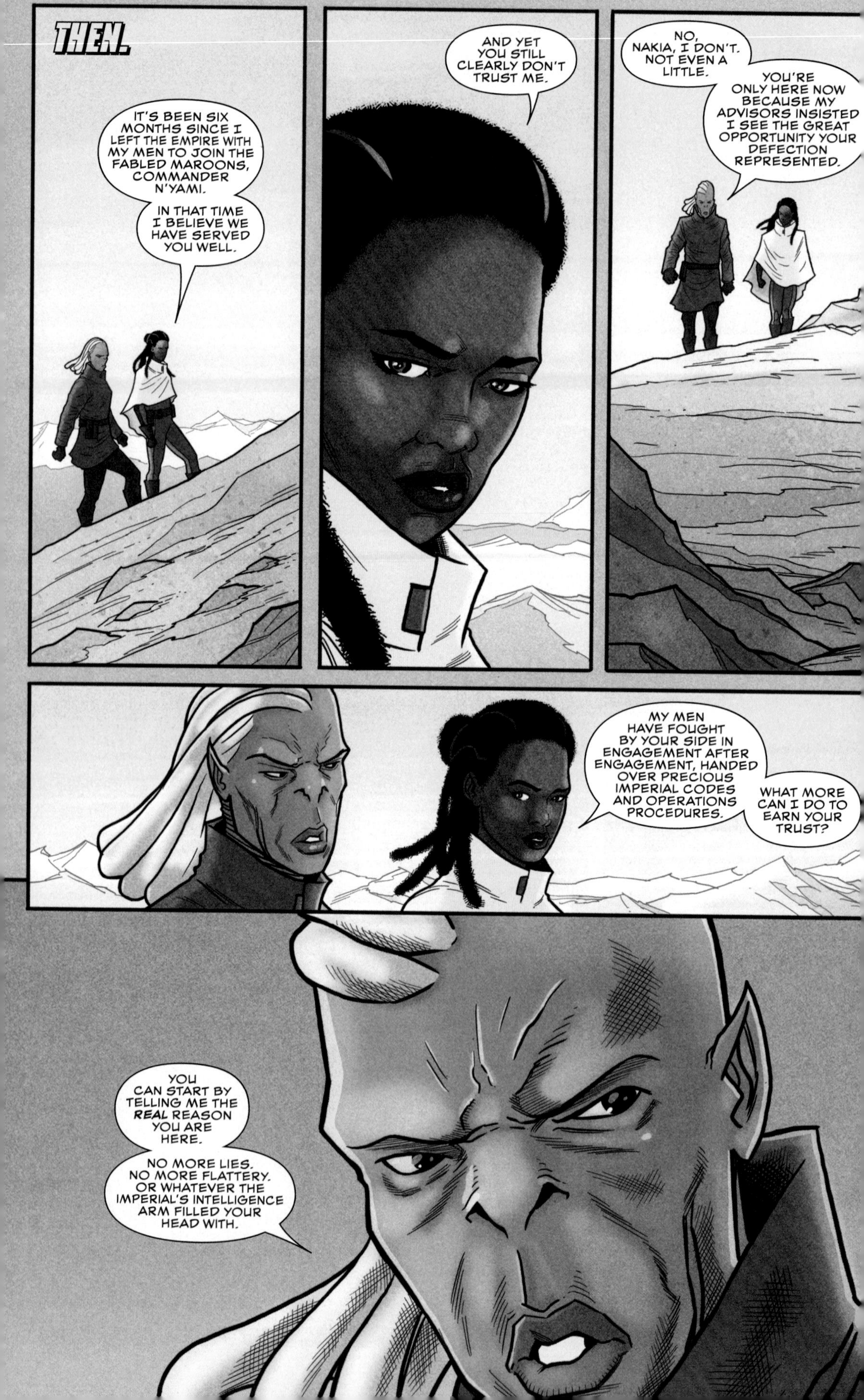
THEN.
IT'S BEEN SIX MONTHS SINCE I LEFT THE EMPIRE WITH MY MEN TO JOIN THE FABLED MAROONS, COMMANDER N'YAMI.
IN THAT TIME I BELIEVE WE HAVE SERVED YOU WELL.
AND YET YOU STILL CLEARLY DON'T TRUST ME.
NO, NAKIA, I DON'T. NOT EVEN A LITTLE.
YOU'RE ONLY HERE NOW BECAUSE MY ADVISORS INSISTED I SEE THE GREAT OPPORTUNITY YOUR DEFECTION REPRESENTED.
MY MEN HAVE FOUGHT BY YOUR SIDE IN ENGAGEMENT AFTER ENGAGEMENT, HANDED OVER PRECIOUS IMPERIAL CODES AND OPERATIONS PROCEDURES.
WHAT MORE CAN I DO TO EARN YOUR TRUST?
YOU CAN START BY TELLING ME THE *REAL* REASON YOU ARE HERE.
NO MORE LIES. NO MORE FLATTERY. OR WHATEVER THE IMPERIAL'S INTELLIGENCE ARM FILLED YOUR HEAD WITH.

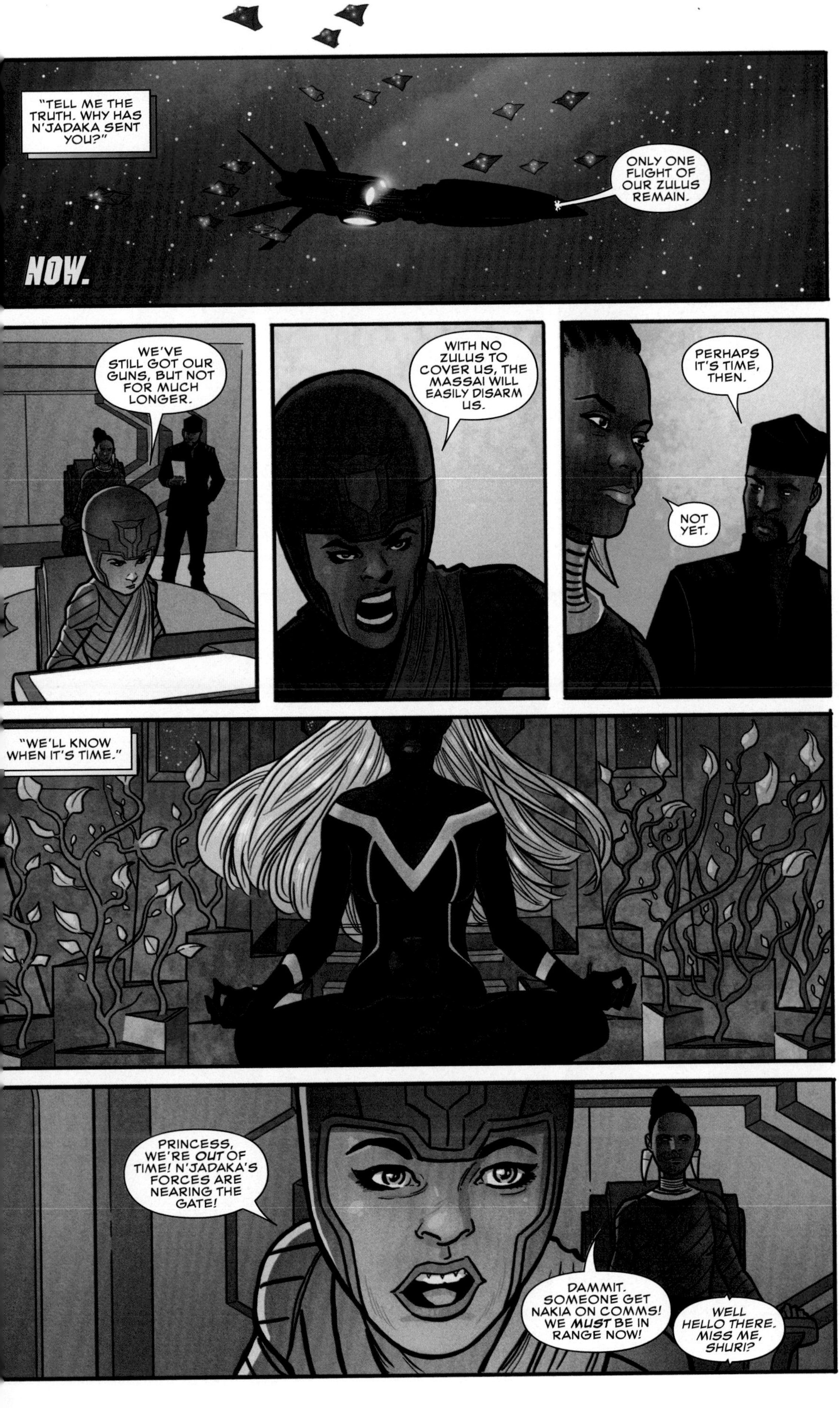
"TELL ME THE TRUTH. WHY HAS N'JADAKA SENT YOU?"
ONLY ONE FLIGHT OF OUR ZULUS REMAIN.
NOW.
WE'VE STILL GOT OUR GUNS, BUT NOT FOR MUCH LONGER.
WITH NO ZULUS TO COVER US, THE MASSAI WILL EASILY DISARM US.
PERHAPS IT'S TIME, THEN.
NOT YET.
"WE'LL KNOW WHEN IT'S TIME."
PRINCESS, WE'RE *OUT* OF TIME! N'JADAKA'S FORCES ARE NEARING THE GATE!
DAMMIT. SOMEONE GET NAKIA ON COMMS! WE *MUST* BE IN RANGE NOW!
WELL HELLO THERE. MISS ME, SHURI?

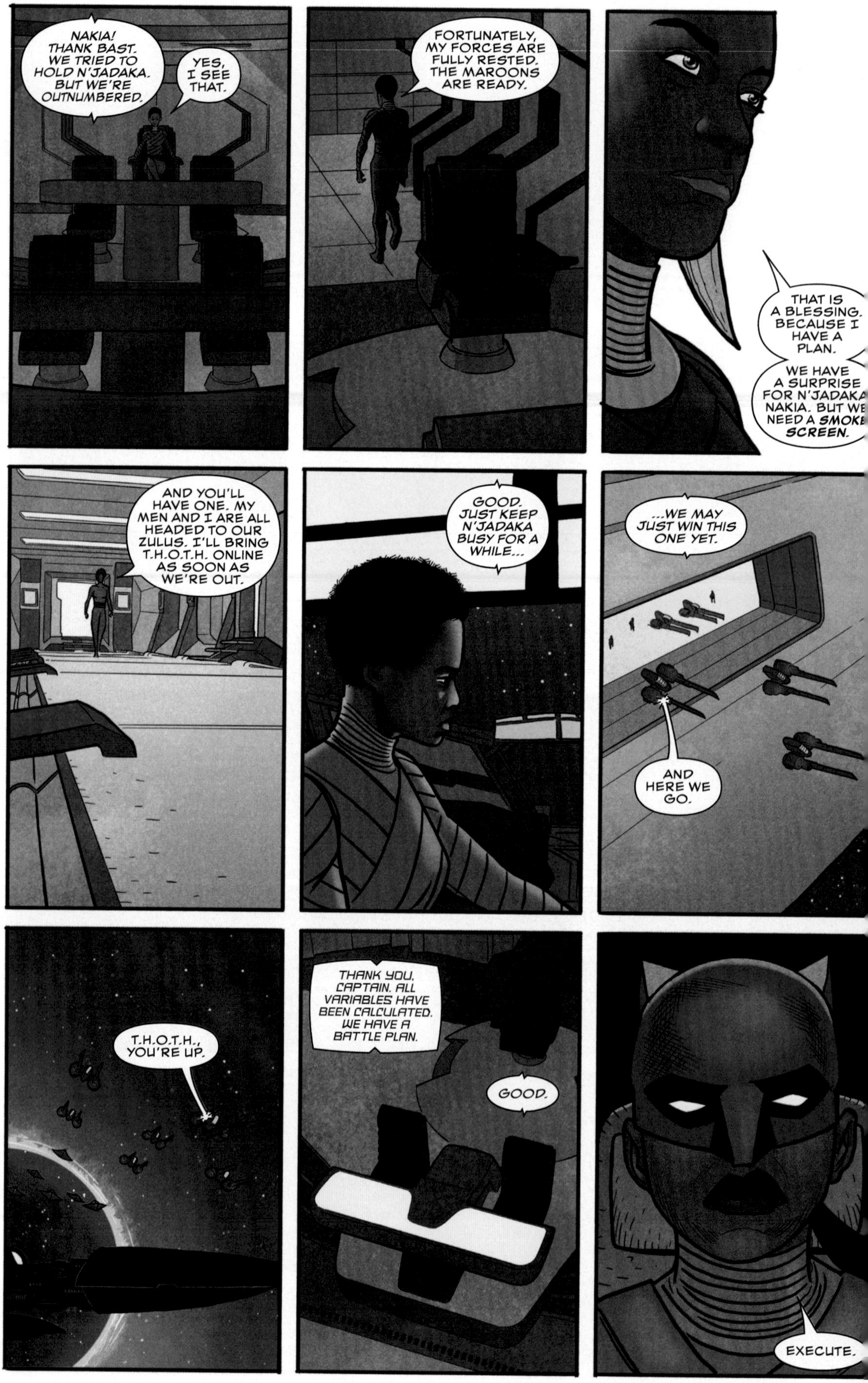
NAKIA! THANK BAST. WE TRIED TO HOLD N'JADAKA. BUT WE'RE OUTNUMBERED.
YES, I SEE THAT.
FORTUNATELY, MY FORCES ARE FULLY RESTED. THE MAROONS ARE READY.
THAT IS A BLESSING. BECAUSE I HAVE A PLAN.
WE HAVE A SURPRISE FOR N'JADAKA NAKIA. BUT WE NEED A SMOKE SCREEN.
AND YOU'LL HAVE ONE. MY MEN AND I ARE ALL HEADED TO OUR ZULUS. I'LL BRING T.H.O.T.H. ONLINE AS SOON AS WE'RE OUT.
GOOD. JUST KEEP N'JADAKA BUSY FOR A WHILE...
...WE MAY JUST WIN THIS ONE YET.
AND HERE WE GO.
T.H.O.T.H., YOU'RE UP.
THANK YOU, CAPTAIN. ALL VARIABLES HAVE BEEN CALCULATED. WE HAVE A BATTLE PLAN.
GOOD.
EXECUTE.

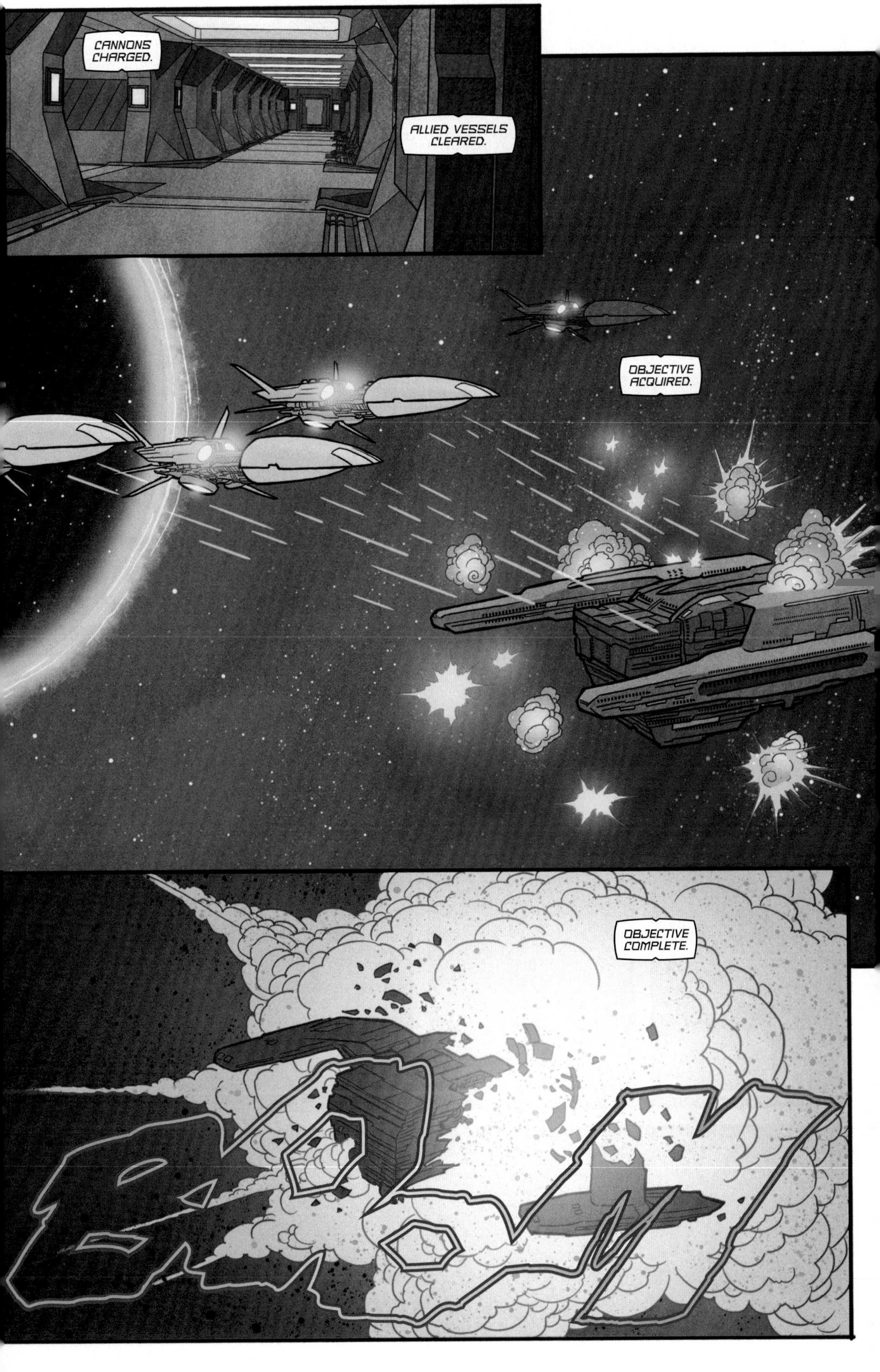

CANNONS CHARGED.
ALLIED VESSELS CLEARED.
OBJECTIVE ACQUIRED.
OBJECTIVE COMPLETE.
BOOM

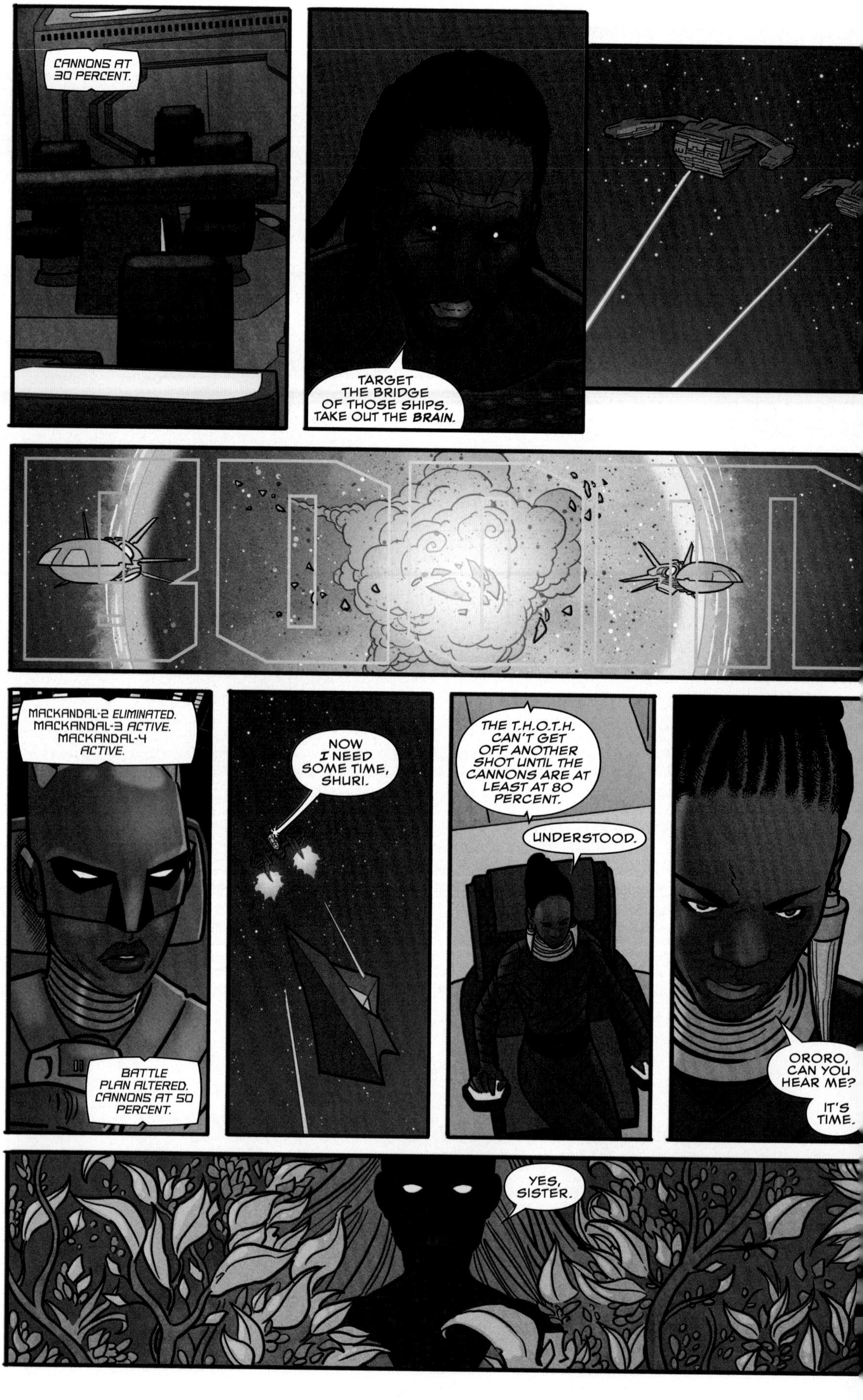
CANNONS AT 30 PERCENT.
TARGET THE BRIDGE OF THOSE SHIPS. TAKE OUT THE BRAIN.
MACKANDAL-2 ELIMINATED. MACKANDAL-3 ACTIVE. MACKANDAL-4 ACTIVE.
BATTLE PLAN ALTERED. CANNONS AT 50 PERCENT.
NOW I NEED SOME TIME, SHURI.
THE T.H.O.T.H. CAN'T GET OFF ANOTHER SHOT UNTIL THE CANNONS ARE AT LEAST AT 80 PERCENT.
UNDERSTOOD.
ORORO, CAN YOU HEAR ME?
IT'S TIME.
YES, SISTER.

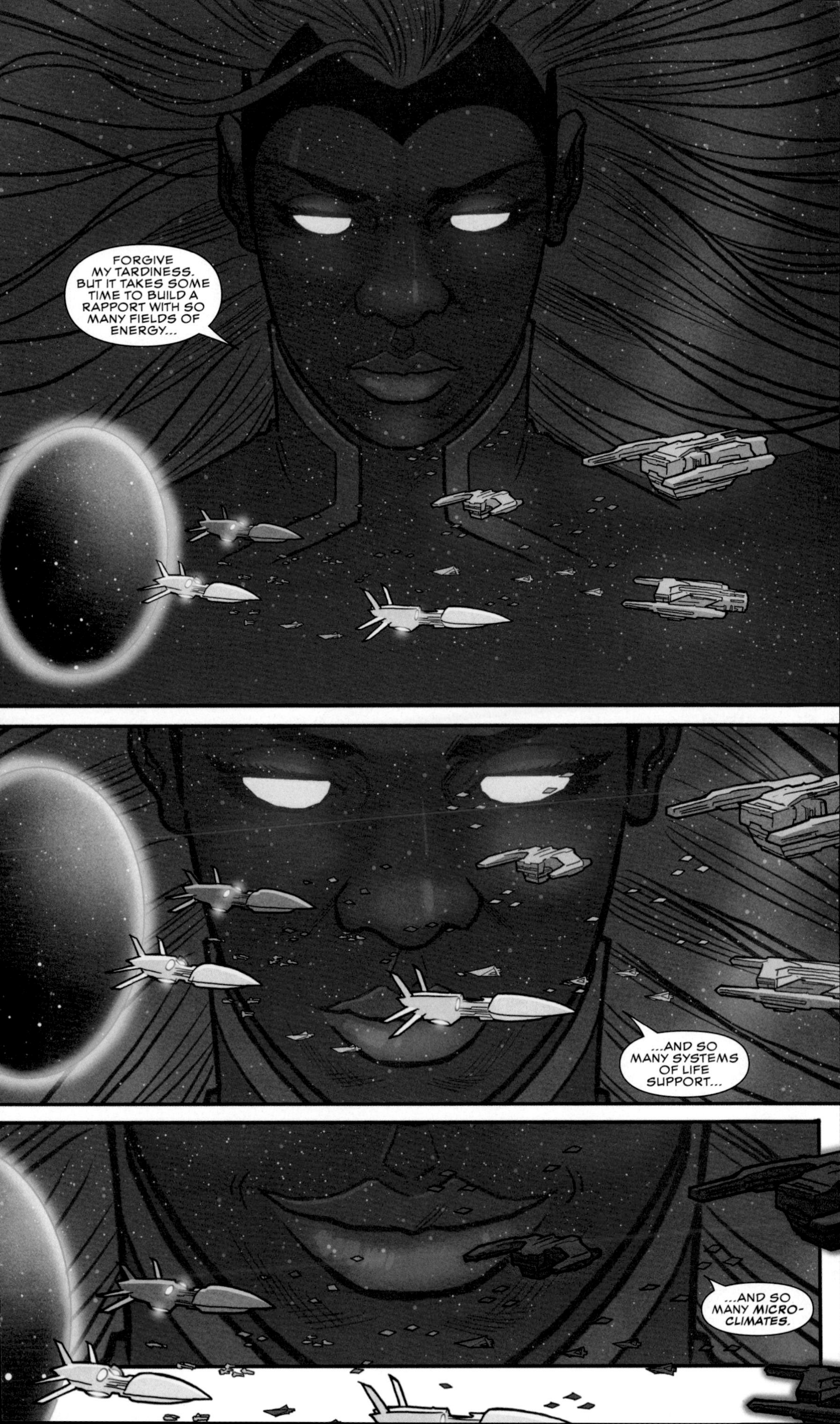
FORGIVE MY TARDINESS. BUT IT TAKES SOME TIME TO BUILD A RAPPORT WITH SO MANY FIELDS OF ENERGY...
...AND SO MANY SYSTEMS OF LIFE SUPPORT...
...AND SO MANY MICRO-CLIMATES.

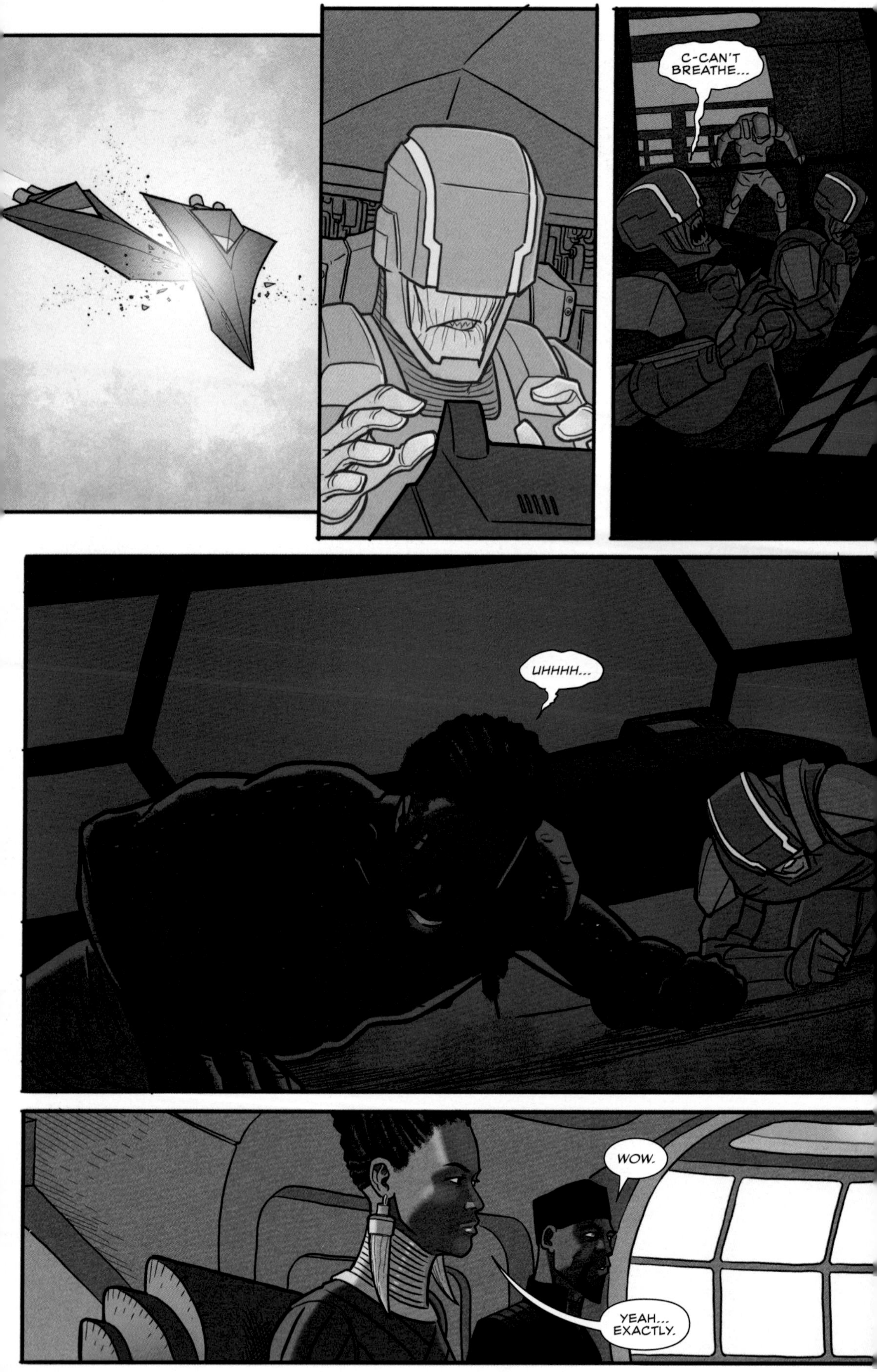
C-CAN'T BREATHE...
UHHHH...
WOW.
YEAH... EXACTLY.

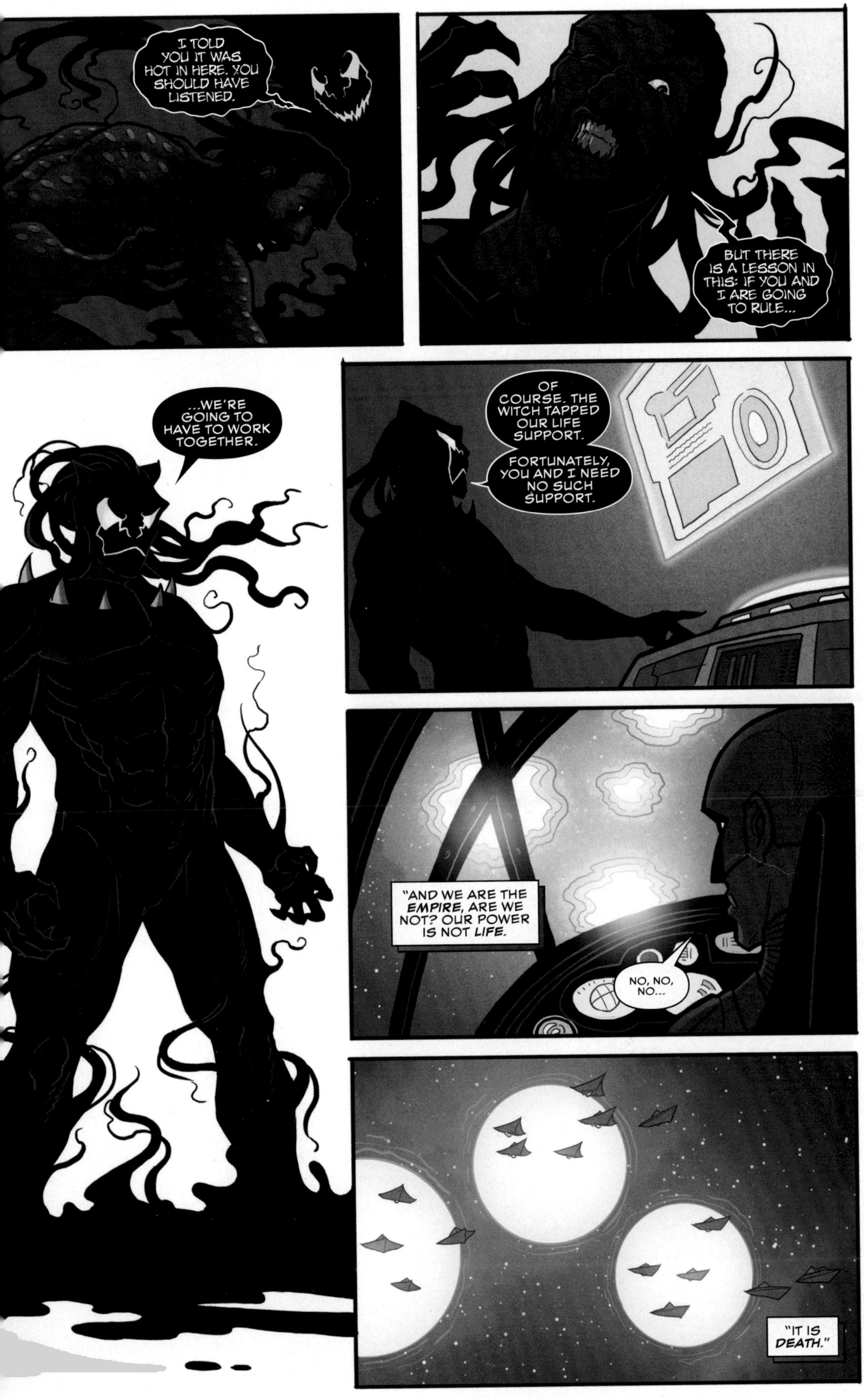
I TOLD YOU IT WAS HOT IN HERE. YOU SHOULD HAVE LISTENED.
BUT THERE IS A LESSON IN THIS: IF YOU AND I ARE GOING TO RULE...
...WE'RE GOING TO HAVE TO WORK TOGETHER.
OF COURSE. THE WITCH TAPPED OUR LIFE SUPPORT.
FORTUNATELY, YOU AND I NEED NO SUCH SUPPORT.
"AND WE ARE THE *EMPIRE*, ARE WE NOT? OUR POWER IS NOT *LIFE*.
NO, NO, NO...
"IT IS *DEATH*."

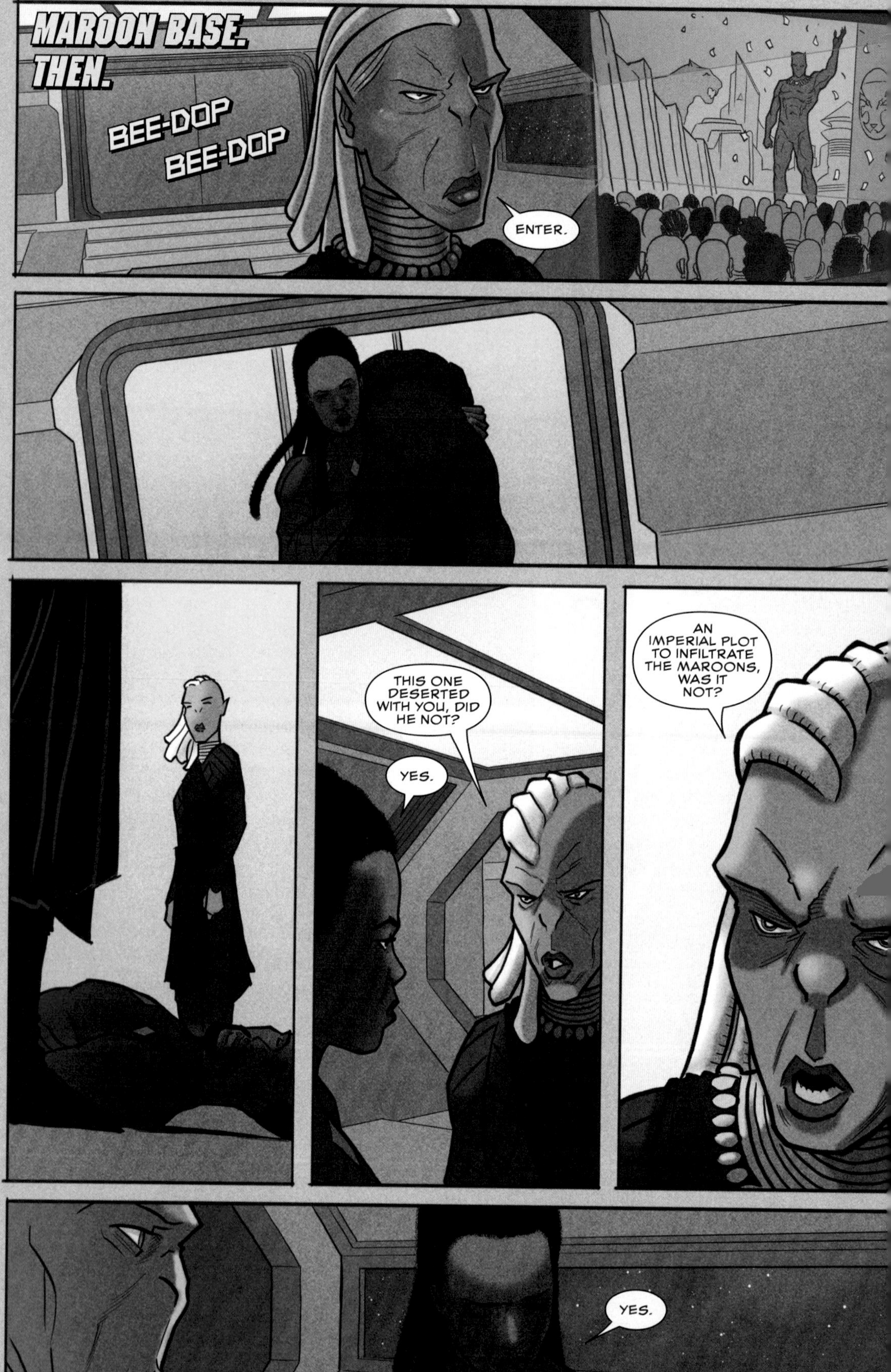
MAROON BASE. THEN.
BEE-DOP BEE-DOP
ENTER.
THIS ONE DESERTED WITH YOU, DID HE NOT?
YES.
AN IMPERIAL PLOT TO INFILTRATE THE MAROONS, WAS IT NOT?
YES.

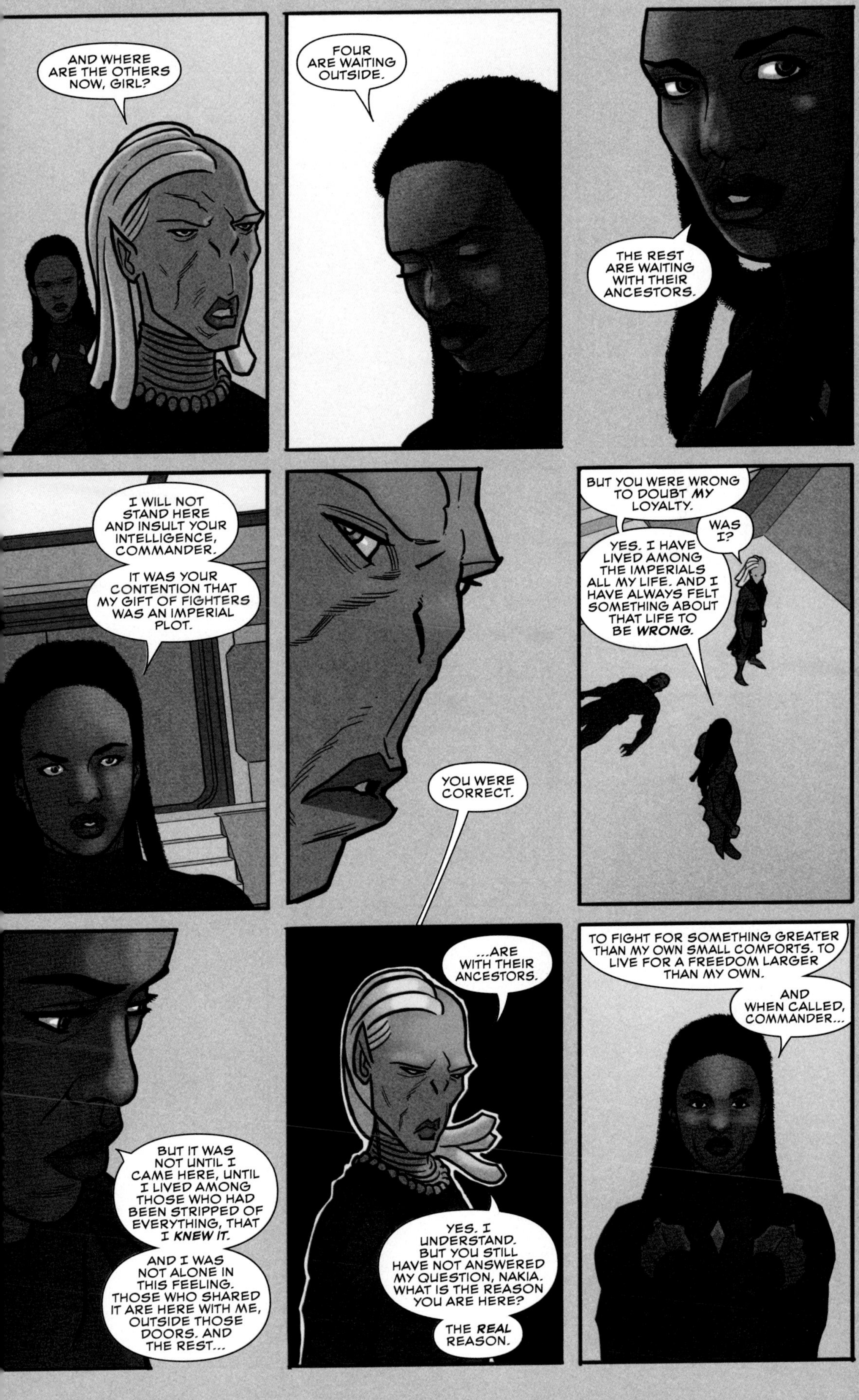
AND WHERE ARE THE OTHERS NOW, GIRL?
FOUR ARE WAITING OUTSIDE.
THE REST ARE WAITING WITH THEIR ANCESTORS.
I WILL NOT STAND HERE AND INSULT YOUR INTELLIGENCE, COMMANDER.
IT WAS YOUR CONTENTION THAT MY GIFT OF FIGHTERS WAS AN IMPERIAL PLOT.
YOU WERE CORRECT.
BUT YOU WERE WRONG TO DOUBT *MY* LOYALTY.
WAS I?
YES. I HAVE LIVED AMONG THE IMPERIALS ALL MY LIFE. AND I HAVE ALWAYS FELT SOMETHING ABOUT THAT LIFE TO BE *WRONG*.
BUT IT WAS NOT UNTIL I CAME HERE, UNTIL I LIVED AMONG THOSE WHO HAD BEEN STRIPPED OF EVERYTHING, THAT I *KNEW IT*.
AND I WAS NOT ALONE IN THIS FEELING. THOSE WHO SHARED IT ARE HERE WITH ME, OUTSIDE THOSE DOORS. AND THE REST...
...ARE WITH THEIR ANCESTORS.
YES. I UNDERSTAND. BUT YOU STILL HAVE NOT ANSWERED MY QUESTION, NAKIA. WHAT IS THE REASON YOU ARE HERE?
THE *REAL* REASON.
TO FIGHT FOR SOMETHING GREATER THAN MY OWN SMALL COMFORTS. TO LIVE FOR A FREEDOM LARGER THAN MY OWN.
AND WHEN CALLED, COMMANDER...

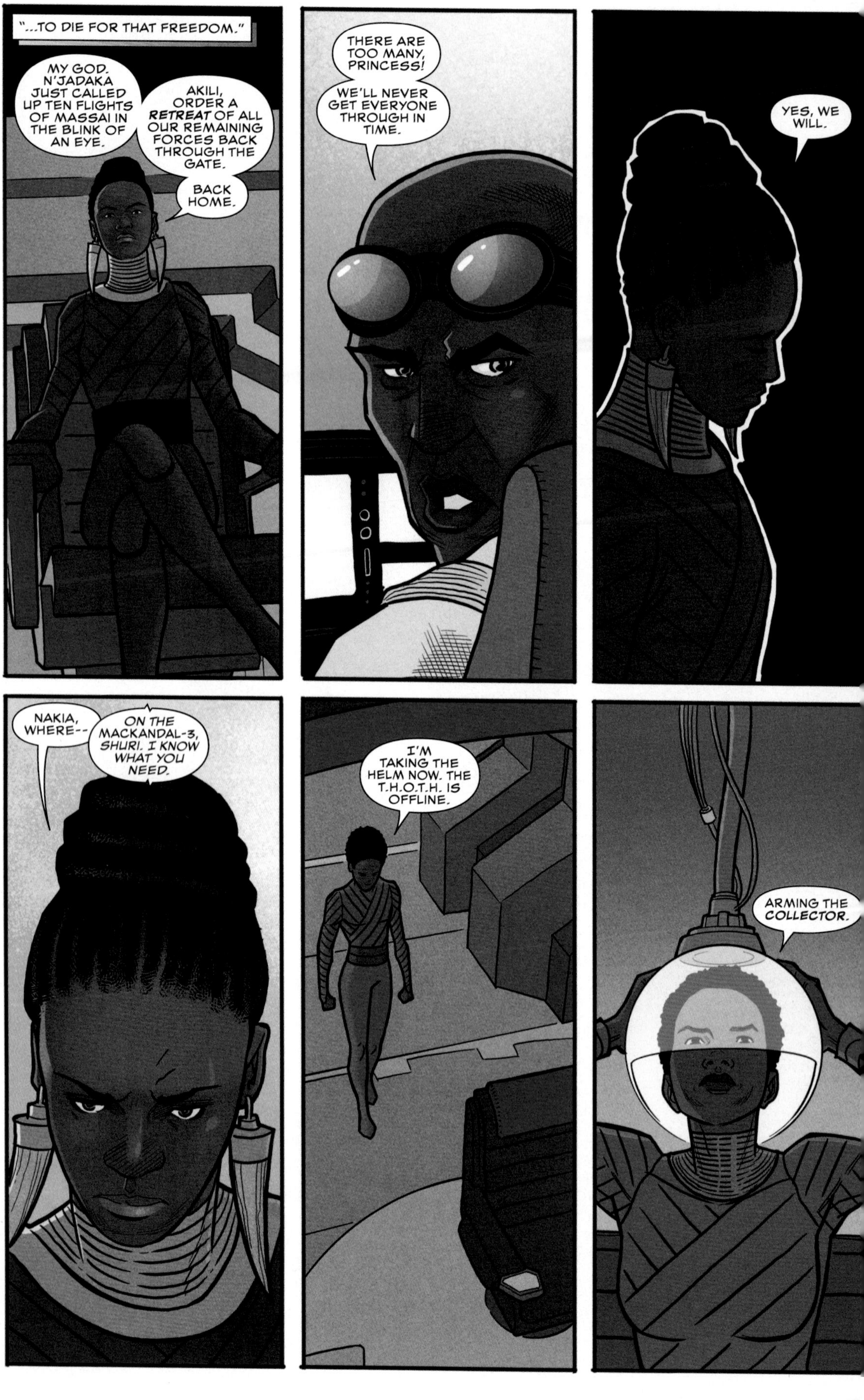
"...TO DIE FOR THAT FREEDOM."
MY GOD. N'JADAKA JUST CALLED UP TEN FLIGHTS OF MASSAI IN THE BLINK OF AN EYE.
AKILI, ORDER A **RETREAT** OF ALL OUR REMAINING FORCES BACK THROUGH THE GATE.
BACK HOME.
THERE ARE TOO MANY, PRINCESS!
WE'LL NEVER GET EVERYONE THROUGH IN TIME.
YES, WE WILL.
NAKIA, WHERE--
ON THE MACKANDAL-3, SHURI. I KNOW WHAT YOU NEED.
I'M TAKING THE HELM NOW. THE T.H.O.T.H. IS OFFLINE.
ARMING THE **COLLECTOR**.

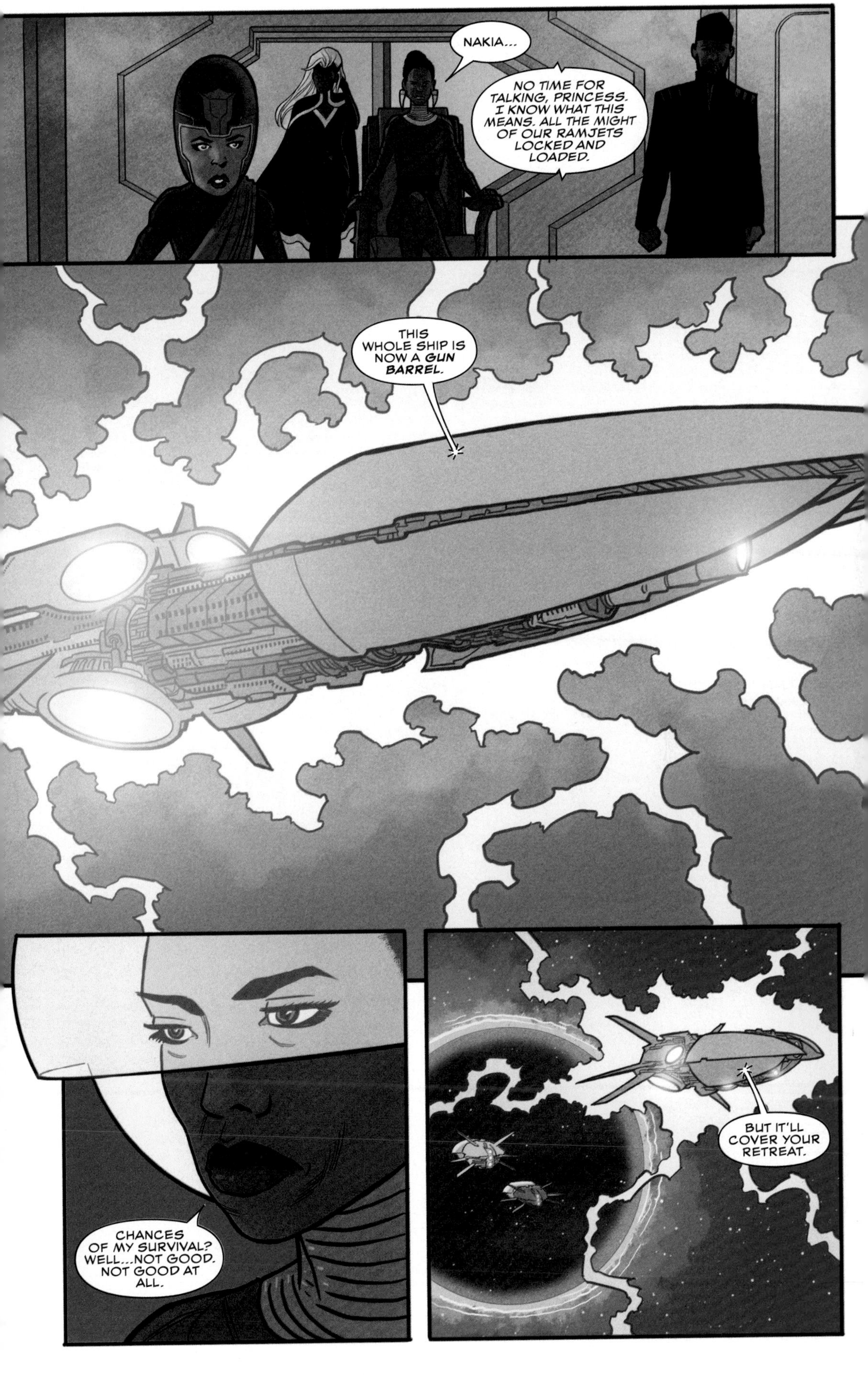

NAKIA...
NO TIME FOR TALKING, PRINCESS. I KNOW WHAT THIS MEANS. ALL THE MIGHT OF OUR RAMJETS LOCKED AND LOADED.
THIS WHOLE SHIP IS NOW A GUN BARREL.
CHANCES OF MY SURVIVAL? WELL...NOT GOOD. NOT GOOD AT ALL.
BUT IT'LL COVER YOUR RETREAT.

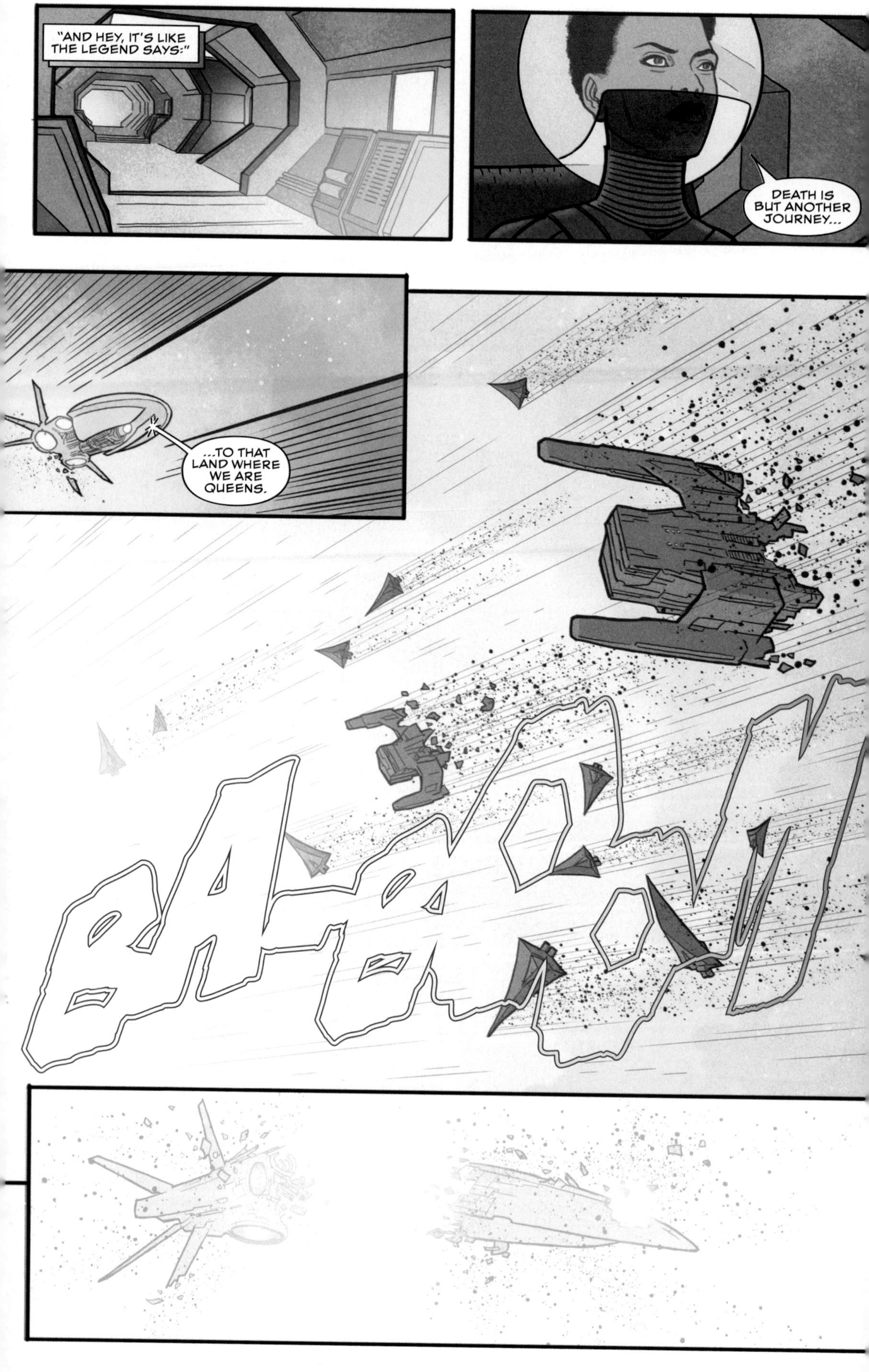
"AND HEY, IT'S LIKE THE LEGEND SAYS:"
DEATH IS BUT ANOTHER JOURNEY...
...TO THAT LAND WHERE WE ARE QUEENS.
BA-BOOM

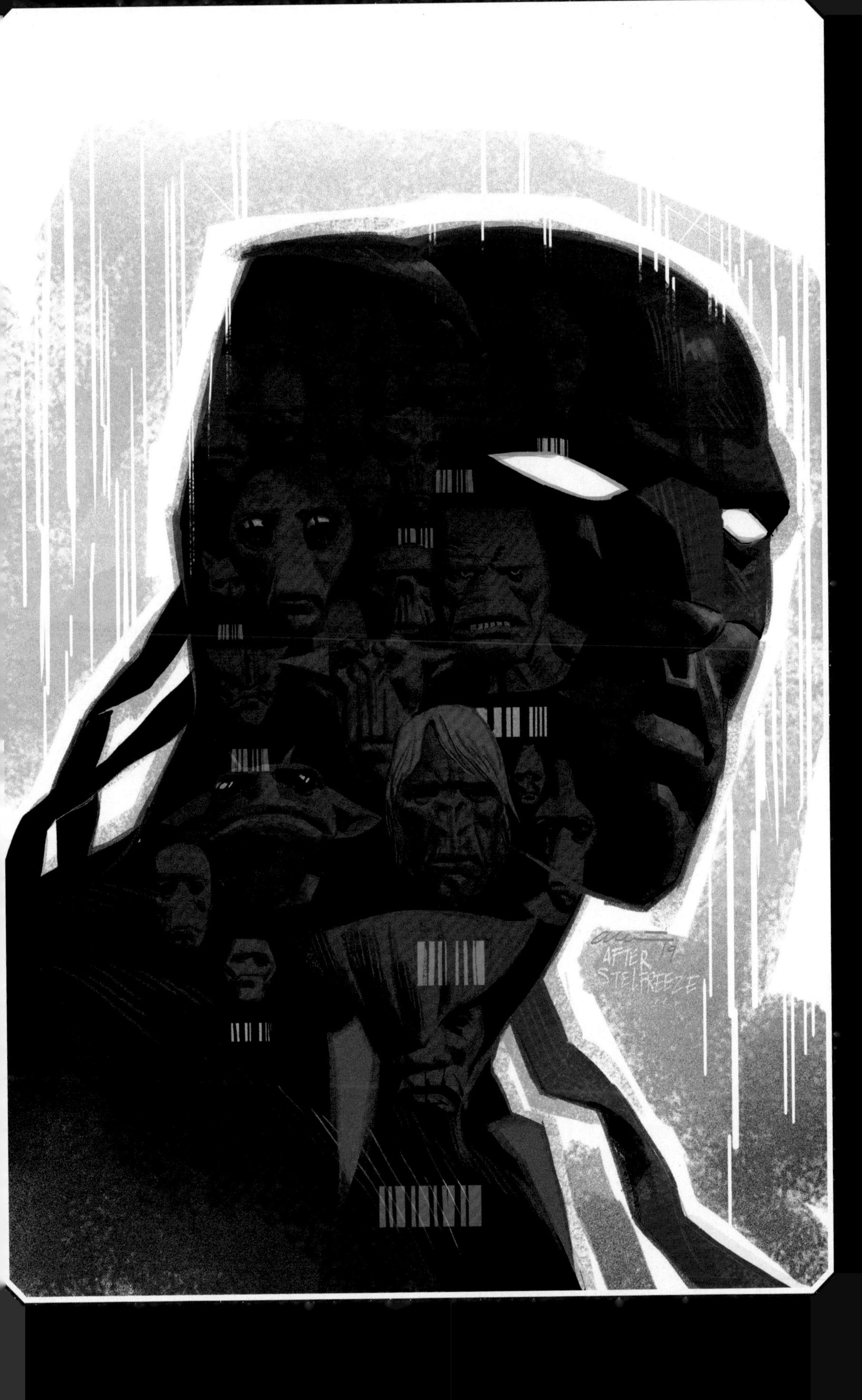
AFTER STELFREEZE

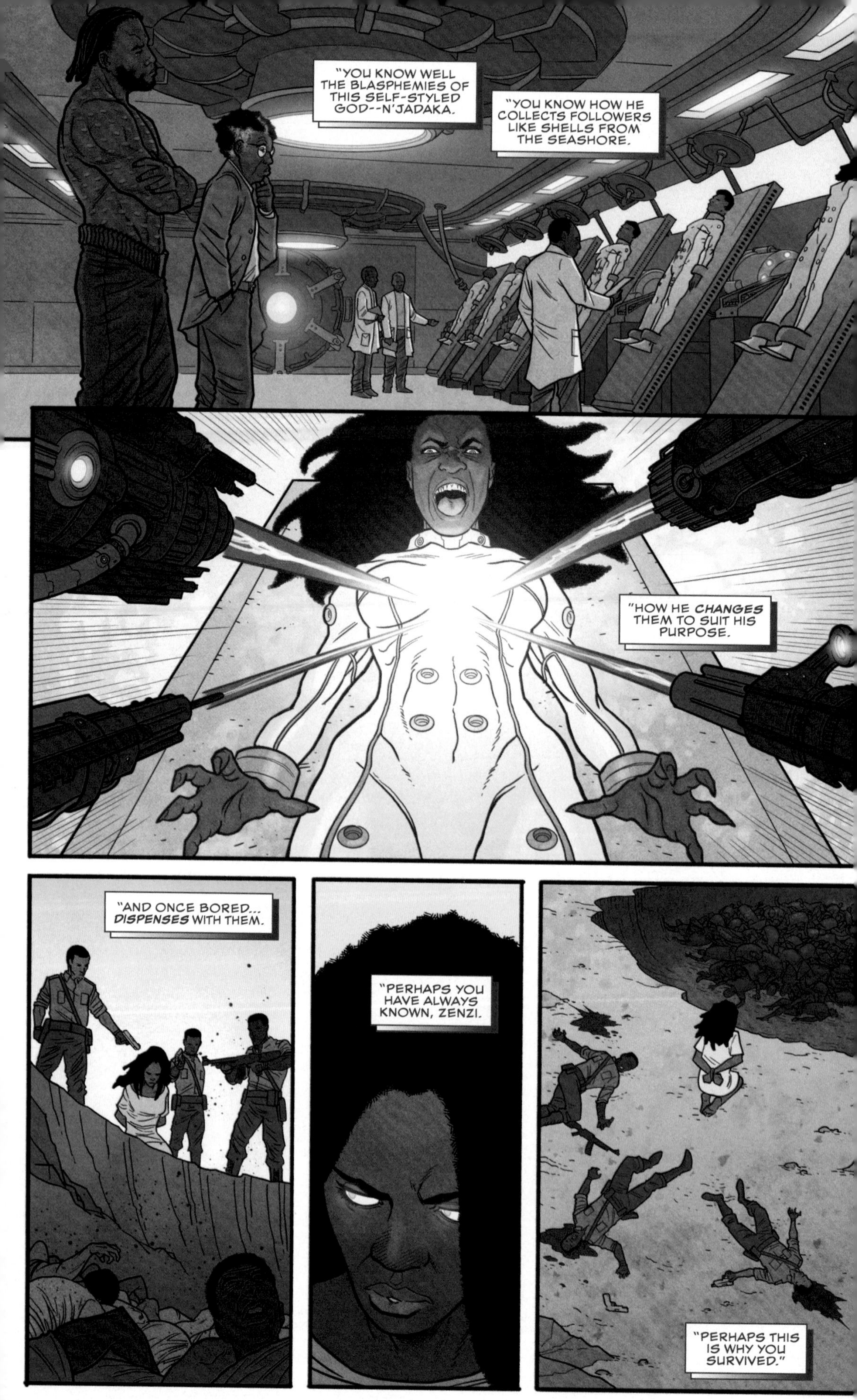
"YOU KNOW WELL THE BLASPHEMIES OF THIS SELF-STYLED GOD--N'JADAKA.
"YOU KNOW HOW HE COLLECTS FOLLOWERS LIKE SHELLS FROM THE SEASHORE.
"HOW HE CHANGES THEM TO SUIT HIS PURPOSE.
"AND ONCE BORED... DISPENSES WITH THEM.
"PERHAPS YOU HAVE ALWAYS KNOWN, ZENZI.
"PERHAPS THIS IS WHY YOU SURVIVED."

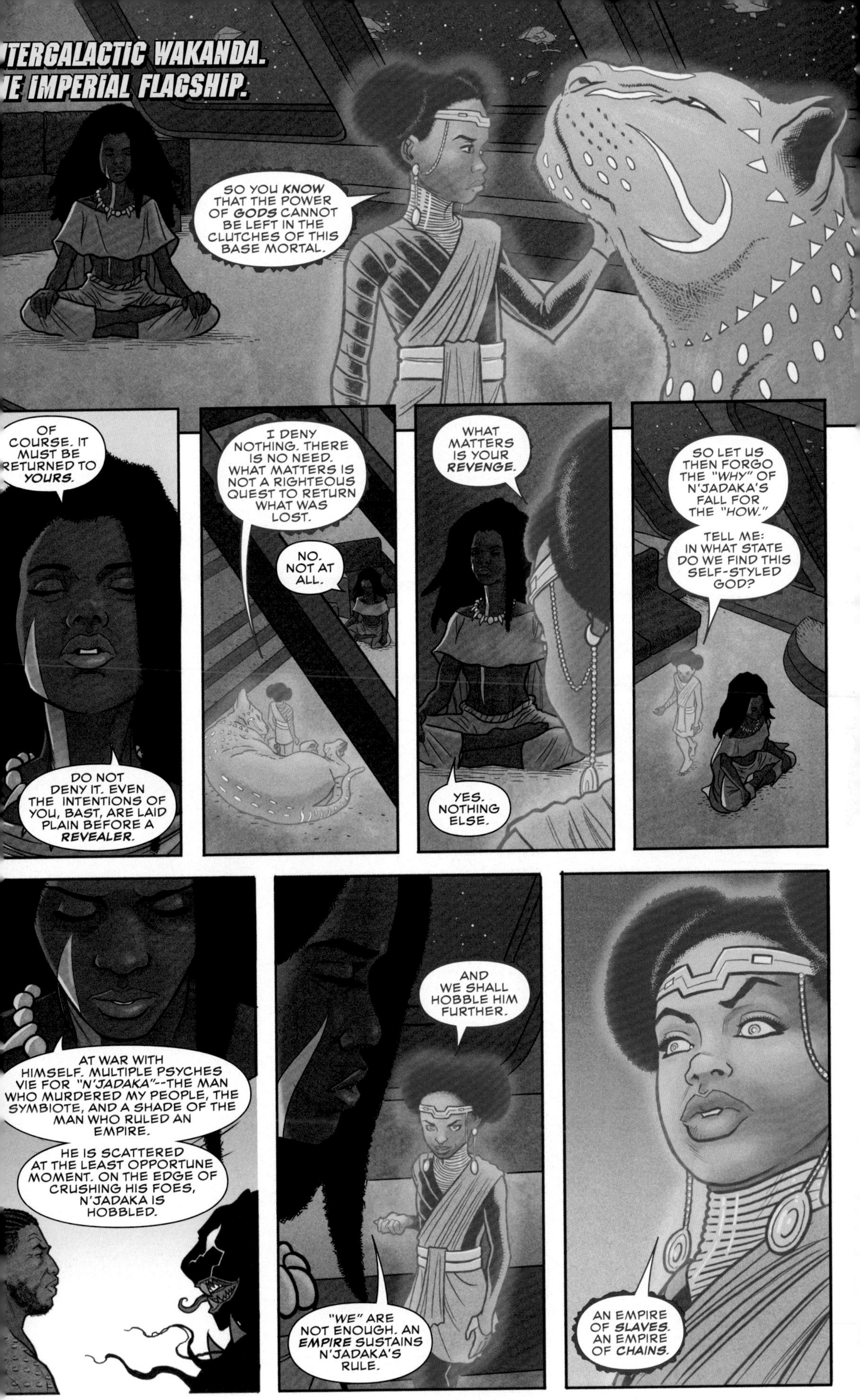

TERGALACTIC WAKANDA.
E IMPERIAL FLAGSHIP.
SO YOU KNOW THAT THE POWER OF GODS CANNOT BE LEFT IN THE CLUTCHES OF THIS BASE MORTAL.
OF COURSE. IT MUST BE RETURNED TO YOURS.
DO NOT DENY IT. EVEN THE INTENTIONS OF YOU, BAST, ARE LAID PLAIN BEFORE A REVEALER.
I DENY NOTHING. THERE IS NO NEED. WHAT MATTERS IS NOT A RIGHTEOUS QUEST TO RETURN WHAT WAS LOST.
NO. NOT AT ALL.
WHAT MATTERS IS YOUR REVENGE.
YES. NOTHING ELSE.
SO LET US THEN FORGO THE "WHY" OF N'JADAKA'S FALL FOR THE "HOW."
TELL ME: IN WHAT STATE DO WE FIND THIS SELF-STYLED GOD?
AT WAR WITH HIMSELF. MULTIPLE PSYCHES VIE FOR "N'JADAKA"--THE MAN WHO MURDERED MY PEOPLE, THE SYMBIOTE, AND A SHADE OF THE MAN WHO RULED AN EMPIRE.
HE IS SCATTERED AT THE LEAST OPPORTUNE MOMENT. ON THE EDGE OF CRUSHING HIS FOES, N'JADAKA IS HOBBLED.
AND WE SHALL HOBBLE HIM FURTHER.
"WE" ARE NOT ENOUGH. AN EMPIRE SUSTAINS N'JADAKA'S RULE.
AN EMPIRE OF SLAVES. AN EMPIRE OF CHAINS.

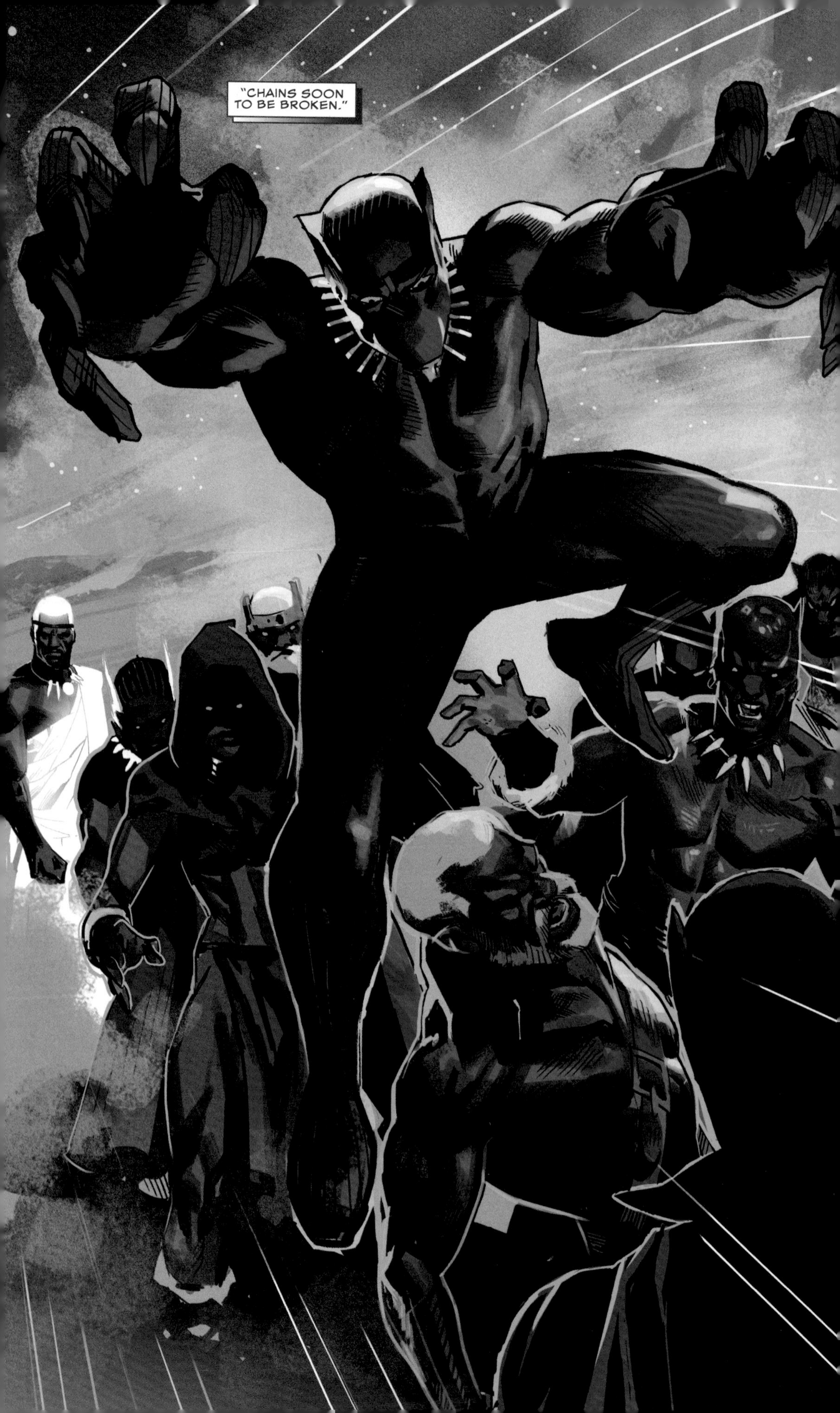
"CHAINS SOON TO BE BROKEN."

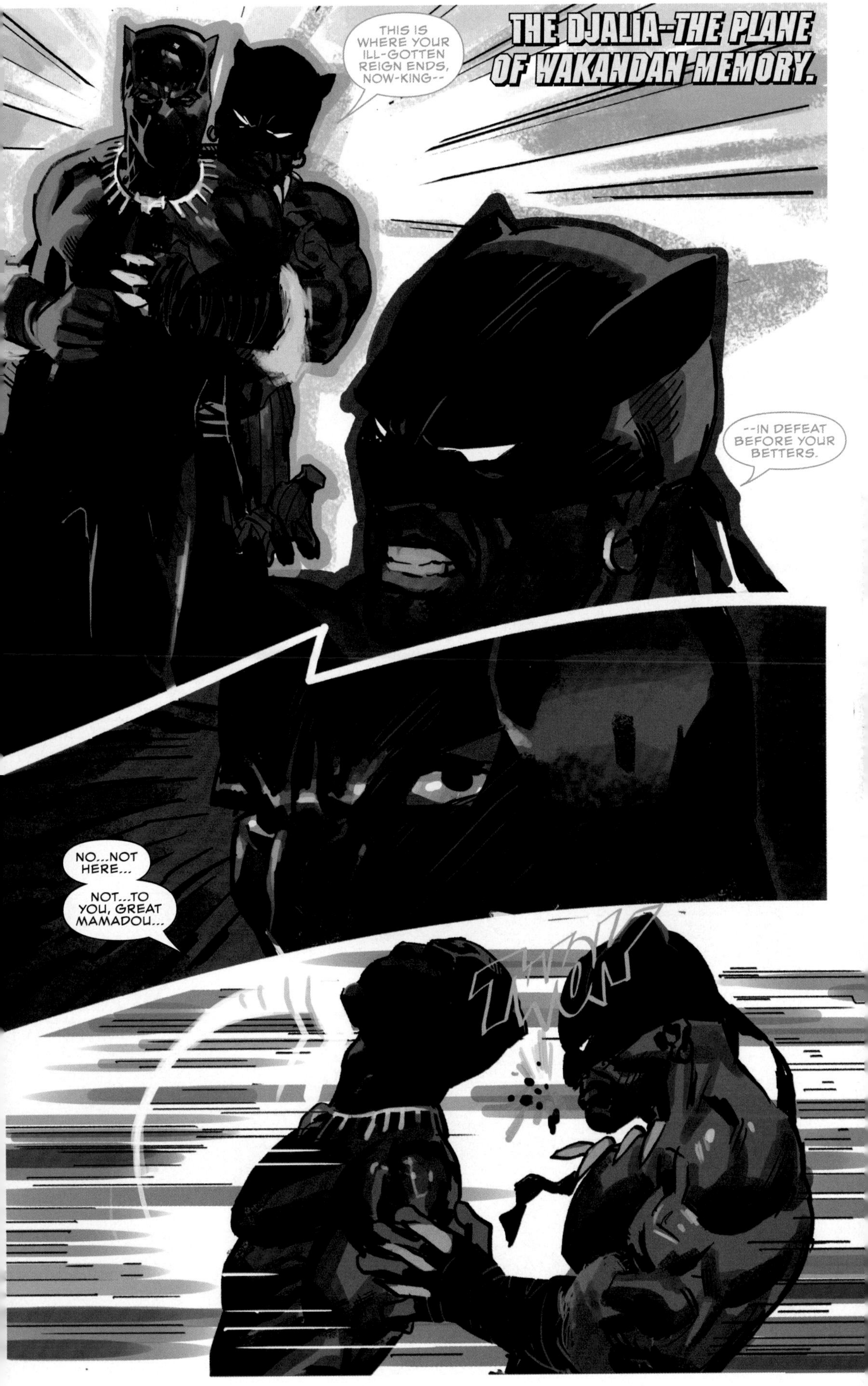
THE DJALIA--THE PLANE OF WAKANDAN MEMORY.
THIS IS WHERE YOUR ILL-GOTTEN REIGN ENDS, NOW-KING--
--IN DEFEAT BEFORE YOUR BETTERS.
NO...NOT HERE...
NOT...TO YOU, GREAT MAMADOU...
THOK

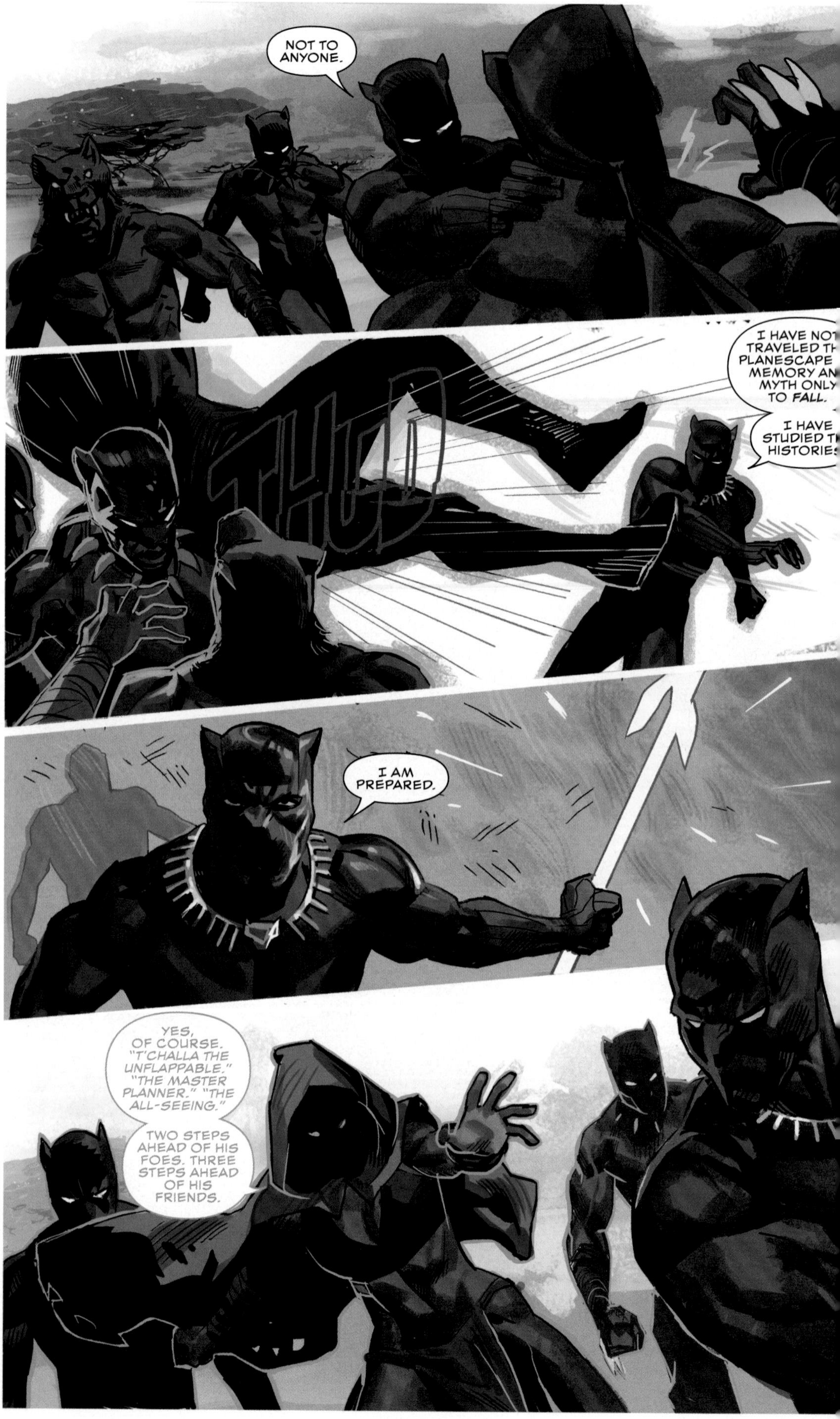
NOT TO ANYONE.
I HAVE NOT TRAVELED TH PLANESCAPE MEMORY AN MYTH ONLY TO FALL.
I HAVE STUDIED T HISTORIES
THUD
I AM PREPARED.
YES, OF COURSE. "T'CHALLA THE UNFLAPPABLE." "THE MASTER PLANNER." "THE ALL-SEEING."
TWO STEPS AHEAD OF HIS FOES. THREE STEPS AHEAD OF HIS FRIENDS.

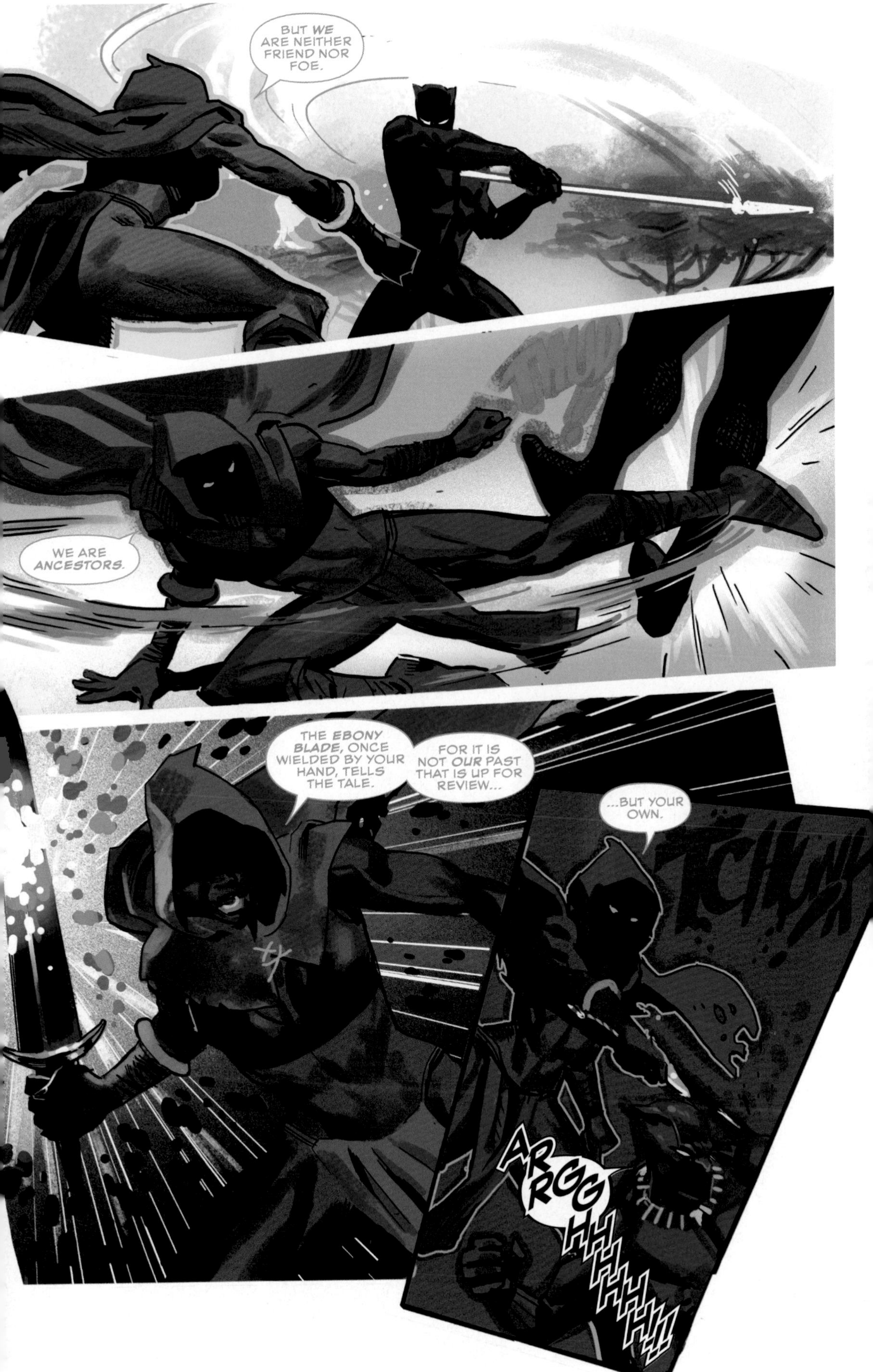
BUT WE ARE NEITHER FRIEND NOR FOE.
WE ARE ANCESTORS.
THE EBONY BLADE, ONCE WIELDED BY YOUR HAND, TELLS THE TALE.
FOR IT IS NOT OUR PAST THAT IS UP FOR REVIEW...
...BUT YOUR OWN.
TCHUNK
ARRGGHHHHHH!!

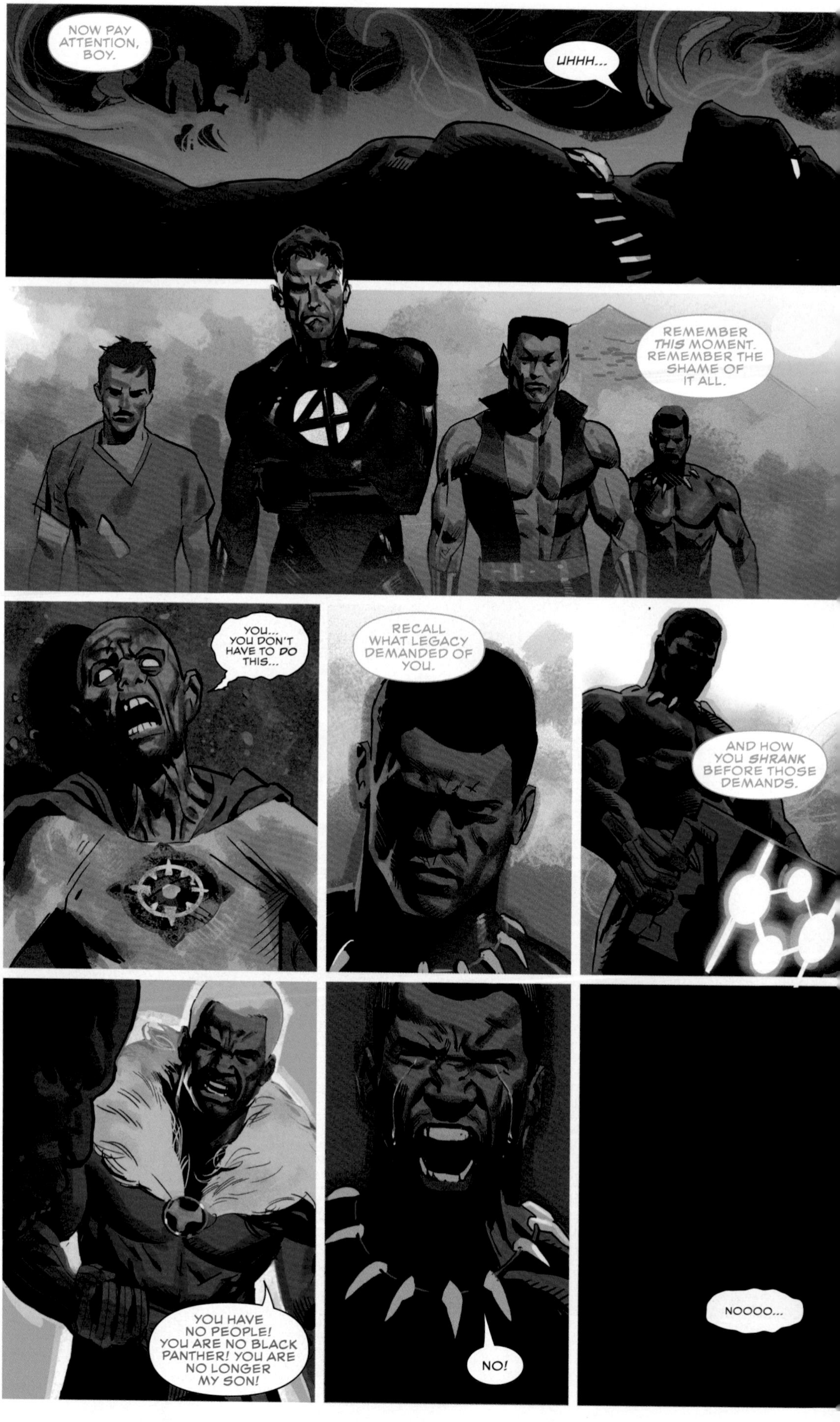
NOW PAY ATTENTION, BOY.
UHHH...
REMEMBER *THIS* MOMENT. REMEMBER THE SHAME OF IT ALL.
YOU... YOU DON'T HAVE TO *DO* THIS...
RECALL WHAT LEGACY DEMANDED OF YOU.
AND HOW YOU *SHRANK* BEFORE THOSE DEMANDS.
YOU HAVE NO PEOPLE! YOU ARE NO BLACK PANTHER! YOU ARE NO LONGER MY SON!
NO!
NOOOO...

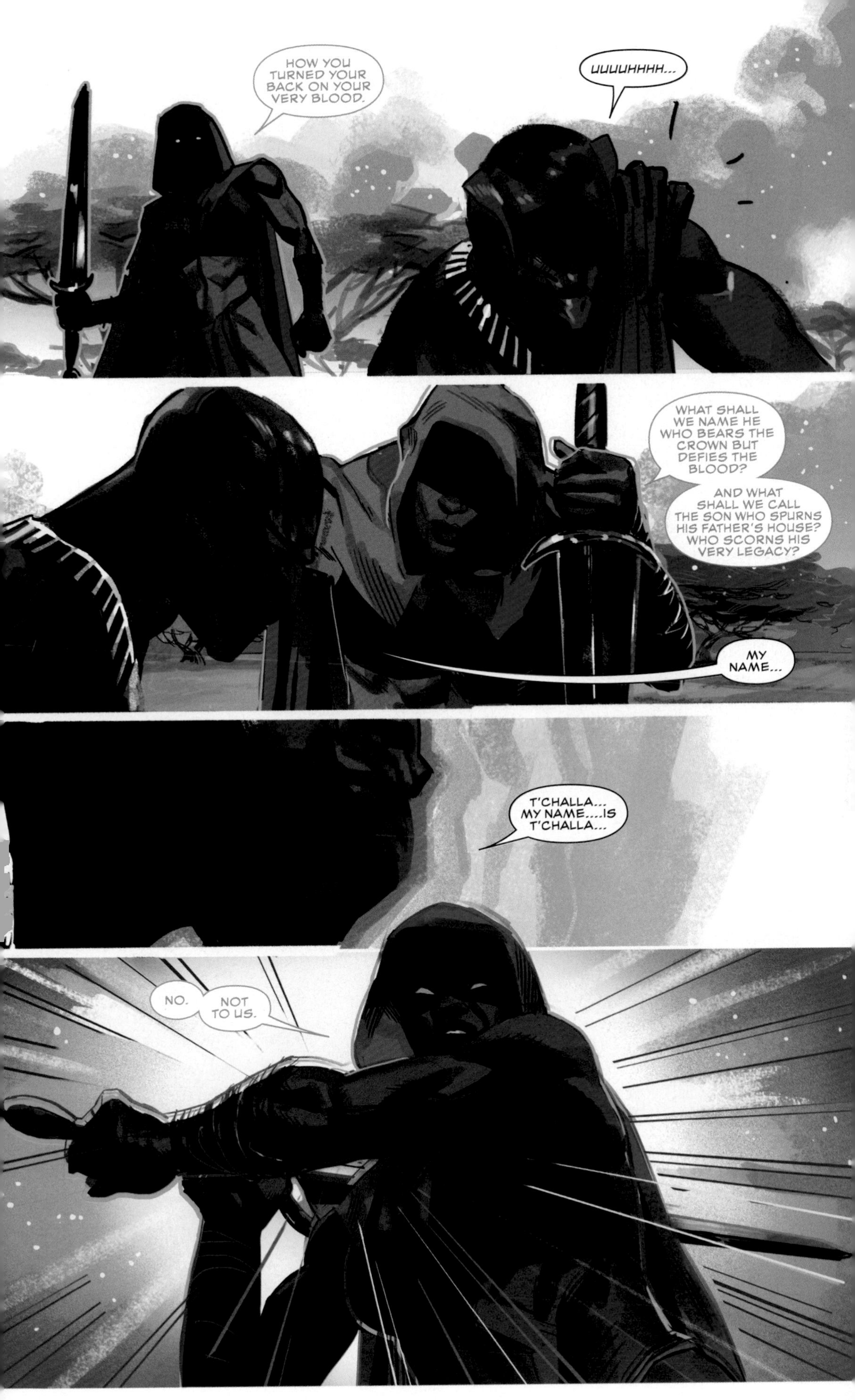
HOW YOU TURNED YOUR BACK ON YOUR VERY BLOOD.
UUUUHHHH...
WHAT SHALL WE NAME HE WHO BEARS THE CROWN BUT DEFIES THE BLOOD?
AND WHAT SHALL WE CALL THE SON WHO SPURNS HIS FATHER'S HOUSE? WHO SCORNS HIS VERY LEGACY?
MY NAME...
T'CHALLA... MY NAME....IS T'CHALLA...
NO.
NOT TO US.

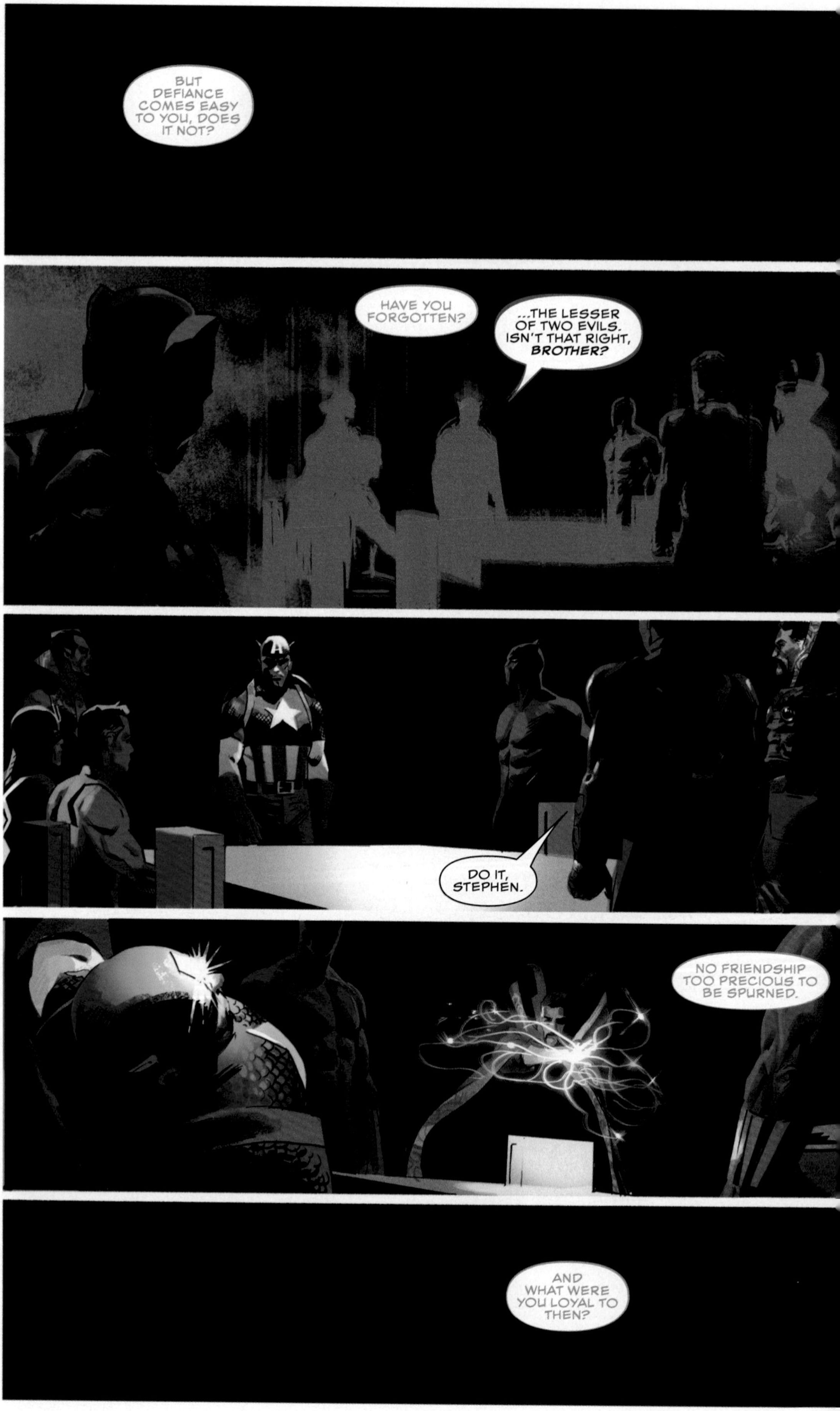

BUT DEFIANCE COMES EASY TO YOU, DOES IT NOT?
HAVE YOU FORGOTTEN?
...THE LESSER OF TWO EVILS. ISN'T THAT RIGHT, *BROTHER?*
DO IT, STEPHEN.
NO FRIENDSHIP TOO PRECIOUS TO BE SPURNED.
AND WHAT WERE YOU LOYAL TO THEN?

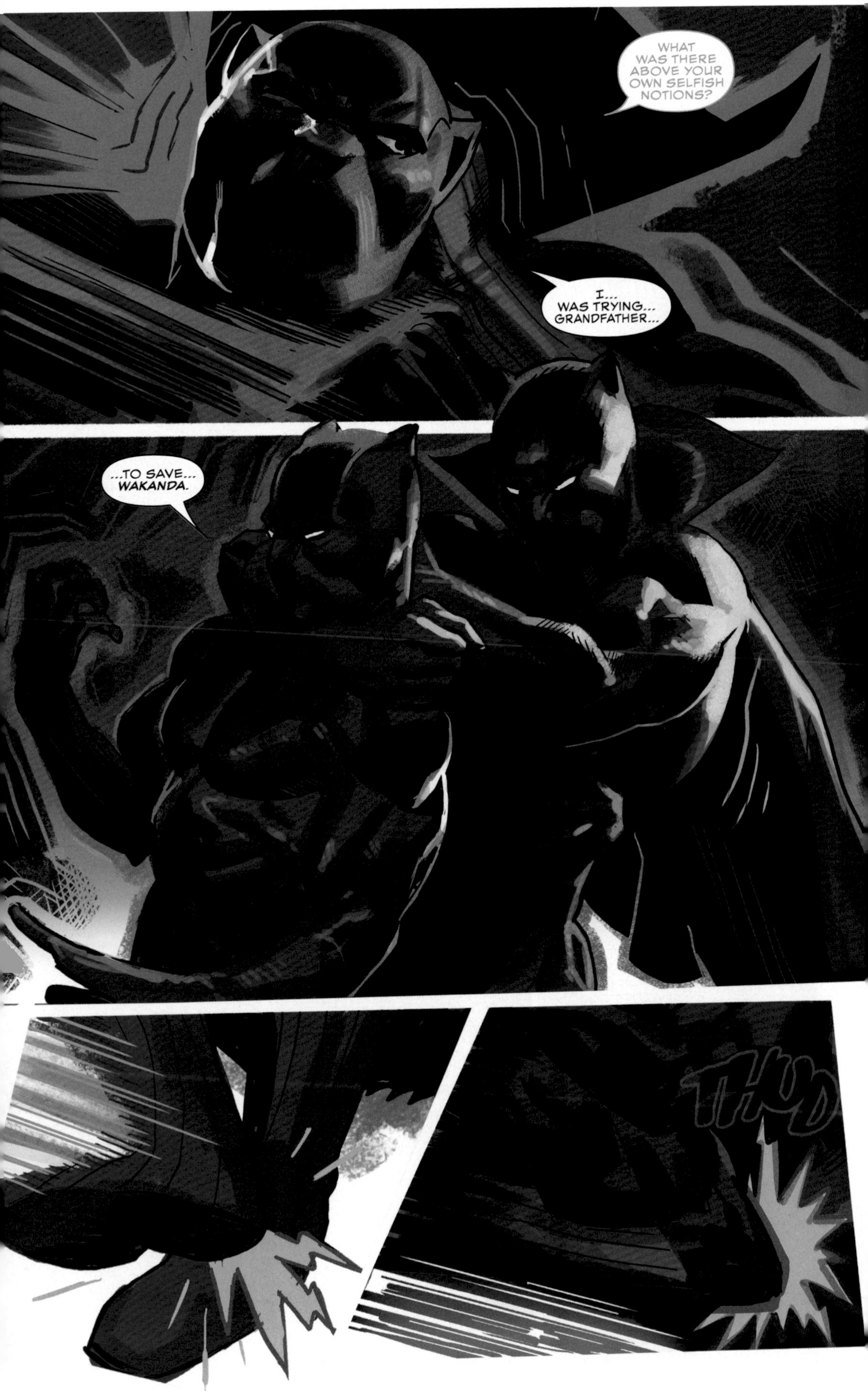
WHAT WAS THERE ABOVE YOUR OWN SELFISH NOTIONS?
I... WAS TRYING... GRANDFATHER...
...TO SAVE... WAKANDA.
THUD

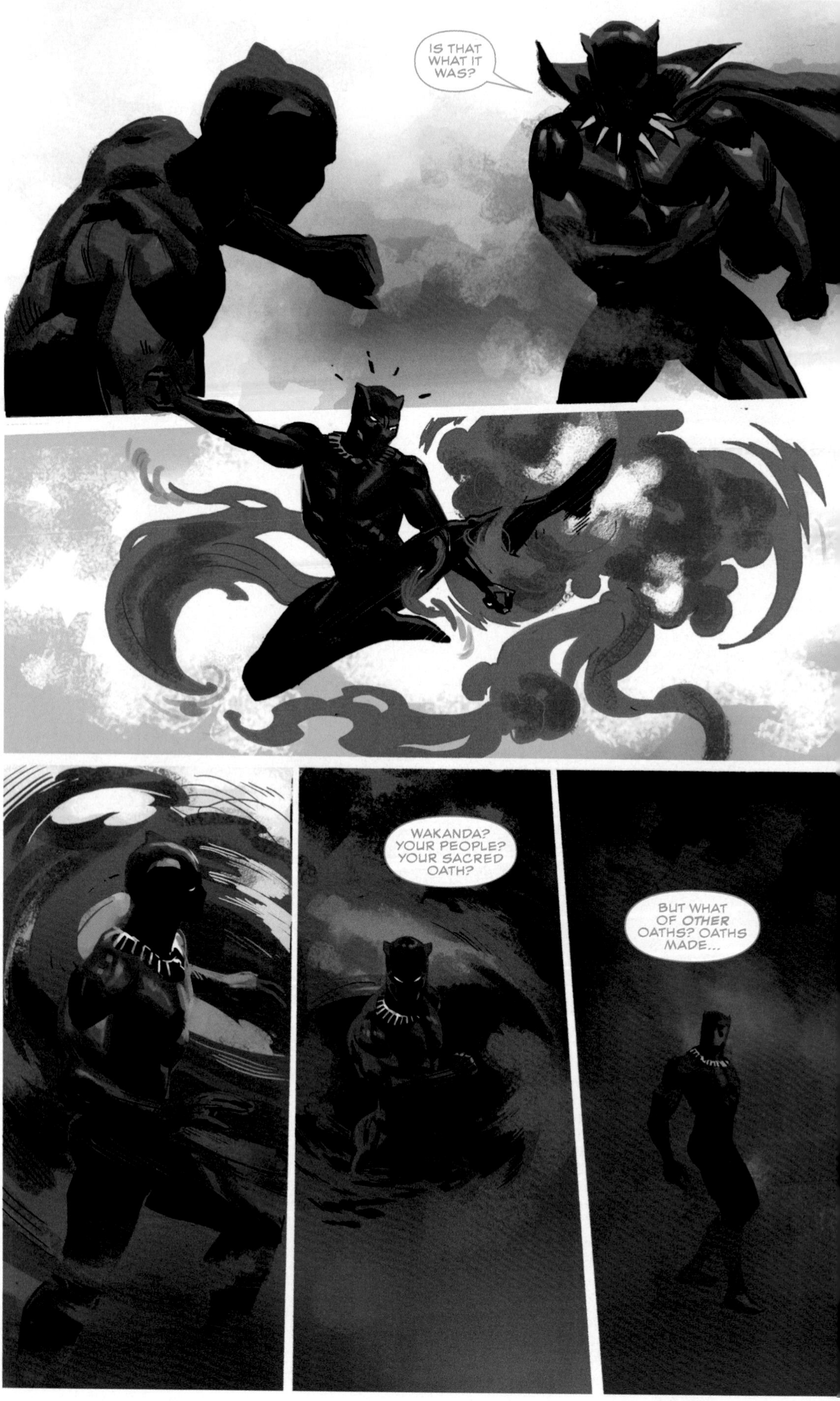
IS THAT WHAT IT WAS?
WAKANDA? YOUR PEOPLE? YOUR SACRED OATH?
BUT WHAT OF OTHER OATHS? OATHS MADE...

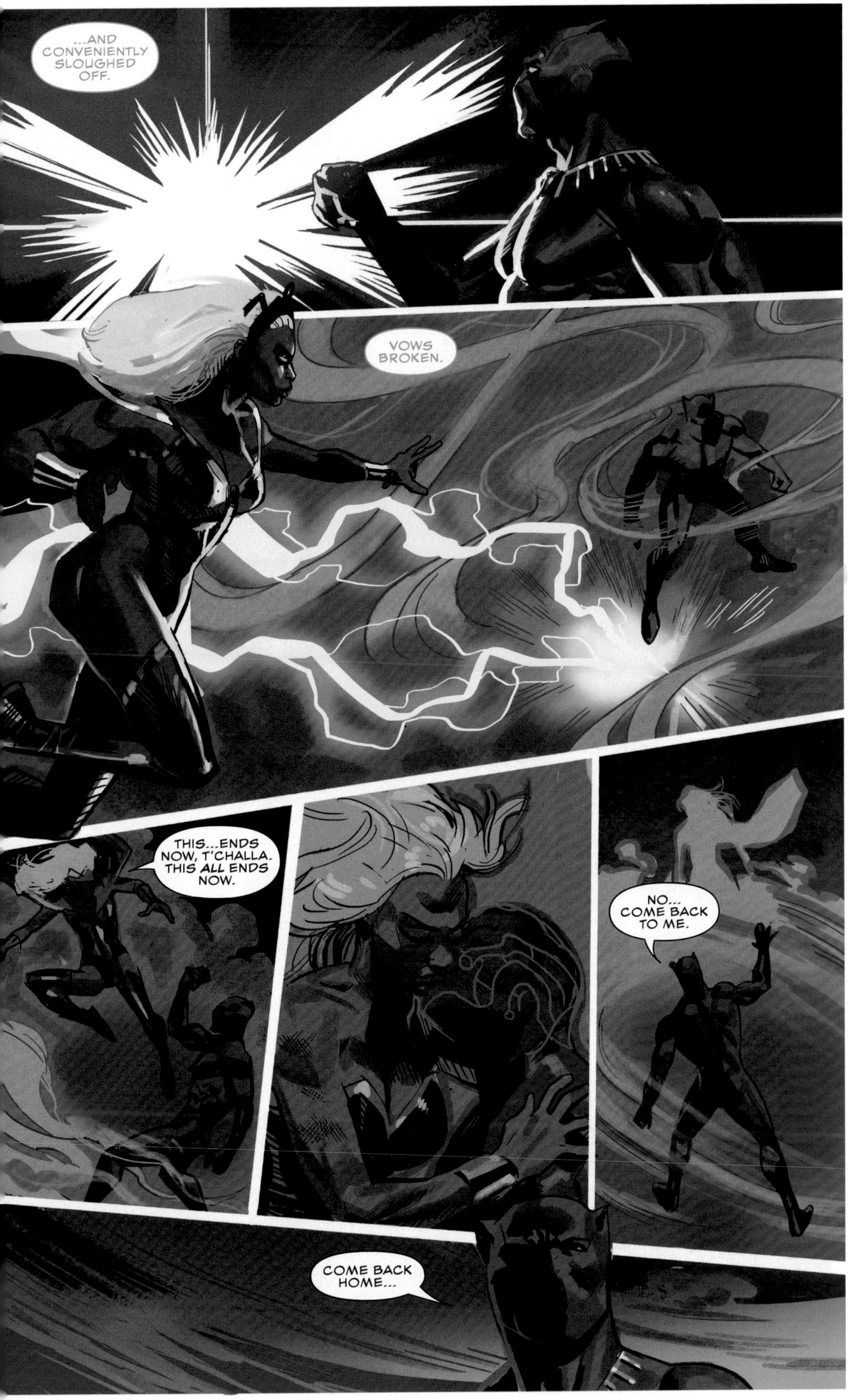
...AND CONVENIENTLY SLOUGHED OFF.
VOWS BROKEN.
THIS...ENDS NOW, T'CHALLA. THIS ALL ENDS NOW.
NO... COME BACK TO ME.
COME BACK HOME...

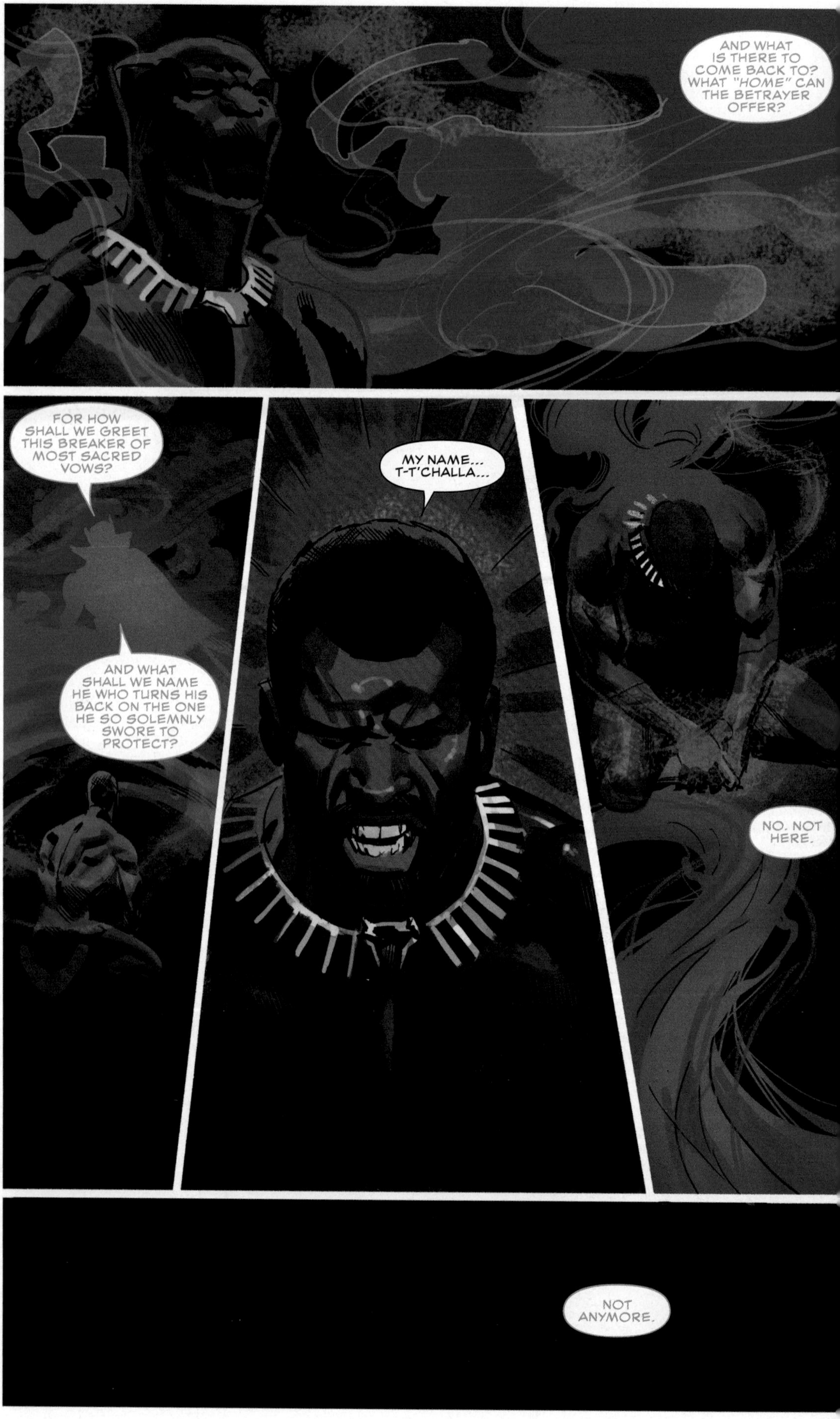
AND WHAT IS THERE TO COME BACK TO? WHAT "HOME" CAN THE BETRAYER OFFER?
FOR HOW SHALL WE GREET THIS BREAKER OF MOST SACRED VOWS?
AND WHAT SHALL WE NAME HE WHO TURNS HIS BACK ON THE ONE HE SO SOLEMNLY SWORE TO PROTECT?
MY NAME... T-T'CHALLA...
NO. NOT HERE.
NOT ANYMORE.

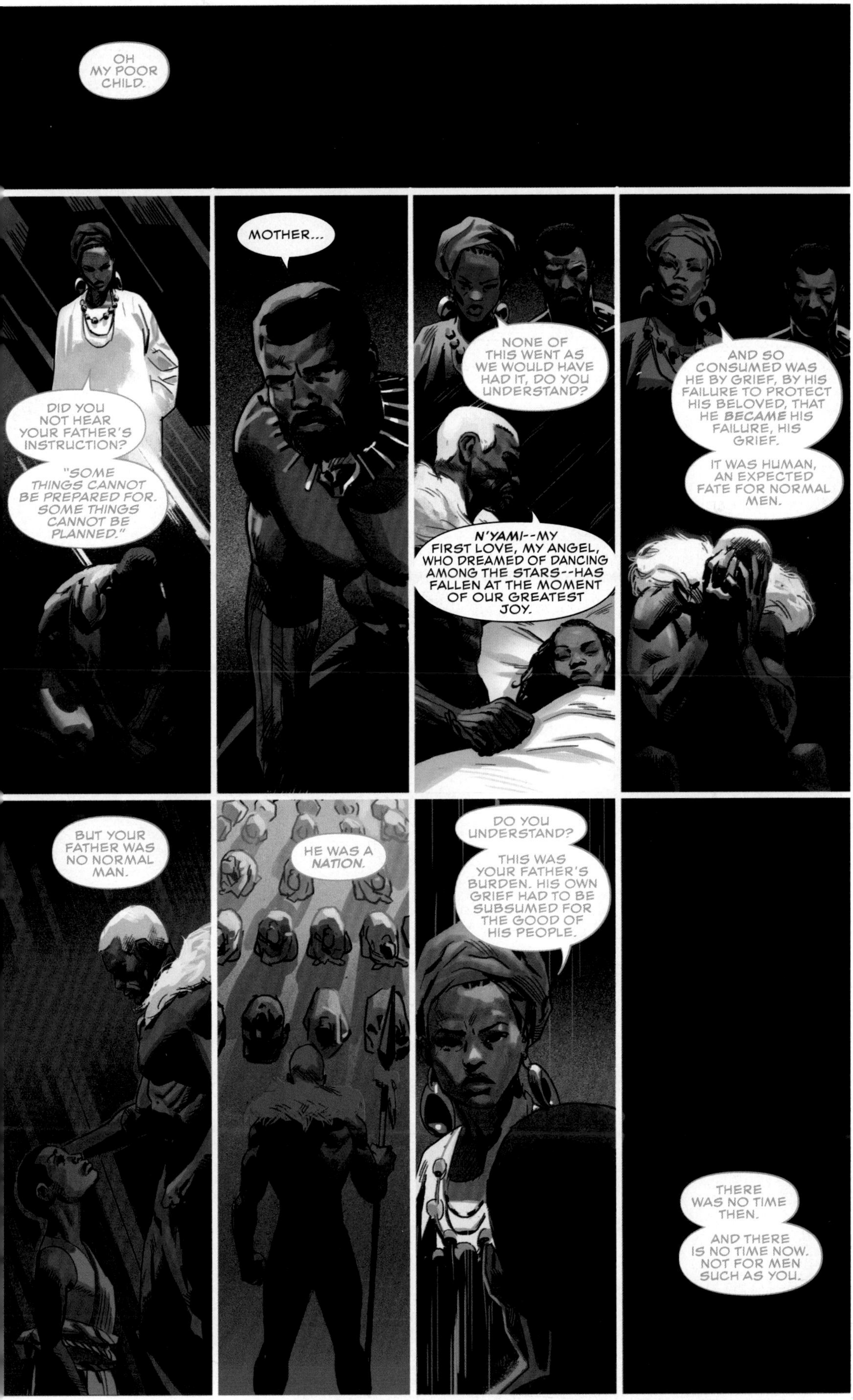
OH MY POOR CHILD.
DID YOU NOT HEAR YOUR FATHER'S INSTRUCTION?
"SOME THINGS CANNOT BE PREPARED FOR. SOME THINGS CANNOT BE PLANNED."
MOTHER...
NONE OF THIS WENT AS WE WOULD HAVE HAD IT, DO YOU UNDERSTAND?
N'YAMI--MY FIRST LOVE, MY ANGEL, WHO DREAMED OF DANCING AMONG THE STARS--HAS FALLEN AT THE MOMENT OF OUR GREATEST JOY.
AND SO CONSUMED WAS HE BY GRIEF, BY HIS FAILURE TO PROTECT HIS BELOVED, THAT HE BECAME HIS FAILURE, HIS GRIEF.
IT WAS HUMAN, AN EXPECTED FATE FOR NORMAL MEN.
BUT YOUR FATHER WAS NO NORMAL MAN.
HE WAS A NATION.
DO YOU UNDERSTAND?
THIS WAS YOUR FATHER'S BURDEN. HIS OWN GRIEF HAD TO BE SUBSUMED FOR THE GOOD OF HIS PEOPLE.
THERE WAS NO TIME THEN.
AND THERE IS NO TIME NOW. NOT FOR MEN SUCH AS YOU.

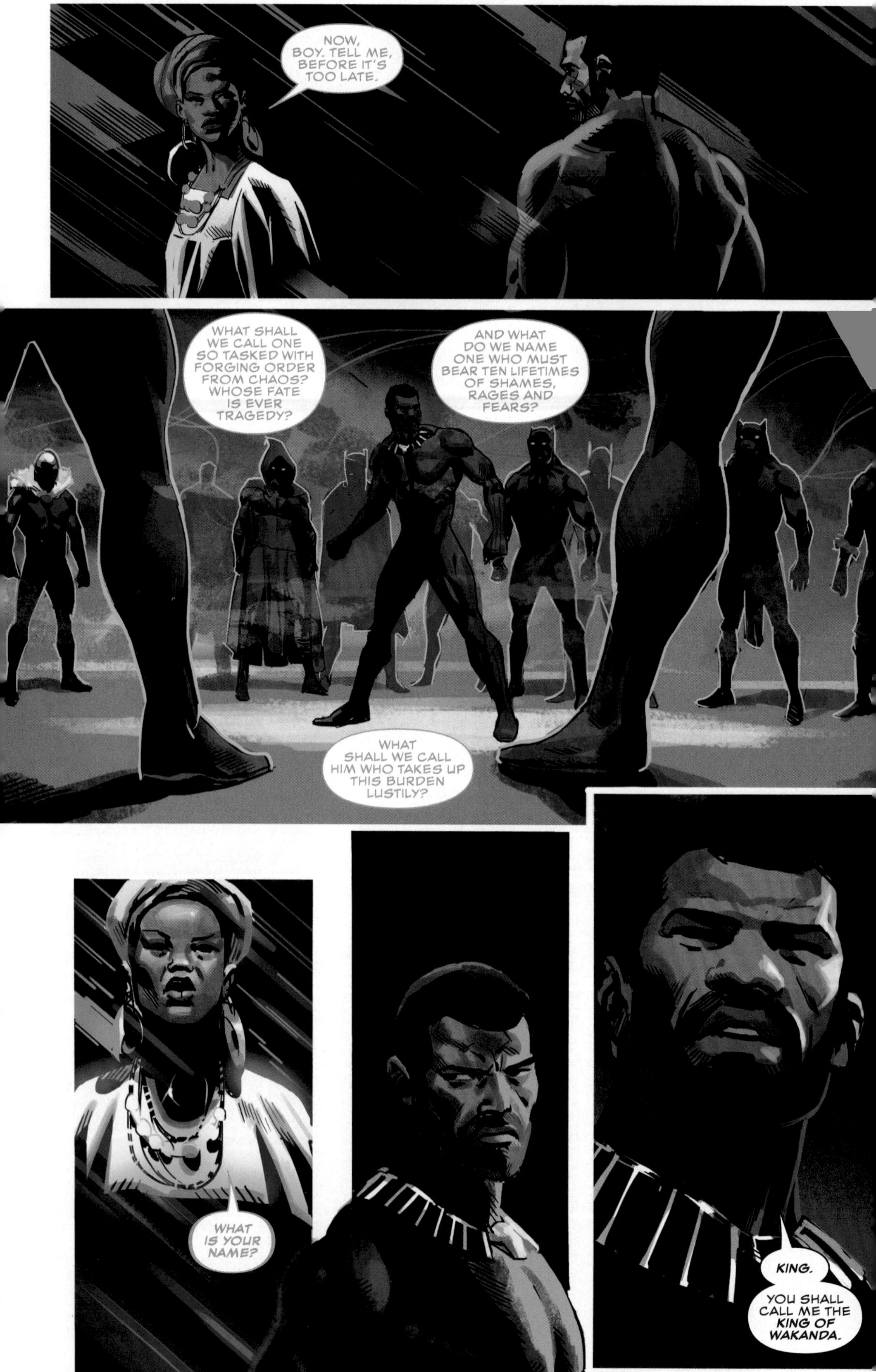
NOW, BOY. TELL ME, BEFORE IT'S TOO LATE.
WHAT SHALL WE CALL ONE SO TASKED WITH FORGING ORDER FROM CHAOS? WHOSE FATE IS EVER TRAGEDY?
AND WHAT DO WE NAME ONE WHO MUST BEAR TEN LIFETIMES OF SHAMES, RAGES AND FEARS?
WHAT SHALL WE CALL HIM WHO TAKES UP THIS BURDEN LUSTILY?
WHAT IS YOUR NAME?
KING.
YOU SHALL CALL ME THE KING OF WAKANDA.

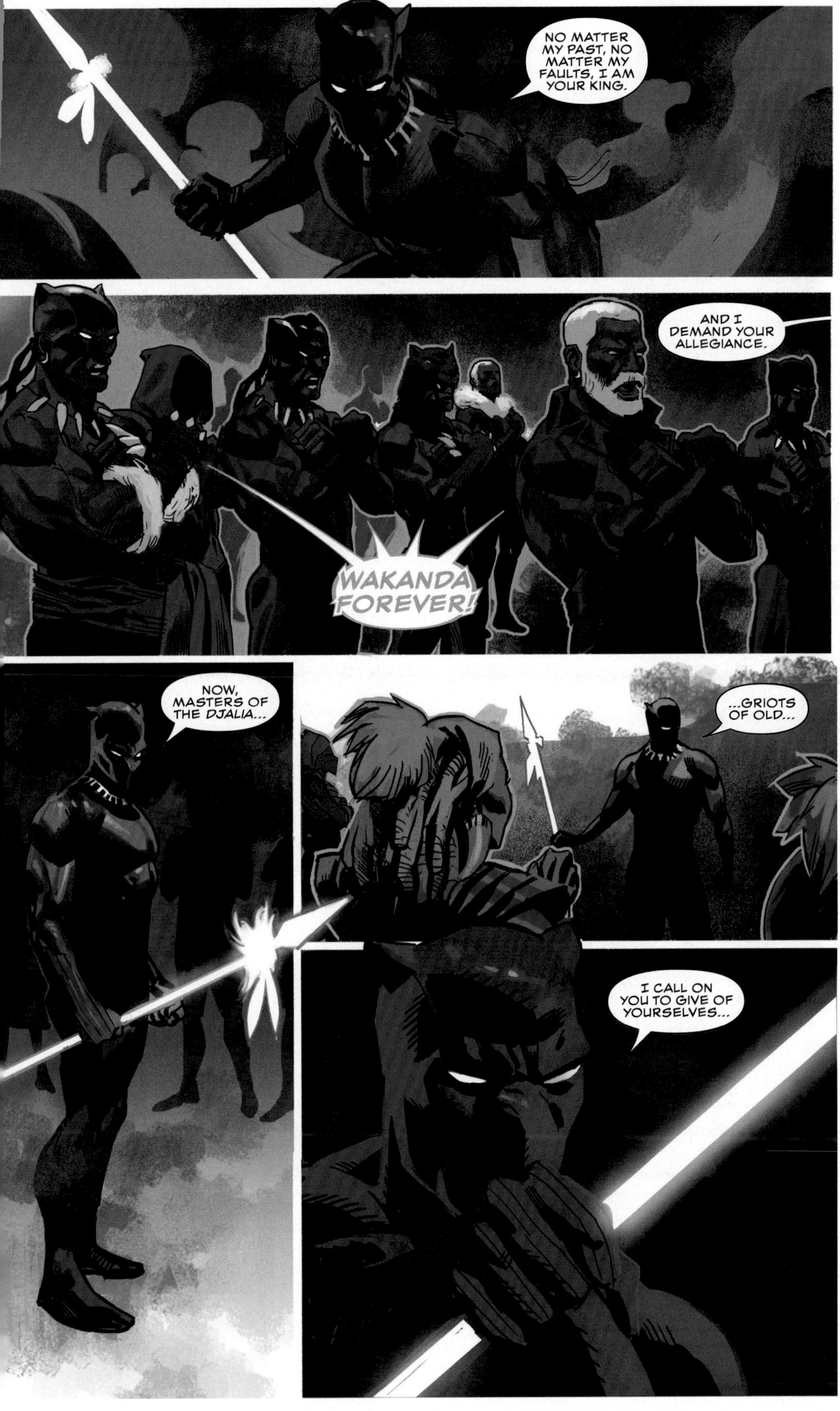
NO MATTER MY PAST, NO MATTER MY FAULTS, I AM YOUR KING.
AND I DEMAND YOUR ALLEGIANCE.
WAKANDA FOREVER!
NOW, MASTERS OF THE *DJALIA*...
...GRIOTS OF OLD...
I CALL ON YOU TO GIVE OF YOURSELVES...

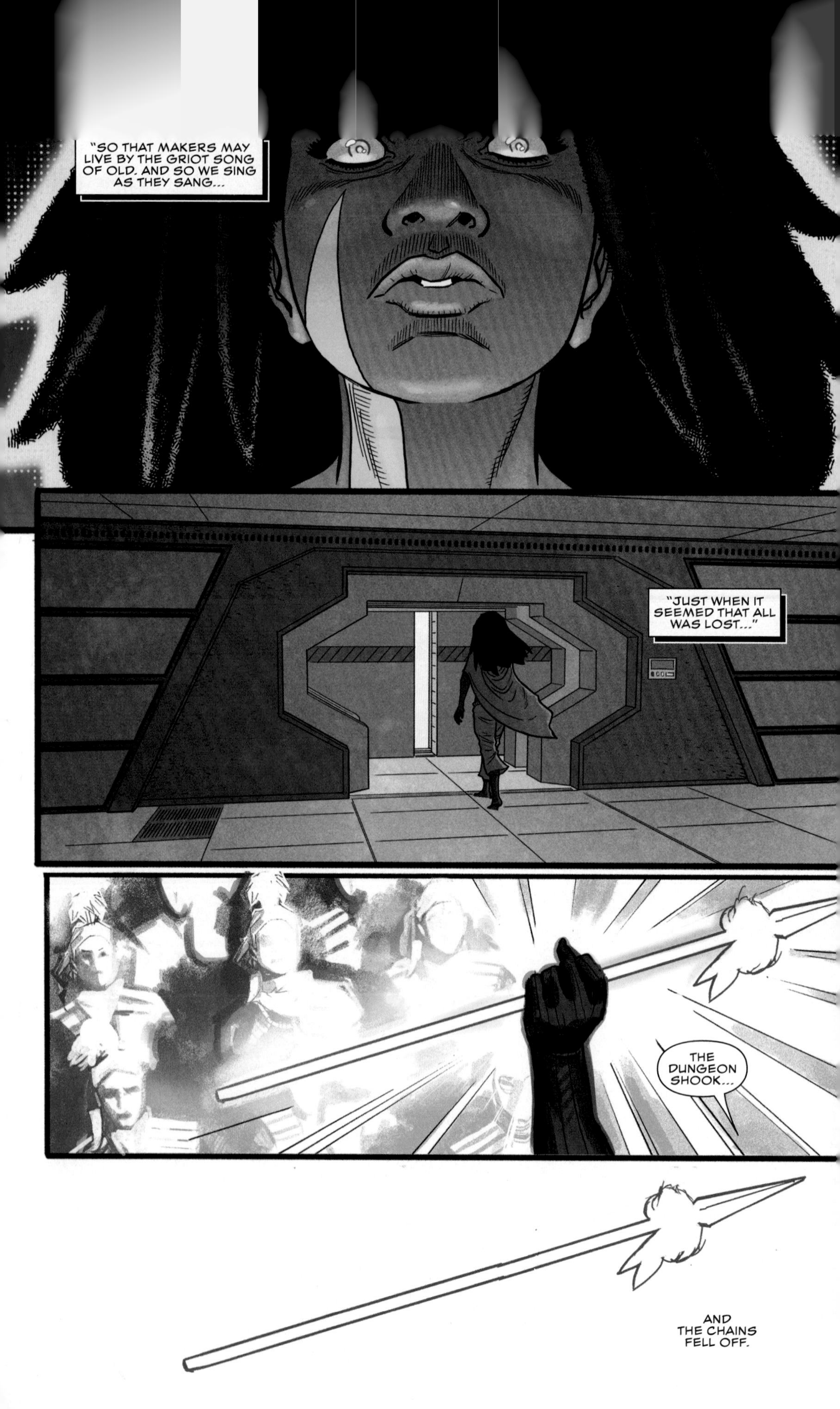
"SO THAT MAKERS MAY LIVE BY THE GRIOT SONG OF OLD. AND SO WE SING AS THEY SANG...
"JUST WHEN IT SEEMED THAT ALL WAS LOST..."
THE DUNGEON SHOOK...
AND THE CHAINS FELL OFF.

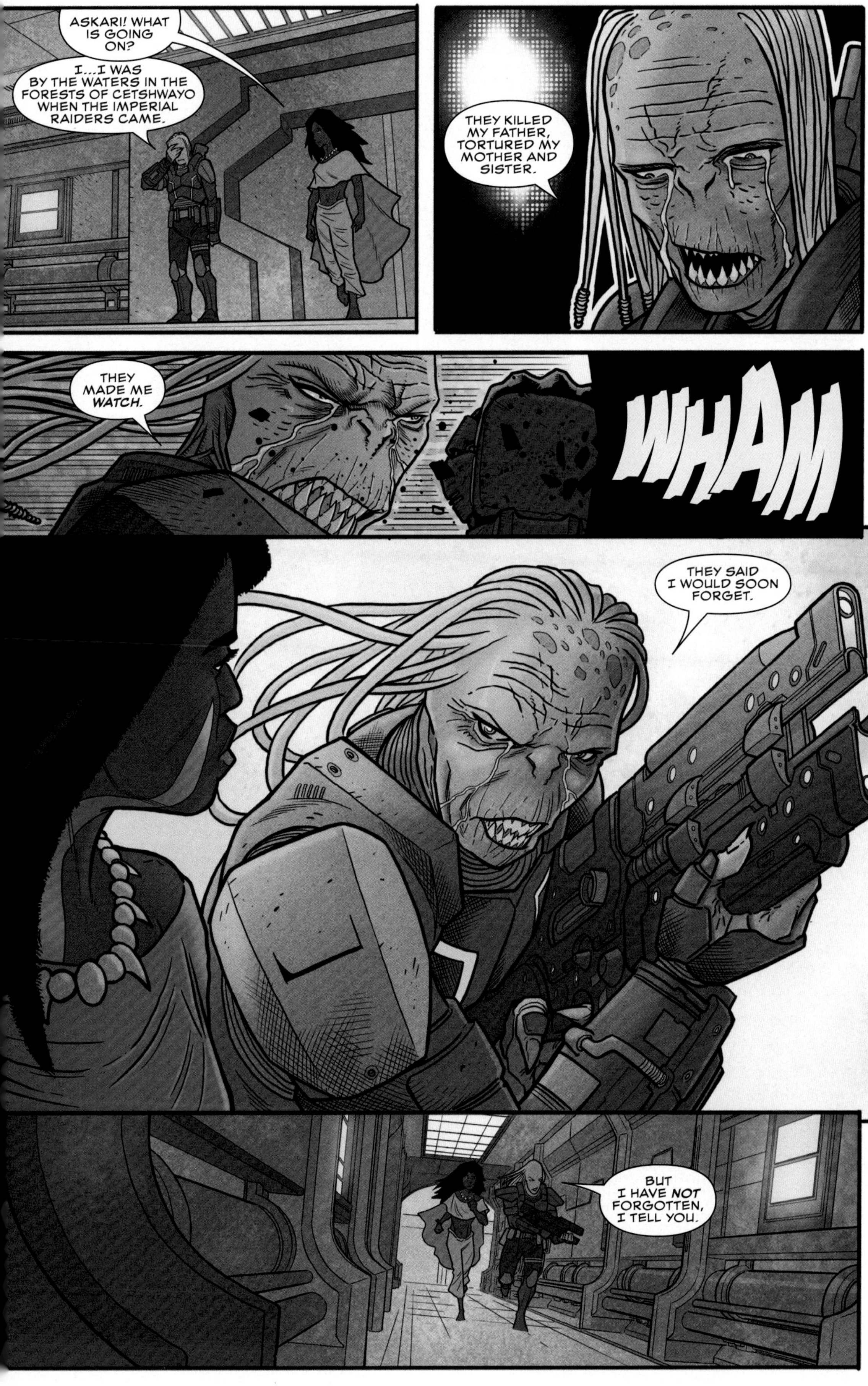
ASKARI! WHAT IS GOING ON?
I...I WAS BY THE WATERS IN THE FORESTS OF CETSHWAYO WHEN THE IMPERIAL RAIDERS CAME.
THEY KILLED MY FATHER, TORTURED MY MOTHER AND SISTER.
THEY MADE ME *WATCH*.
WHAM
THEY SAID I WOULD SOON FORGET.
BUT I HAVE ***NOT*** FORGOTTEN, I TELL YOU.

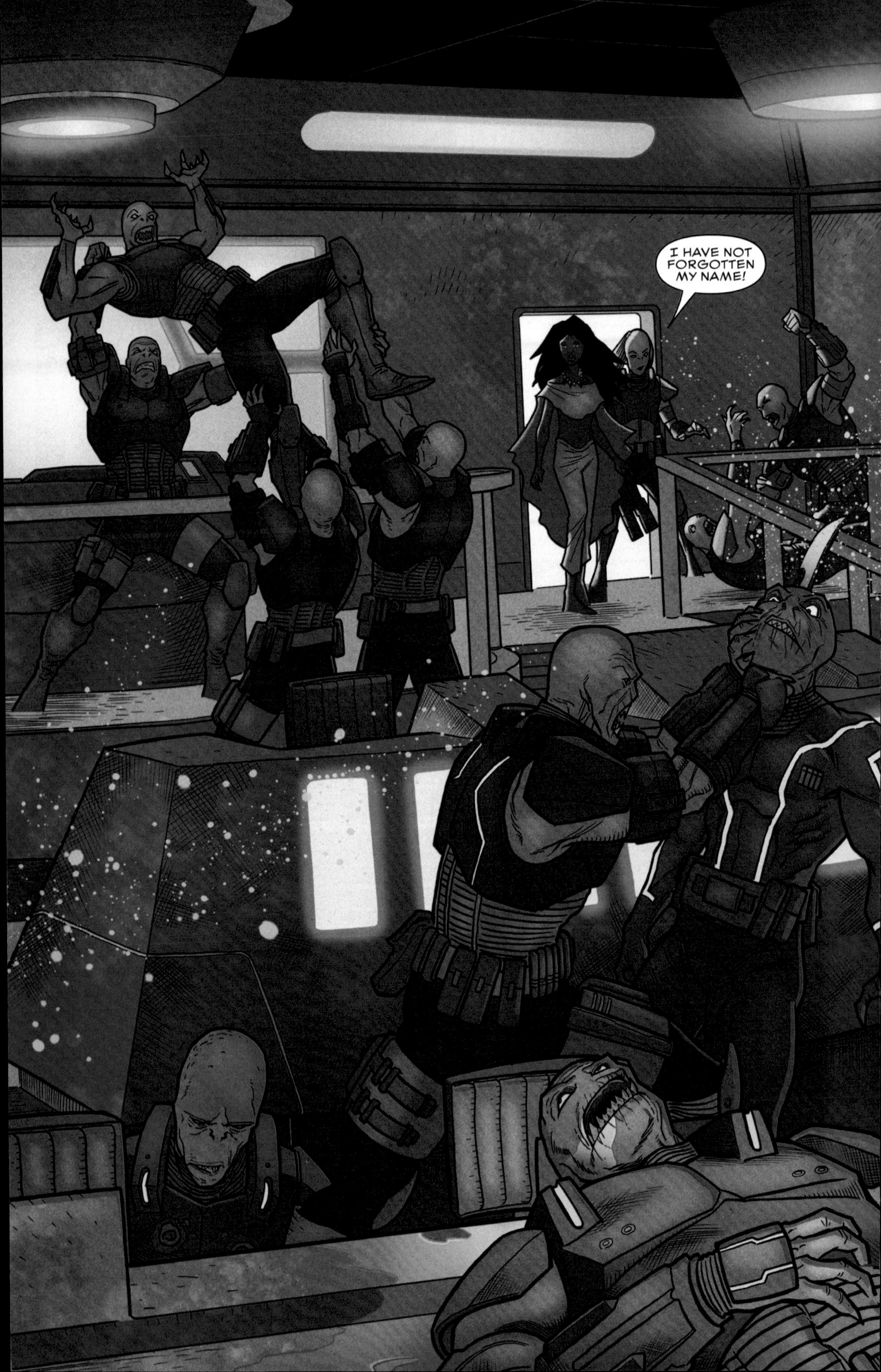
I HAVE NOT FORGOTTEN MY NAME!

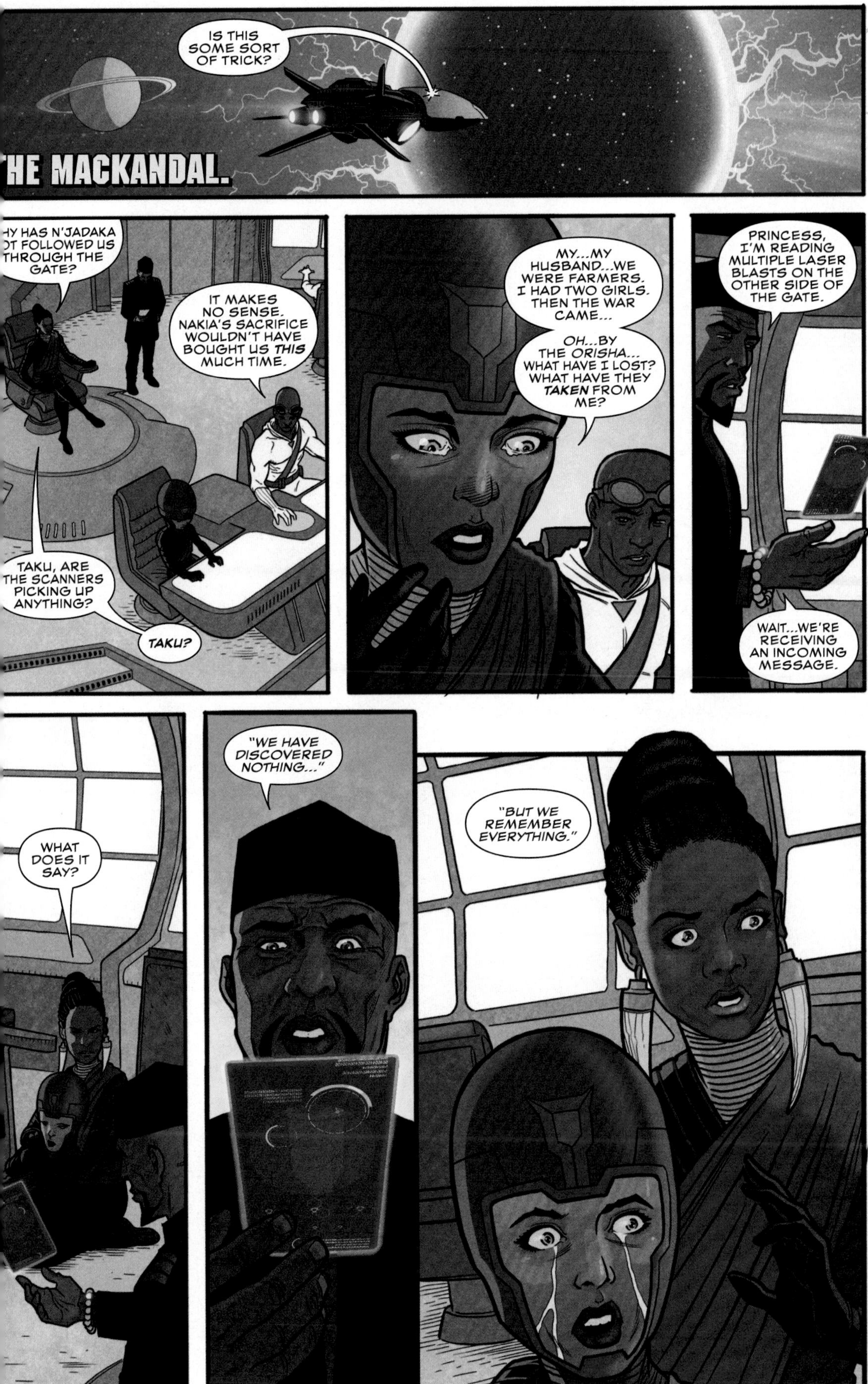
IS THIS SOME SORT OF TRICK?
THE MACKANDAL.
HY HAS N'JADAKA OT FOLLOWED US THROUGH THE GATE?
IT MAKES NO SENSE. NAKIA'S SACRIFICE WOULDN'T HAVE BOUGHT US *THIS* MUCH TIME.
TAKU, ARE THE SCANNERS PICKING UP ANYTHING?
TAKU?
MY...MY HUSBAND...WE WERE FARMERS. I HAD TWO GIRLS. THEN THE WAR CAME...
OH...BY THE *ORISHA*... WHAT HAVE I LOST? WHAT HAVE THEY *TAKEN* FROM ME?
PRINCESS, I'M READING MULTIPLE LASER BLASTS ON THE OTHER SIDE OF THE GATE.
WAIT...WE'RE RECEIVING AN INCOMING MESSAGE.
WHAT DOES IT SAY?
"WE HAVE DISCOVERED NOTHING..."
"BUT WE REMEMBER EVERYTHING."

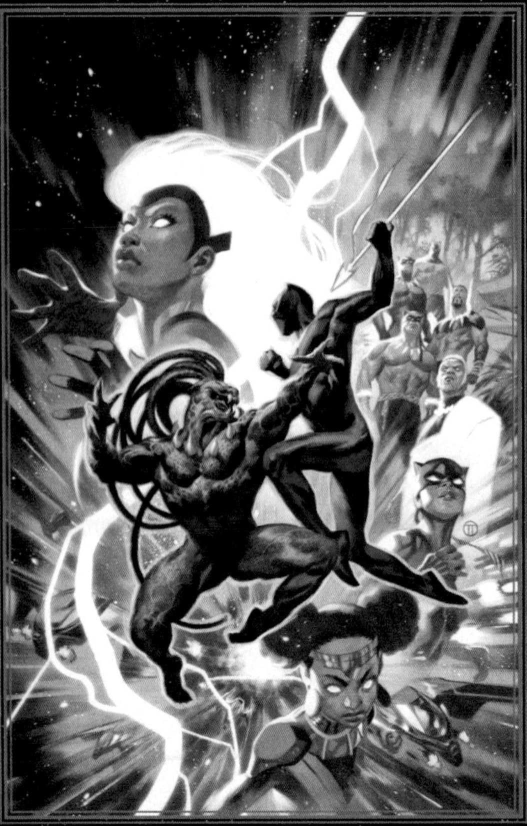

Julian Totino Tedesco
23 VARIANT

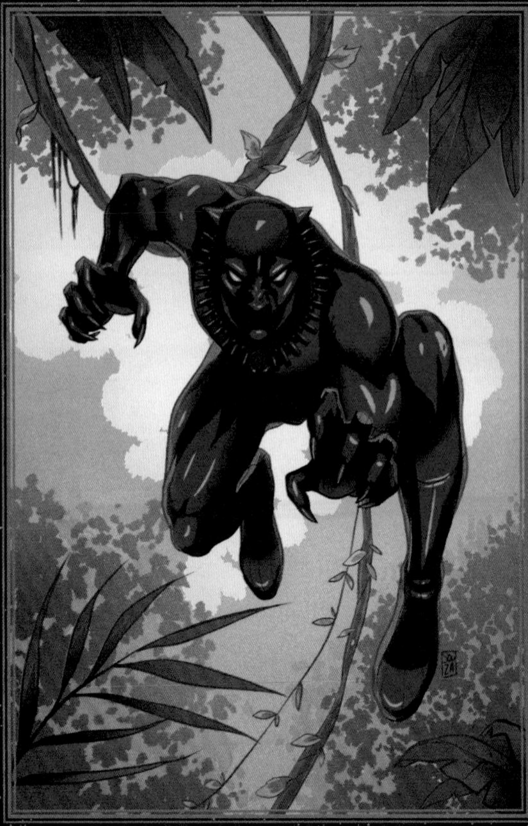

Ernanda Souza
23 VARIANT

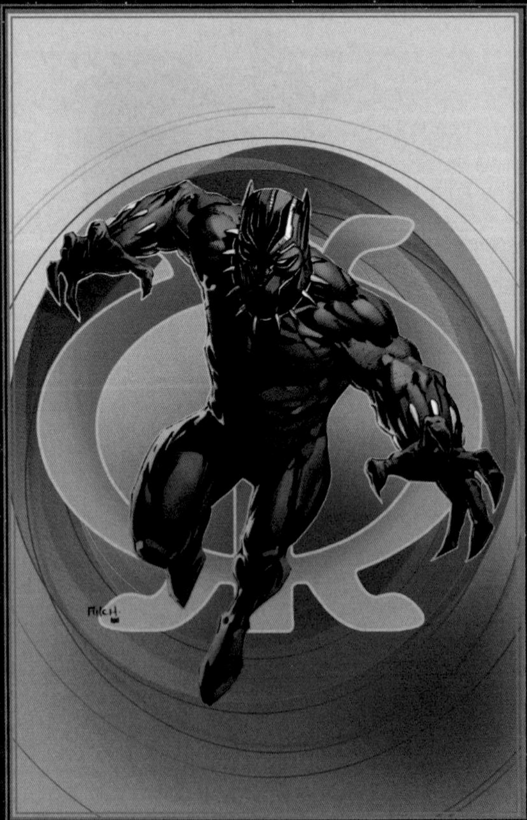

David Finch & Frank D'armata
23 VARIANT

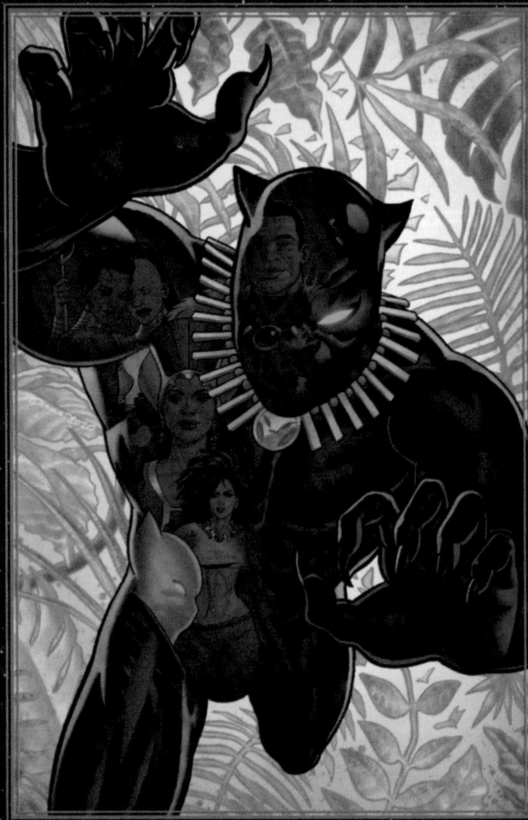

Joe Quinones
24 VARIANT

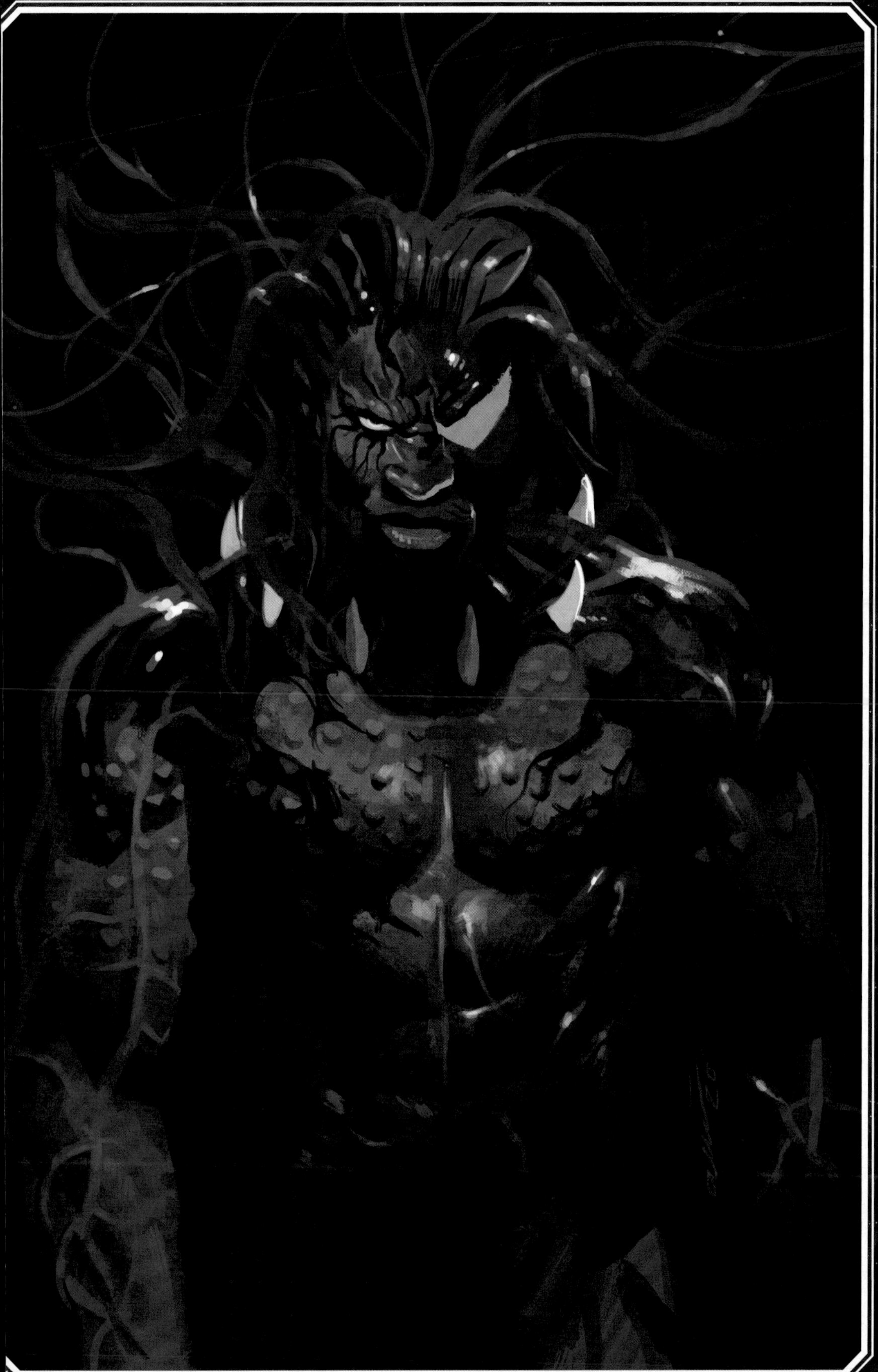

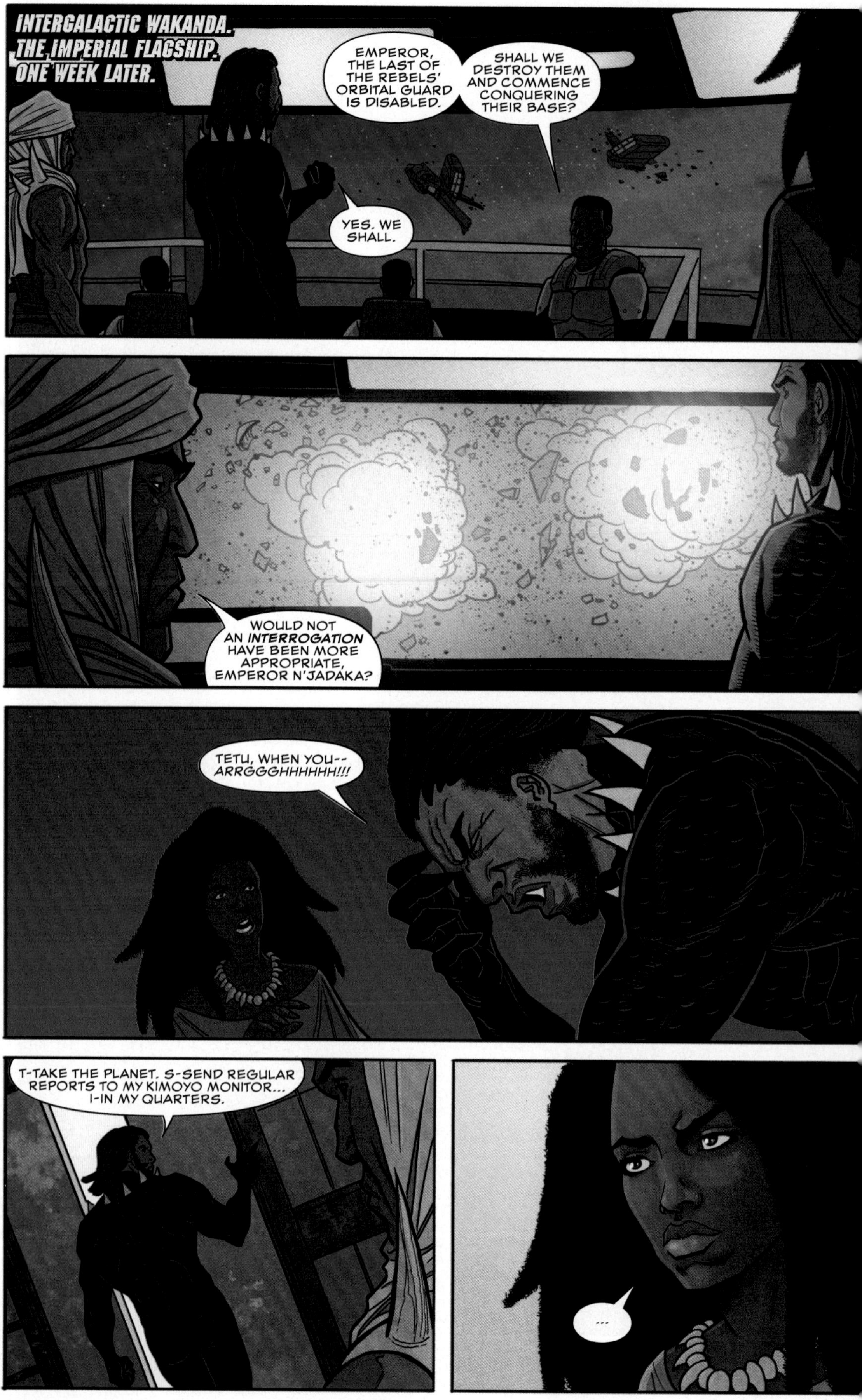
INTERGALACTIC WAKANDA. THE IMPERIAL FLAGSHIP. ONE WEEK LATER.
EMPEROR, THE LAST OF THE REBELS' ORBITAL GUARD IS DISABLED.
SHALL WE DESTROY THEM AND COMMENCE CONQUERING THEIR BASE?
YES. WE SHALL.
WOULD NOT AN INTERROGATION HAVE BEEN MORE APPROPRIATE, EMPEROR N'JADAKA?
TETU, WHEN YOU-- ARRGGGHHHHHH!!!
T-TAKE THE PLANET. S-SEND REGULAR REPORTS TO MY KIMOYO MONITOR... I-IN MY QUARTERS.
...

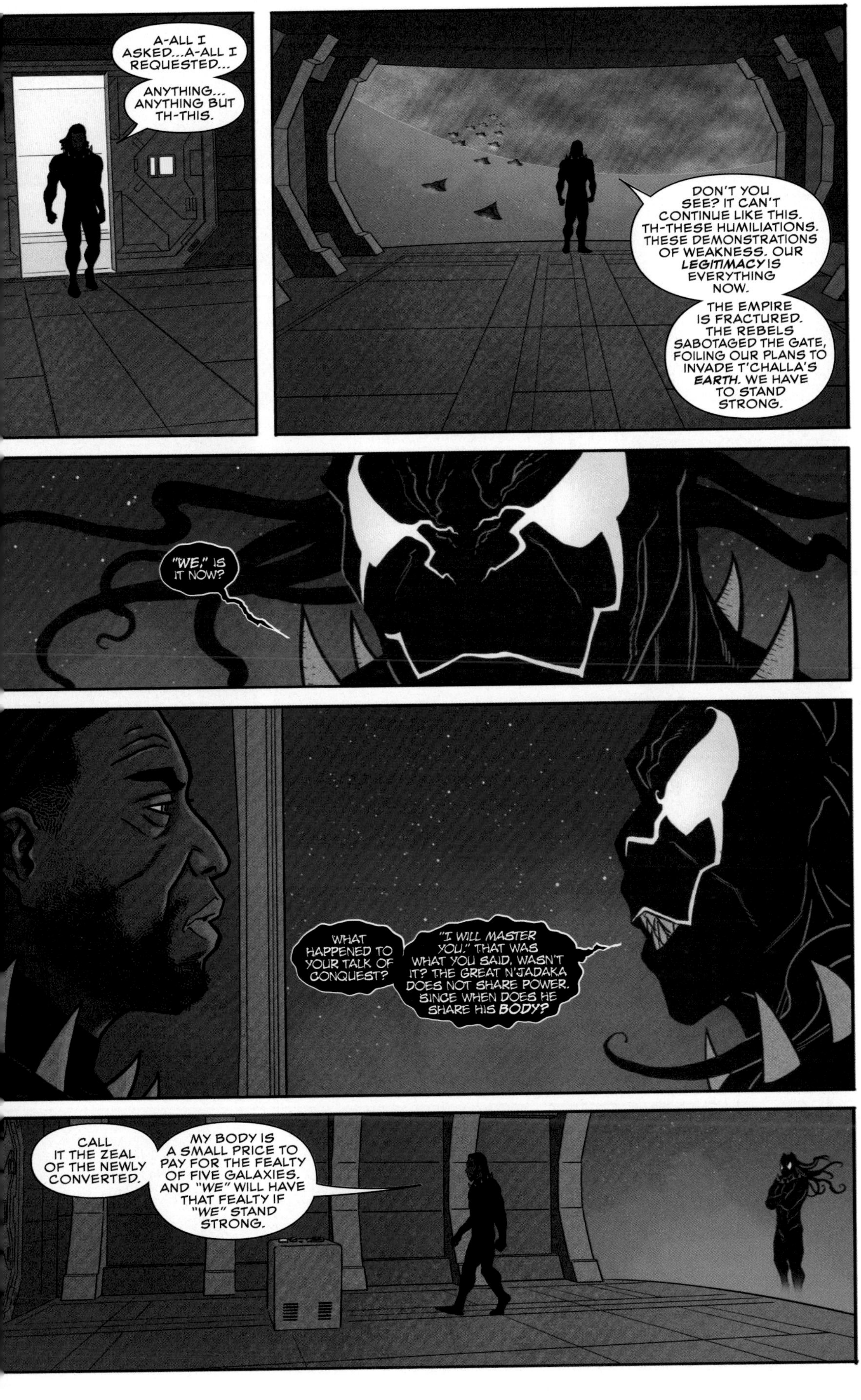
A-ALL I ASKED... A-ALL I REQUESTED...
ANYTHING... ANYTHING BUT TH-THIS.
DON'T YOU SEE? IT CAN'T CONTINUE LIKE THIS. TH-THESE HUMILIATIONS. THESE DEMONSTRATIONS OF WEAKNESS. OUR LEGITIMACY IS EVERYTHING NOW.
THE EMPIRE IS FRACTURED. THE REBELS SABOTAGED THE GATE, FOILING OUR PLANS TO INVADE T'CHALLA'S EARTH. WE HAVE TO STAND STRONG.
"WE," IS IT NOW?
WHAT HAPPENED TO YOUR TALK OF CONQUEST?
"I WILL MASTER YOU." THAT WAS WHAT YOU SAID, WASN'T IT? THE GREAT N'JADAKA DOES NOT SHARE POWER. SINCE WHEN DOES HE SHARE HIS BODY?
CALL IT THE ZEAL OF THE NEWLY CONVERTED.
MY BODY IS A SMALL PRICE TO PAY FOR THE FEALTY OF FIVE GALAXIES. AND "WE" WILL HAVE THAT FEALTY IF "WE" STAND STRONG.

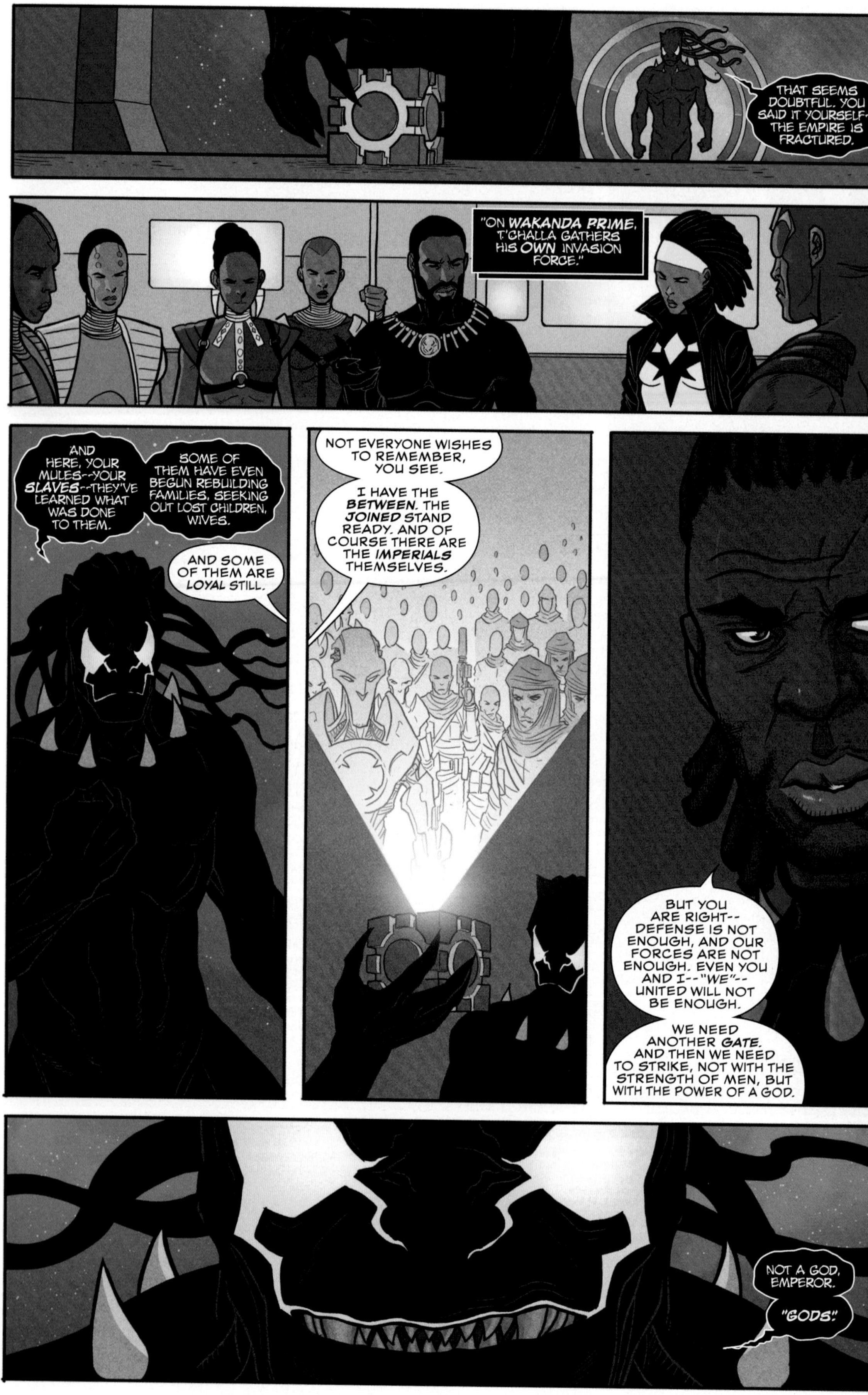
THAT SEEMS DOUBTFUL. YOU SAID IT YOURSELF--THE EMPIRE IS FRACTURED.
"ON WAKANDA PRIME, T'CHALLA GATHERS HIS OWN INVASION FORCE."
AND HERE, YOUR MULES--YOUR SLAVES--THEY'VE LEARNED WHAT WAS DONE TO THEM.
SOME OF THEM HAVE EVEN BEGUN REBUILDING FAMILIES, SEEKING OUT LOST CHILDREN, WIVES.
AND SOME OF THEM ARE LOYAL STILL.
NOT EVERYONE WISHES TO REMEMBER, YOU SEE.
I HAVE THE BETWEEN. THE JOINED STAND READY. AND OF COURSE THERE ARE THE IMPERIALS THEMSELVES.
BUT YOU ARE RIGHT--DEFENSE IS NOT ENOUGH, AND OUR FORCES ARE NOT ENOUGH. EVEN YOU AND I--"WE"--UNITED WILL NOT BE ENOUGH.
WE NEED ANOTHER GATE. AND THEN WE NEED TO STRIKE, NOT WITH THE STRENGTH OF MEN, BUT WITH THE POWER OF A GOD.
NOT A GOD, EMPEROR.
"GODS."

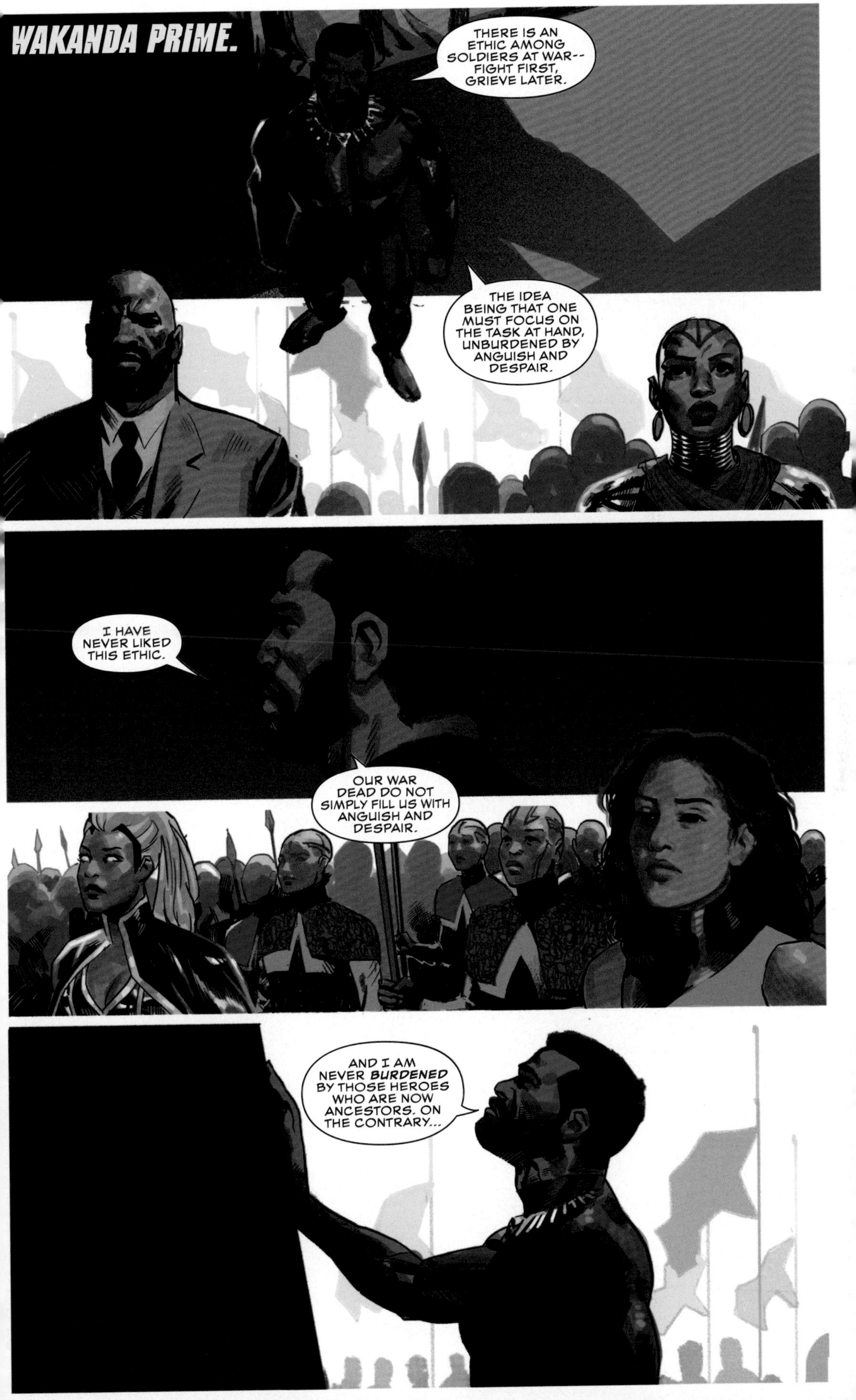
WAKANDA PRIME.
THERE IS AN ETHIC AMONG SOLDIERS AT WAR-- FIGHT FIRST, GRIEVE LATER.
THE IDEA BEING THAT ONE MUST FOCUS ON THE TASK AT HAND, UNBURDENED BY ANGUISH AND DESPAIR.
I HAVE NEVER LIKED THIS ETHIC.
OUR WAR DEAD DO NOT SIMPLY FILL US WITH ANGUISH AND DESPAIR.
AND I AM NEVER BURDENED BY THOSE HEROES WHO ARE NOW ANCESTORS. ON THE CONTRARY...

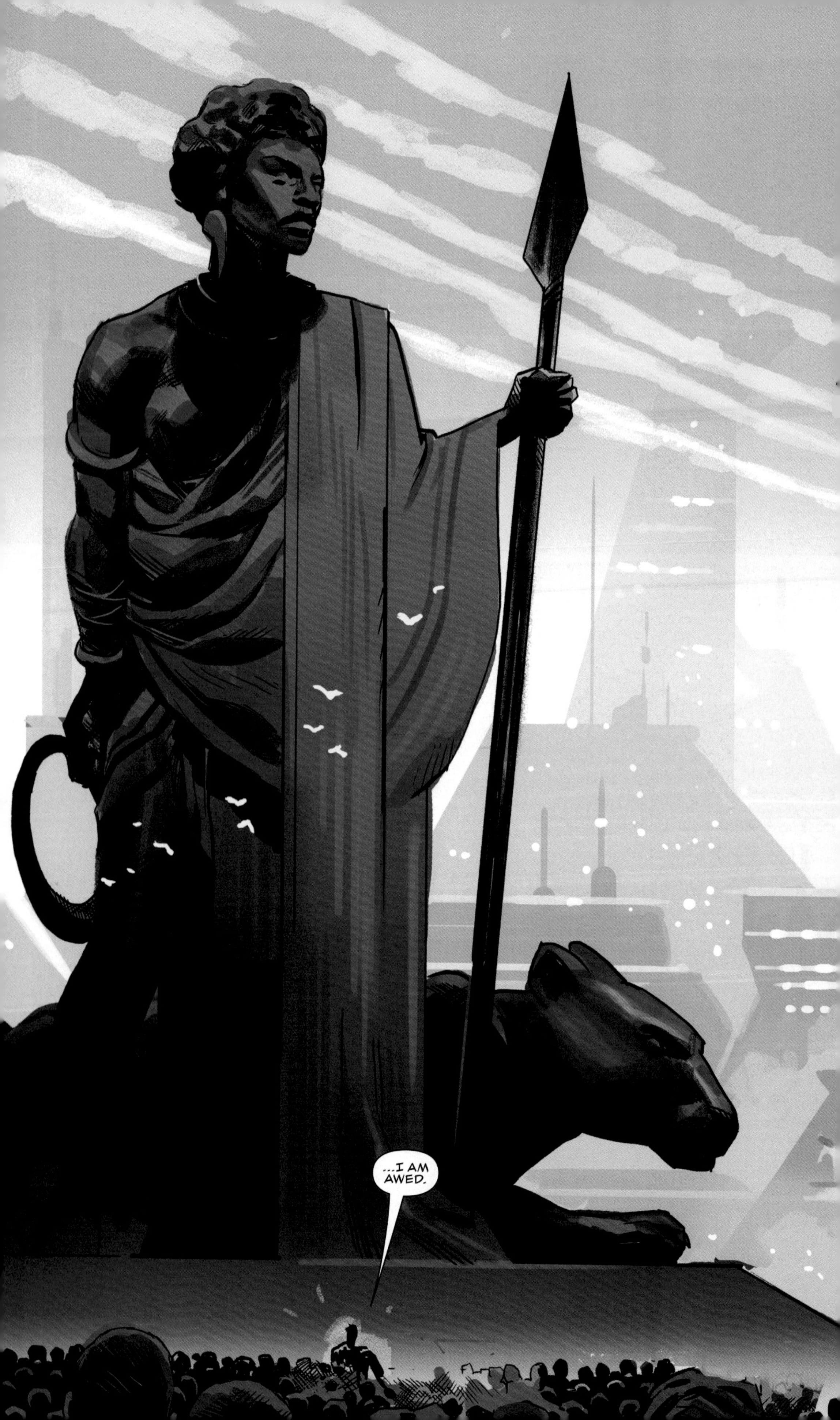
...I AM AWED.

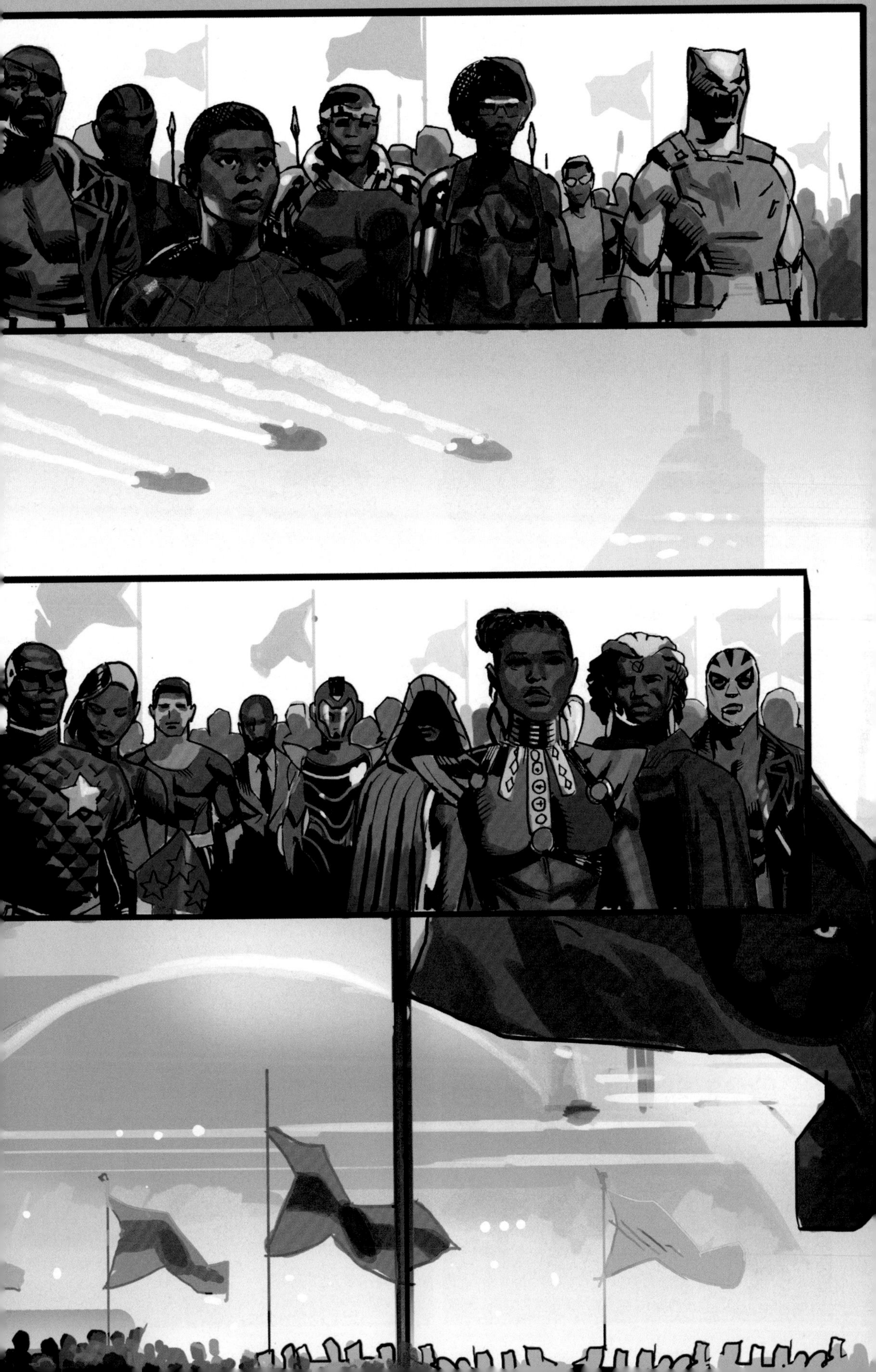

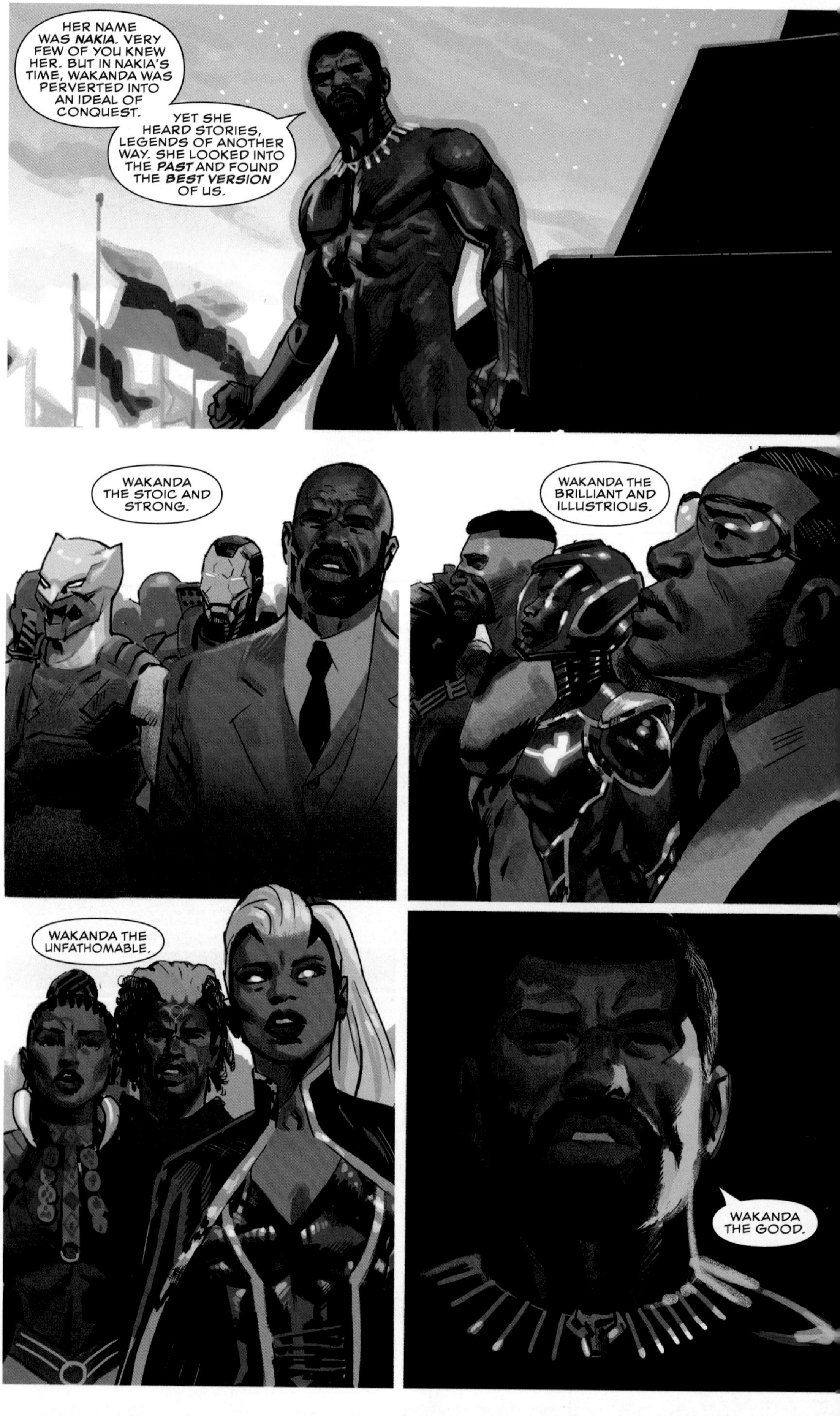
HER NAME WAS NAKIA. VERY FEW OF YOU KNEW HER. BUT IN NAKIA'S TIME, WAKANDA WAS PERVERTED INTO AN IDEAL OF CONQUEST.
YET SHE HEARD STORIES, LEGENDS OF ANOTHER WAY. SHE LOOKED INTO THE PAST AND FOUND THE BEST VERSION OF US.
WAKANDA THE STOIC AND STRONG.
WAKANDA THE BRILLIANT AND ILLUSTRIOUS.
WAKANDA THE UNFATHOMABLE.
WAKANDA THE GOOD.

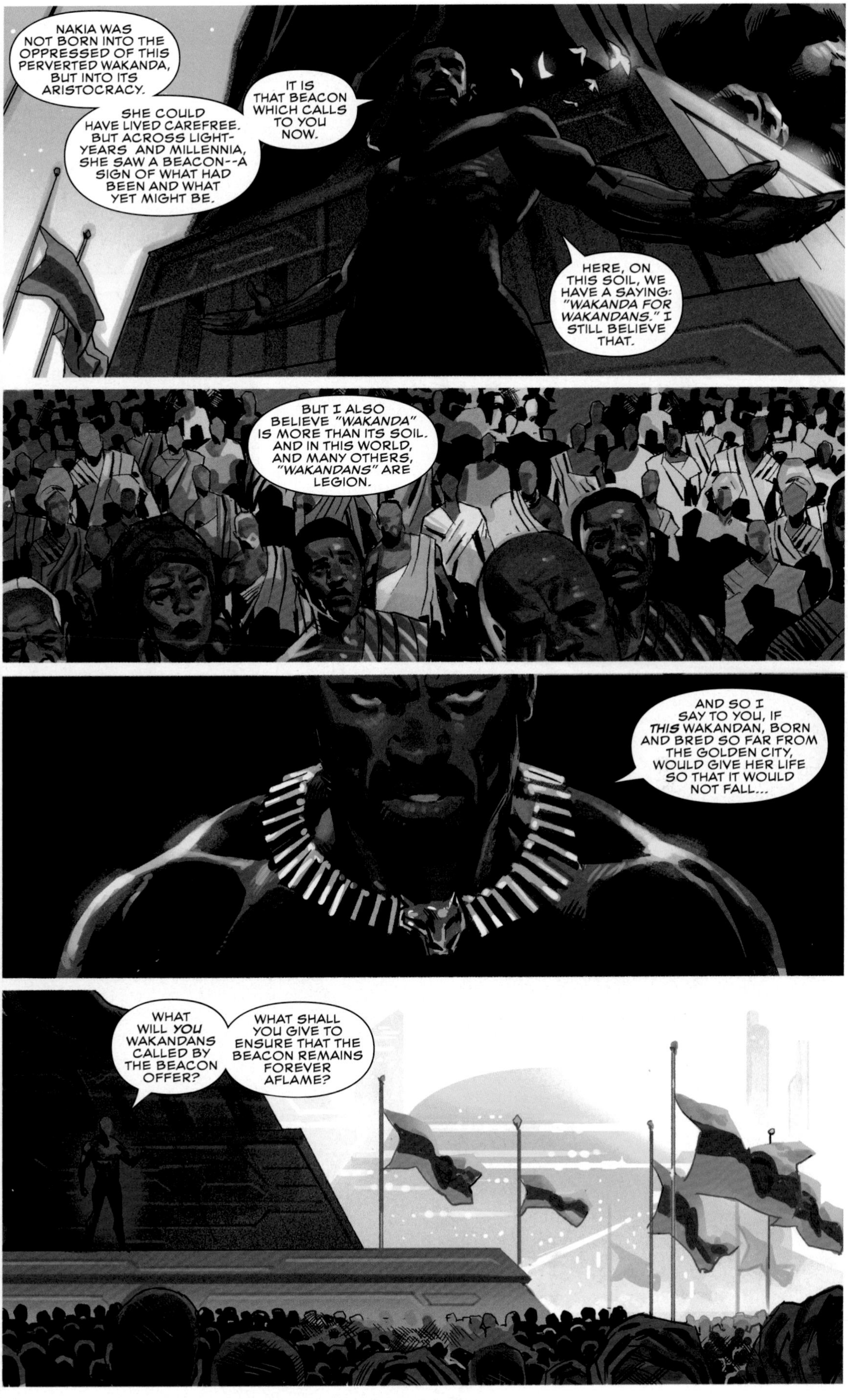
NAKIA WAS NOT BORN INTO THE OPPRESSED OF THIS PERVERTED WAKANDA, BUT INTO ITS ARISTOCRACY.
SHE COULD HAVE LIVED CAREFREE. BUT ACROSS LIGHT-YEARS AND MILLENNIA, SHE SAW A BEACON--A SIGN OF WHAT HAD BEEN AND WHAT YET MIGHT BE.
IT IS THAT BEACON WHICH CALLS TO YOU NOW.
HERE, ON THIS SOIL, WE HAVE A SAYING: "WAKANDA FOR WAKANDANS." I STILL BELIEVE THAT.
BUT I ALSO BELIEVE "WAKANDA" IS MORE THAN ITS SOIL. AND IN THIS WORLD, AND MANY OTHERS, "WAKANDANS" ARE LEGION.
AND SO I SAY TO YOU, IF THIS WAKANDAN, BORN AND BRED SO FAR FROM THE GOLDEN CITY, WOULD GIVE HER LIFE SO THAT IT WOULD NOT FALL...
WHAT WILL YOU WAKANDANS CALLED BY THE BEACON OFFER?
WHAT SHALL YOU GIVE TO ENSURE THAT THE BEACON REMAINS FOREVER AFLAME?

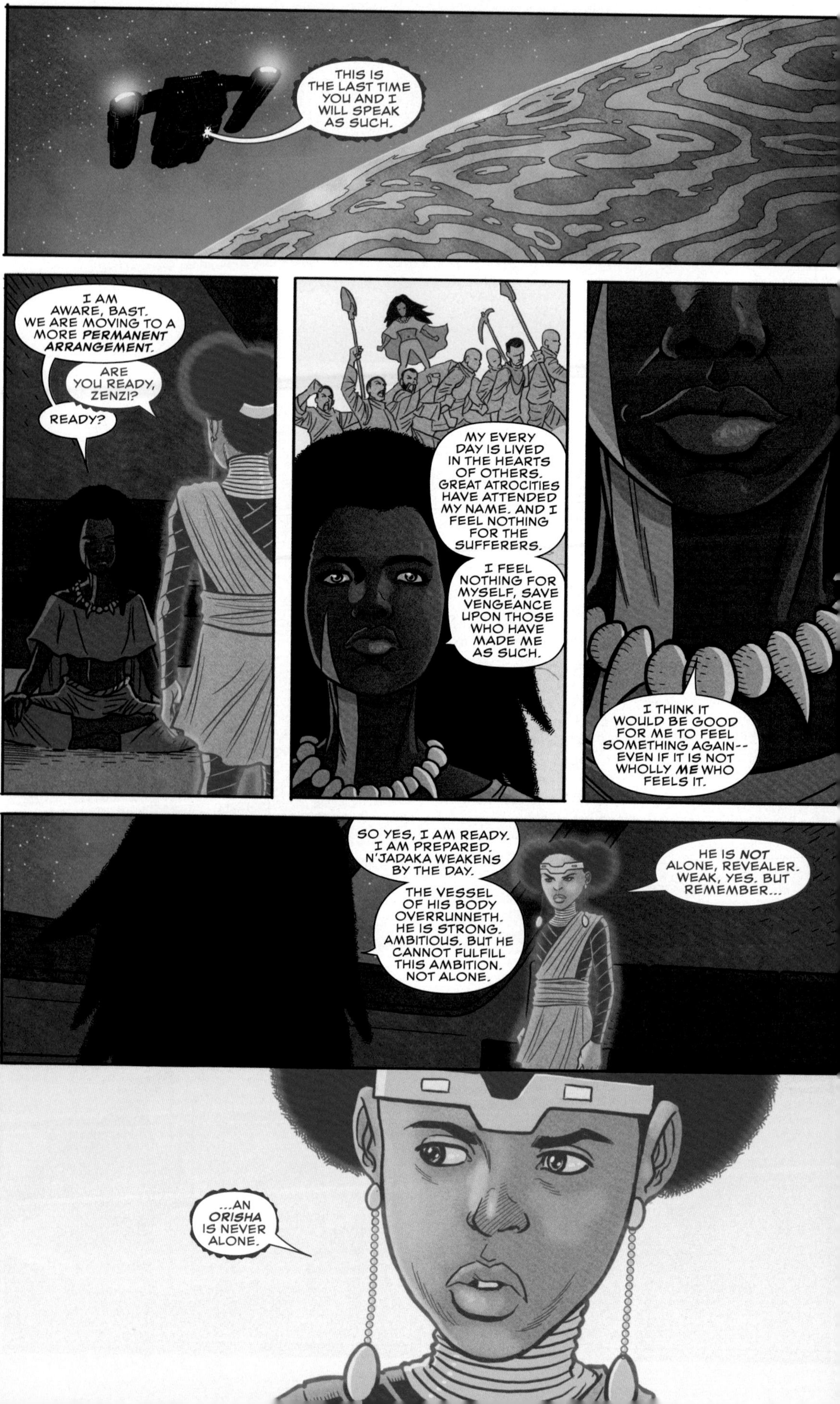

THIS IS THE LAST TIME YOU AND I WILL SPEAK AS SUCH.
I AM AWARE, BAST. WE ARE MOVING TO A MORE *PERMANENT ARRANGEMENT.*
ARE YOU READY, ZENZI?
READY?
MY EVERY DAY IS LIVED IN THE HEARTS OF OTHERS. GREAT ATROCITIES HAVE ATTENDED MY NAME. AND I FEEL NOTHING FOR THE SUFFERERS.
I FEEL NOTHING FOR MYSELF, SAVE VENGEANCE UPON THOSE WHO HAVE MADE ME AS SUCH.
I THINK IT WOULD BE GOOD FOR ME TO FEEL SOMETHING AGAIN-- EVEN IF IT IS NOT WHOLLY *ME* WHO FEELS IT.
SO YES, I AM READY. I AM PREPARED. N'JADAKA WEAKENS BY THE DAY.
THE VESSEL OF HIS BODY OVERRUNNETH. HE IS STRONG. AMBITIOUS. BUT HE CANNOT FULFILL THIS AMBITION. NOT ALONE.
HE IS *NOT* ALONE, REVEALER. WEAK, YES. BUT REMEMBER...
...AN *ORISHA* IS NEVER ALONE.

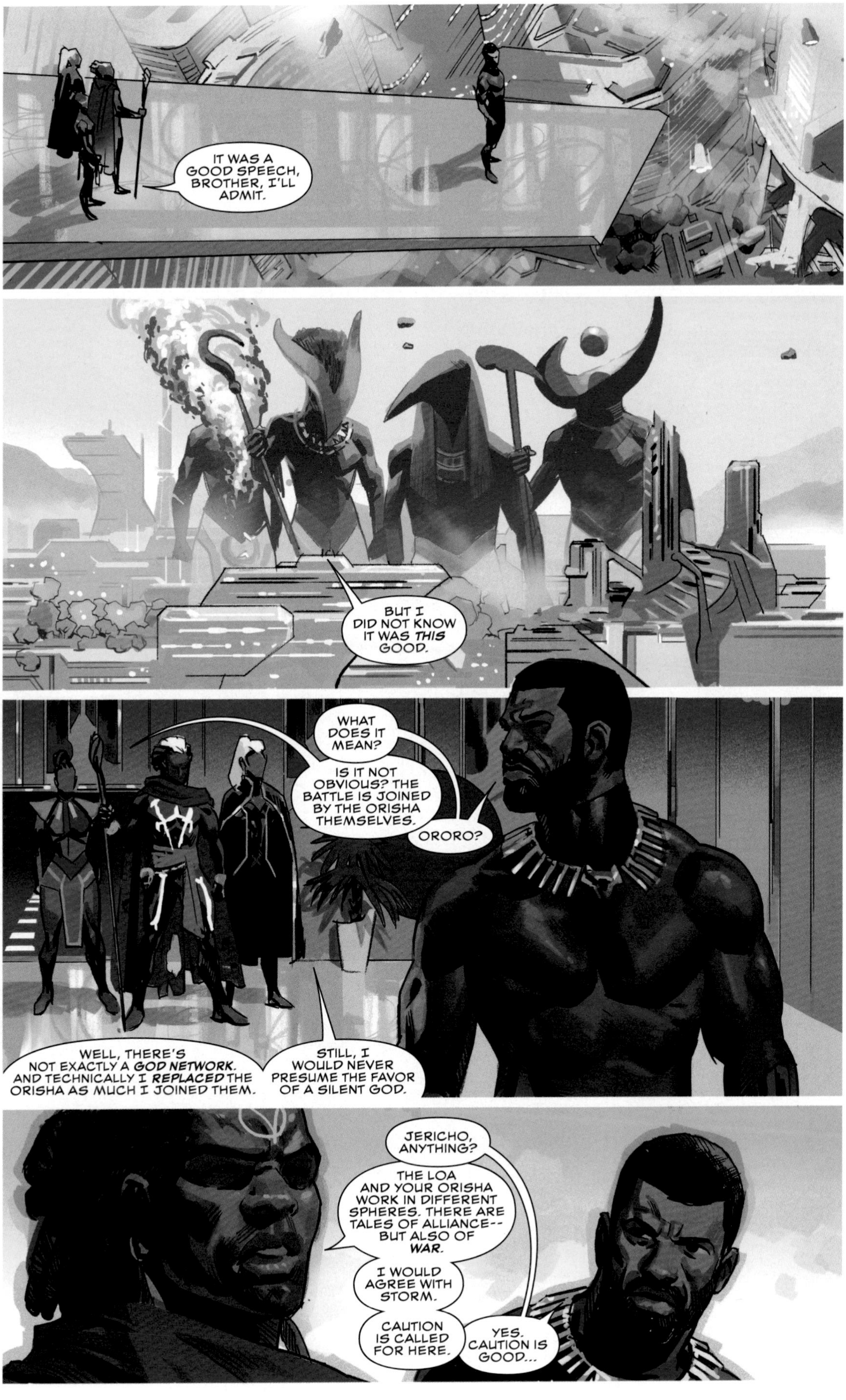
IT WAS A GOOD SPEECH, BROTHER, I'LL ADMIT.
BUT I DID NOT KNOW IT WAS *THIS* GOOD.
WHAT DOES IT MEAN?
IS IT NOT OBVIOUS? THE BATTLE IS JOINED BY THE ORISHA THEMSELVES.
ORORO?
WELL, THERE'S NOT EXACTLY A *GOD NETWORK*. AND TECHNICALLY I *REPLACED* THE ORISHA AS MUCH I JOINED THEM.
STILL, I WOULD NEVER PRESUME THE FAVOR OF A SILENT GOD.
JERICHO, ANYTHING?
THE LOA AND YOUR ORISHA WORK IN DIFFERENT SPHERES. THERE ARE TALES OF ALLIANCE-- BUT ALSO OF *WAR*.
I WOULD AGREE WITH STORM.
CAUTION IS CALLED FOR HERE.
YES. CAUTION IS GOOD...

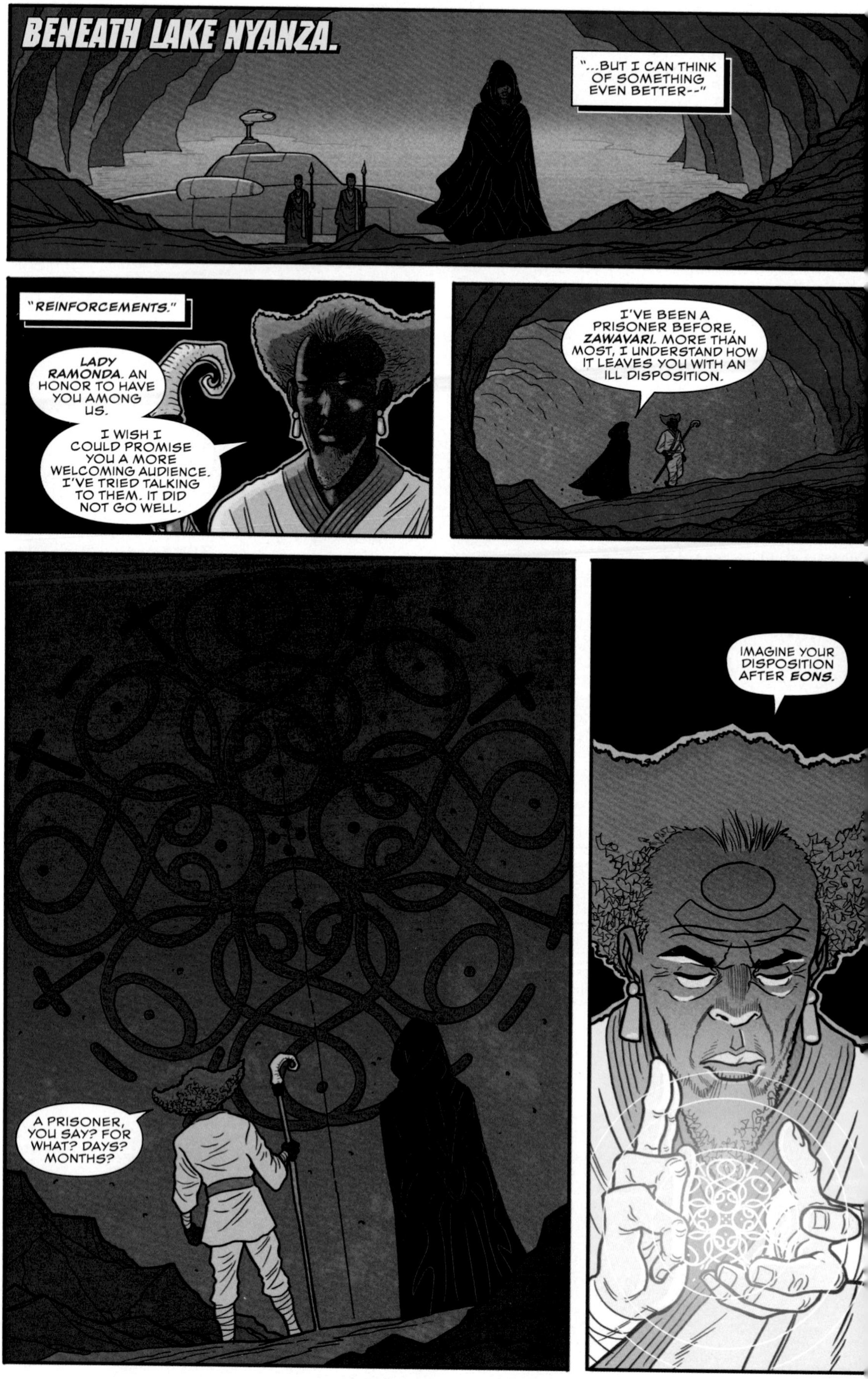
BENEATH LAKE NYANZA.
"...BUT I CAN THINK OF SOMETHING EVEN BETTER--"
"REINFORCEMENTS."
LADY RAMONDA. AN HONOR TO HAVE YOU AMONG US.
I WISH I COULD PROMISE YOU A MORE WELCOMING AUDIENCE. I'VE TRIED TALKING TO THEM. IT DID NOT GO WELL.
I'VE BEEN A PRISONER BEFORE, ZAWAVARI. MORE THAN MOST, I UNDERSTAND HOW IT LEAVES YOU WITH AN ILL DISPOSITION.
A PRISONER, YOU SAY? FOR WHAT? DAYS? MONTHS?
IMAGINE YOUR DISPOSITION AFTER EONS.

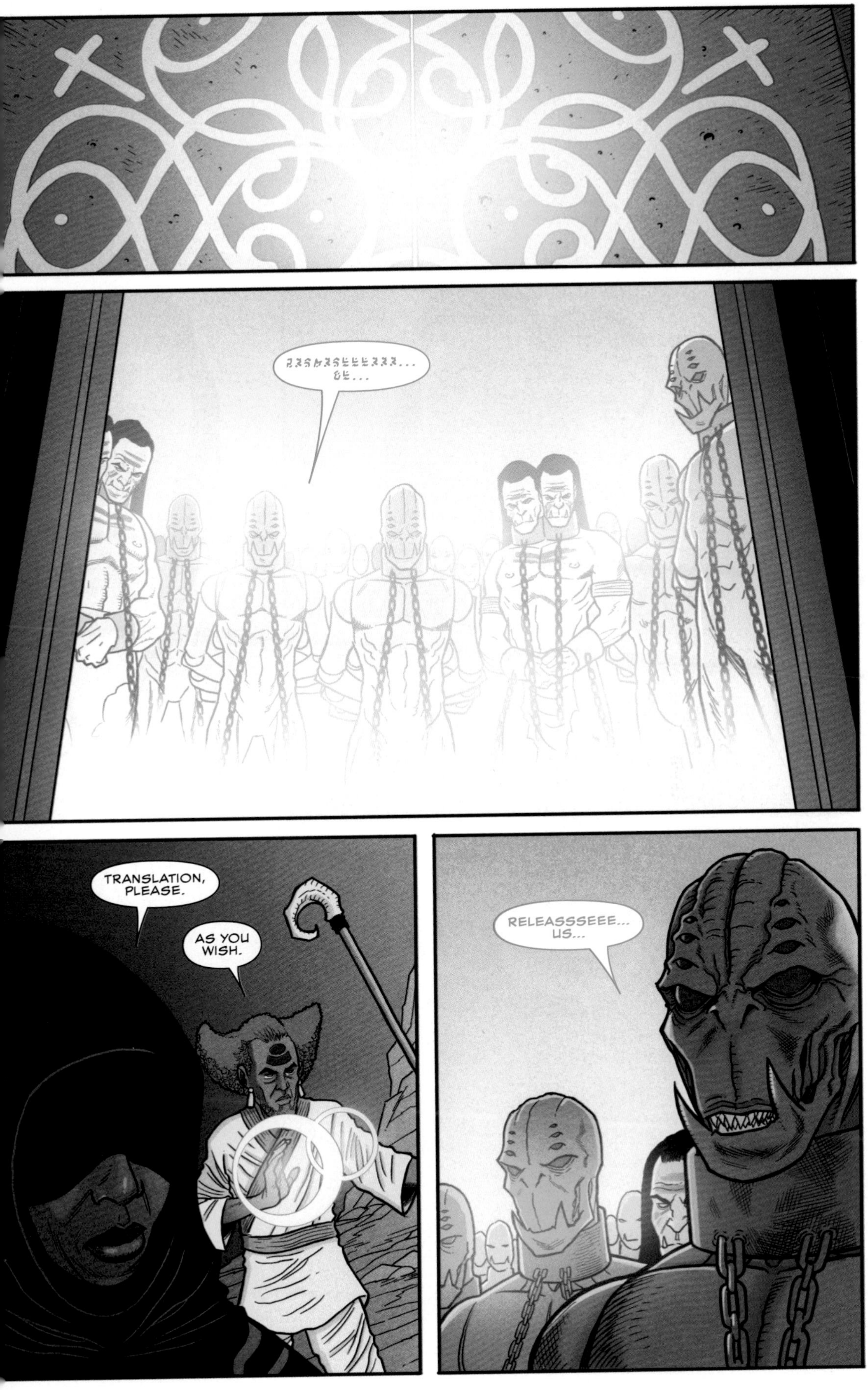
TRANSLATION, PLEASE.
AS YOU WISH.
RELEASSSEEE... US...

NO. NOT LIKE THIS. NOT UNTIL OUR TERMS ARE ESTABLISHED.

TERMS?

YOU ROB US OF OUR LAND, IMPRISON US HERE, AND SPEAK OF TERMS?

WE SHOULD CALL DOWN THE FURY OF THE HEAVENS UPON YOU AND ALL YOUR KIND.

BUT THE HEAVENS BETRAYED US LONG AGO. AND THE GOD OF THE *JUST* IS THE GOD OF THE *WEAK*, WHILE THE GOD OF *CONQUEST* REIGNS OVER *ALL* CREATION.

WE UNDERSTAND IT AS OUR LOT. YOU HAVE DIMINISHED THE *ORIGINATORS* TWICE NOW. WE ACCEPT IT.

BUT DO NOT STOO TO MOCKER

I COME NOT IN SERVICE OF MOCKERY, ORIGINATOR...

...BUT REPARATION.

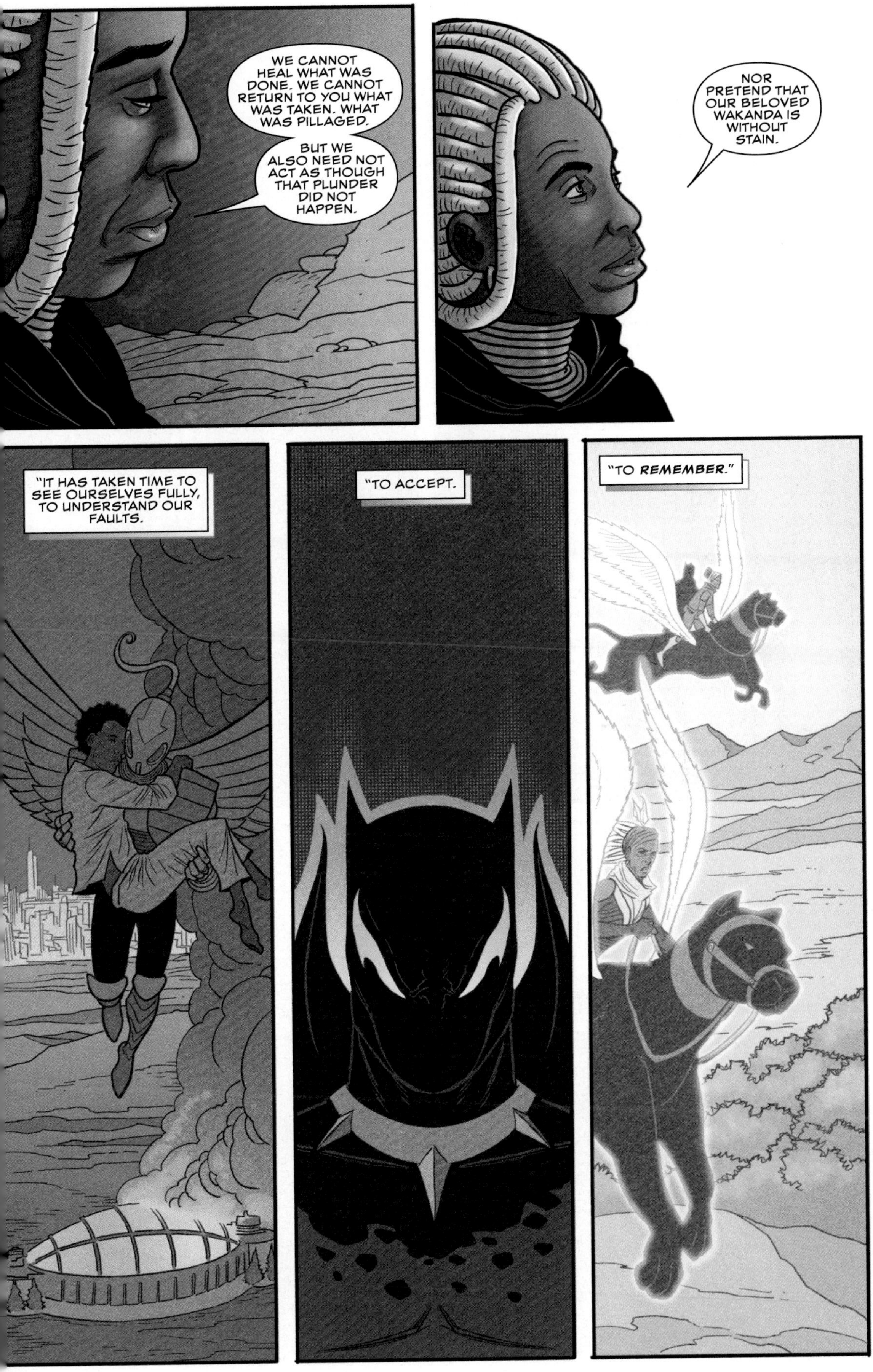
WE CANNOT HEAL WHAT WAS DONE. WE CANNOT RETURN TO YOU WHAT WAS TAKEN. WHAT WAS PILLAGED.
BUT WE ALSO NEED NOT ACT AS THOUGH THAT PLUNDER DID NOT HAPPEN.
NOR PRETEND THAT OUR BELOVED WAKANDA IS WITHOUT STAIN.
"IT HAS TAKEN TIME TO SEE OURSELVES FULLY, TO UNDERSTAND OUR FAULTS.
"TO ACCEPT.
"TO REMEMBER."

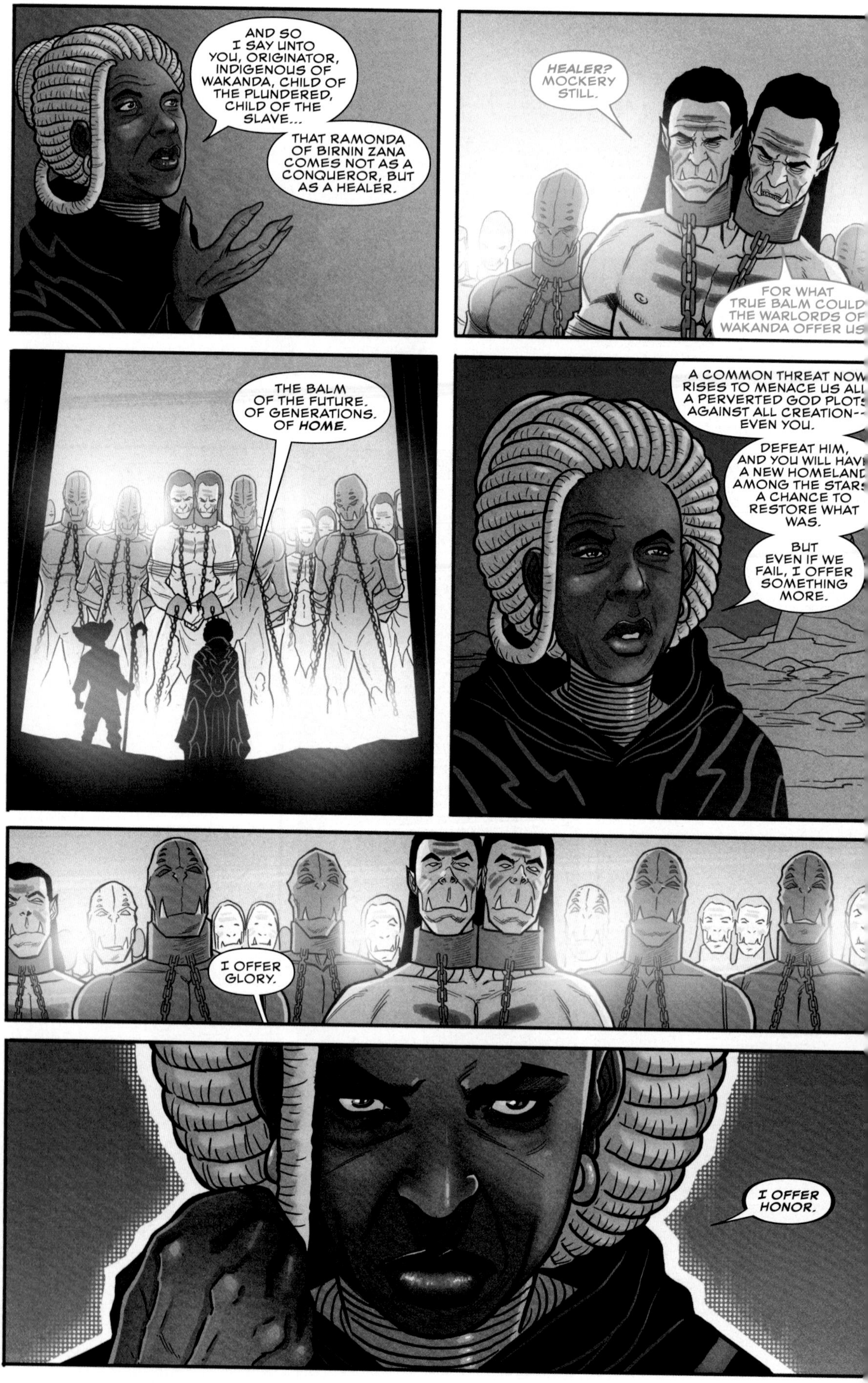
AND SO I SAY UNTO YOU, ORIGINATOR, INDIGENOUS OF WAKANDA, CHILD OF THE PLUNDERED, CHILD OF THE SLAVE...
THAT RAMONDA OF BIRNIN ZANA COMES NOT AS A CONQUEROR, BUT AS A HEALER.
HEALER? MOCKERY STILL.
FOR WHAT TRUE BALM COULD THE WARLORDS OF WAKANDA OFFER US
THE BALM OF THE FUTURE. OF GENERATIONS. OF HOME.
A COMMON THREAT NOW RISES TO MENACE US ALL A PERVERTED GOD PLOTS AGAINST ALL CREATION-- EVEN YOU.
DEFEAT HIM, AND YOU WILL HAVE A NEW HOMELAND AMONG THE STARS A CHANCE TO RESTORE WHAT WAS.
BUT EVEN IF WE FAIL, I OFFER SOMETHING MORE.
I OFFER GLORY.
I OFFER HONOR.

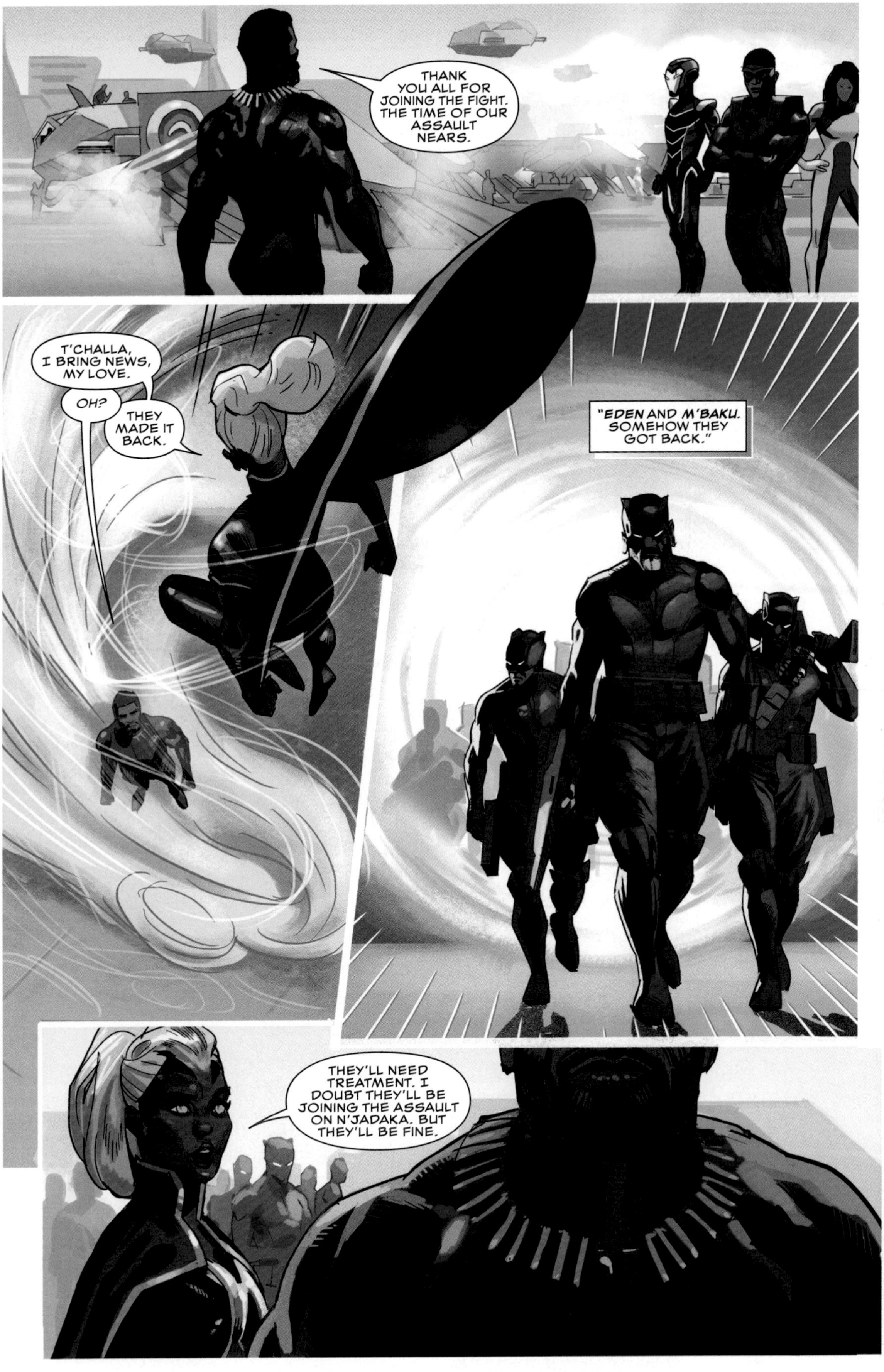
THANK YOU ALL FOR JOINING THE FIGHT. THE TIME OF OUR ASSAULT NEARS.
T'CHALLA, I BRING NEWS, MY LOVE.
OH?
THEY MADE IT BACK.
"EDEN AND M'BAKU. SOMEHOW THEY GOT BACK."
THEY'LL NEED TREATMENT. I DOUBT THEY'LL BE JOINING THE ASSAULT ON N'JADAKA. BUT THEY'LL BE FINE.

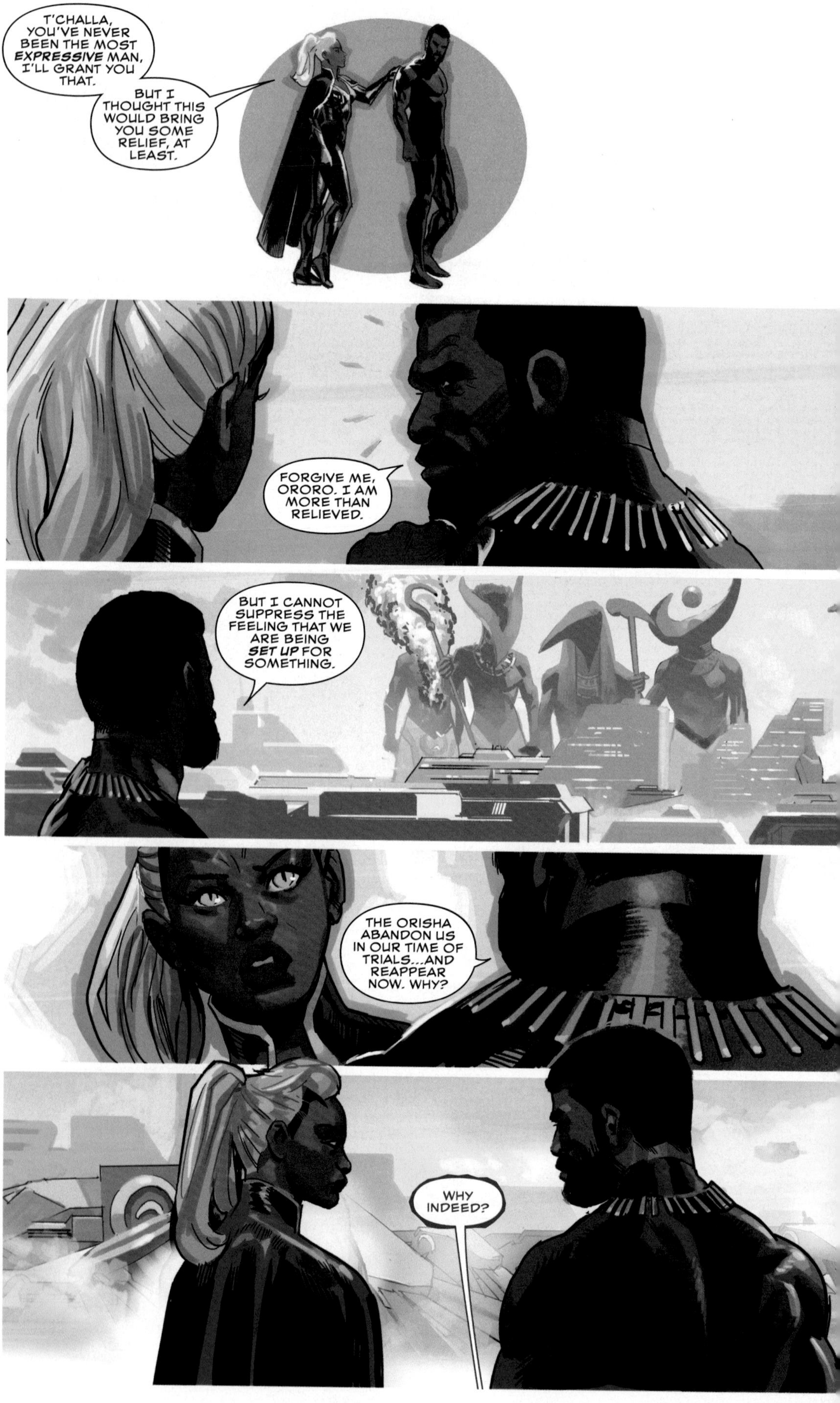
T'CHALLA, YOU'VE NEVER BEEN THE MOST EXPRESSIVE MAN, I'LL GRANT YOU THAT.
BUT I THOUGHT THIS WOULD BRING YOU SOME RELIEF, AT LEAST.
FORGIVE ME, ORORO. I AM MORE THAN RELIEVED.
BUT I CANNOT SUPPRESS THE FEELING THAT WE ARE BEING SET UP FOR SOMETHING.
THE ORISHA ABANDON US IN OUR TIME OF TRIALS...AND REAPPEAR NOW. WHY?
WHY INDEED?

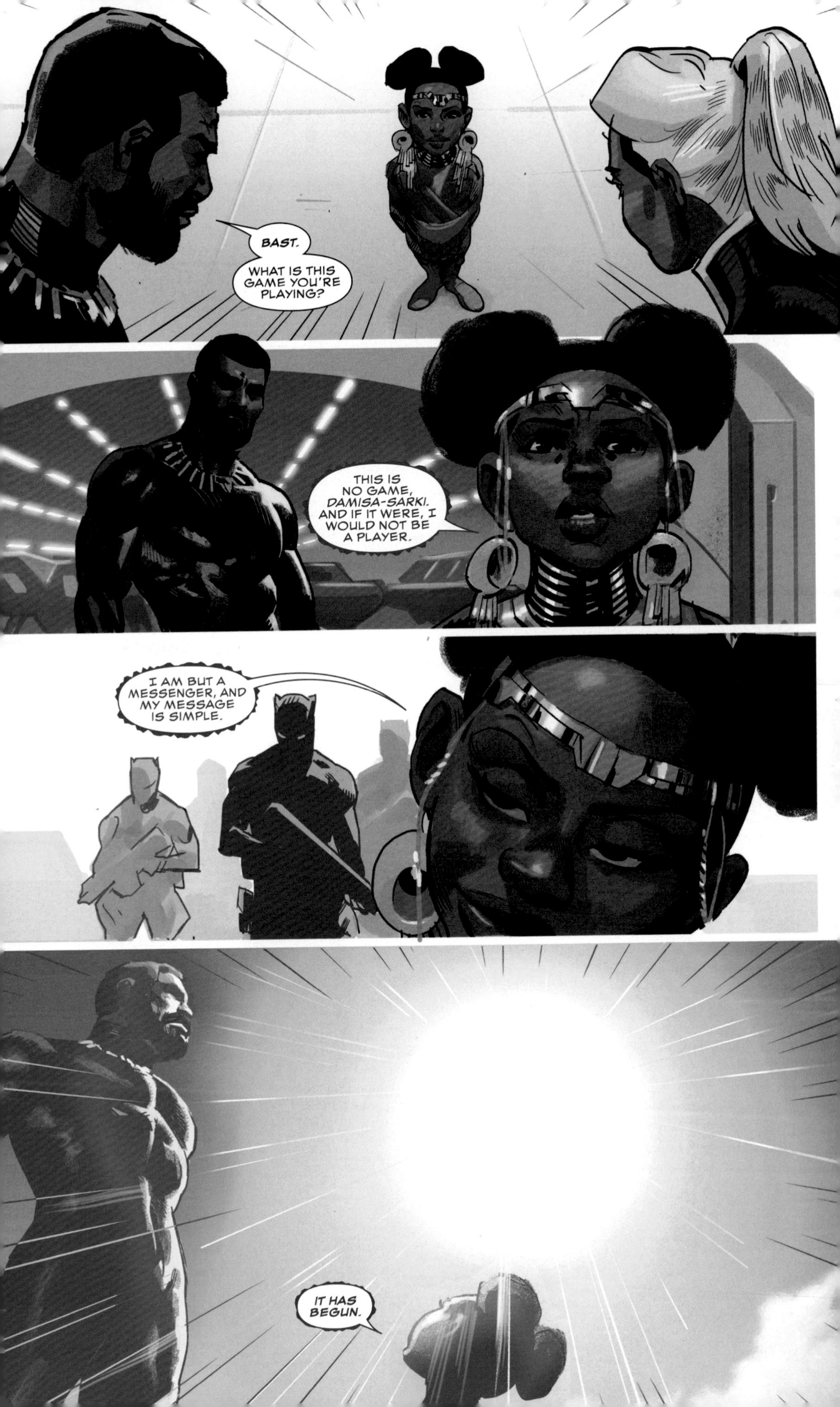
BAST.
WHAT IS THIS GAME YOU'RE PLAYING?
THIS IS NO GAME, *DAMISA-SARKI*. AND IF IT WERE, I WOULD NOT BE A PLAYER.
I AM BUT A MESSENGER, AND MY MESSAGE IS SIMPLE.
IT HAS BEGUN.

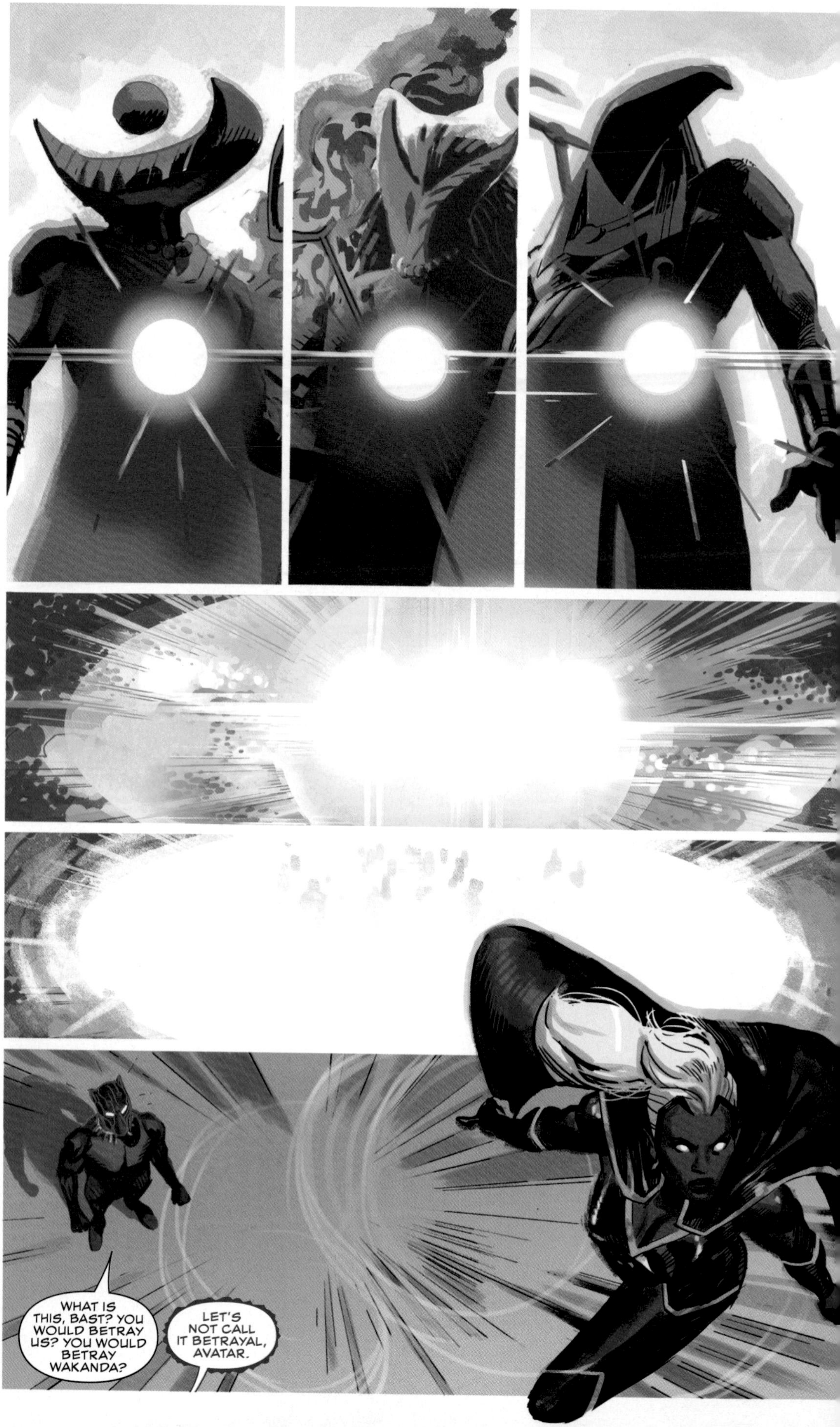
WHAT IS THIS, BAST? YOU WOULD BETRAY US? YOU WOULD BETRAY WAKANDA?
LET'S NOT CALL IT BETRAYAL, AVATAR.

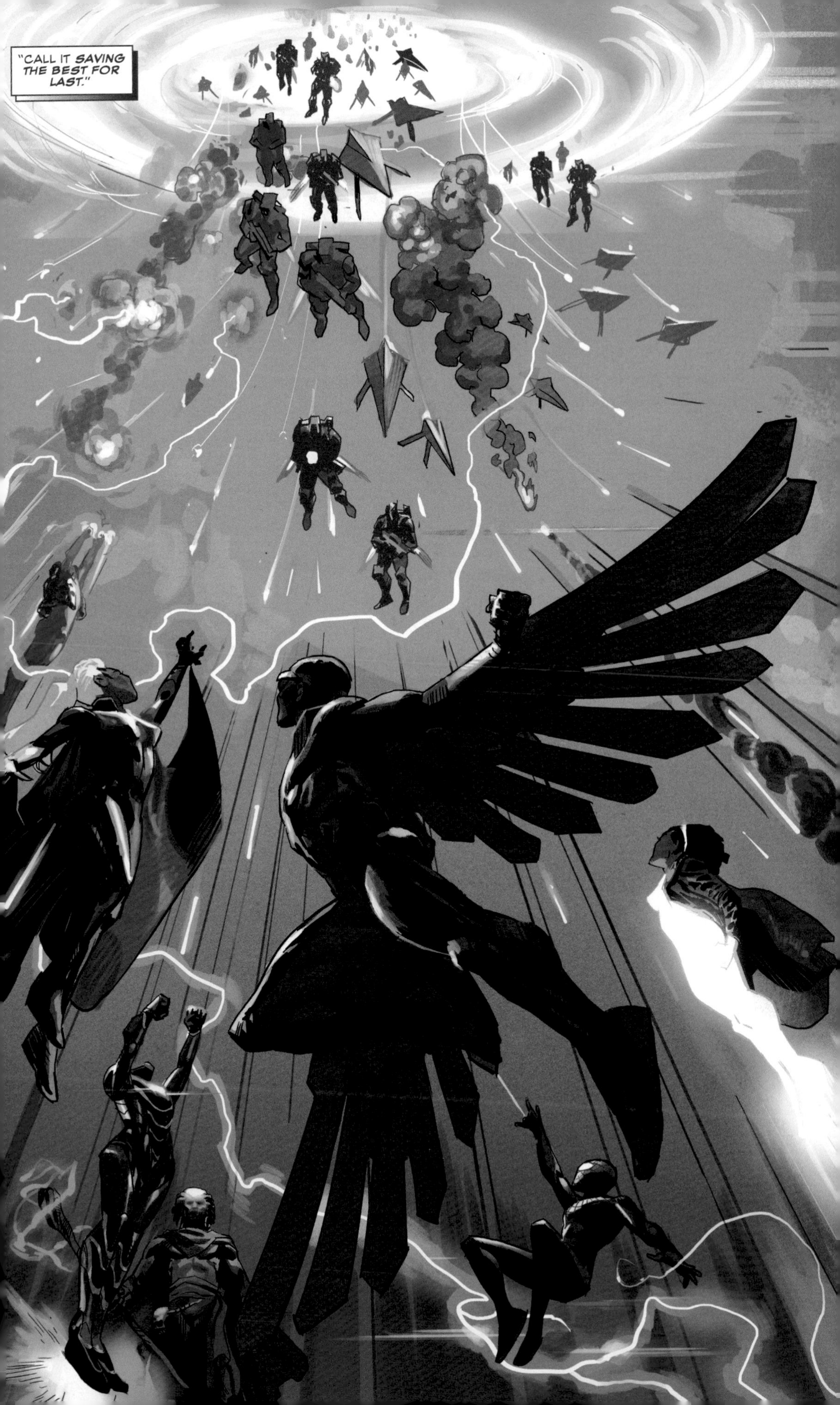
"CALL IT SAVING THE BEST FOR LAST."

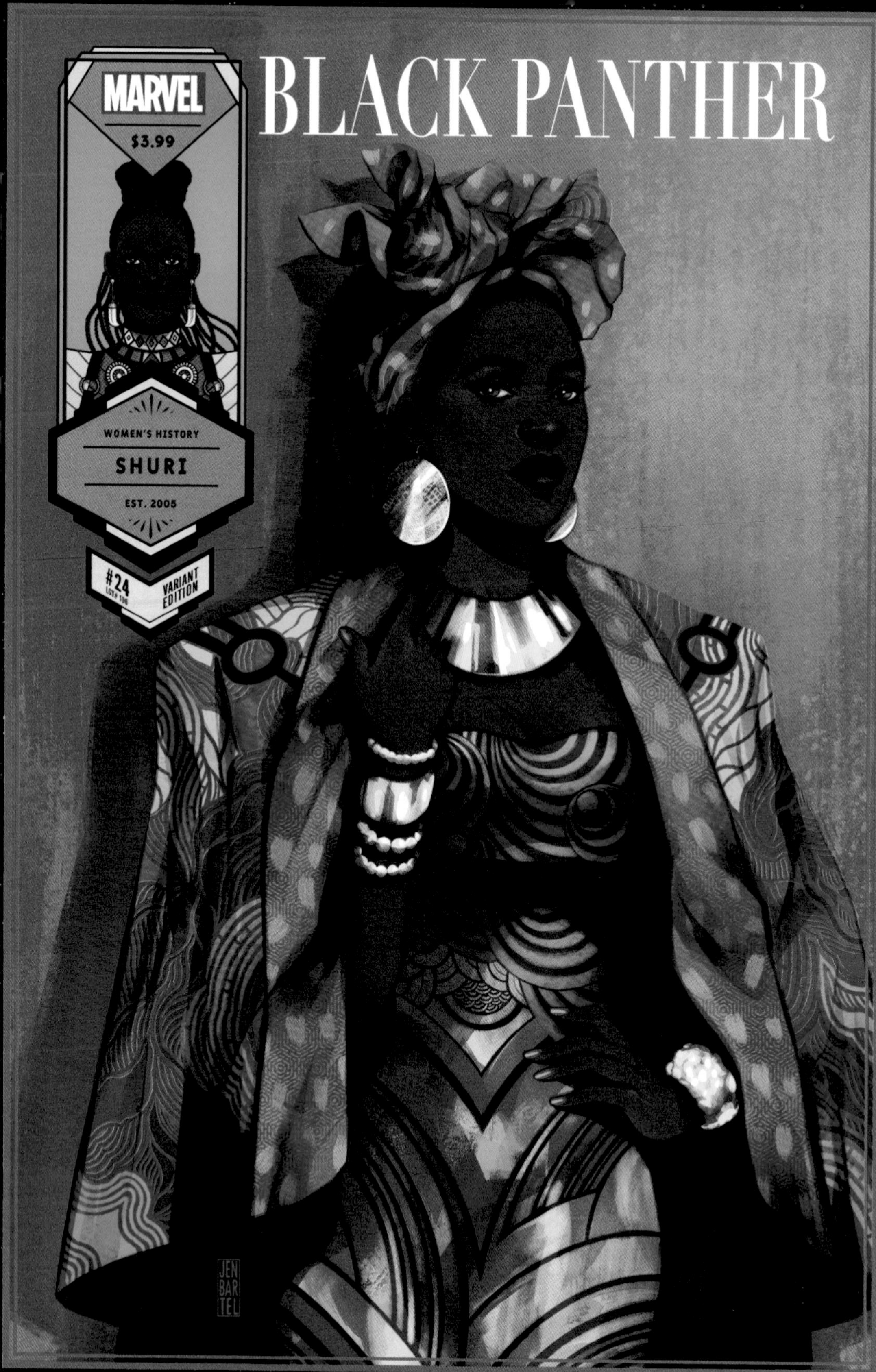

BLACK PANTHER
MARVEL
$3.99
WOMEN'S HISTORY
SHURI
EST. 2005
#24
VARIANT EDITION
JEN BARTEL

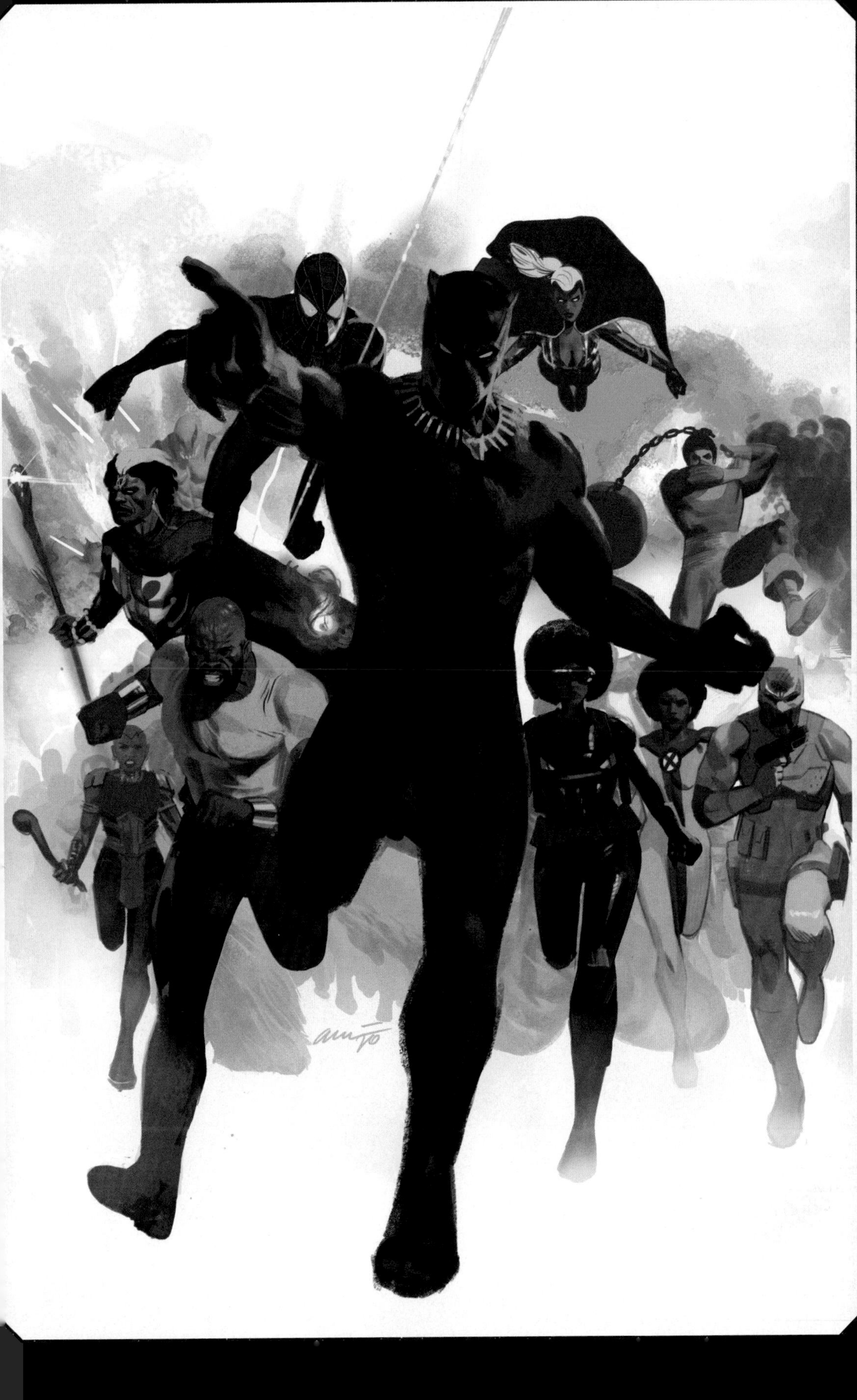

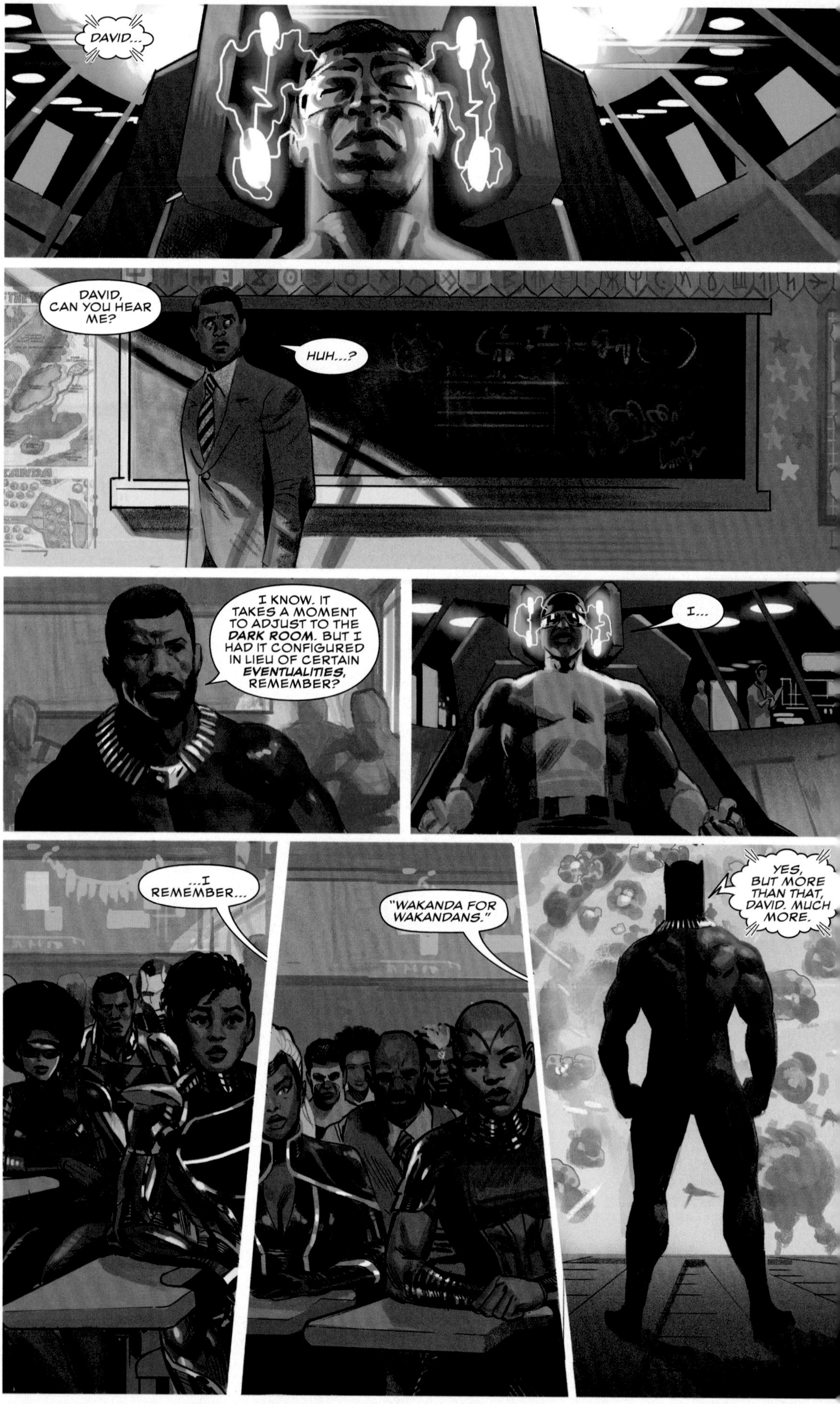
DAVID...
DAVID, CAN YOU HEAR ME?
HUH...?
I KNOW. IT TAKES A MOMENT TO ADJUST TO THE DARK ROOM. BUT I HAD IT CONFIGURED IN LIEU OF CERTAIN EVENTUALITIES, REMEMBER?
I...
...I REMEMBER...
"WAKANDA FOR WAKANDANS."
YES, BUT MORE THAN THAT, DAVID. MUCH MORE.

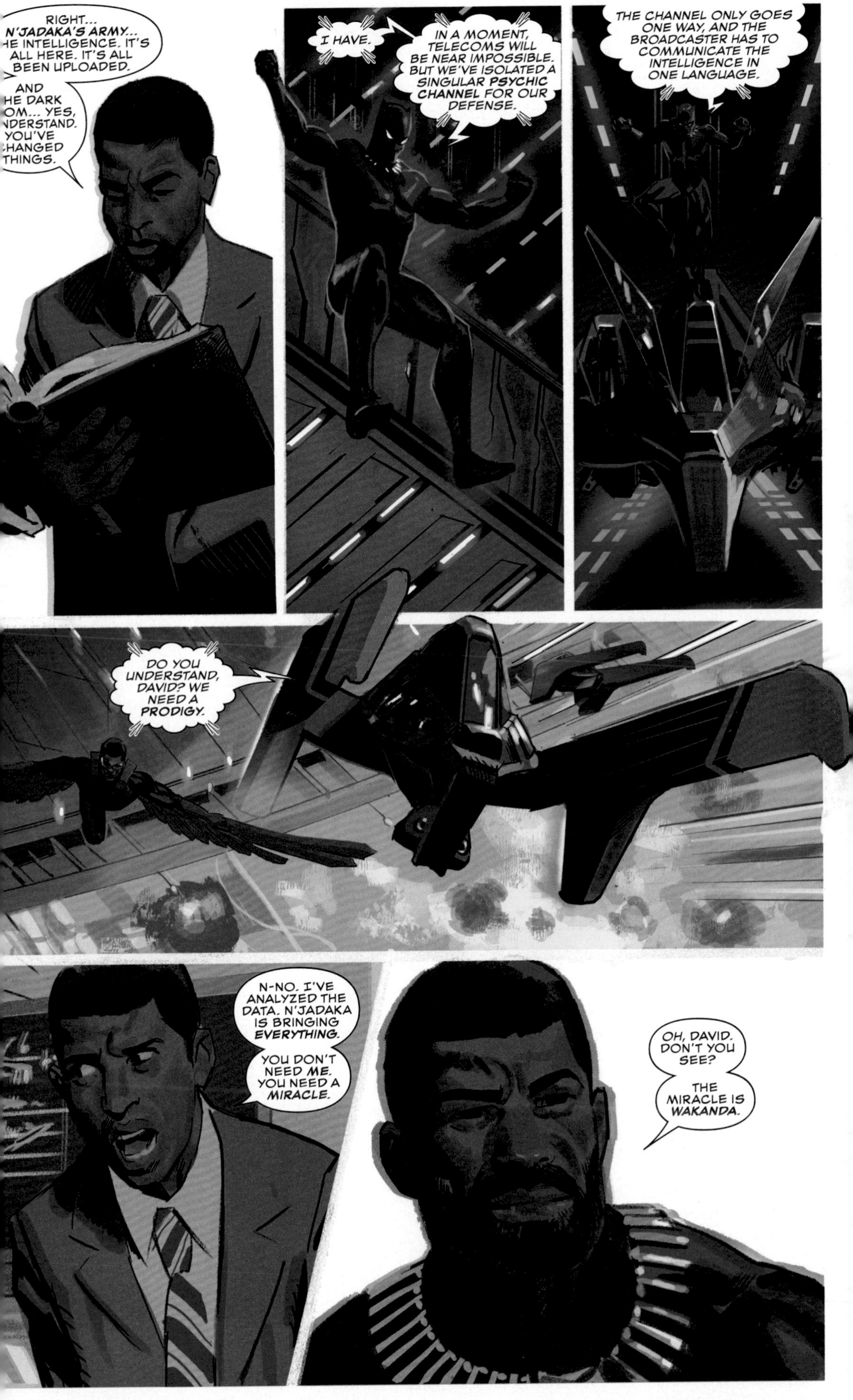
RIGHT... N'JADAKA'S ARMY... HE INTELLIGENCE. IT'S ALL HERE. IT'S ALL BEEN UPLOADED.
AND HE DARK OM... YES, NDERSTAND. YOU'VE HANGED THINGS.
I HAVE.
IN A MOMENT, TELECOMS WILL BE NEAR IMPOSSIBLE. BUT WE'VE ISOLATED A SINGULAR PSYCHIC CHANNEL FOR OUR DEFENSE.
THE CHANNEL ONLY GOES ONE WAY, AND THE BROADCASTER HAS TO COMMUNICATE THE INTELLIGENCE IN ONE LANGUAGE.
DO YOU UNDERSTAND, DAVID? WE NEED A PRODIGY.
N-NO. I'VE ANALYZED THE DATA. N'JADAKA IS BRINGING EVERYTHING.
YOU DON'T NEED ME. YOU NEED A MIRACLE.
OH, DAVID. DON'T YOU SEE?
THE MIRACLE IS WAKANDA.

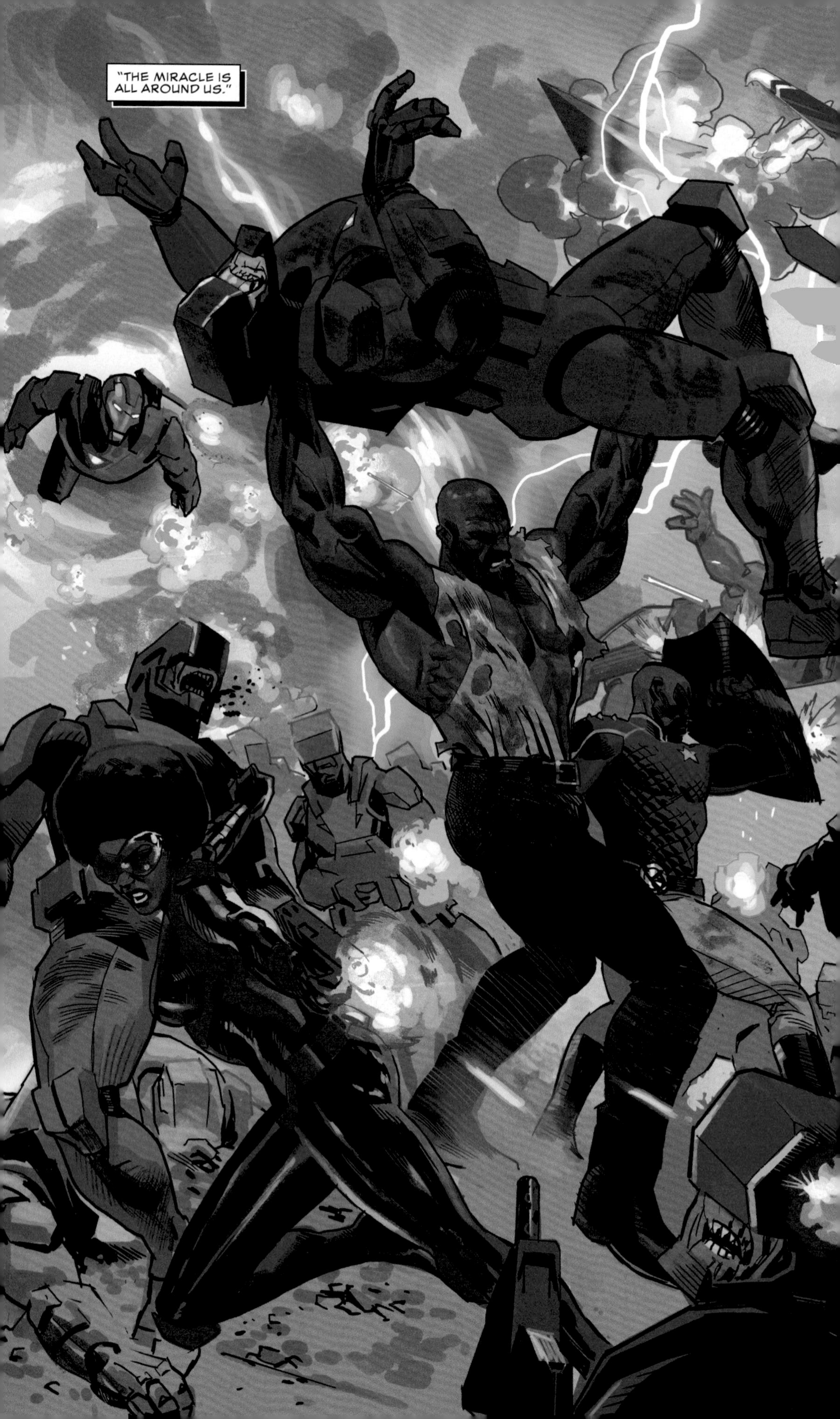
"THE MIRACLE IS ALL AROUND US."

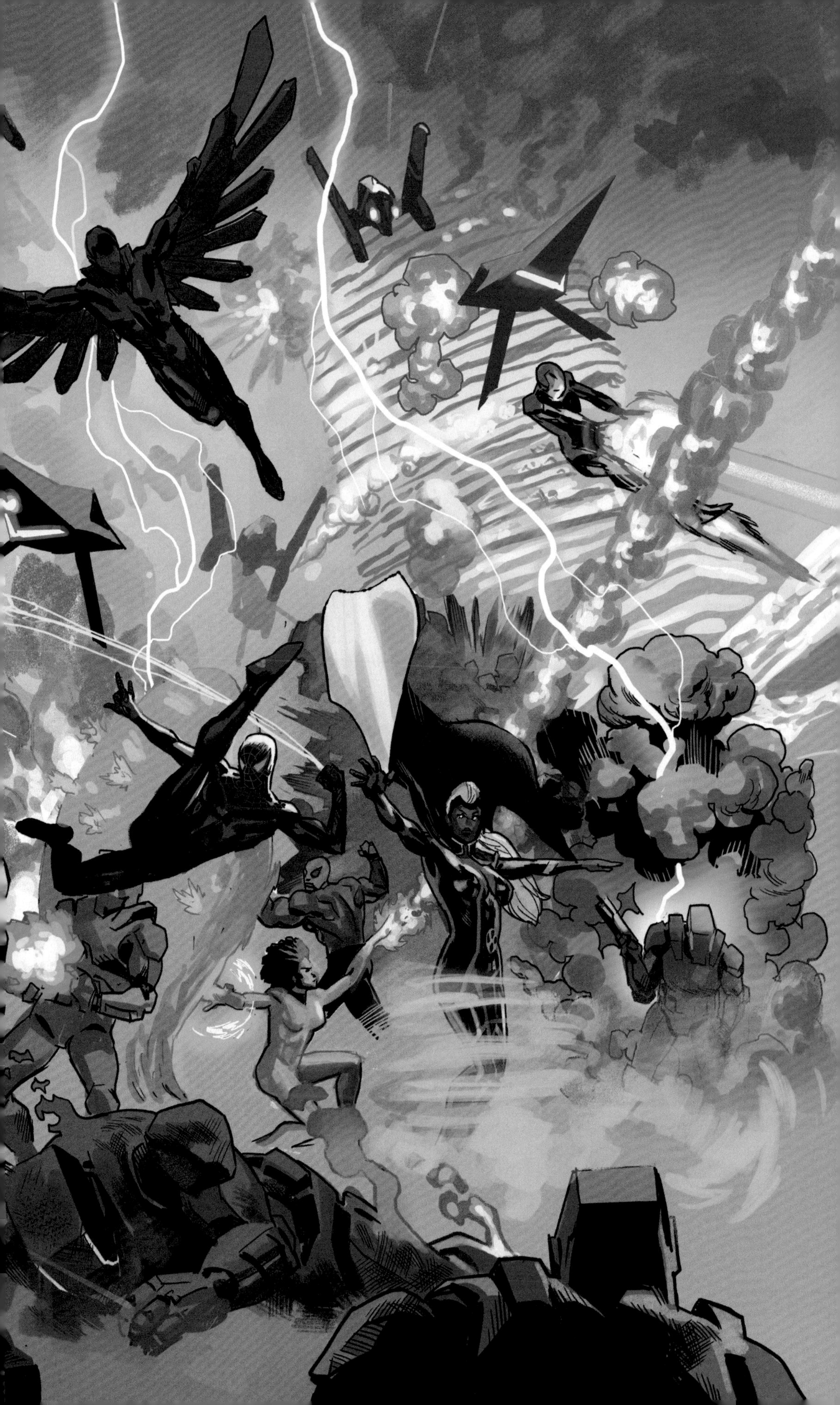

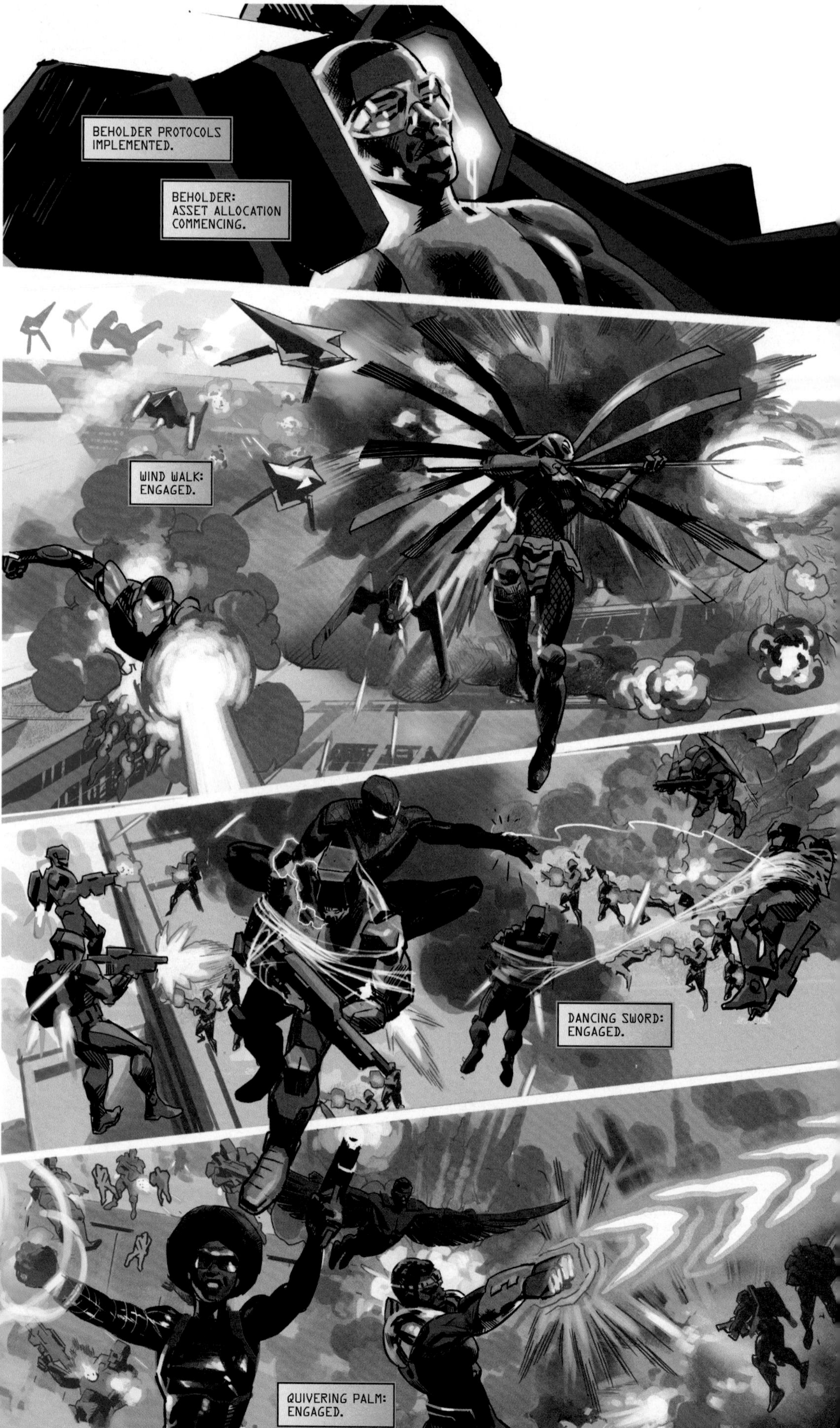
BEHOLDER PROTOCOLS IMPLEMENTED.
BEHOLDER: ASSET ALLOCATION COMMENCING.
WIND WALK: ENGAGED.
DANCING SWORD: ENGAGED.
QUIVERING PALM: ENGAGED.

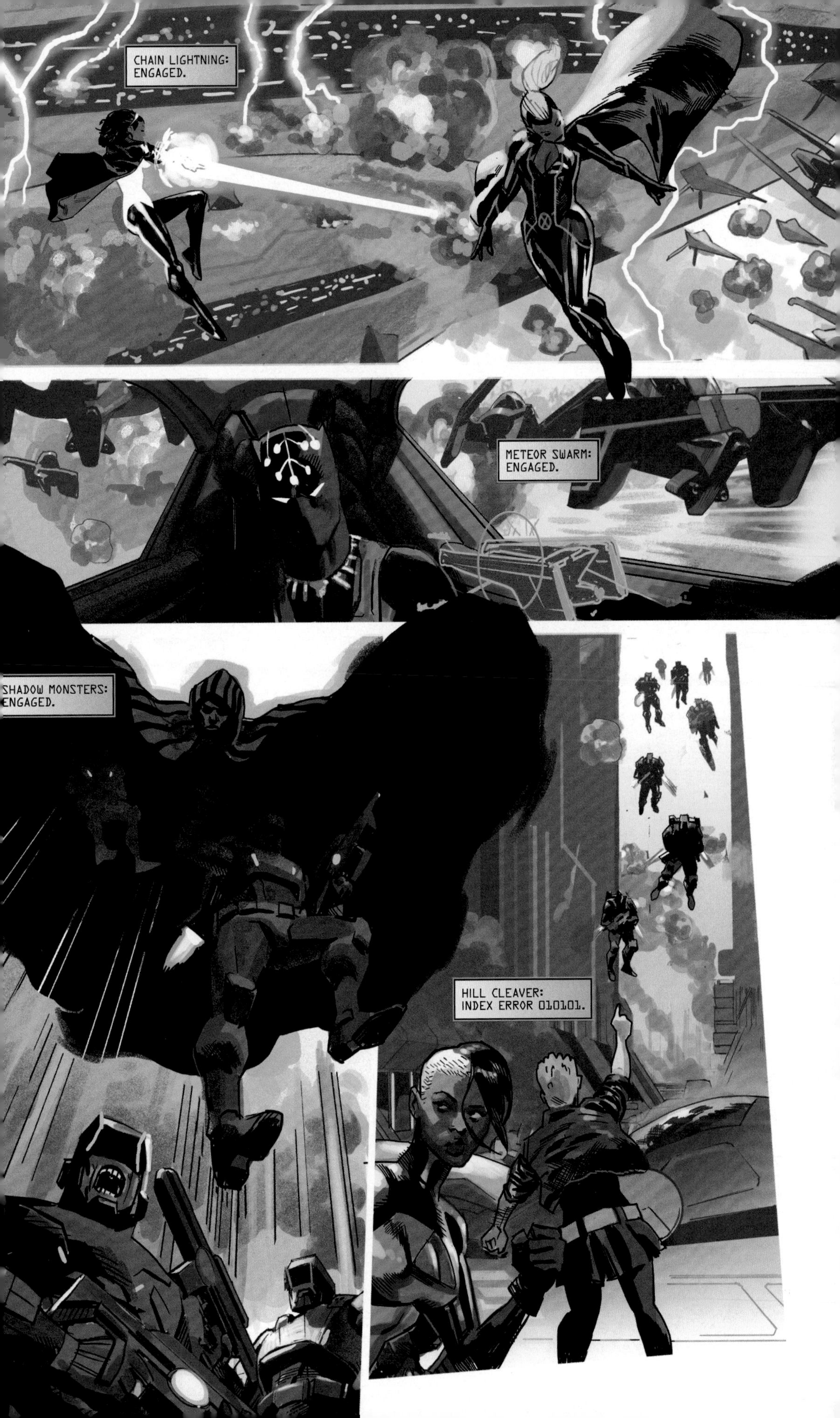
CHAIN LIGHTNING: ENGAGED.
METEOR SWARM: ENGAGED.
SHADOW MONSTERS: ENGAGED.
HILL CLEAVER: INDEX ERROR 010101.

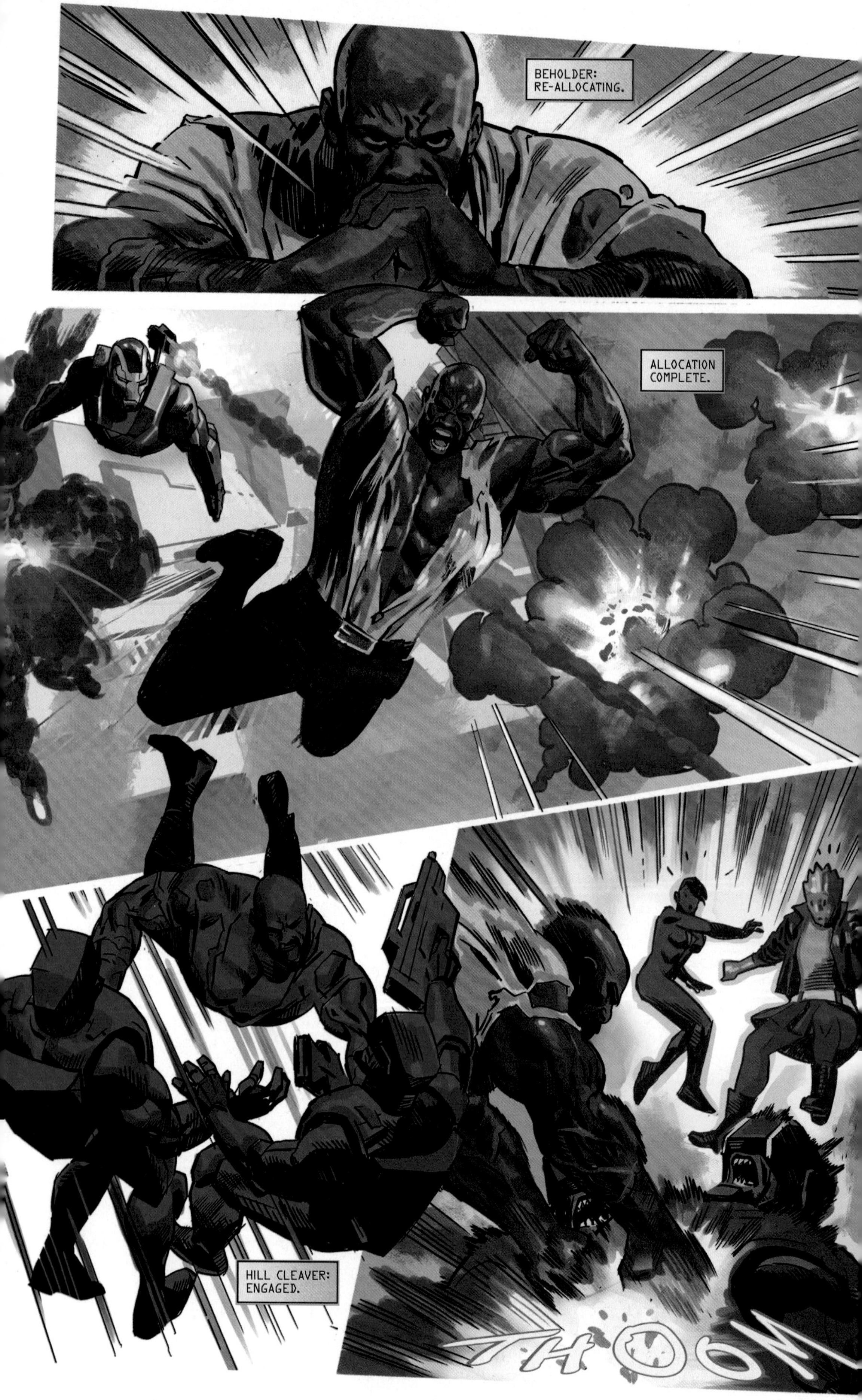
BEHOLDER:
RE-ALLOCATING.
ALLOCATION
COMPLETE.
HILL CLEAVER:
ENGAGED.
THOOM

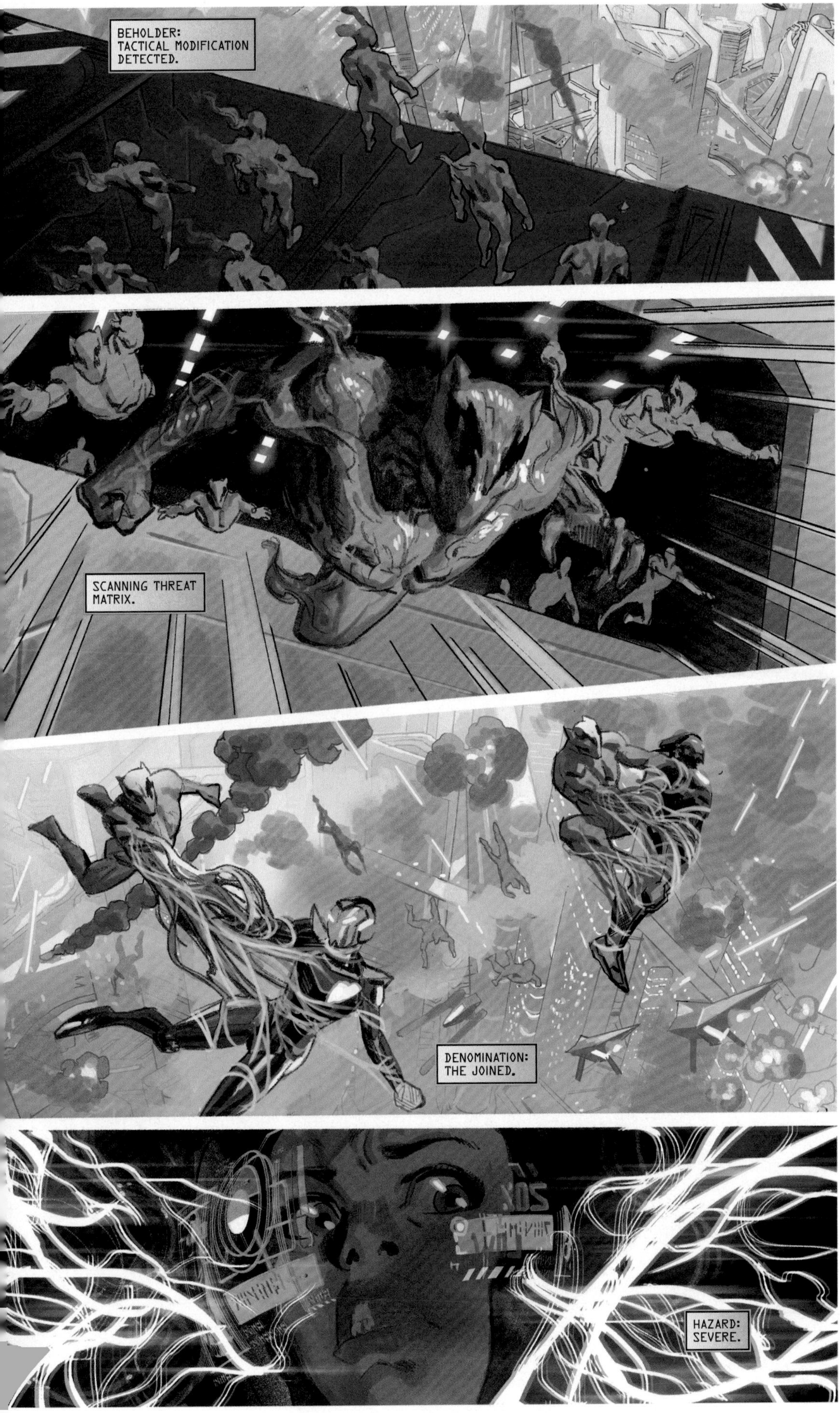
BEHOLDER: TACTICAL MODIFICATION DETECTED.
SCANNING THREAT MATRIX.
DENOMINATION: THE JOINED.
HAZARD: SEVERE.

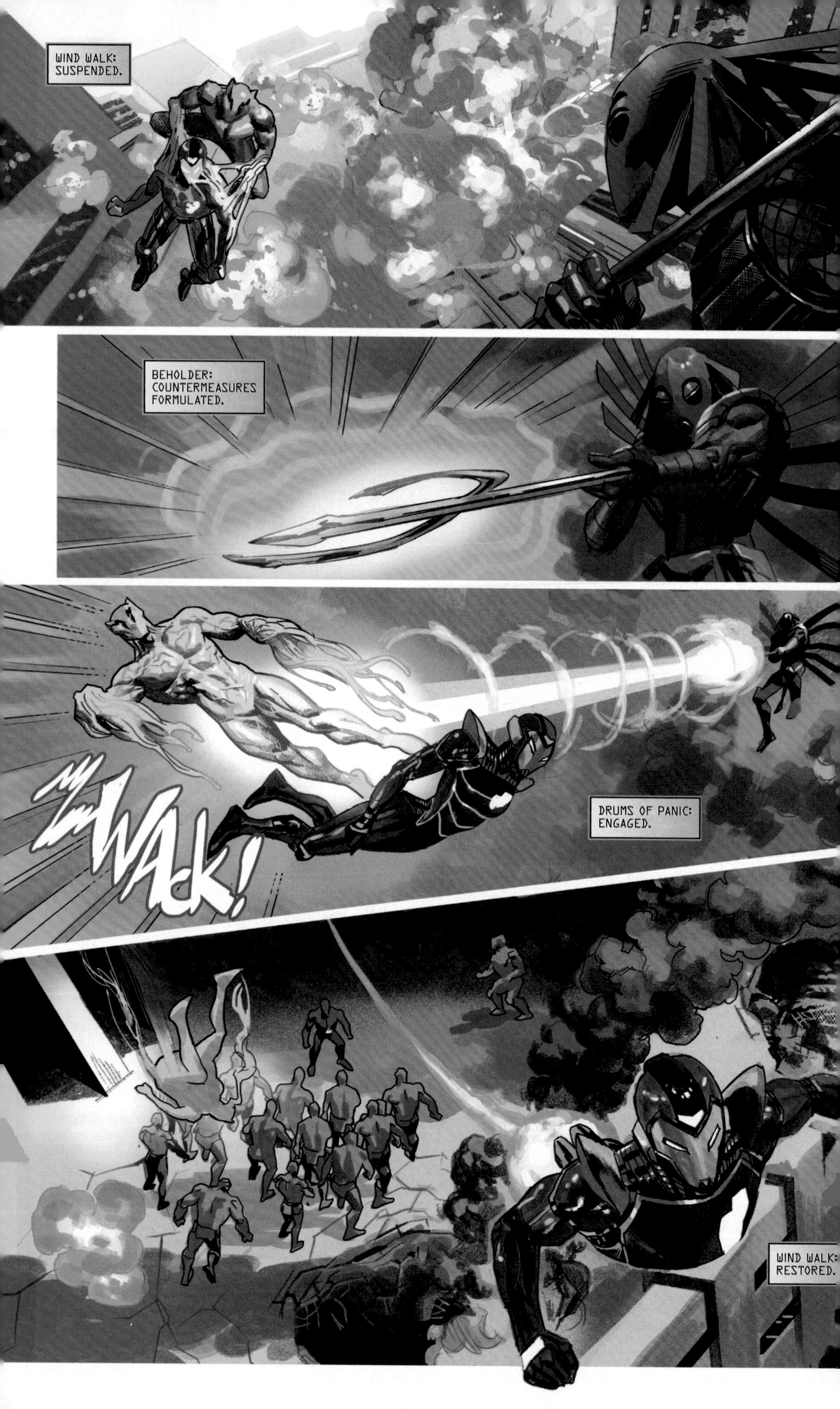
WIND WALK: SUSPENDED.
BEHOLDER: COUNTERMEASURES FORMULATED.
ZWACK!
DRUMS OF PANIC: ENGAGED.
WIND WALK: RESTORED.

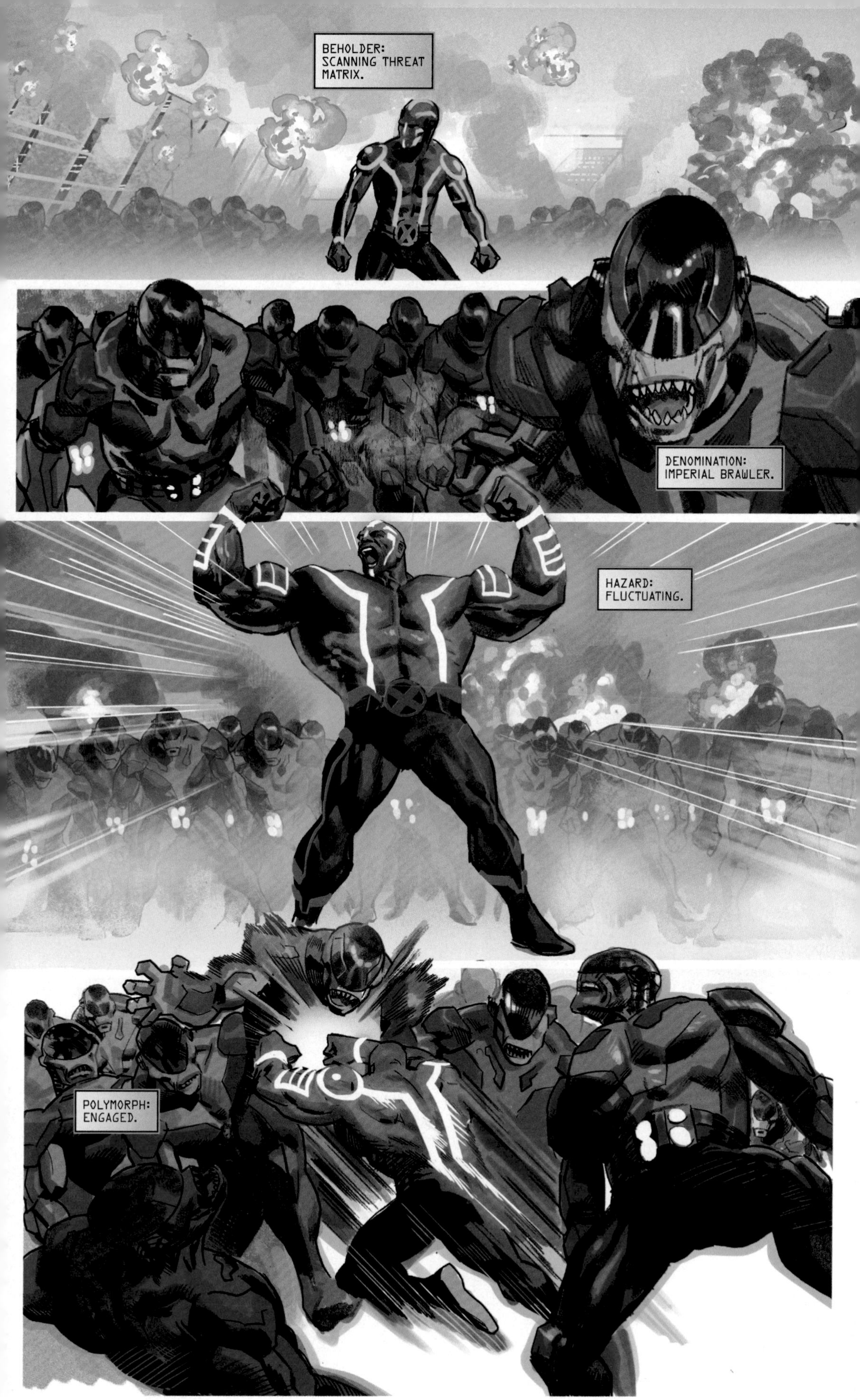
BEHOLDER: SCANNING THREAT MATRIX.
DENOMINATION: IMPERIAL BRAWLER.
HAZARD: FLUCTUATING.
POLYMORPH: ENGAGED.

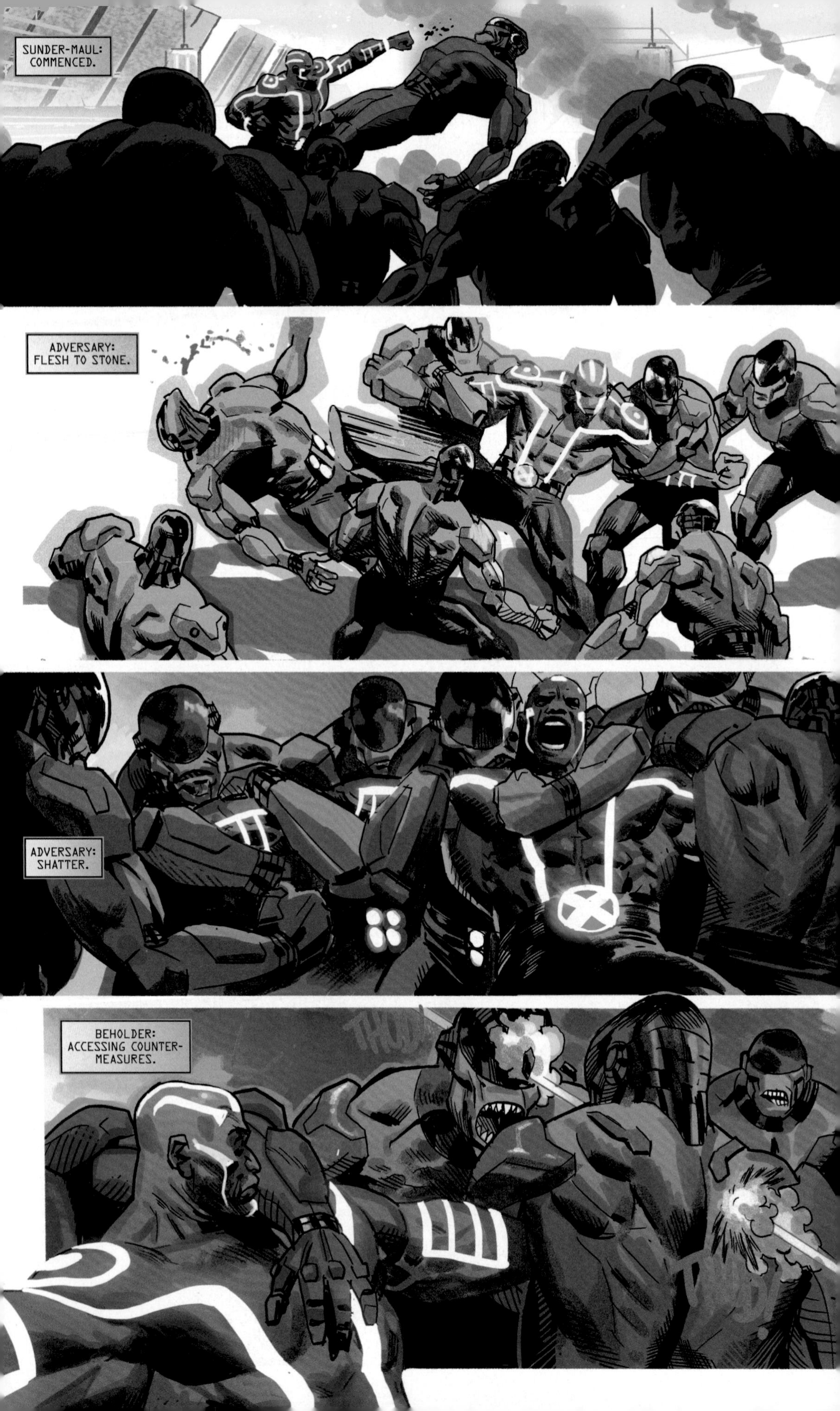
SUNDER-MAUL: COMMENCED.
ADVERSARY: FLESH TO STONE.
ADVERSARY: SHATTER.
BEHOLDER: ACCESSING COUNTER-MEASURES.
THUD

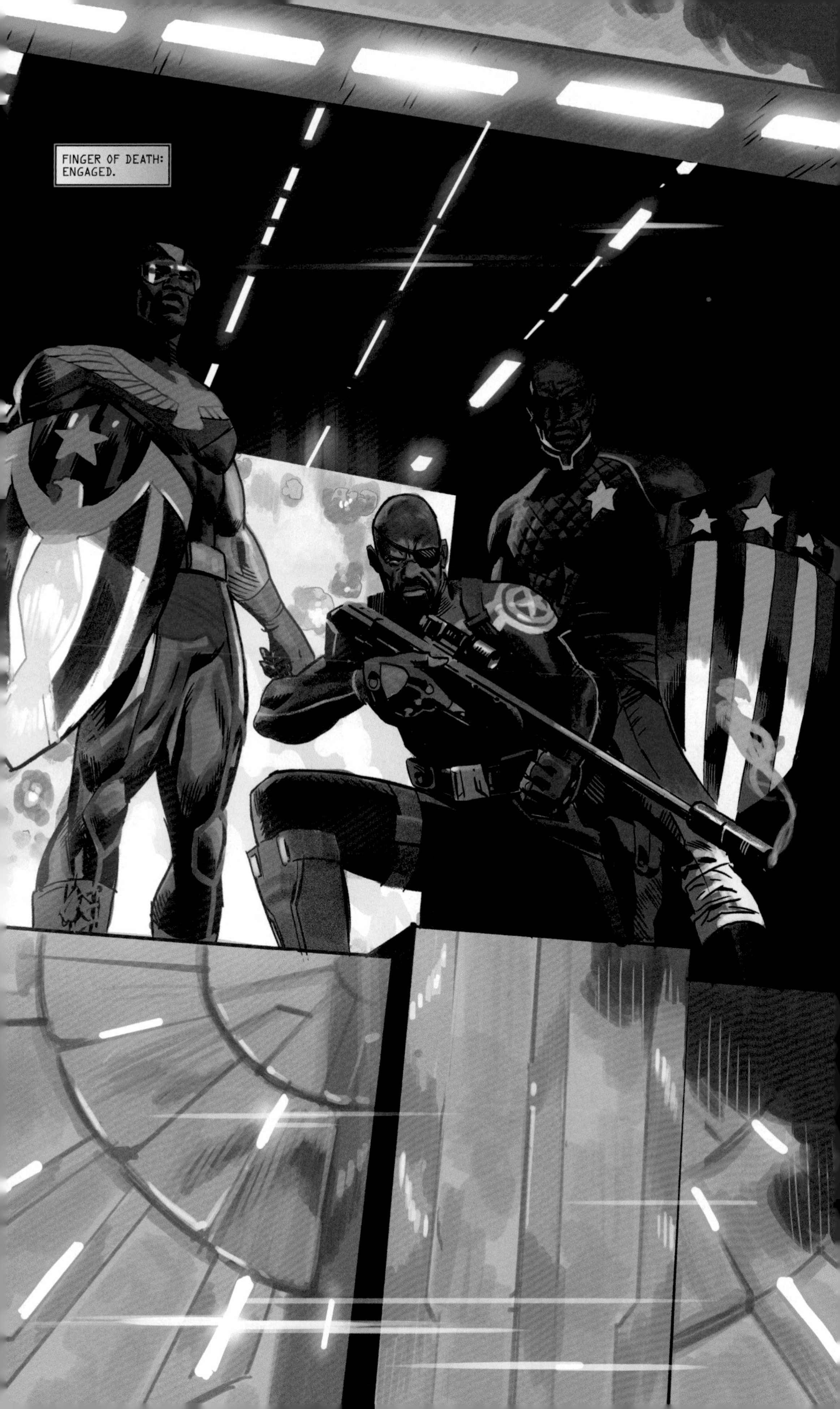
FINGER OF DEATH:
ENGAGED.

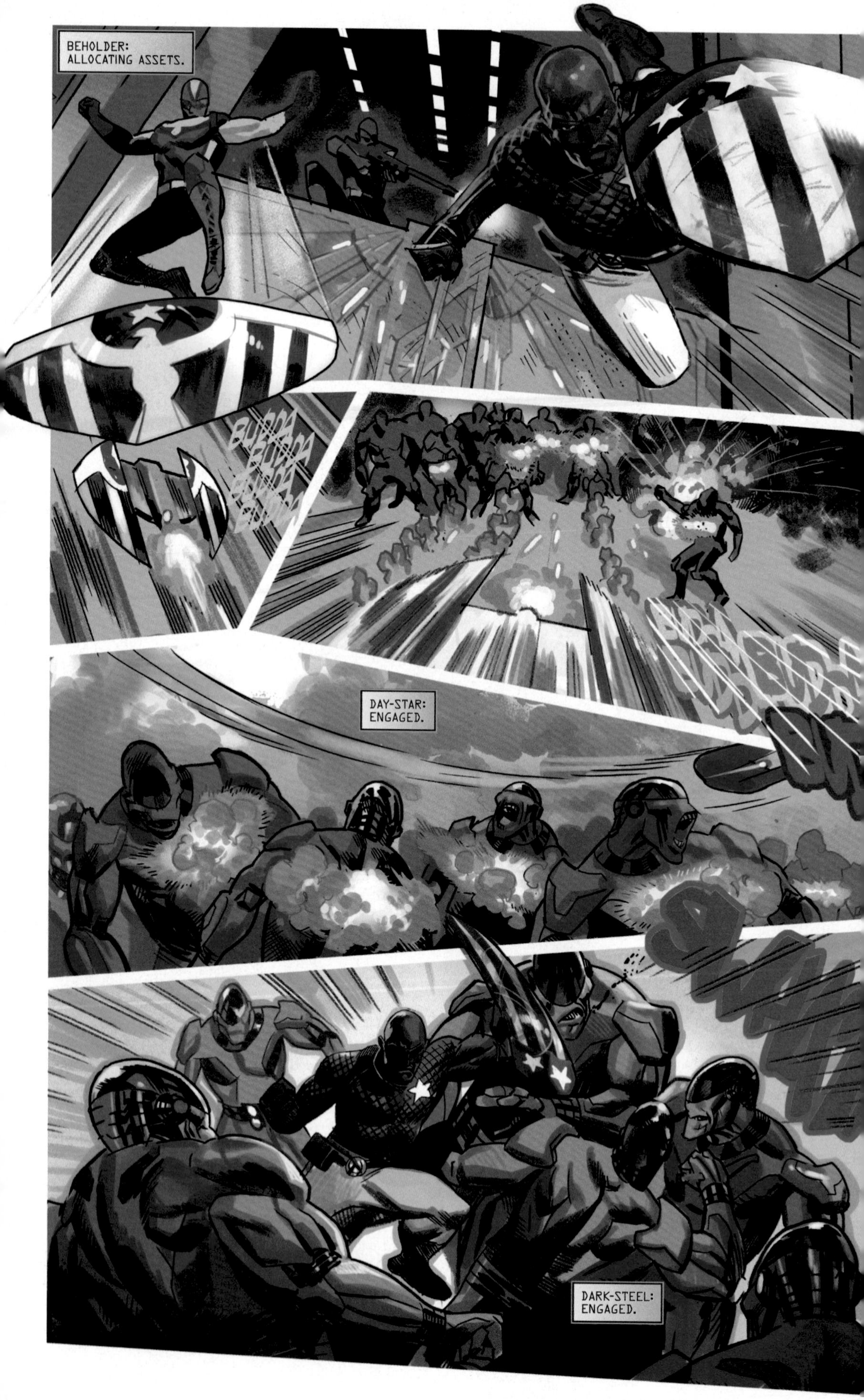
BEHOLDER:
ALLOCATING ASSETS.
DAY-STAR:
ENGAGED.
DARK-STEEL:
ENGAGED.

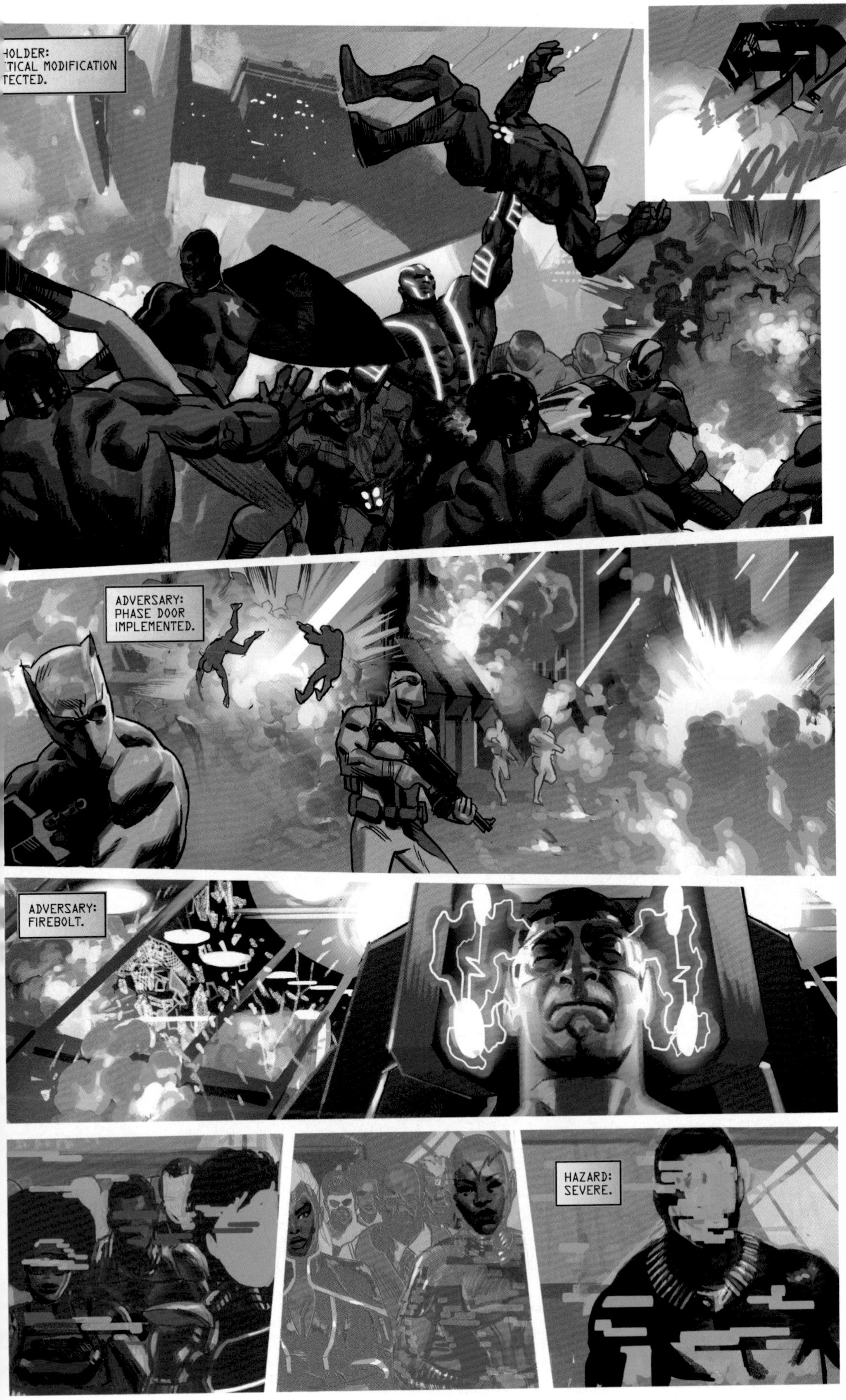
HOLDER:
TICAL MODIFICATION
TECTED.
ADVERSARY:
PHASE DOOR
IMPLEMENTED.
ADVERSARY:
FIREBOLT.
HAZARD:
SEVERE.

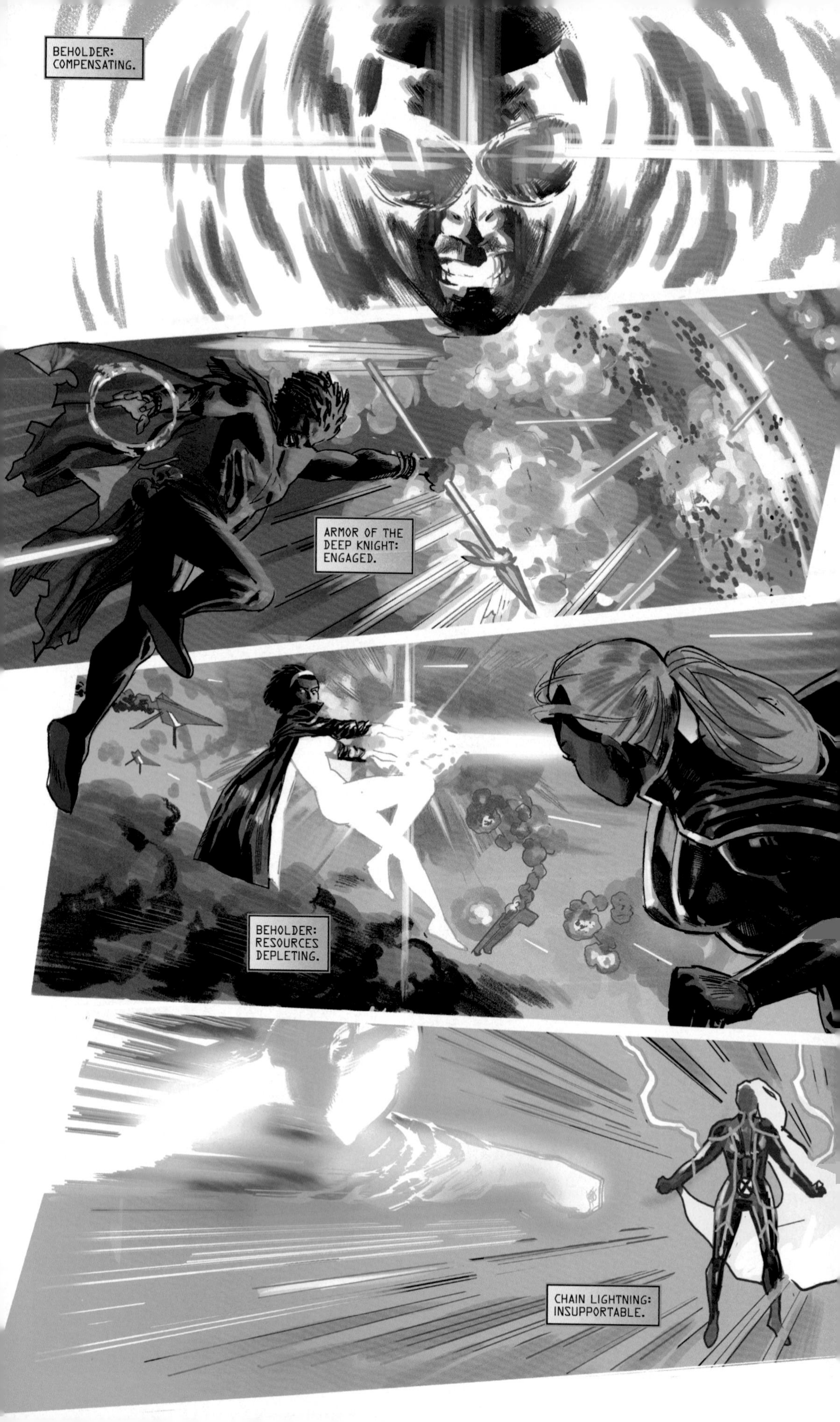
BEHOLDER: COMPENSATING.
ARMOR OF THE DEEP KNIGHT: ENGAGED.
BEHOLDER: RESOURCES DEPLETING.
CHAIN LIGHTNING: INSUPPORTABLE.

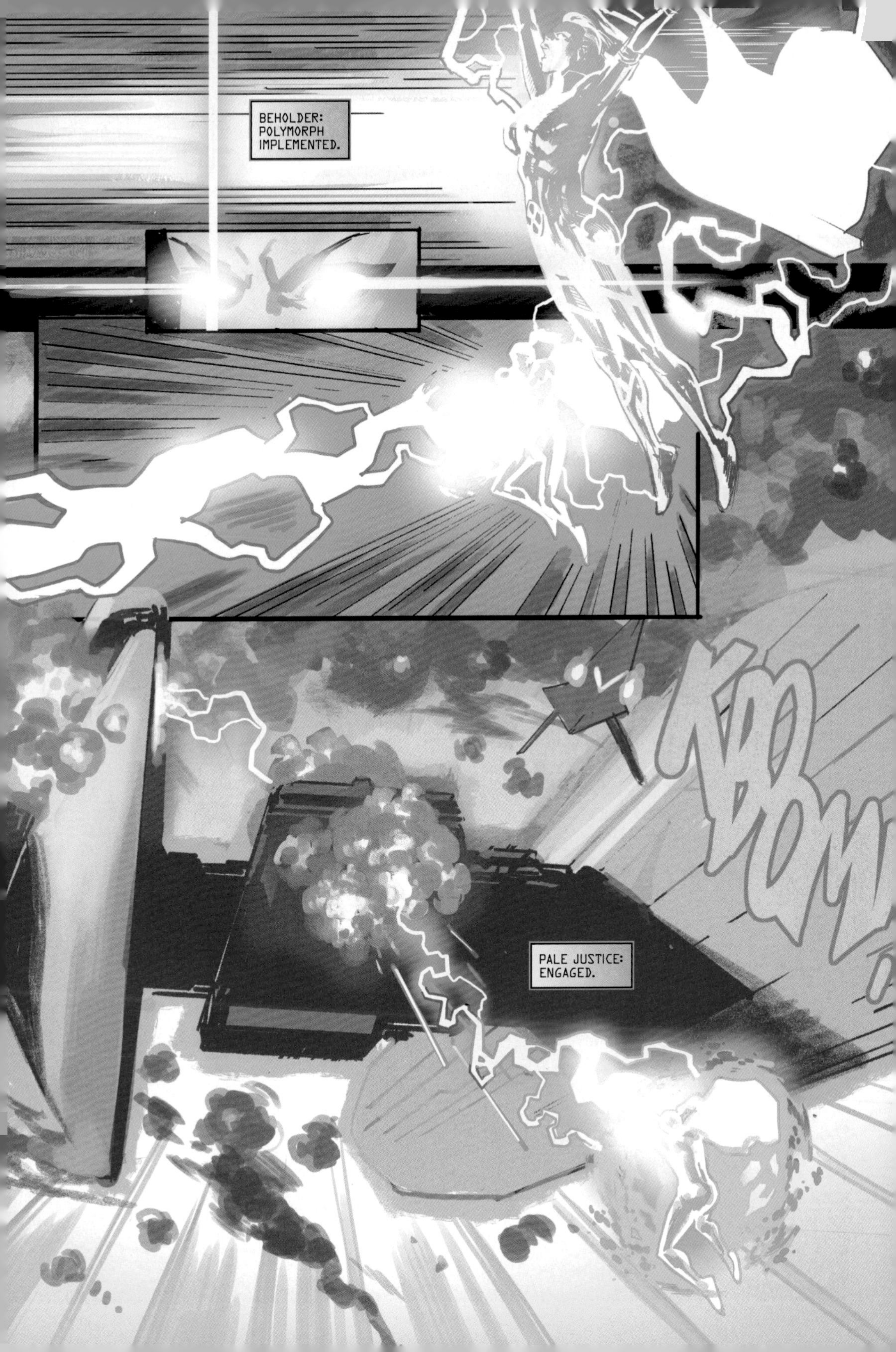
BEHOLDER: POLYMORPH IMPLEMENTED.
PALE JUSTICE: ENGAGED.

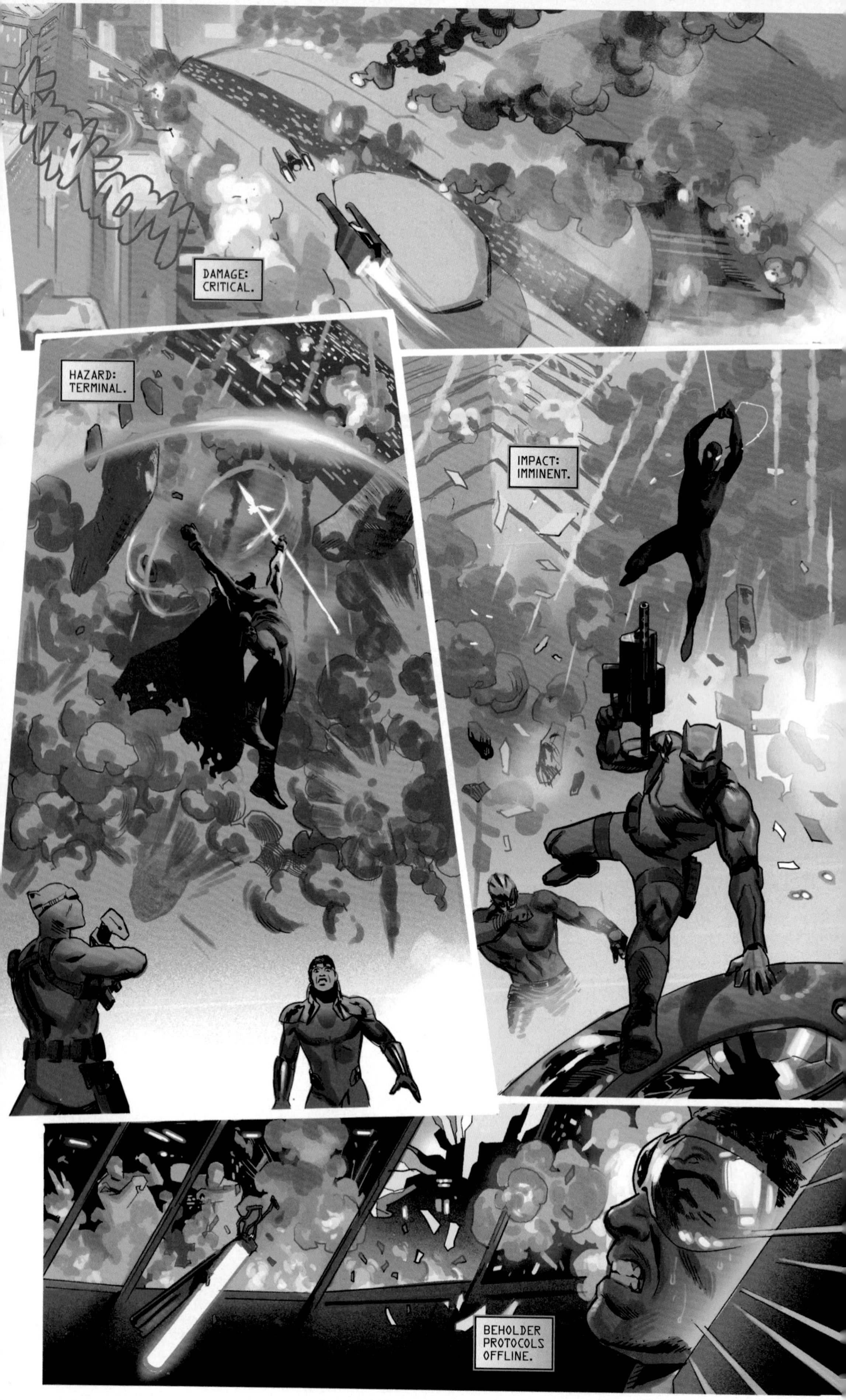
DAMAGE:
CRITICAL.
HAZARD:
TERMINAL.
IMPACT:
IMMINENT.
BEHOLDER
PROTOCOLS
OFFLINE.

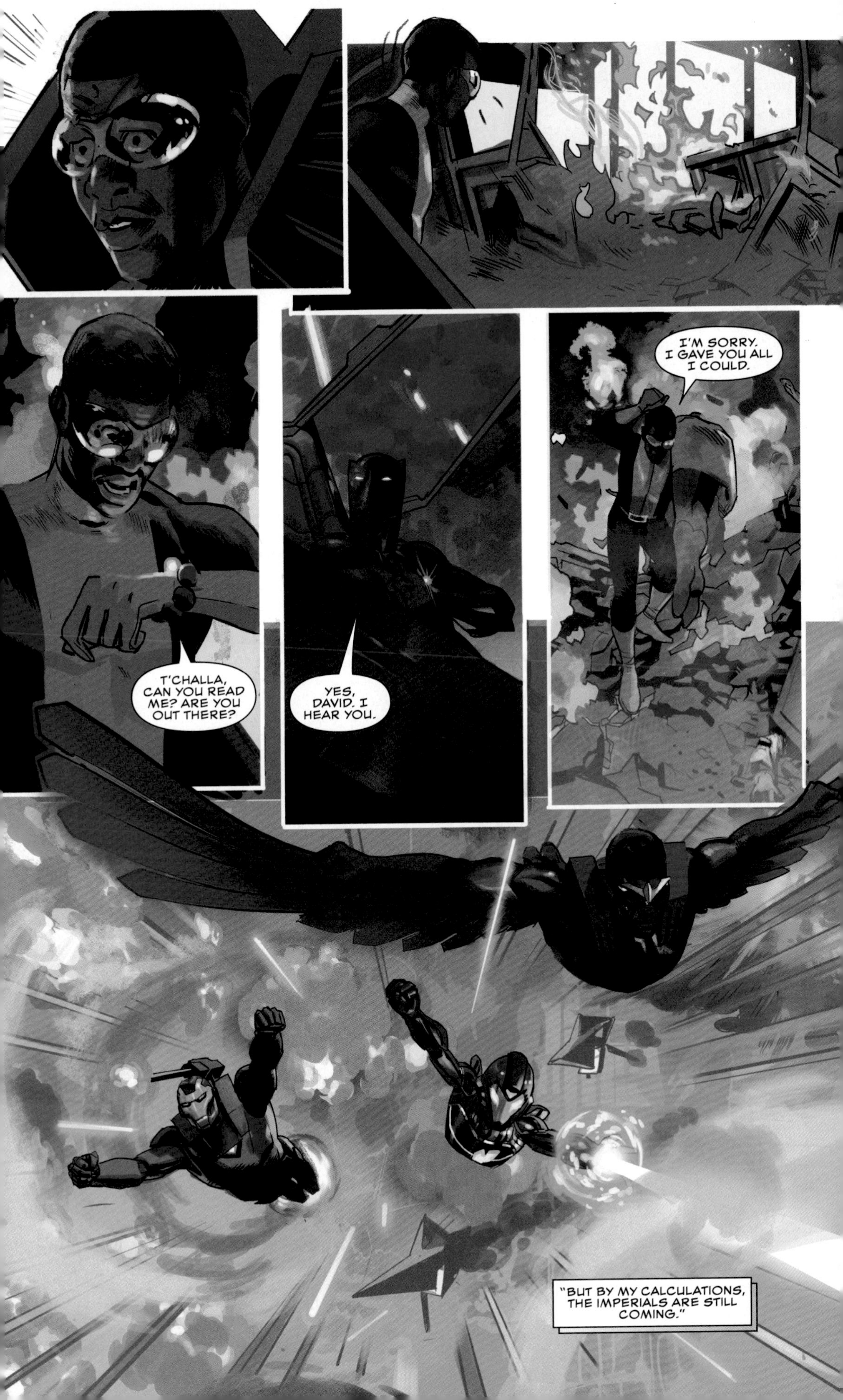
T'CHALLA, CAN YOU READ ME? ARE YOU OUT THERE?
YES, DAVID. I HEAR YOU.
I'M SORRY. I GAVE YOU ALL I COULD.
"BUT BY MY CALCULATIONS, THE IMPERIALS ARE STILL COMING."

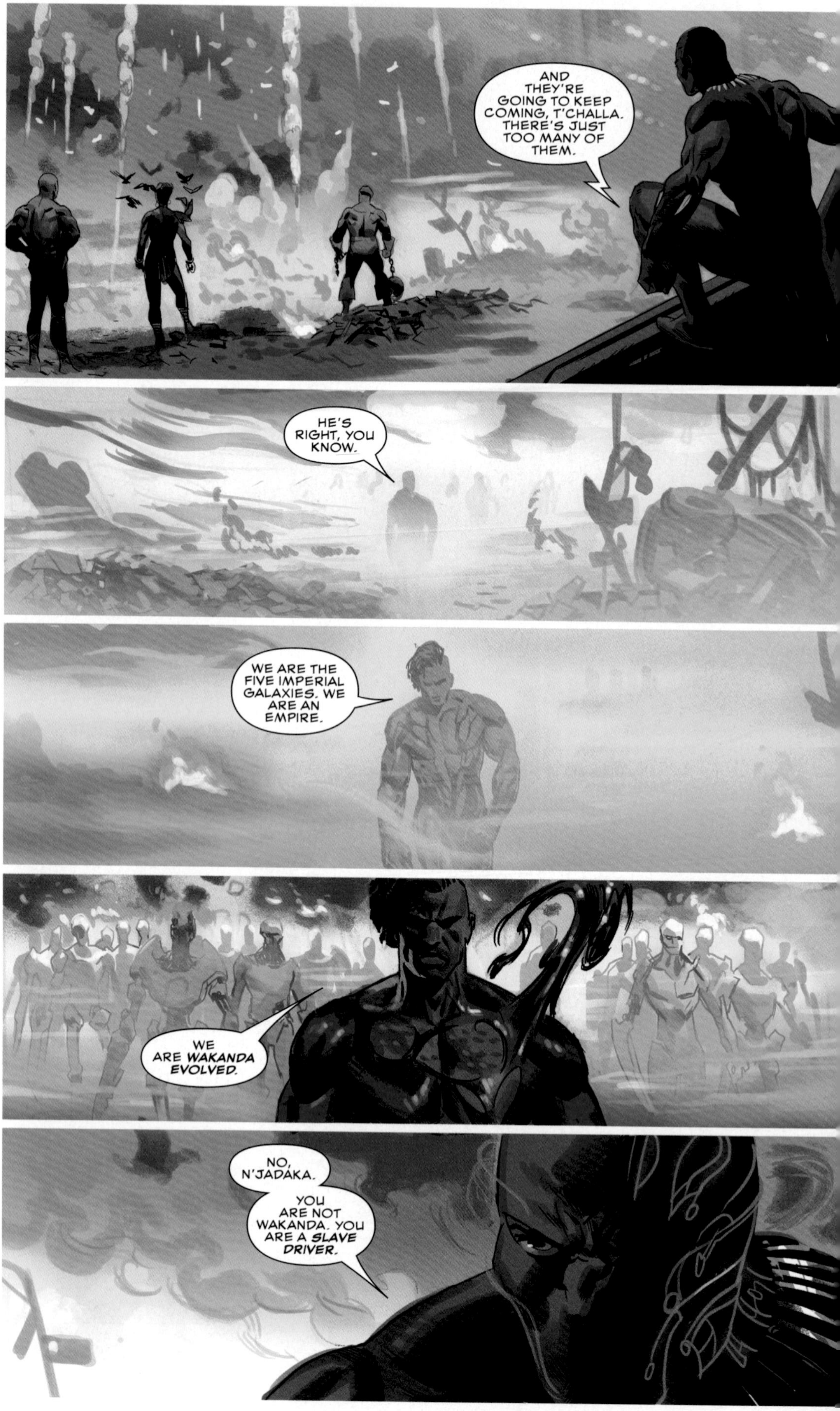
AND THEY'RE GOING TO KEEP COMING, T'CHALLA. THERE'S JUST TOO MANY OF THEM.
HE'S RIGHT, YOU KNOW.
WE ARE THE FIVE IMPERIAL GALAXIES. WE ARE AN EMPIRE.
WE ARE *WAKANDA EVOLVED.*
NO, N'JADAKA.
YOU ARE NOT WAKANDA. YOU ARE A *SLAVE DRIVER.*

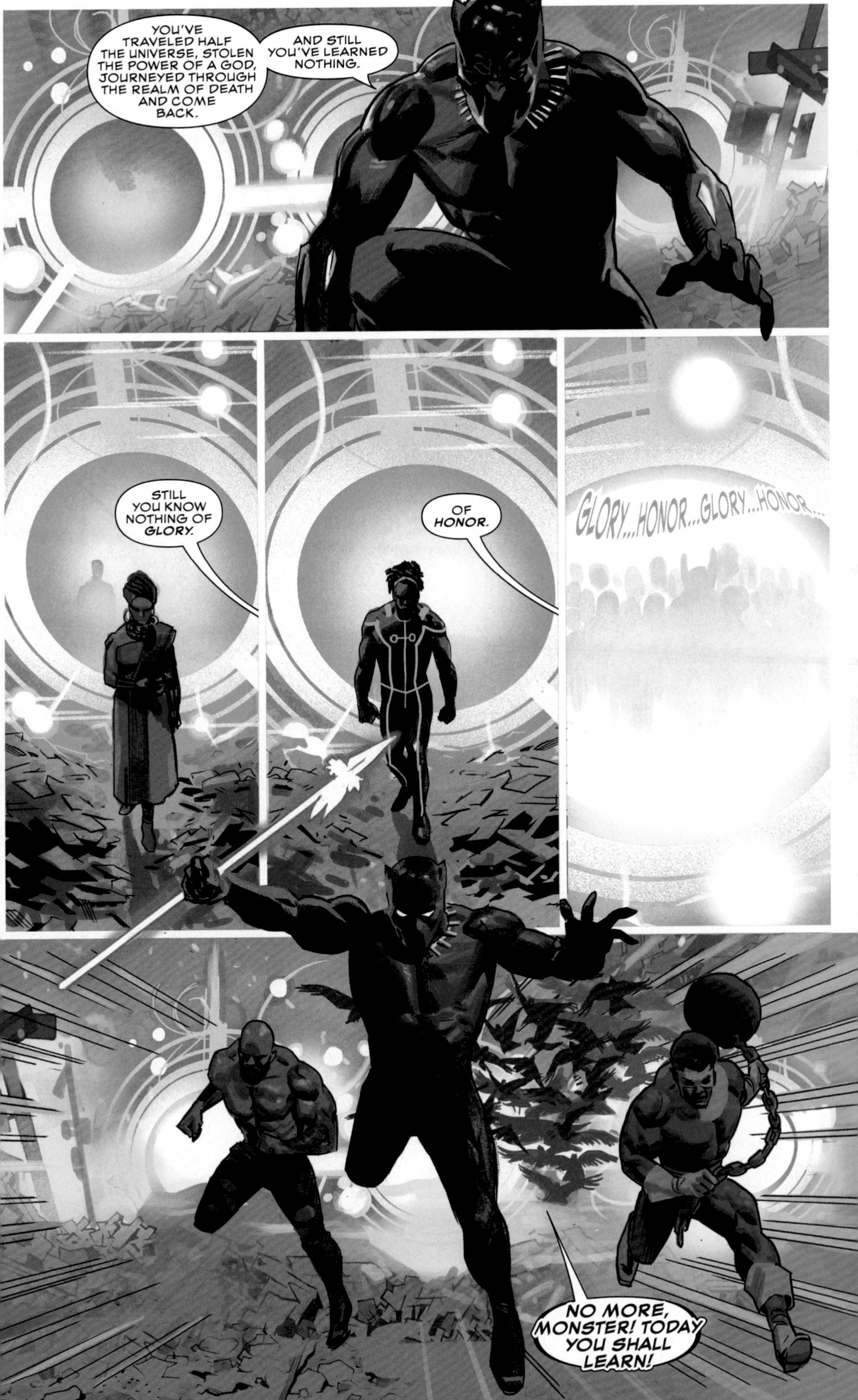
YOU'VE TRAVELED HALF THE UNIVERSE, STOLEN THE POWER OF A GOD, JOURNEYED THROUGH THE REALM OF DEATH AND COME BACK.
AND STILL YOU'VE LEARNED NOTHING.
STILL YOU KNOW NOTHING OF GLORY.
OF HONOR.
GLORY...HONOR...GLORY...HONOR...
NO MORE, MONSTER! TODAY YOU SHALL LEARN!

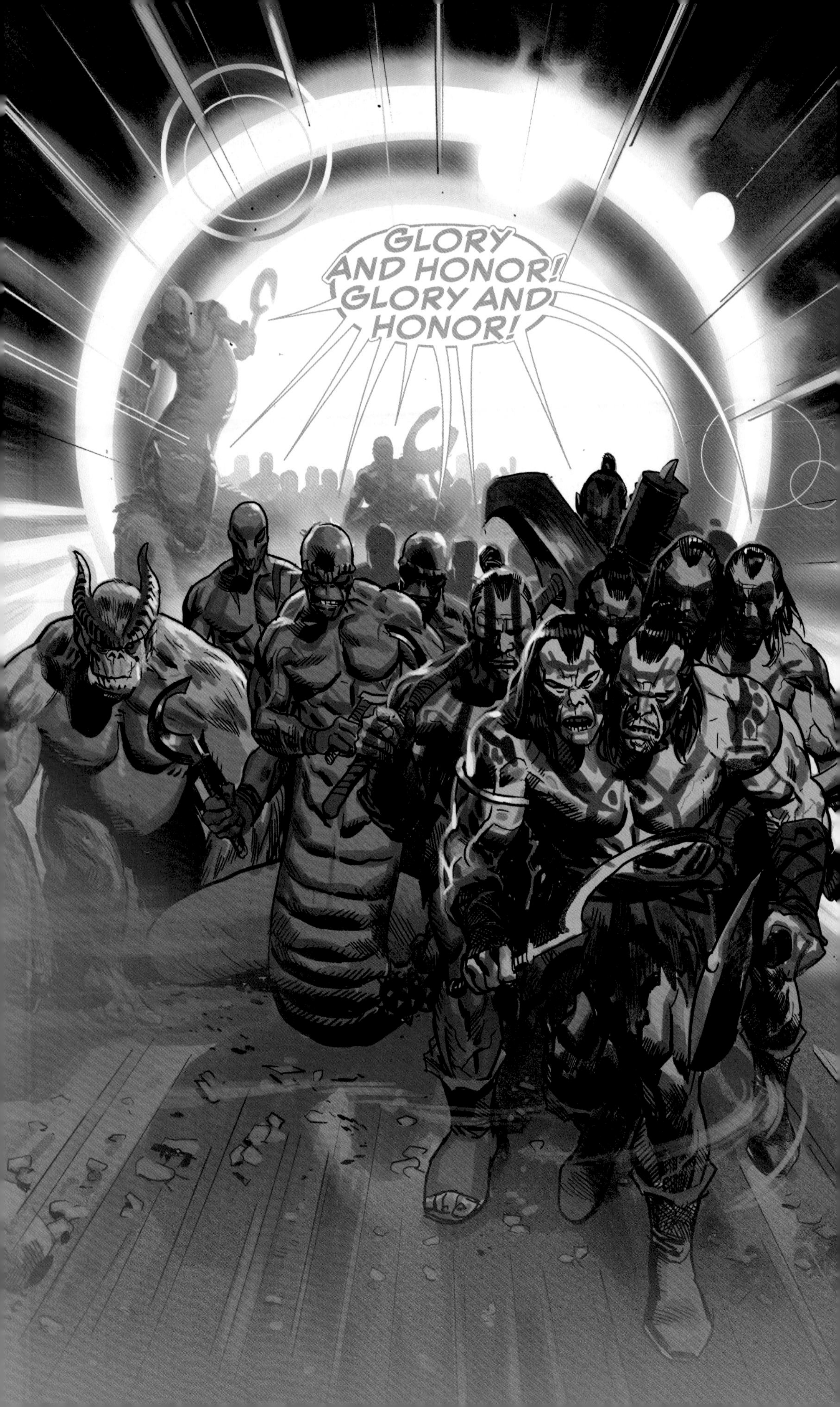
GLORY AND HONOR! GLORY AND HONOR!

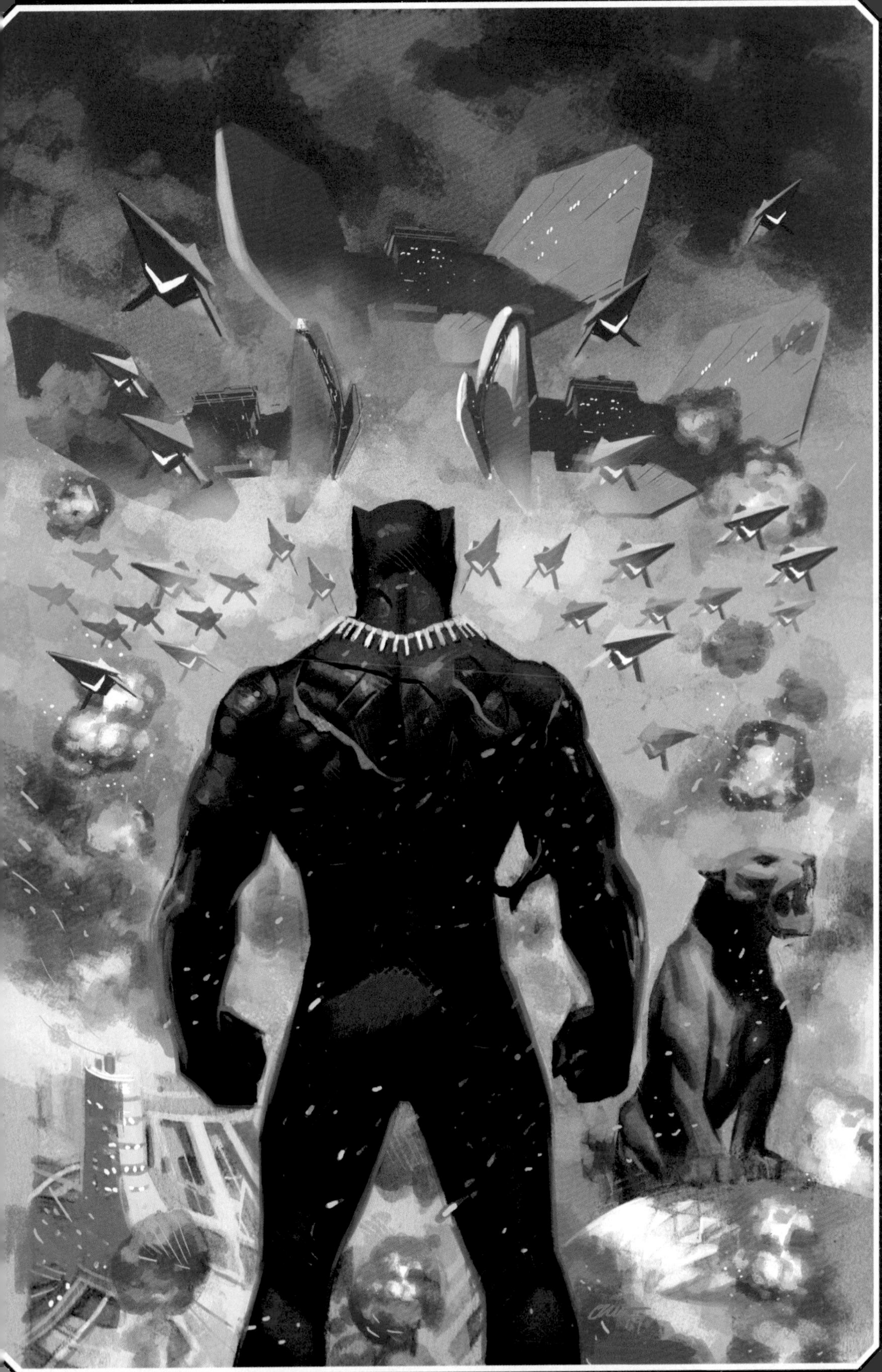

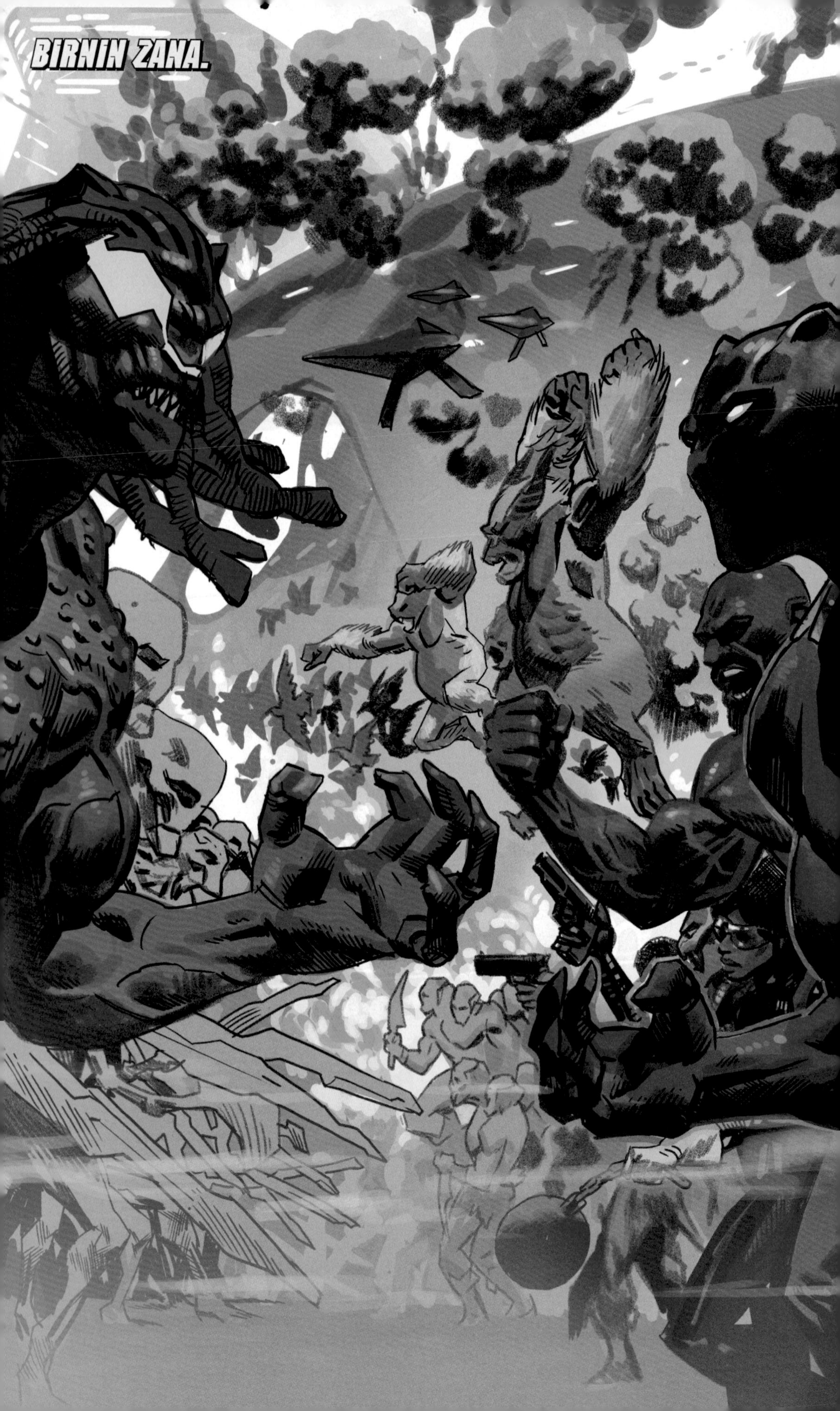
BIRNIN ZANA.

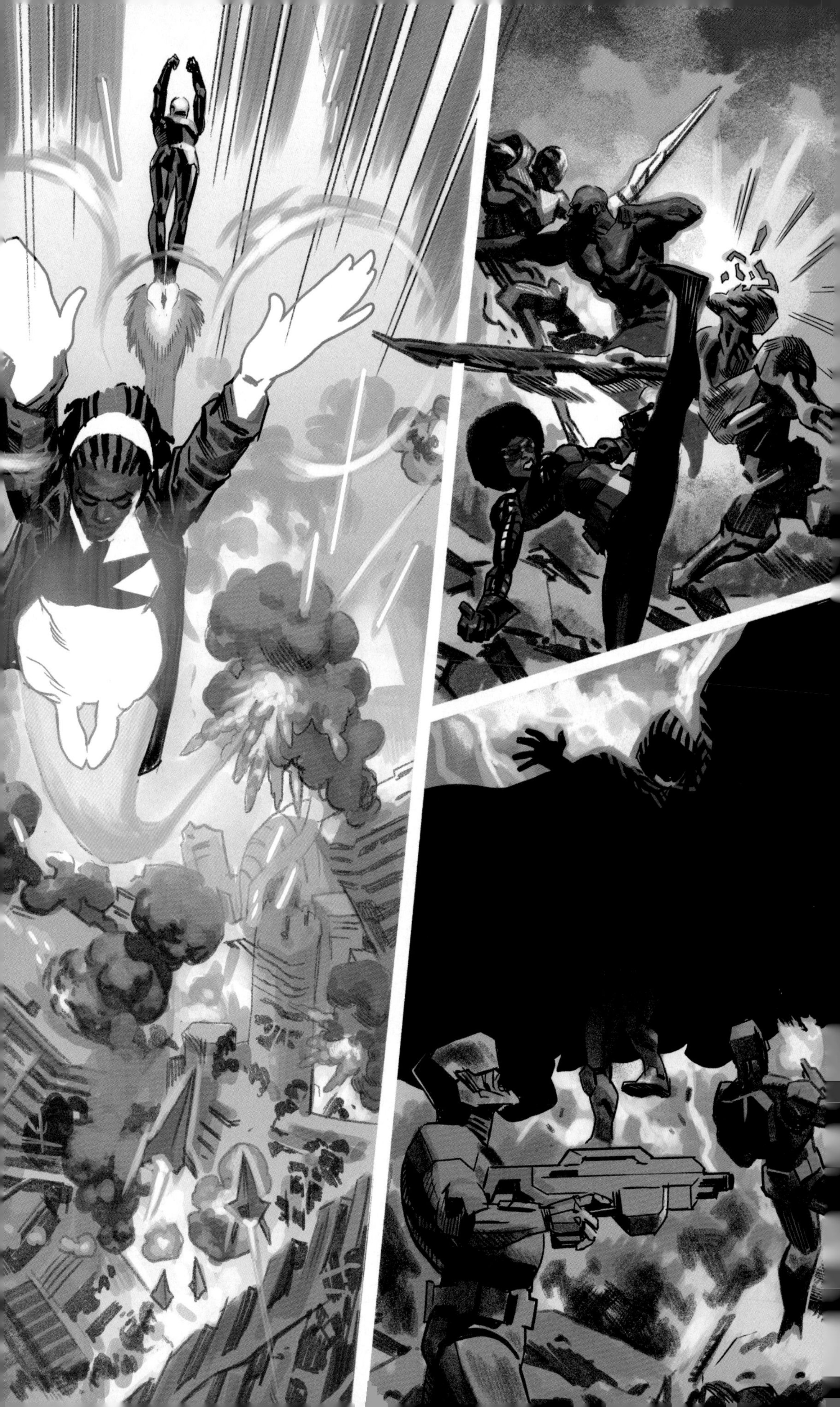

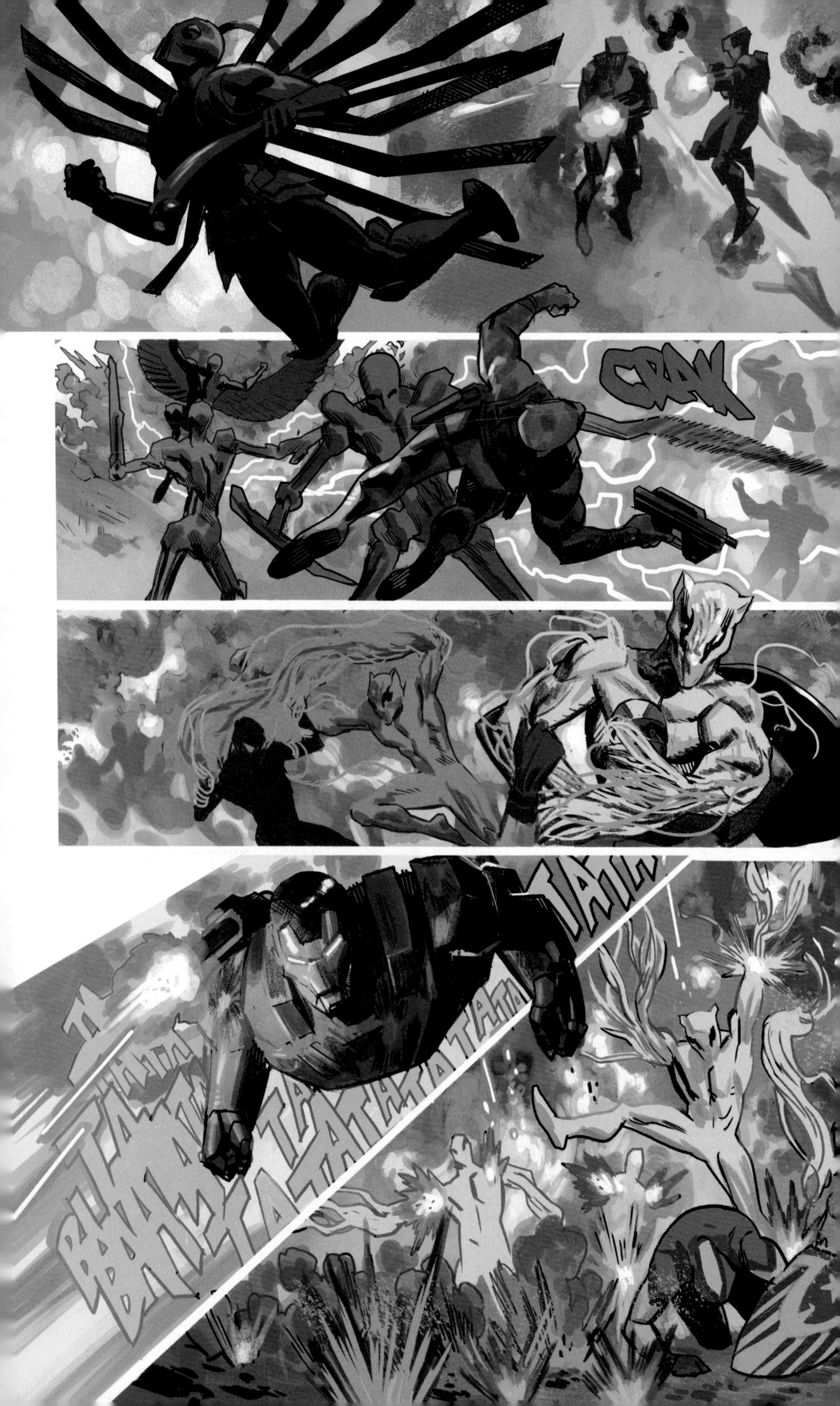
CRAK

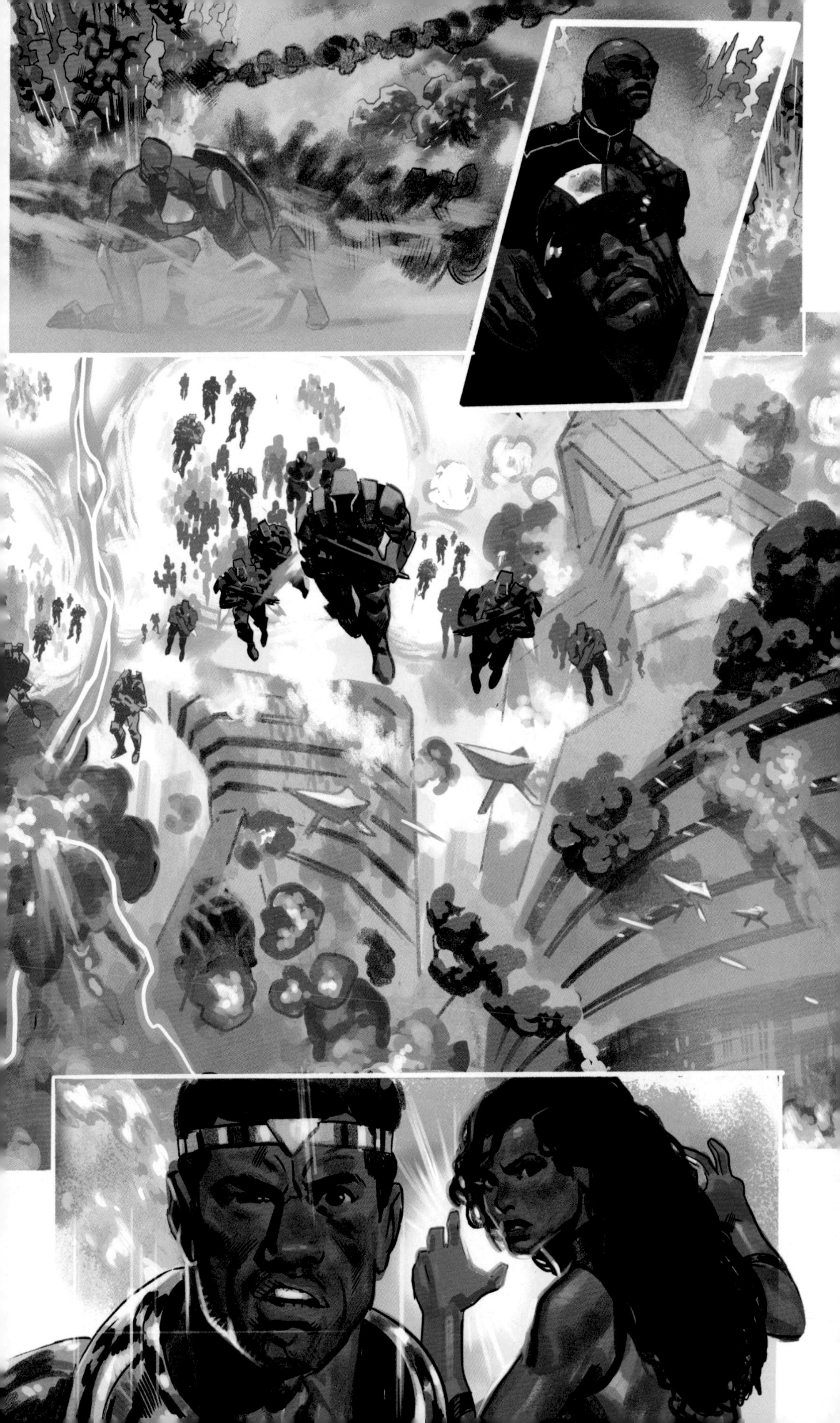

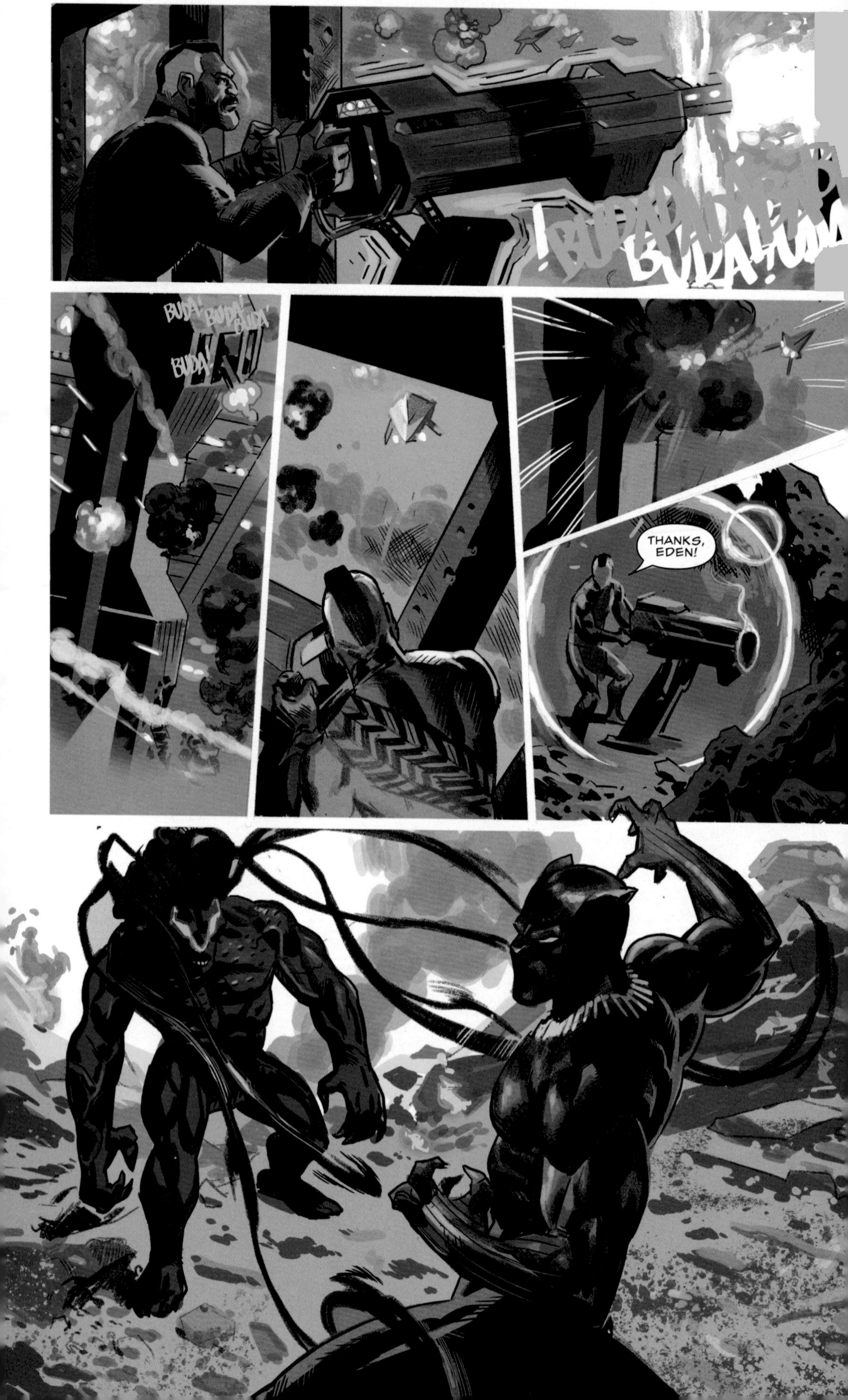
BUDA!
BUDA!
BUDA!
BUDA!
THANKS, EDEN!

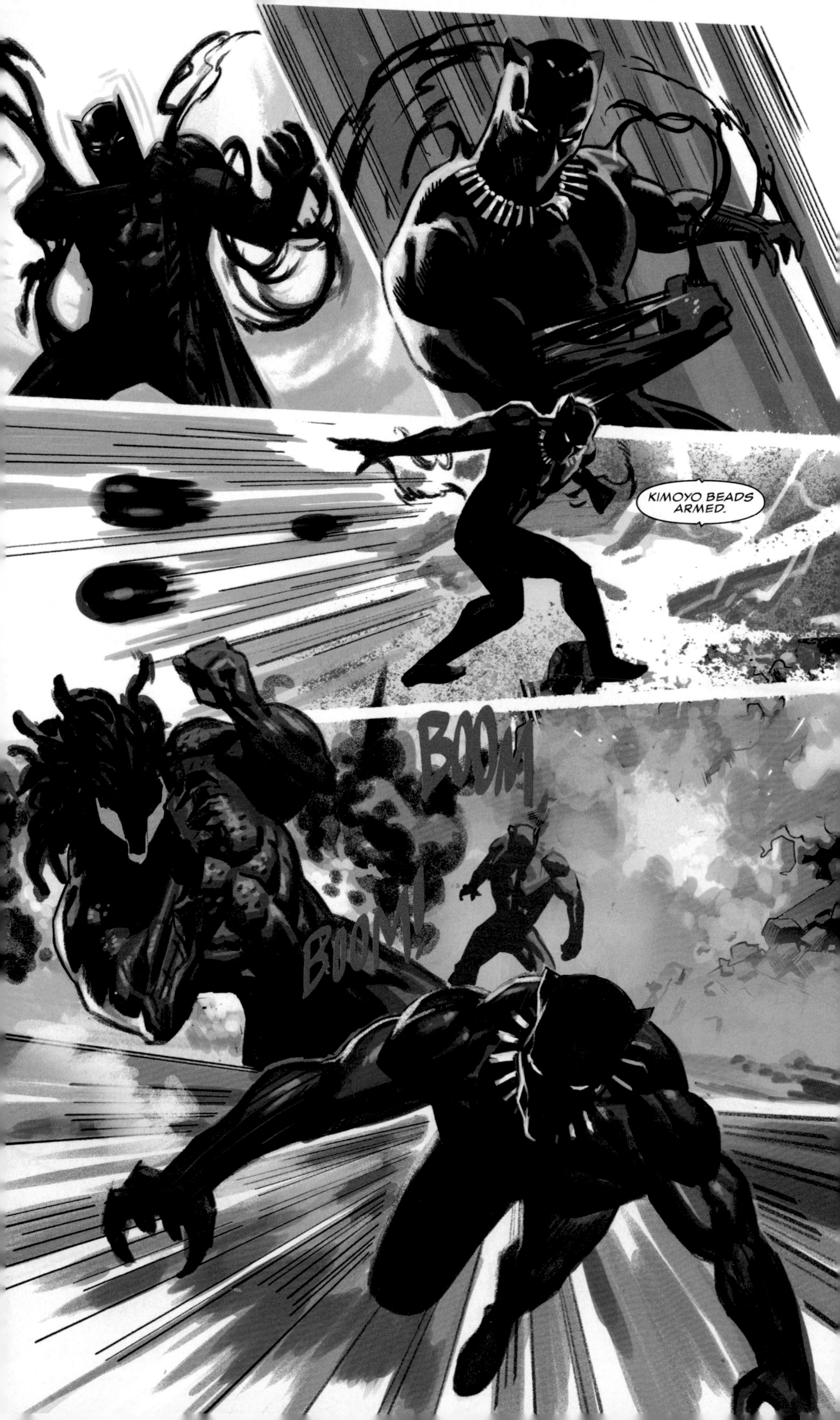
KIMOYO BEADS ARMED.
BOOM
BOOM!

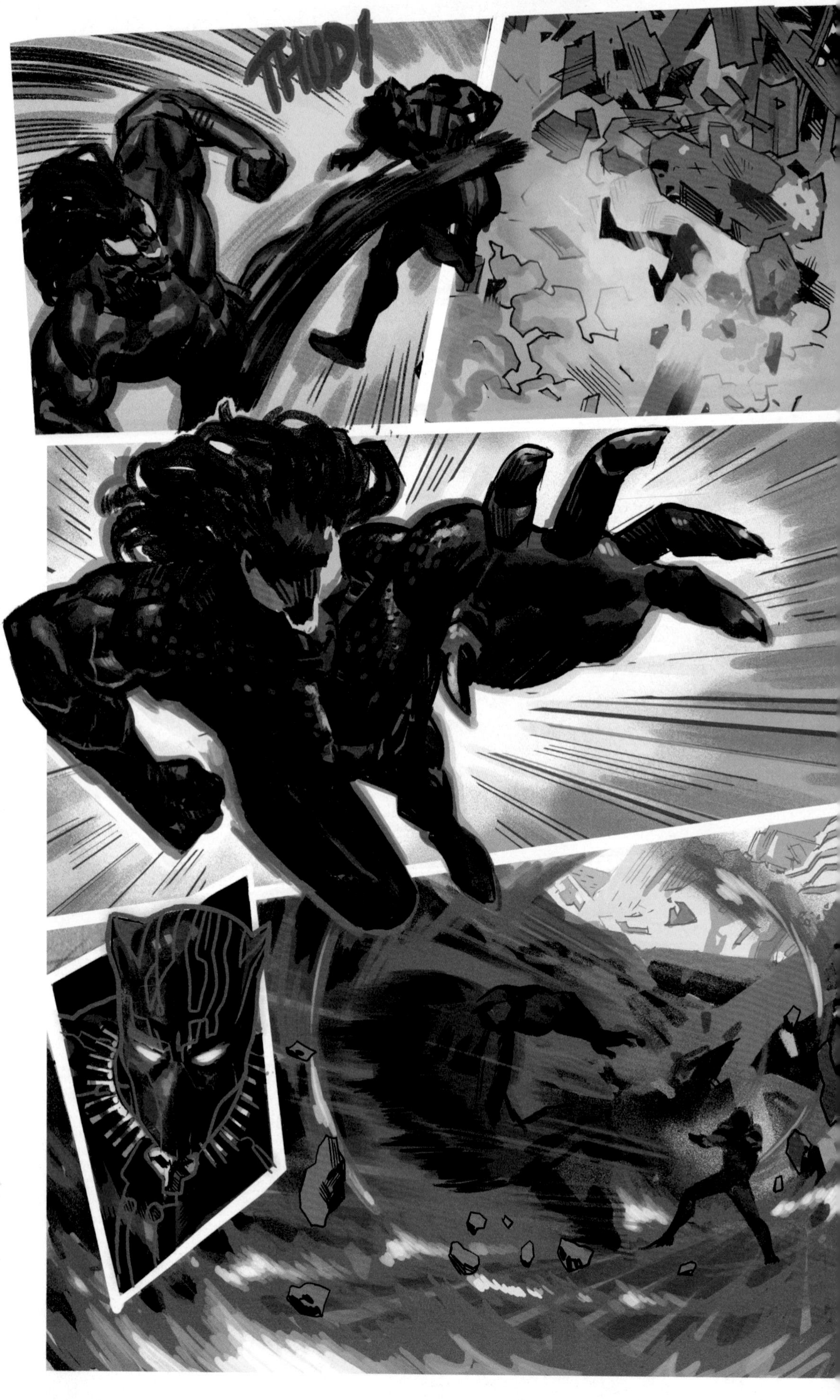
THUD!

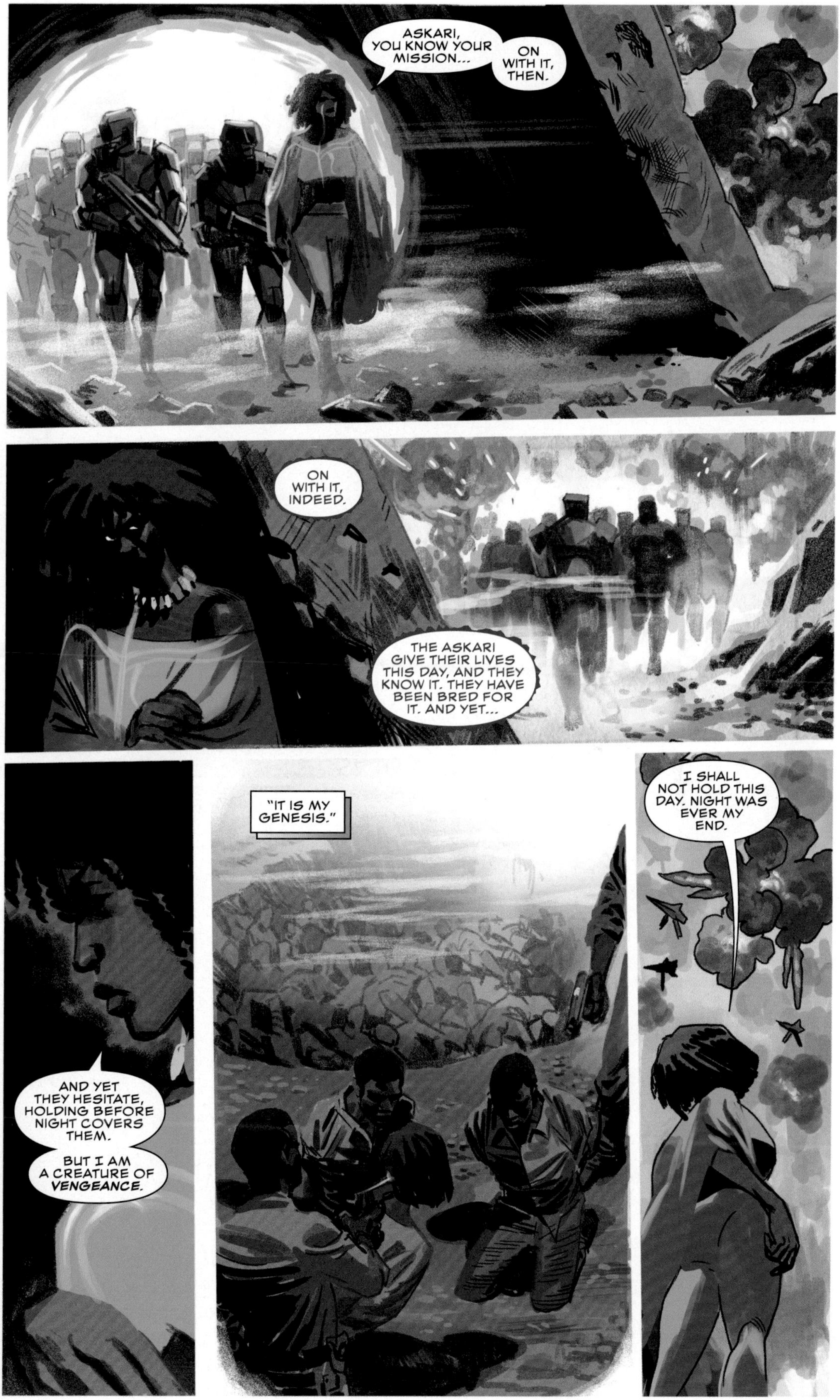
ASKARI, YOU KNOW YOUR MISSION...
ON WITH IT, THEN.
ON WITH IT, INDEED.
THE ASKARI GIVE THEIR LIVES THIS DAY, AND THEY KNOW IT. THEY HAVE BEEN BRED FOR IT. AND YET...
AND YET THEY HESITATE, HOLDING BEFORE NIGHT COVERS THEM.
BUT I AM A CREATURE OF *VENGEANCE*.
"IT IS MY GENESIS."
I SHALL NOT HOLD THIS DAY. NIGHT WAS EVER MY END.

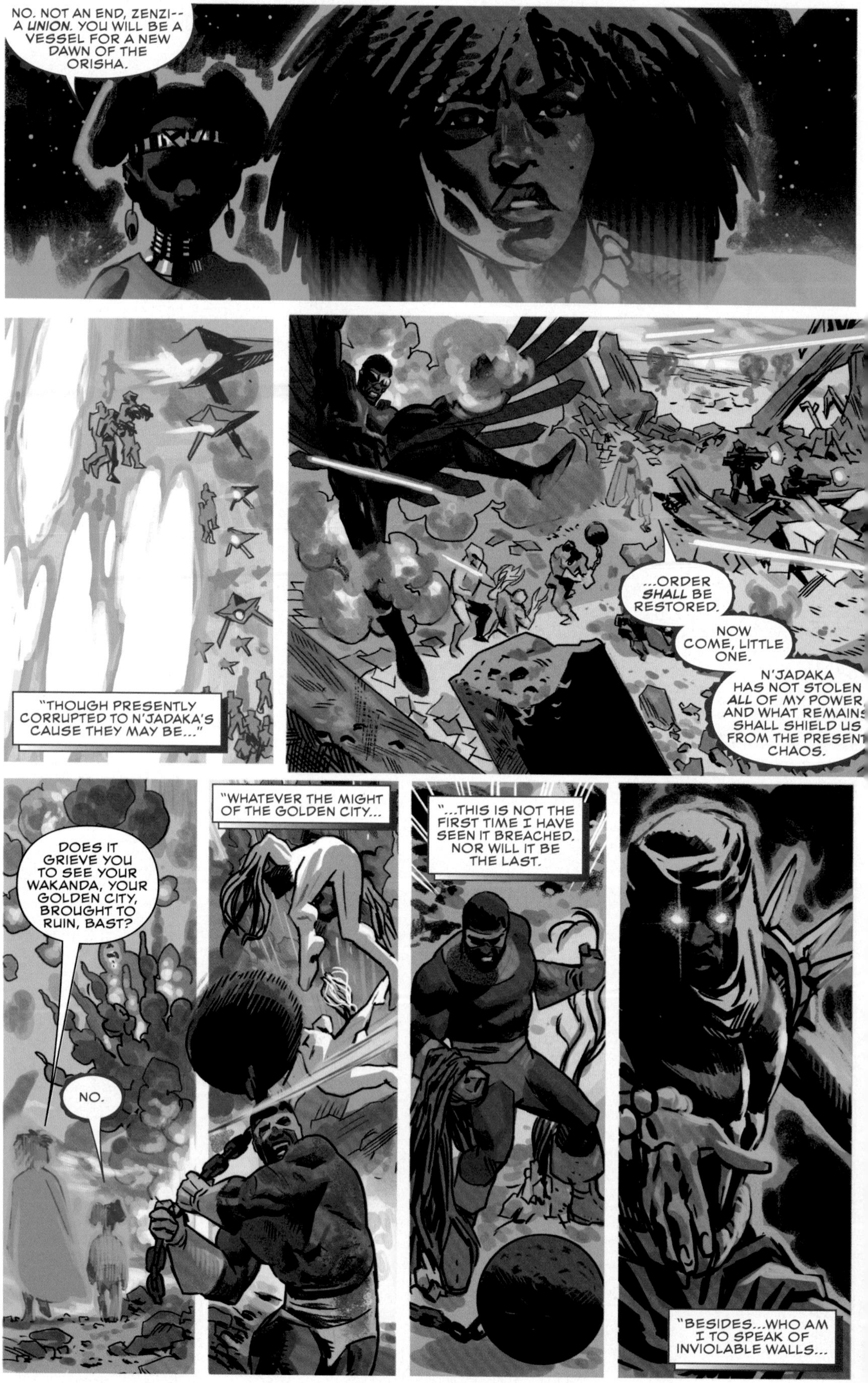

NO. NOT AN END, ZENZI-- A UNION. YOU WILL BE A VESSEL FOR A NEW DAWN OF THE ORISHA.
"THOUGH PRESENTLY CORRUPTED TO N'JADAKA'S CAUSE THEY MAY BE..."
...ORDER SHALL BE RESTORED.
NOW COME, LITTLE ONE.
N'JADAKA HAS NOT STOLEN ALL OF MY POWER AND WHAT REMAINS SHALL SHIELD US FROM THE PRESENT CHAOS.
DOES IT GRIEVE YOU TO SEE YOUR WAKANDA, YOUR GOLDEN CITY, BROUGHT TO RUIN, BAST?
NO.
"WHATEVER THE MIGHT OF THE GOLDEN CITY...
"...THIS IS NOT THE FIRST TIME I HAVE SEEN IT BREACHED. NOR WILL IT BE THE LAST.
"BESIDES...WHO AM I TO SPEAK OF INVIOLABLE WALLS...

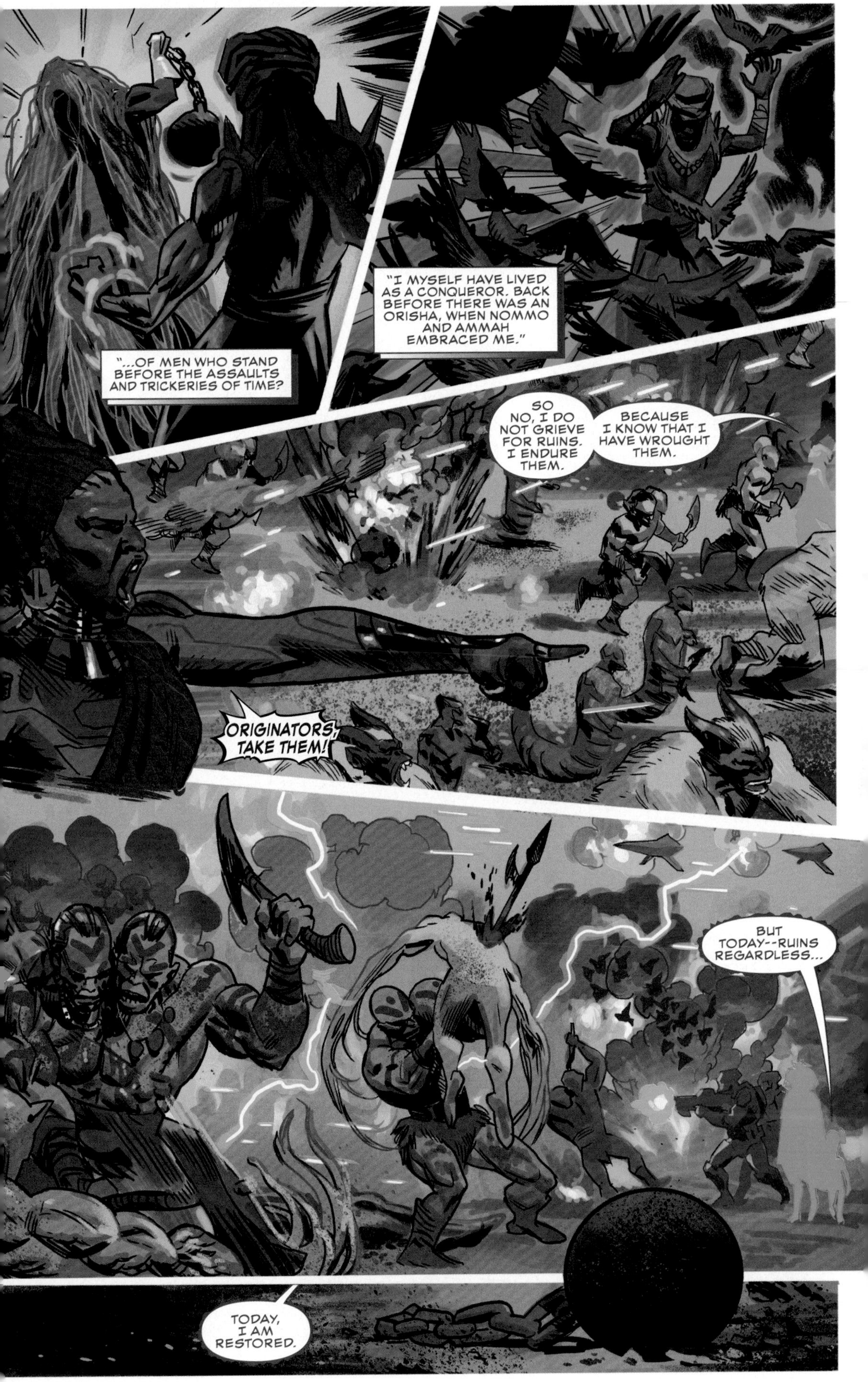
"...OF MEN WHO STAND BEFORE THE ASSAULTS AND TRICKERIES OF TIME?
"I MYSELF HAVE LIVED AS A CONQUEROR. BACK BEFORE THERE WAS AN ORISHA, WHEN NOMMO AND AMMAH EMBRACED ME."
SO NO, I DO NOT GRIEVE FOR RUINS. I ENDURE THEM.
BECAUSE I KNOW THAT I HAVE WROUGHT THEM.
ORIGINATORS, TAKE THEM!
BUT TODAY--RUINS REGARDLESS...
TODAY, I AM RESTORED.

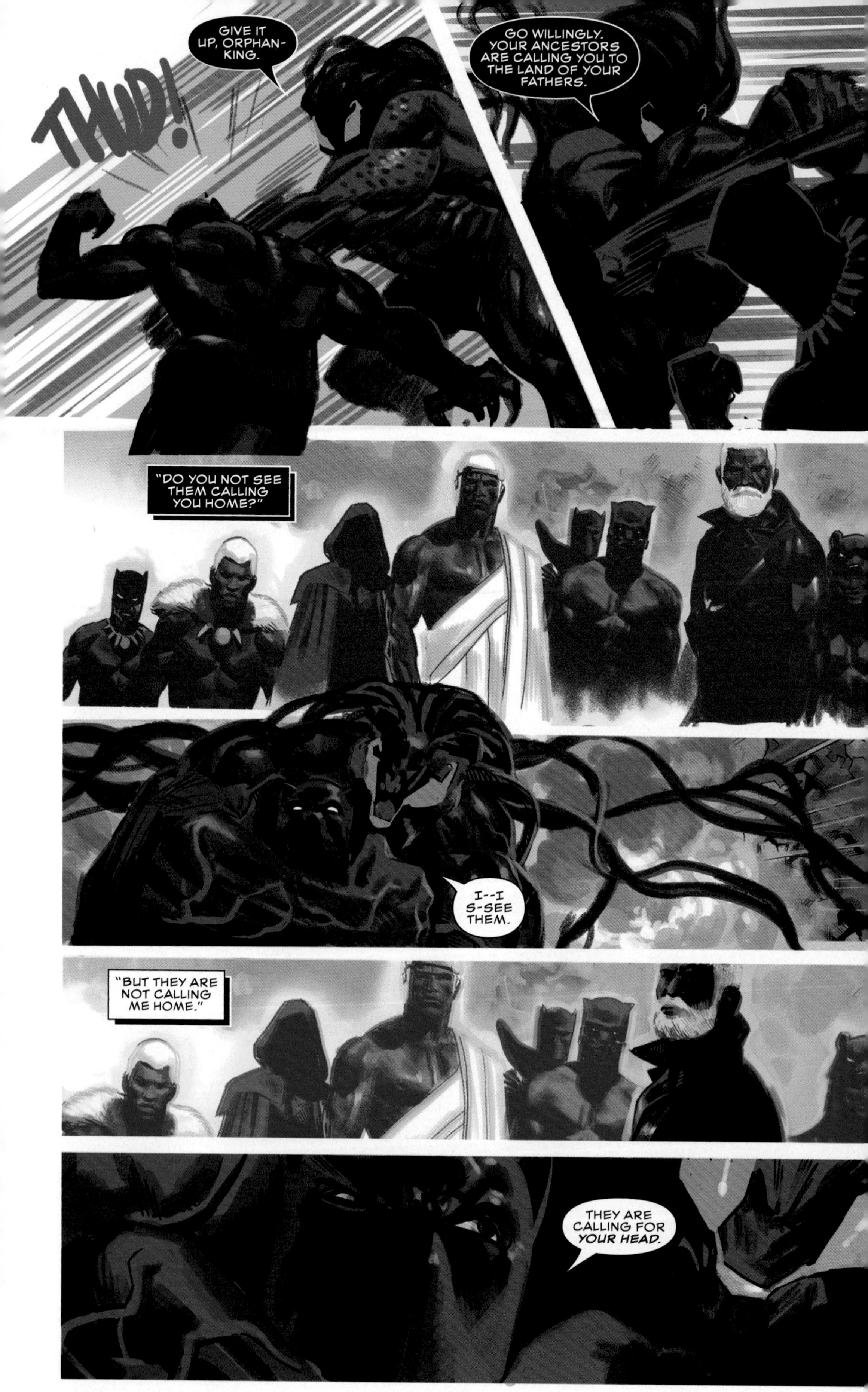
THUD!
GIVE IT UP, ORPHAN-KING.
GO WILLINGLY. YOUR ANCESTORS ARE CALLING YOU TO THE LAND OF YOUR FATHERS.
"DO YOU NOT SEE THEM CALLING YOU HOME?"
I--I S-SEE THEM.
"BUT THEY ARE NOT CALLING ME HOME."
THEY ARE CALLING FOR YOUR HEAD.

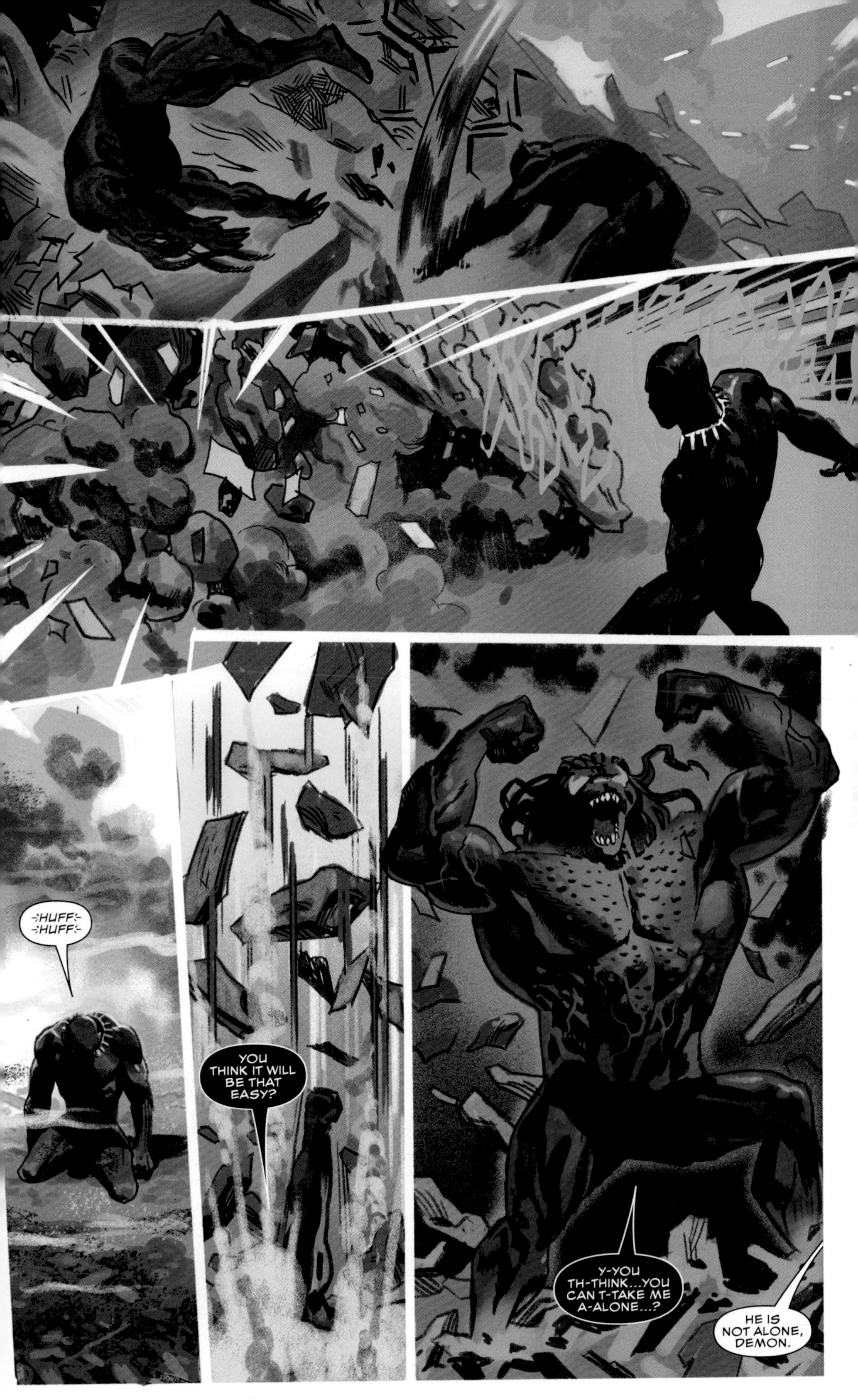

-HUFF- -HUFF-
YOU THINK IT WILL BE THAT EASY?
Y-YOU TH-THINK...YOU CAN T-TAKE ME A-ALONE...?
HE IS NOT ALONE, DEMON.

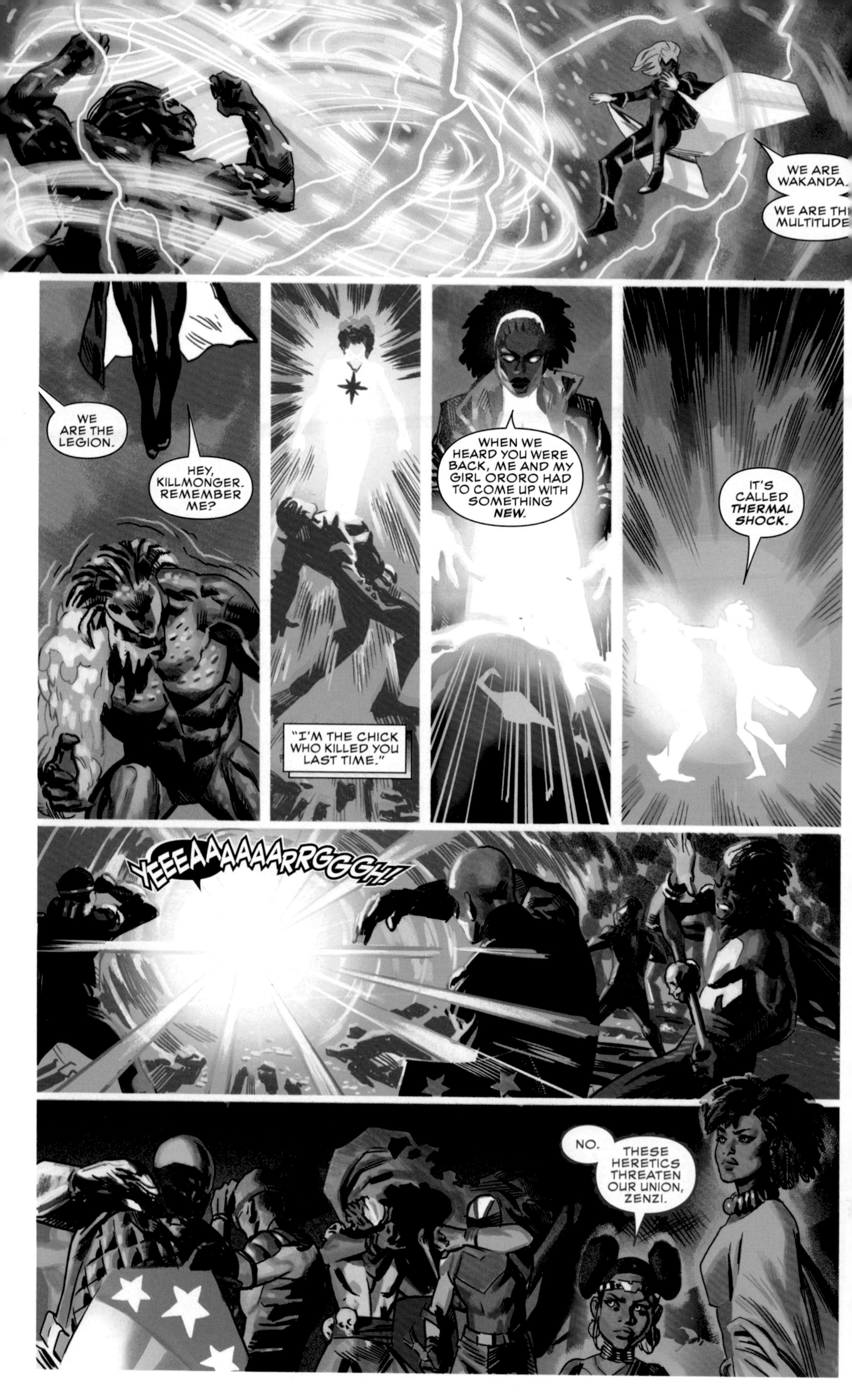
WE ARE WAKANDA.
WE ARE THE MULTITUDE
WE ARE THE LEGION.
HEY, KILLMONGER. REMEMBER ME?
"I'M THE CHICK WHO KILLED YOU LAST TIME."
WHEN WE HEARD YOU WERE BACK, ME AND MY GIRL ORORO HAD TO COME UP WITH SOMETHING NEW.
IT'S CALLED THERMAL SHOCK.
YEEEAAAAAARRGGGH!!
NO.
THESE HERETICS THREATEN OUR UNION, ZENZI.

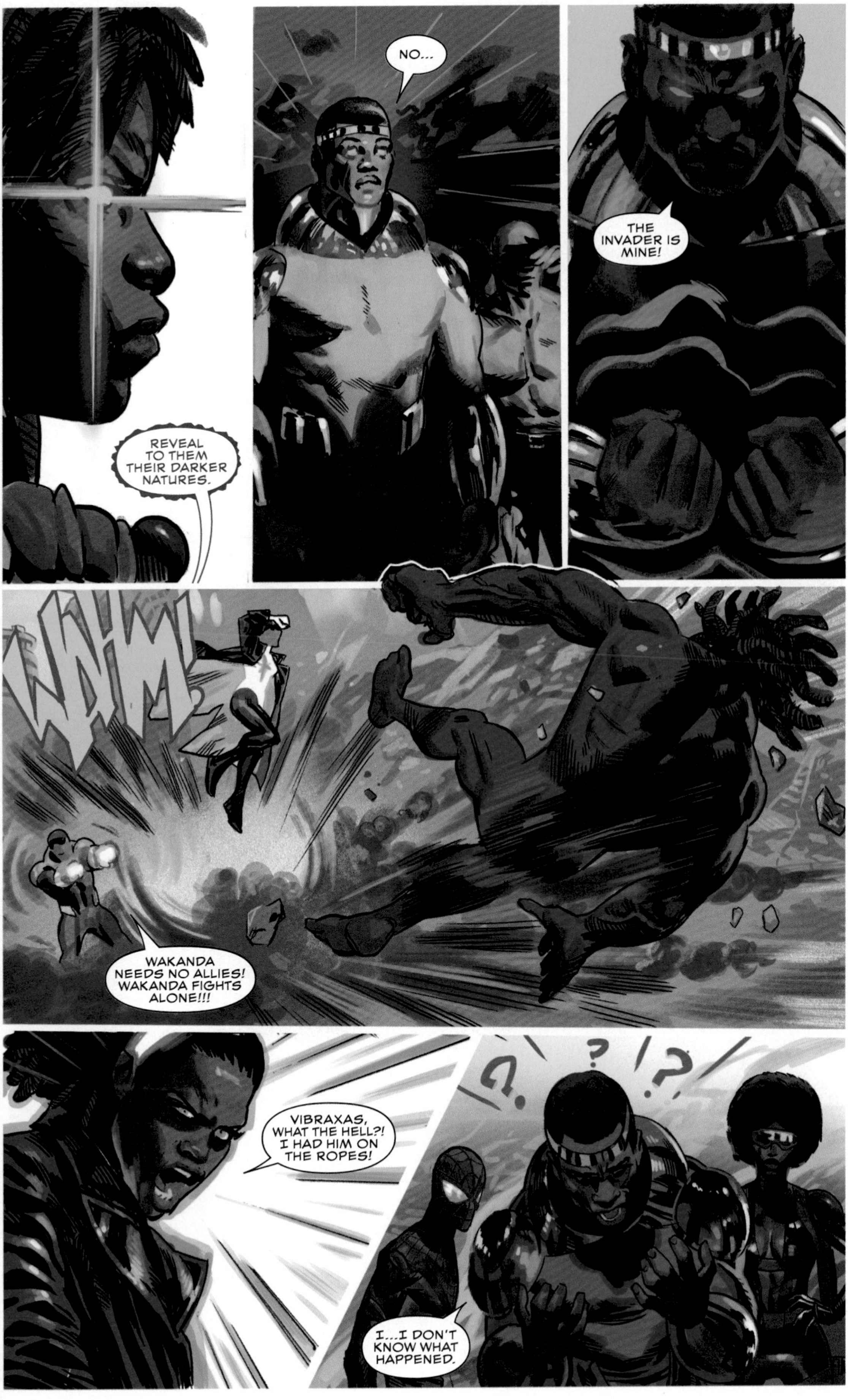
REVEAL TO THEM THEIR DARKER NATURES.
NO...
THE INVADER IS MINE!
WAKANDA NEEDS NO ALLIES! WAKANDA FIGHTS ALONE!!!
VIBRAXAS, WHAT THE HELL?! I HAD HIM ON THE ROPES!
I...I DON'T KNOW WHAT HAPPENED.

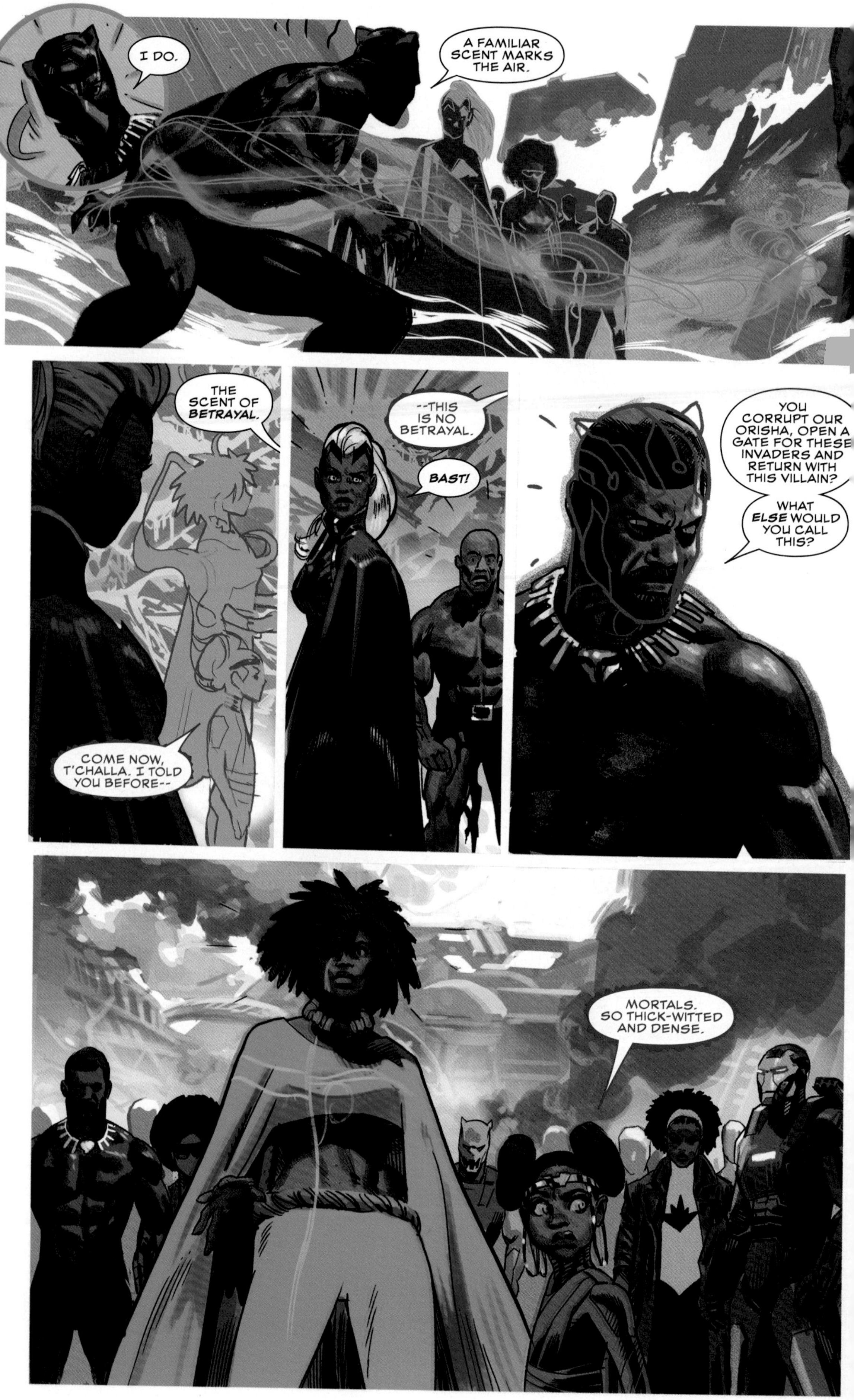
I DO.
A FAMILIAR SCENT MARKS THE AIR.
THE SCENT OF BETRAYAL.
COME NOW, T'CHALLA. I TOLD YOU BEFORE--
--THIS IS NO BETRAYAL.
BAST!
YOU CORRUPT OUR ORISHA, OPEN A GATE FOR THESE INVADERS AND RETURN WITH THIS VILLAIN?
WHAT ELSE WOULD YOU CALL THIS?
MORTALS. SO THICK-WITTED AND DENSE.

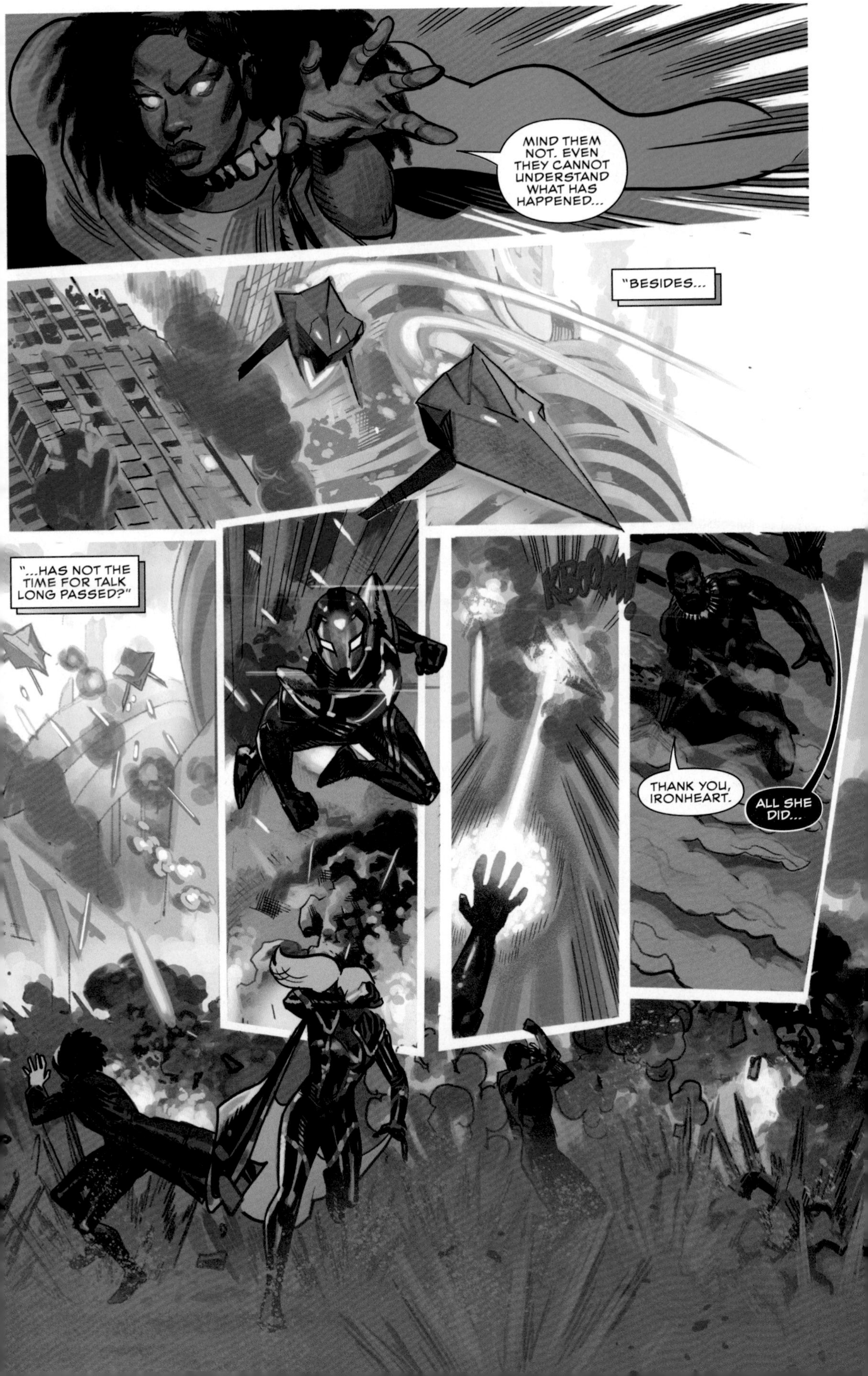
MIND THEM NOT. EVEN THEY CANNOT UNDERSTAND WHAT HAS HAPPENED...
"BESIDES...
"...HAS NOT THE TIME FOR TALK LONG PASSED?"
KBOOM!
THANK YOU, IRONHEART.
ALL SHE DID...

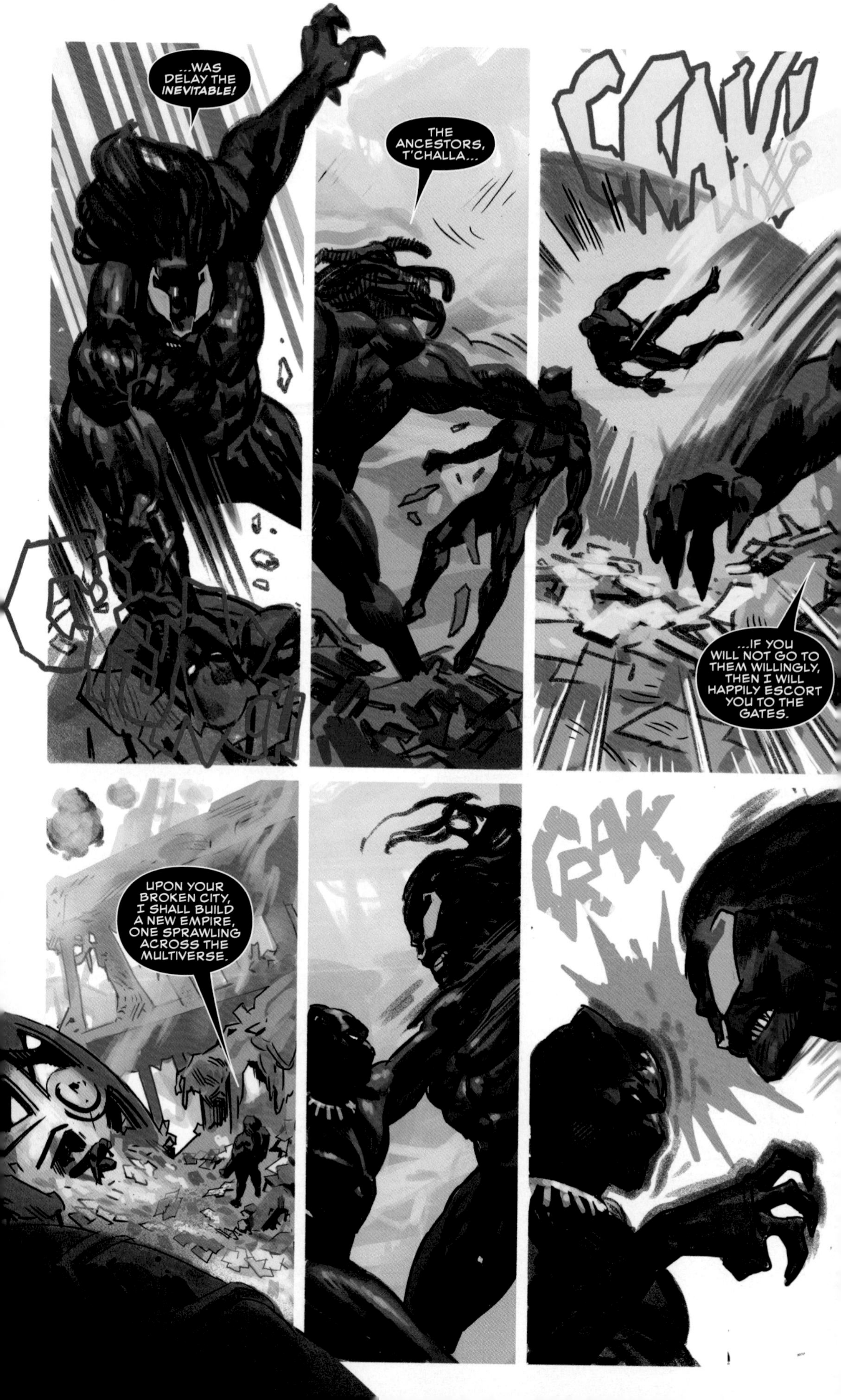

...WAS DELAY THE INEVITABLE!
THE ANCESTORS, T'CHALLA...
...IF YOU WILL NOT GO TO THEM WILLINGLY, THEN I WILL HAPPILY ESCORT YOU TO THE GATES.
UPON YOUR BROKEN CITY, I SHALL BUILD A NEW EMPIRE, ONE SPRAWLING ACROSS THE MULTIVERSE.
KRAK

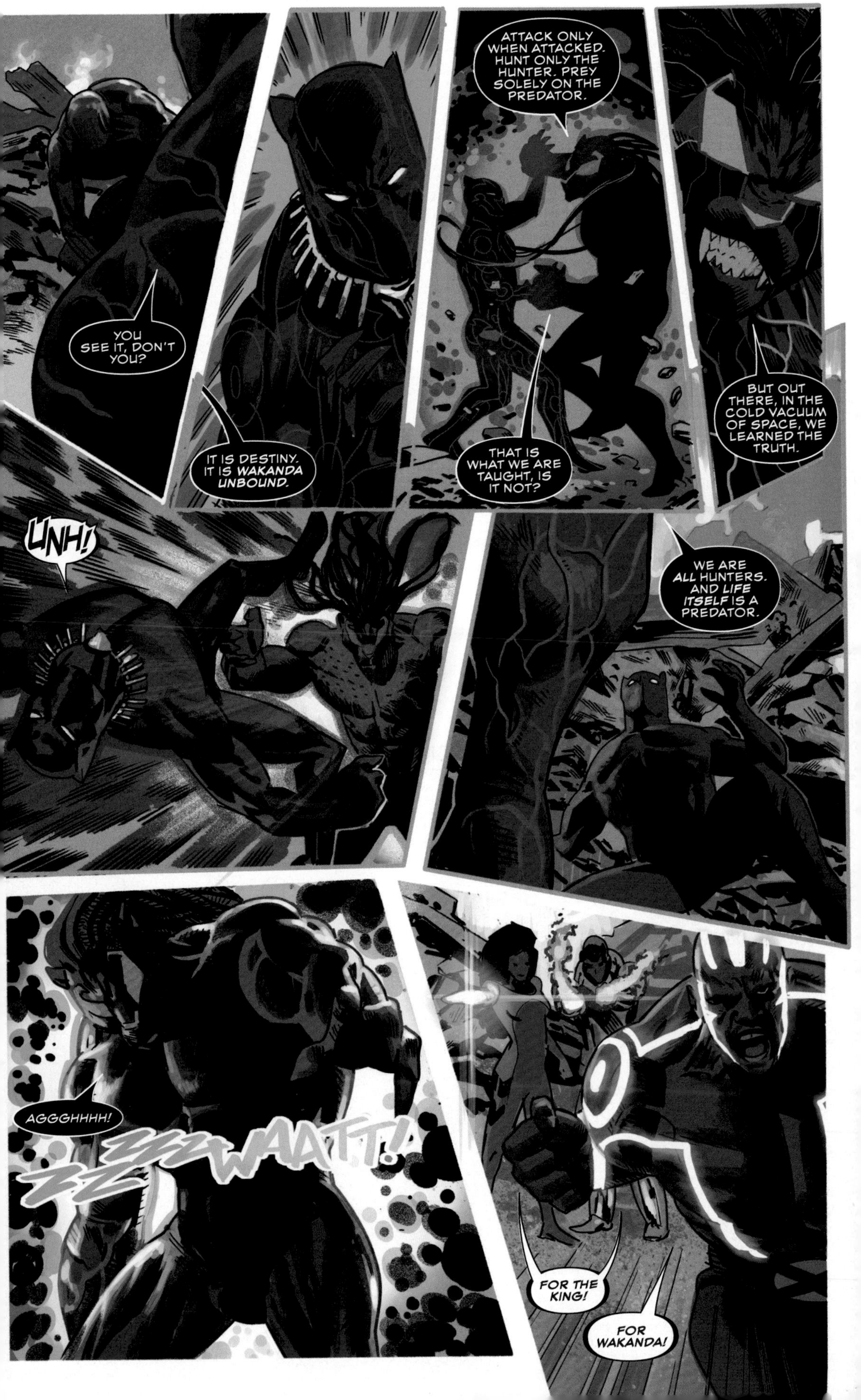
YOU SEE IT, DON'T YOU?
IT IS DESTINY. IT IS WAKANDA UNBOUND.
ATTACK ONLY WHEN ATTACKED. HUNT ONLY THE HUNTER. PREY SOLELY ON THE PREDATOR.
THAT IS WHAT WE ARE TAUGHT, IS IT NOT?
BUT OUT THERE, IN THE COLD VACUUM OF SPACE, WE LEARNED THE TRUTH.
UNH!
WE ARE ALL HUNTERS. AND LIFE ITSELF IS A PREDATOR.
AGGGHHHH!
ZZZZZWAATT!
FOR THE KING!
FOR WAKANDA!

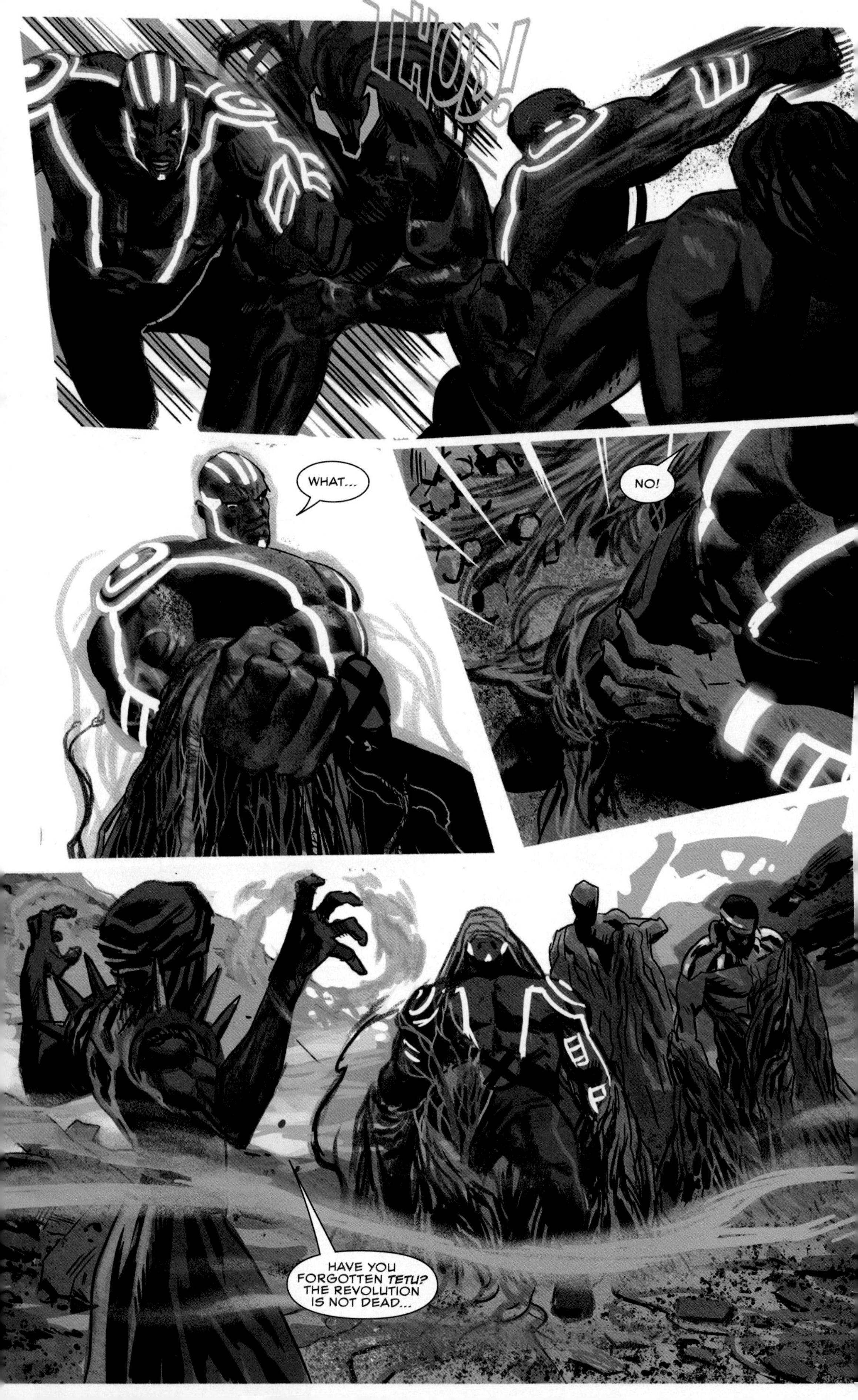
THUD!
WHAT...
NO!
HAVE YOU FORGOTTEN *TETU?* THE REVOLUTION IS NOT DEAD...

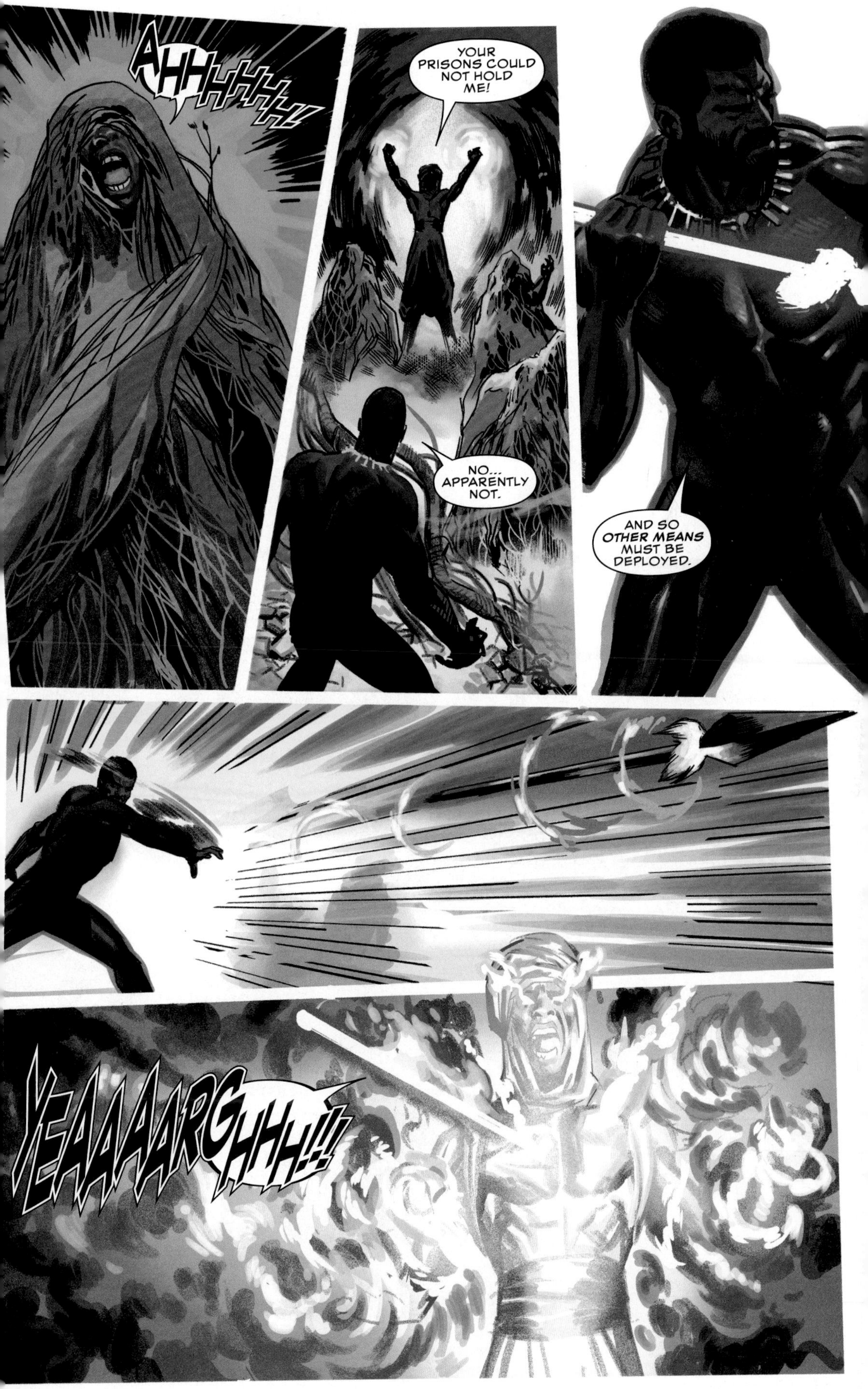
AHHHHHH!
YOUR PRISONS COULD NOT HOLD ME!
NO... APPARENTLY NOT.
AND SO OTHER MEANS MUST BE DEPLOYED.
YEAAAARGHHH!!!

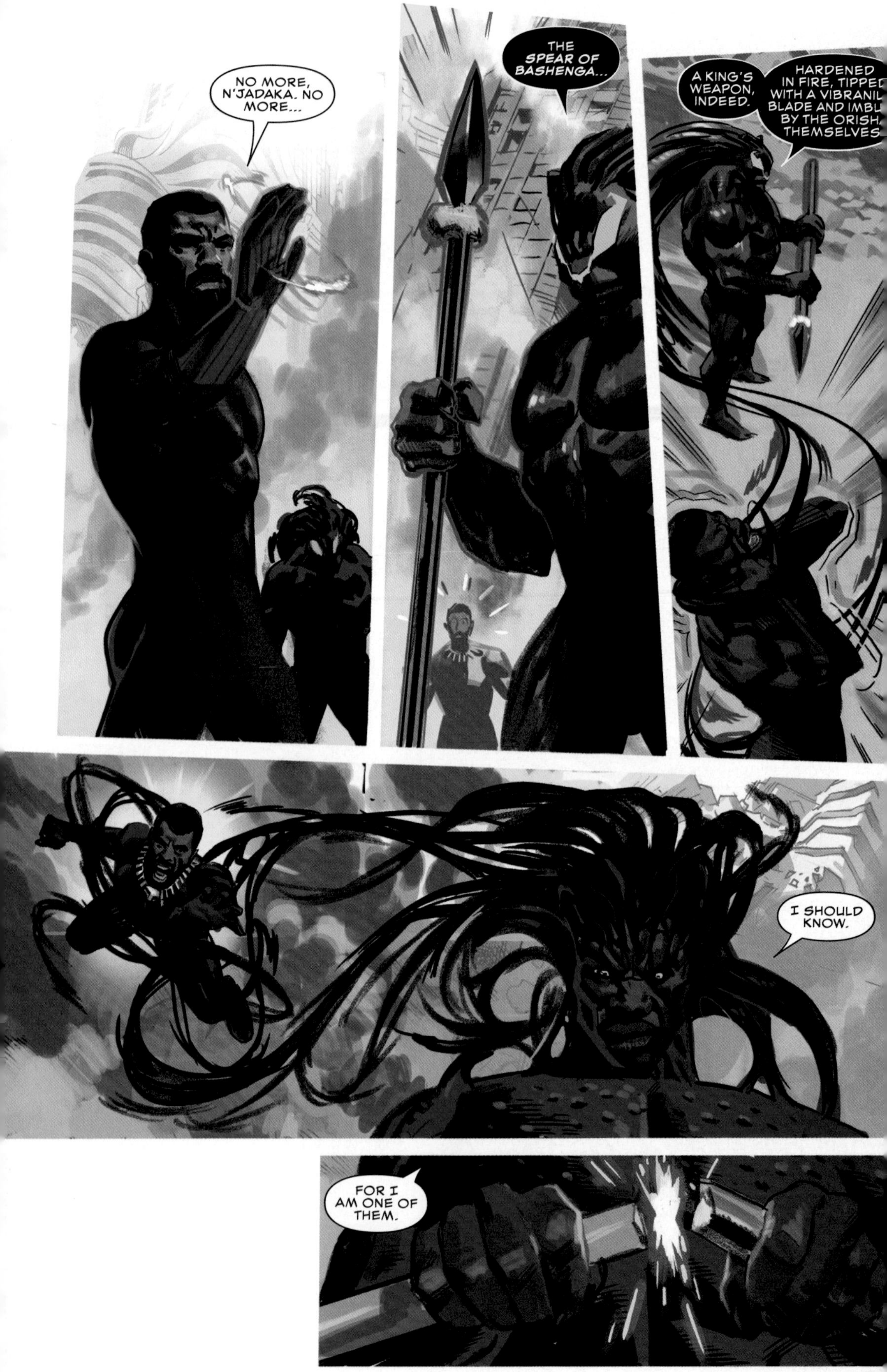
NO MORE, N'JADAKA. NO MORE...
THE SPEAR OF BASHENGA...
A KING'S WEAPON, INDEED.
HARDENED IN FIRE, TIPPED WITH A VIBRANIU BLADE AND IMBU BY THE ORISH THEMSELVES.
I SHOULD KNOW.
FOR I AM ONE OF THEM.

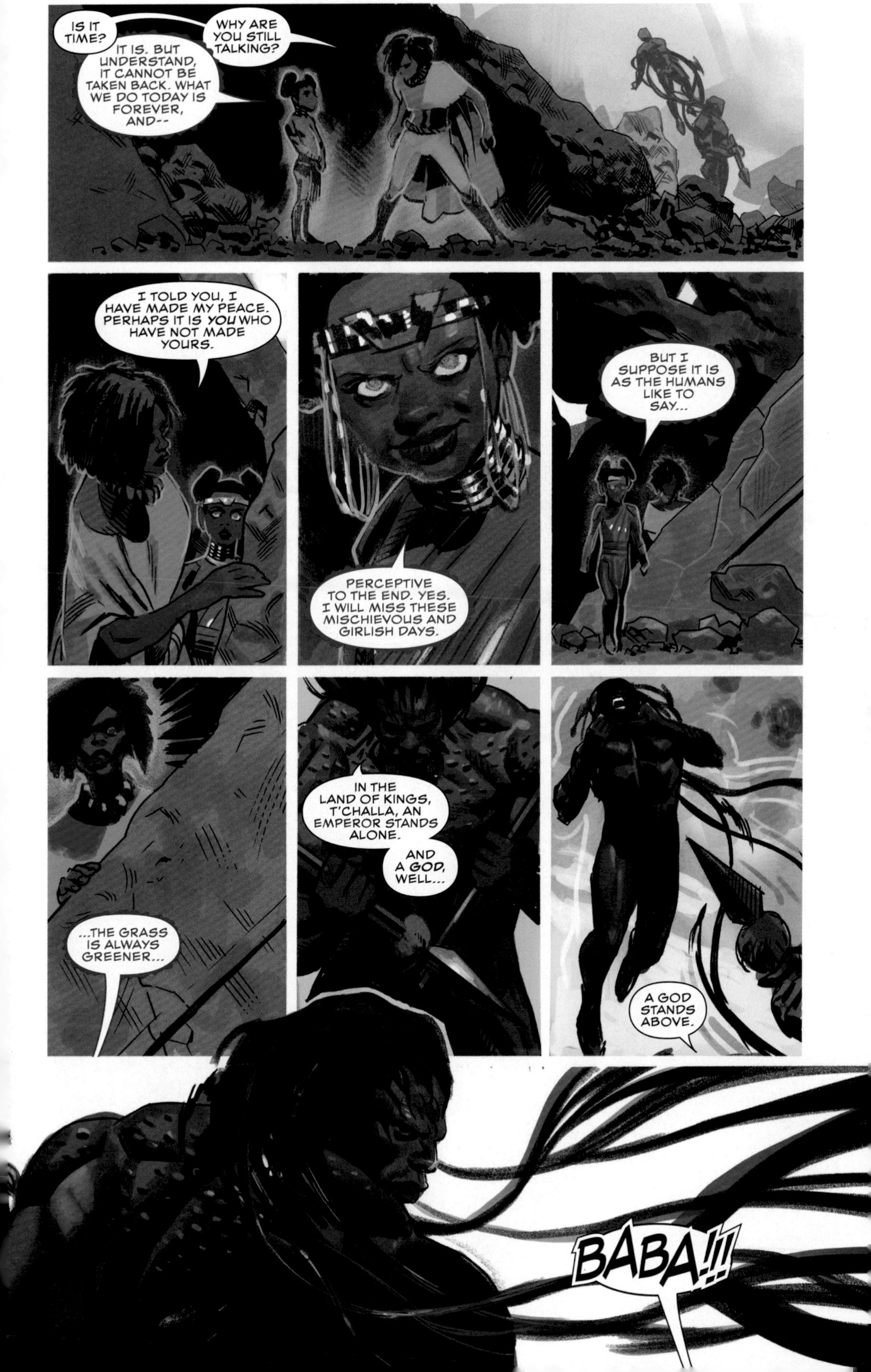
IS IT TIME?
IT IS. BUT UNDERSTAND, IT CANNOT BE TAKEN BACK. WHAT WE DO TODAY IS FOREVER, AND--
WHY ARE YOU STILL TALKING?
I TOLD YOU, I HAVE MADE MY PEACE. PERHAPS IT IS *YOU* WHO HAVE NOT MADE YOURS.
PERCEPTIVE TO THE END. YES. I WILL MISS THESE MISCHIEVOUS AND GIRLISH DAYS.
BUT I SUPPOSE IT IS AS THE HUMANS LIKE TO SAY...
...THE GRASS IS ALWAYS GREENER...
IN THE LAND OF KINGS, T'CHALLA, AN EMPEROR STANDS ALONE.
AND A *GOD*, WELL...
A GOD STANDS ABOVE.
BABA!!!

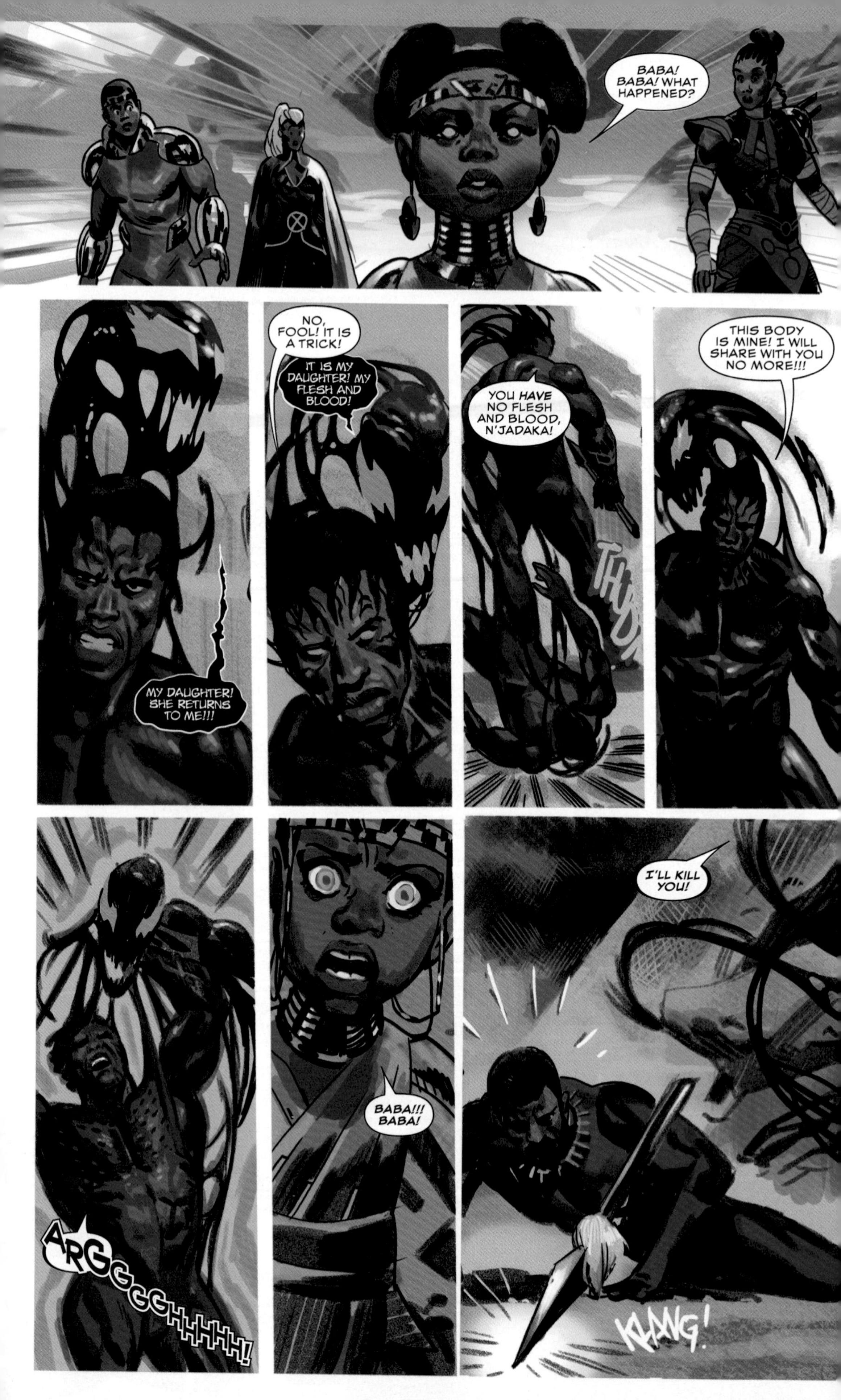
BABA! BABA! WHAT HAPPENED?
MY DAUGHTER! SHE RETURNS TO ME!!!
NO, FOOL! IT IS A TRICK!
IT IS MY DAUGHTER! MY FLESH AND BLOOD!
YOU HAVE NO FLESH AND BLOOD, N'JADAKA!
THUD!
THIS BODY IS MINE! I WILL SHARE WITH YOU NO MORE!!!
ARGGGGHHHHHH!
BABA!!! BABA!
I'LL KILL YOU!
KLANG!

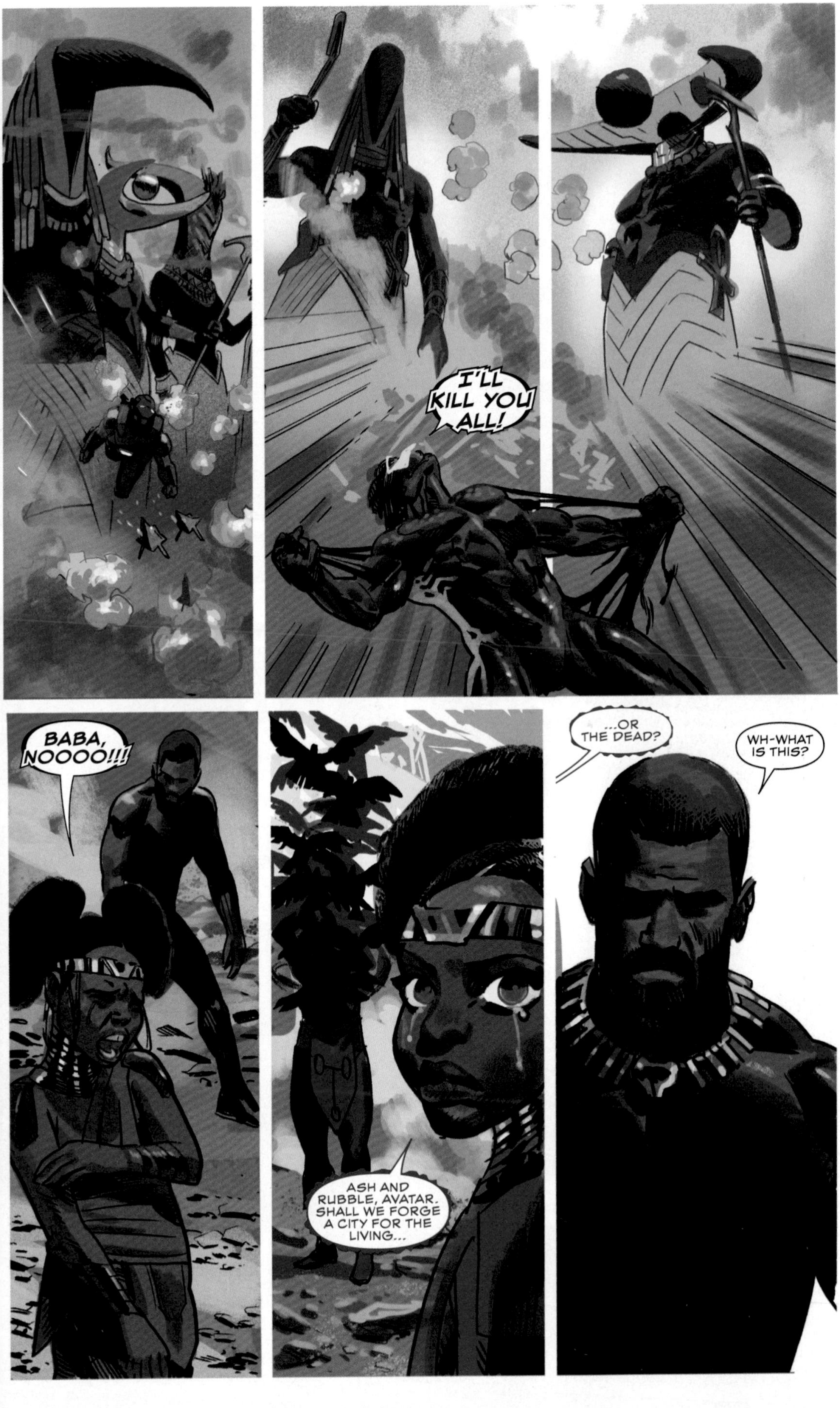
I'LL KILL YOU ALL!
BABA, NOOOO!!!
ASH AND RUBBLE, AVATAR. SHALL WE FORGE A CITY FOR THE LIVING...
...OR THE DEAD?
WH-WHAT IS THIS?

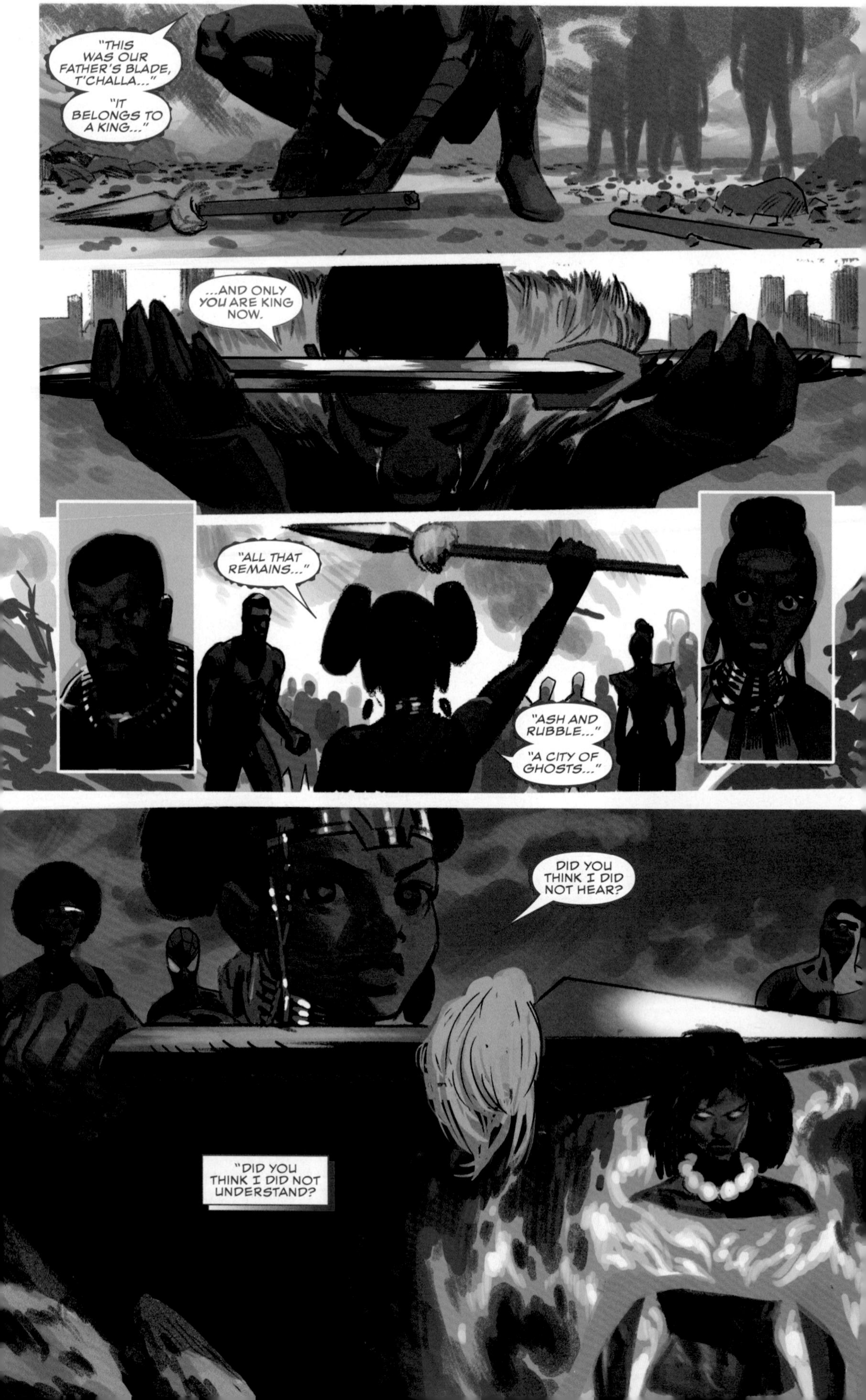
"THIS WAS OUR FATHER'S BLADE, T'CHALLA..."
"IT BELONGS TO A KING..."
...AND ONLY YOU ARE KING NOW.
"ALL THAT REMAINS..."
"ASH AND RUBBLE..."
"A CITY OF GHOSTS..."
DID YOU THINK I DID NOT HEAR?
"DID YOU THINK I DID NOT UNDERSTAND?

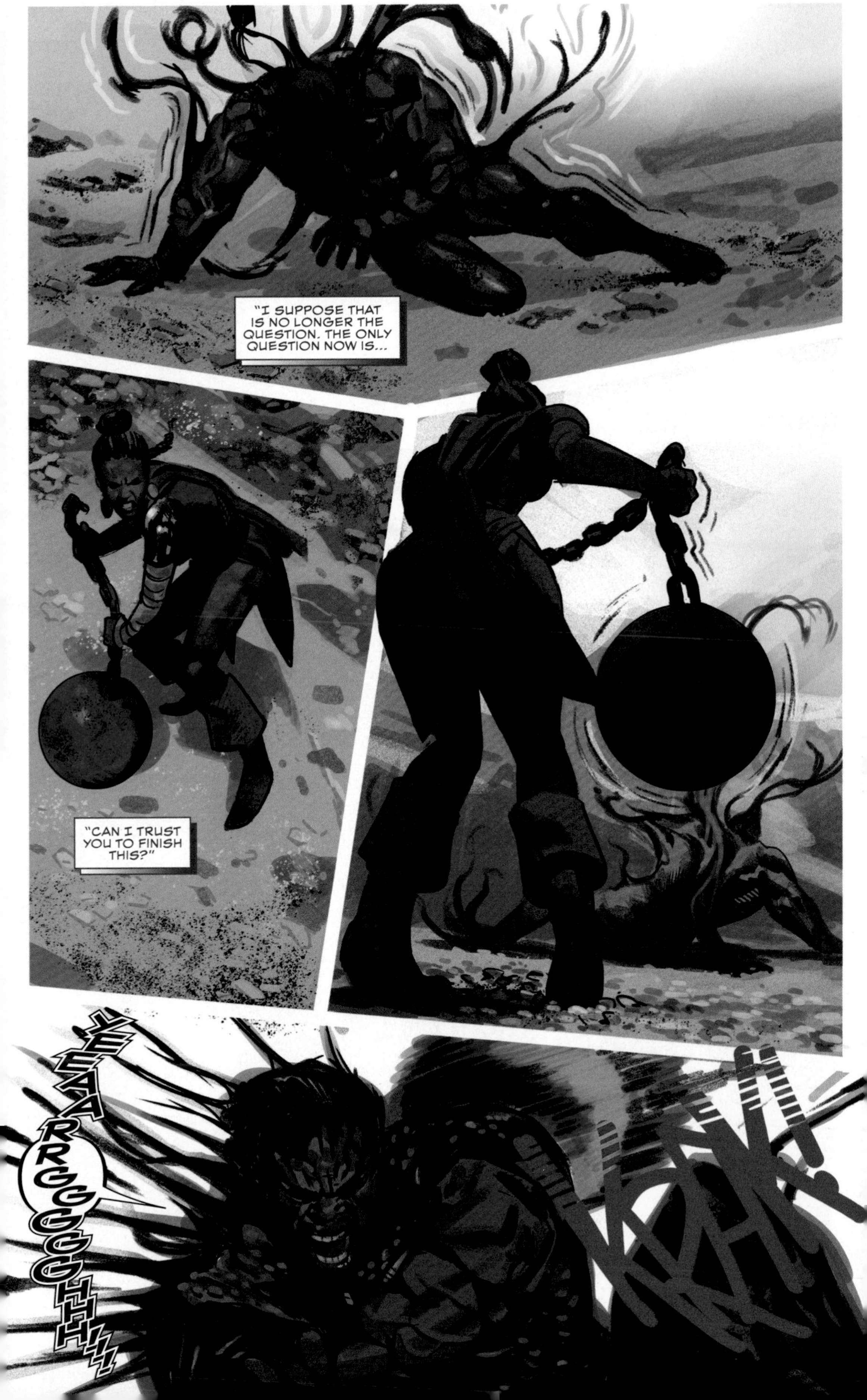
"I SUPPOSE THAT IS NO LONGER THE QUESTION. THE ONLY QUESTION NOW IS...
"CAN I TRUST YOU TO FINISH THIS?"
YEEAARRGGGGHHH!!!
KRAK!!

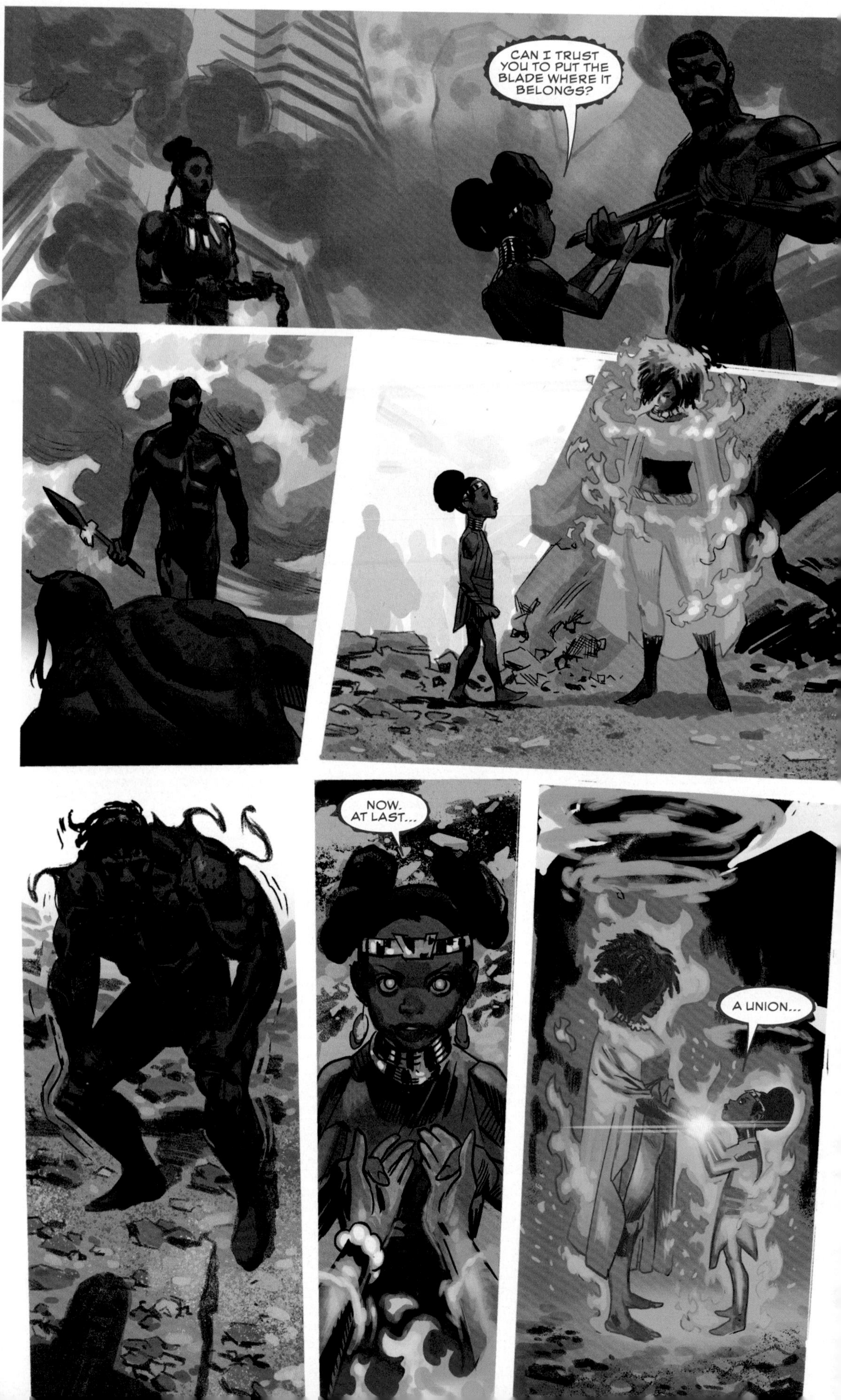
CAN I TRUST YOU TO PUT THE BLADE WHERE IT BELONGS?
NOW. AT LAST...
A UNION...

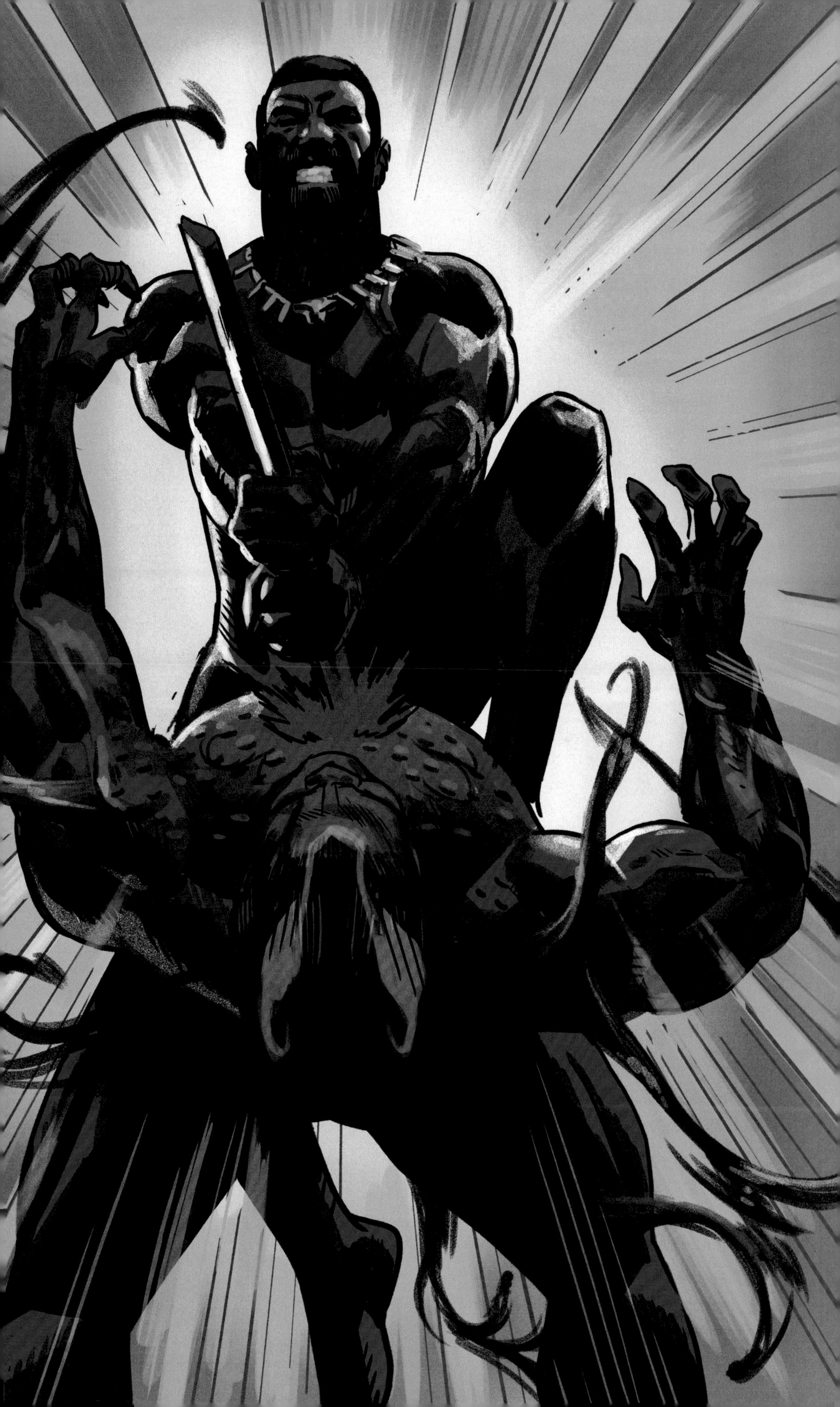

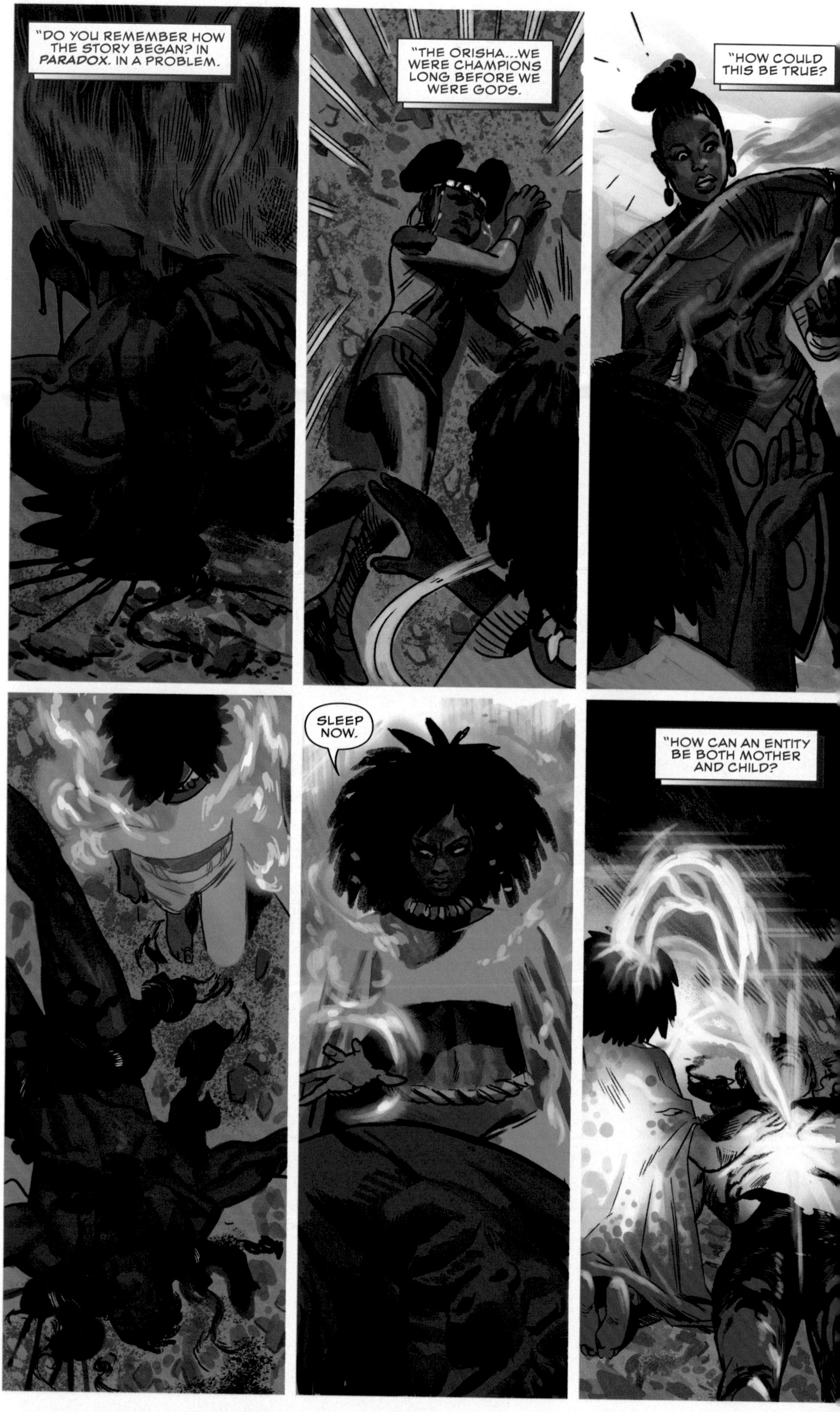
"DO YOU REMEMBER HOW THE STORY BEGAN? IN *PARADOX*. IN A PROBLEM.
"THE ORISHA...WE WERE CHAMPIONS LONG BEFORE WE WERE GODS.
"HOW COULD THIS BE TRUE?
SLEEP NOW.
"HOW CAN AN ENTITY BE BOTH MOTHER AND CHILD?

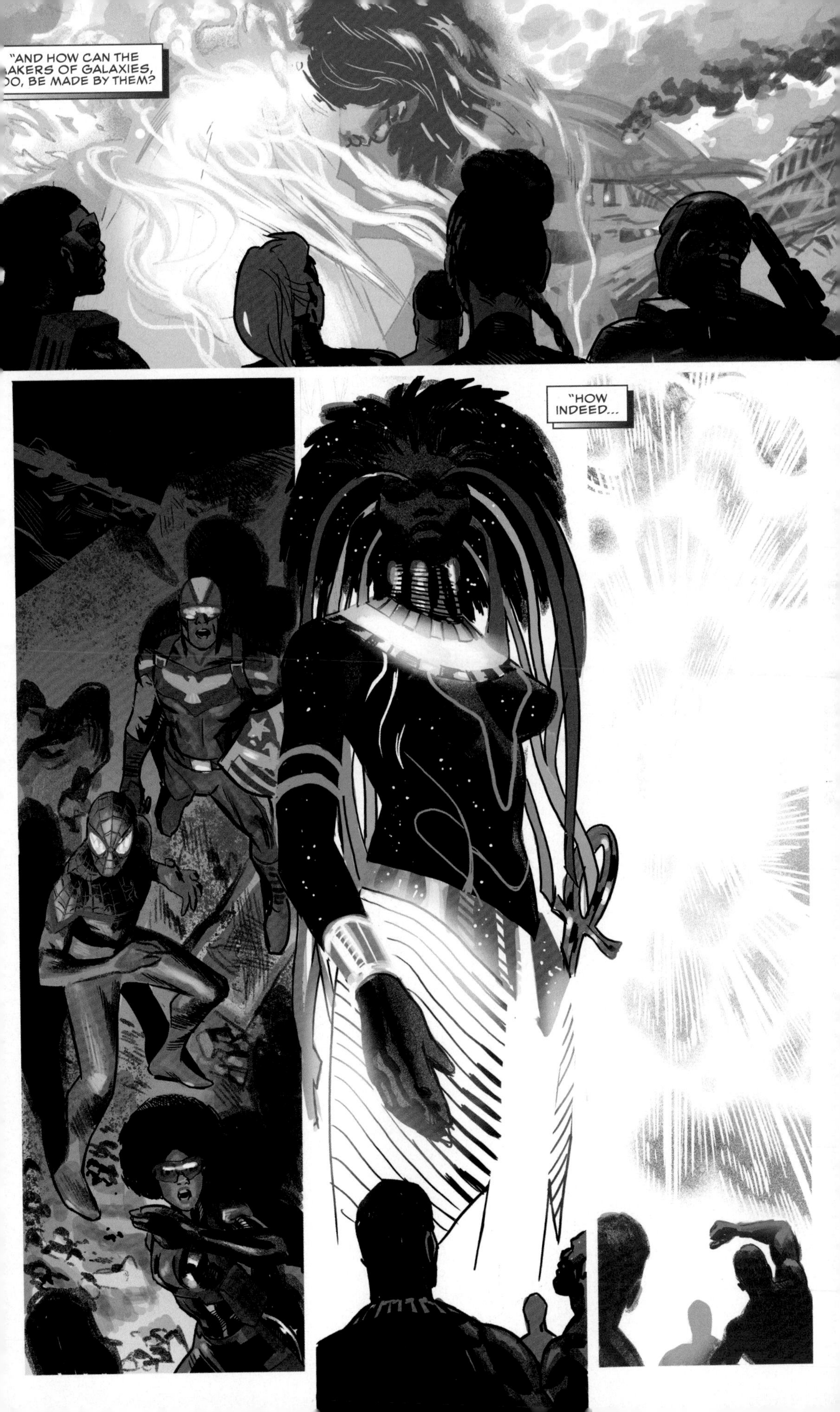
"AND HOW CAN THE
AKERS OF GALAXIES,
DO, BE MADE BY THEM?
"HOW
INDEED...

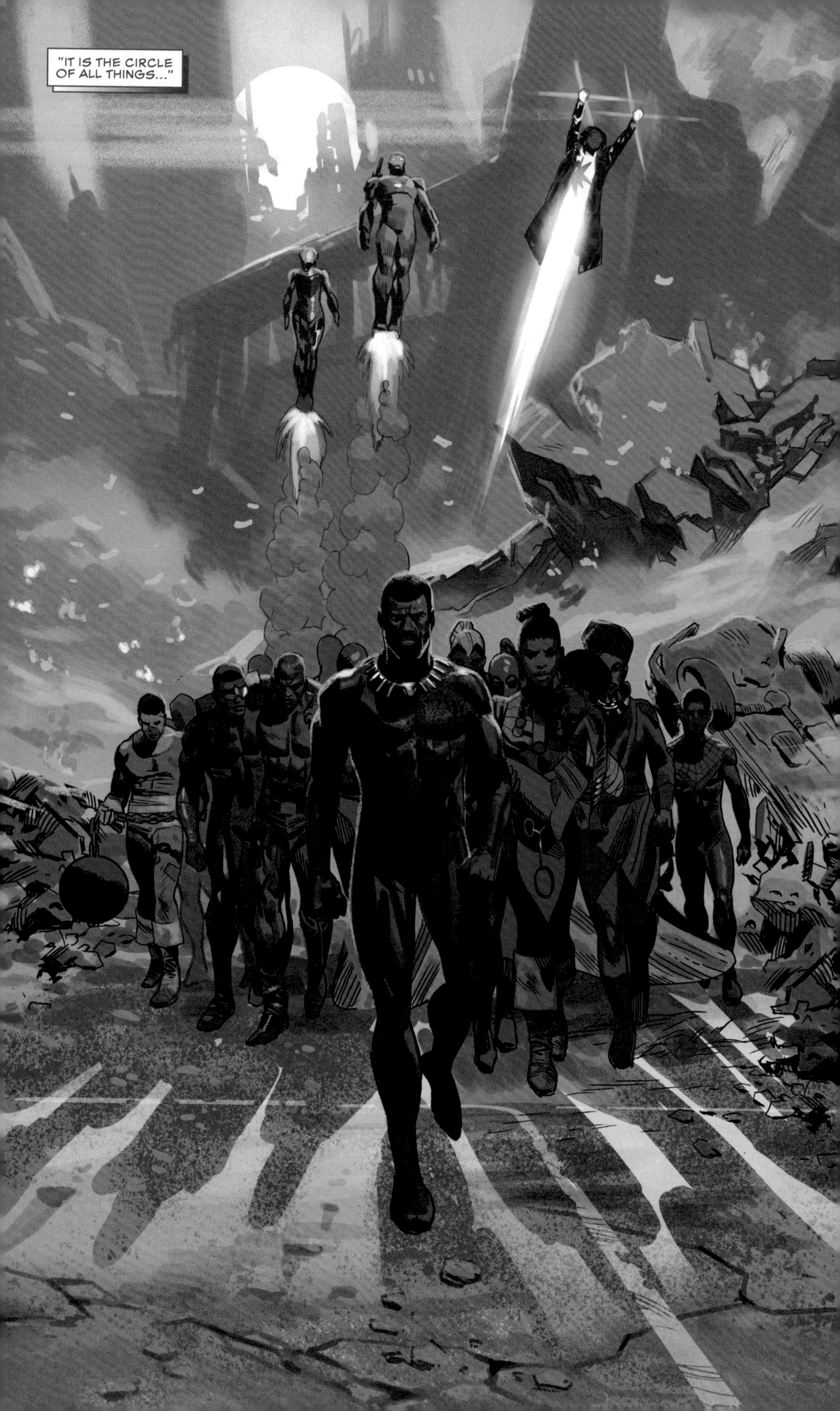
"IT IS THE CIRCLE OF ALL THINGS..."

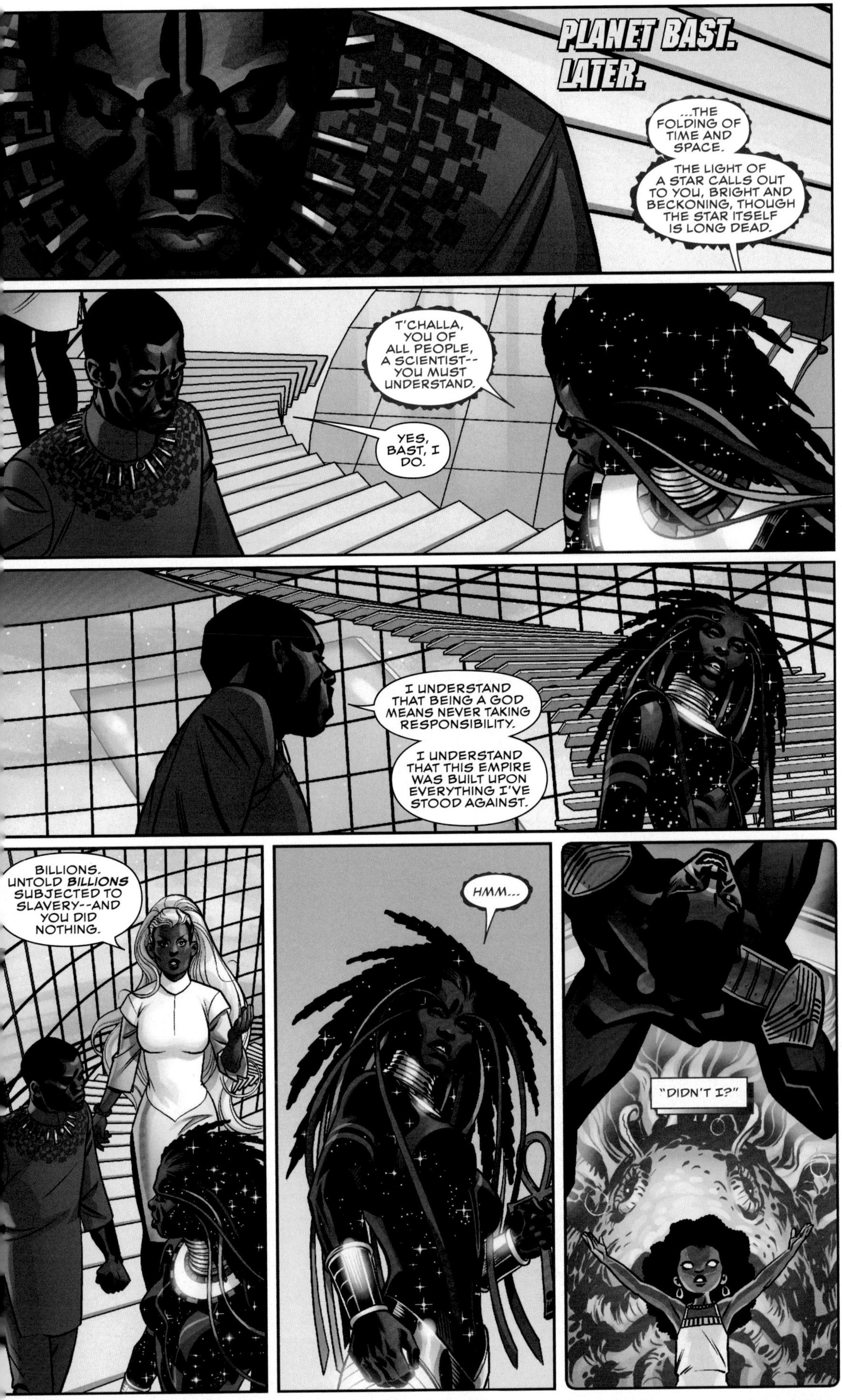
PLANET BAST. LATER.
...THE FOLDING OF TIME AND SPACE.
THE LIGHT OF A STAR CALLS OUT TO YOU, BRIGHT AND BECKONING, THOUGH THE STAR ITSELF IS LONG DEAD.
T'CHALLA, YOU OF ALL PEOPLE, A SCIENTIST-- YOU MUST UNDERSTAND.
YES, BAST, I DO.
I UNDERSTAND THAT BEING A GOD MEANS NEVER TAKING RESPONSIBILITY.
I UNDERSTAND THAT THIS EMPIRE WAS BUILT UPON EVERYTHING I'VE STOOD AGAINST.
BILLIONS. UNTOLD *BILLIONS* SUBJECTED TO SLAVERY--AND YOU DID NOTHING.
HMM...
"DIDN'T I?"

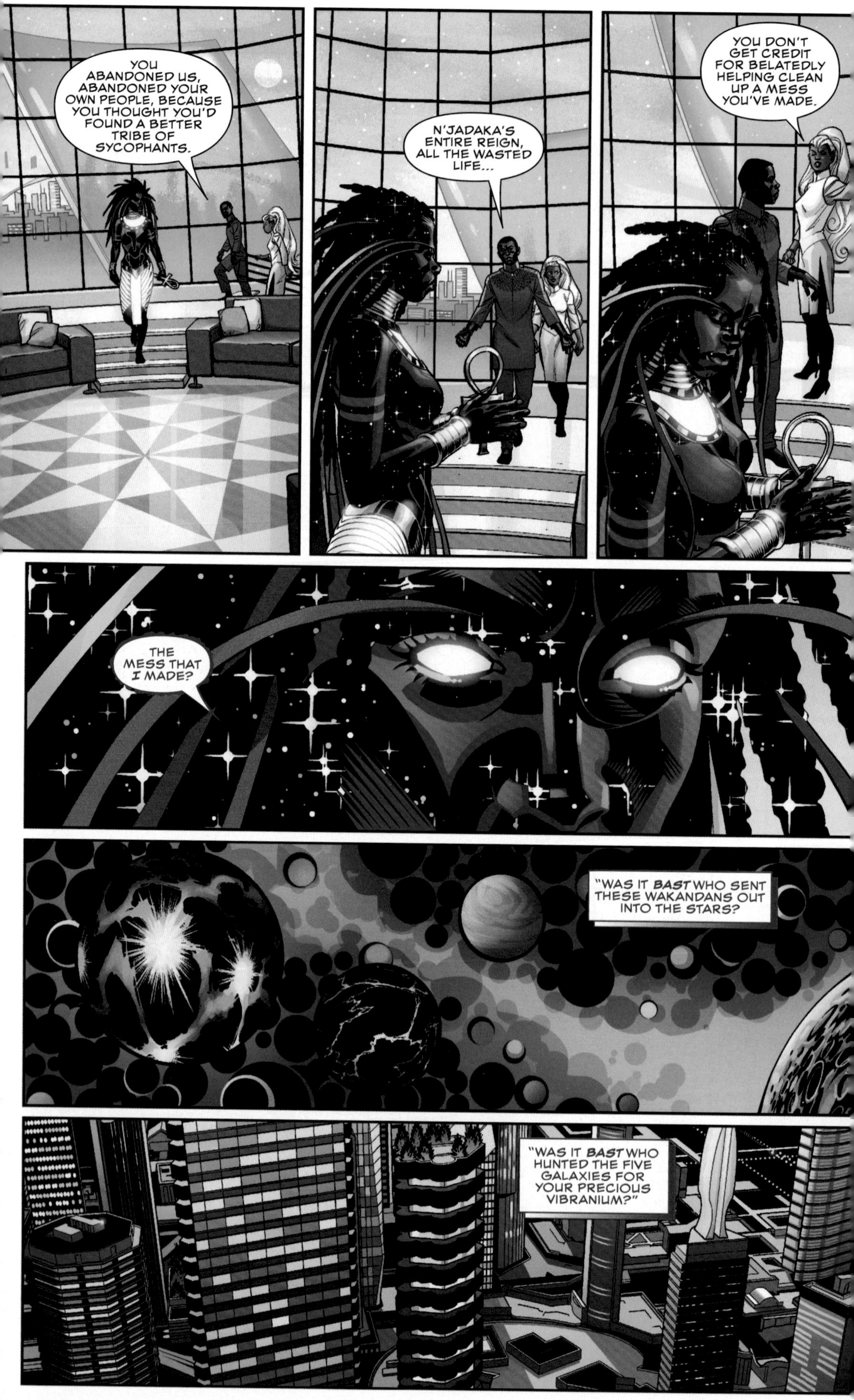
YOU ABANDONED US, ABANDONED YOUR OWN PEOPLE, BECAUSE YOU THOUGHT YOU'D FOUND A BETTER TRIBE OF SYCOPHANTS.
N'JADAKA'S ENTIRE REIGN, ALL THE WASTED LIFE...
YOU DON'T GET CREDIT FOR BELATEDLY HELPING CLEAN UP A MESS YOU'VE MADE.
THE MESS THAT I MADE?
"WAS IT BAST WHO SENT THESE WAKANDANS OUT INTO THE STARS?
"WAS IT BAST WHO HUNTED THE FIVE GALAXIES FOR YOUR PRECIOUS VIBRANIUM?"

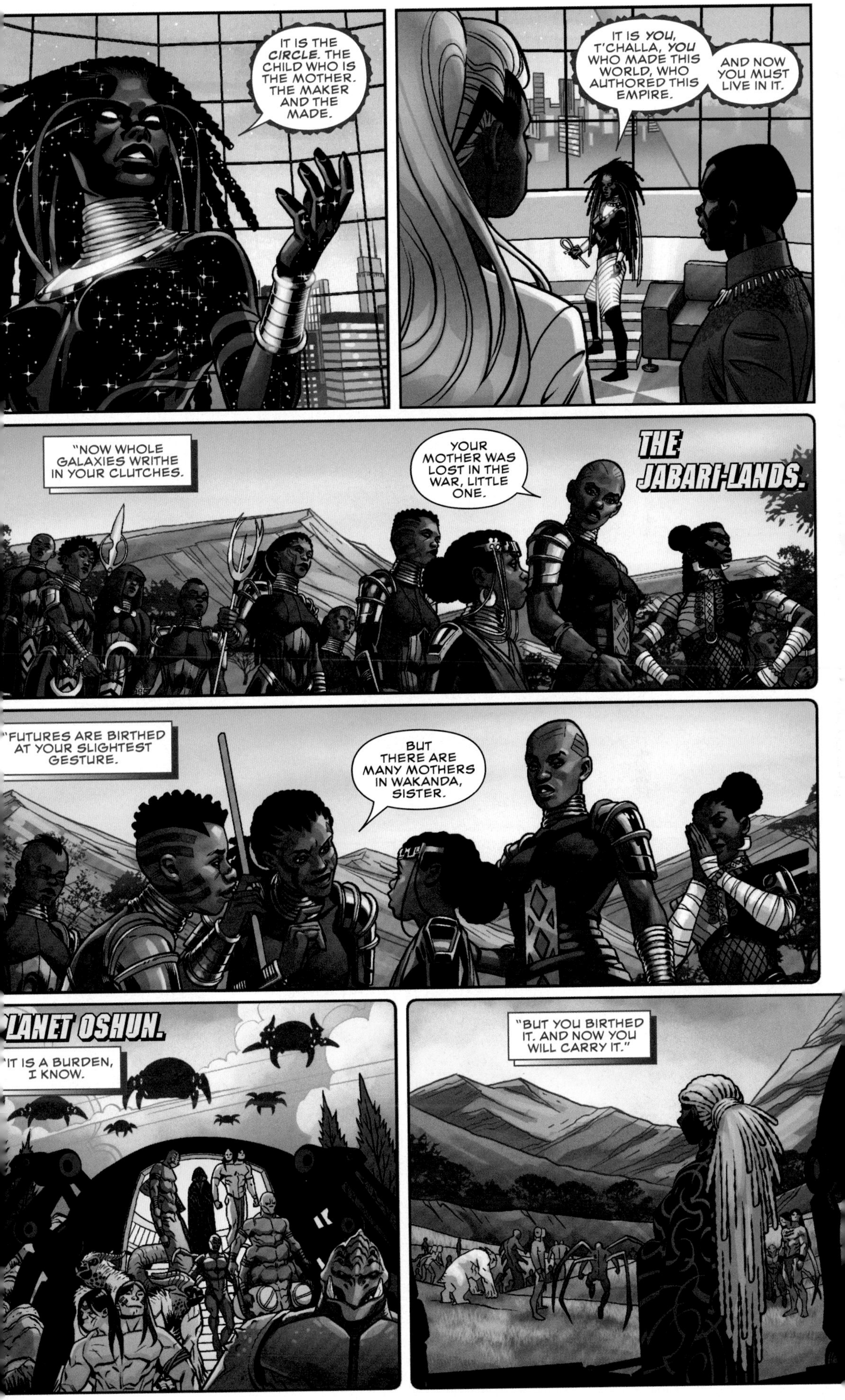

IT IS THE CIRCLE. THE CHILD WHO IS THE MOTHER. THE MAKER AND THE MADE.
IT IS YOU, T'CHALLA, YOU WHO MADE THIS WORLD, WHO AUTHORED THIS EMPIRE.
AND NOW YOU MUST LIVE IN IT.
"NOW WHOLE GALAXIES WRITHE IN YOUR CLUTCHES.
YOUR MOTHER WAS LOST IN THE WAR, LITTLE ONE.
THE JABARI-LANDS.
"FUTURES ARE BIRTHED AT YOUR SLIGHTEST GESTURE.
BUT THERE ARE MANY MOTHERS IN WAKANDA, SISTER.
LANET OSHUN.
"IT IS A BURDEN, I KNOW.
"BUT YOU BIRTHED IT. AND NOW YOU WILL CARRY IT."

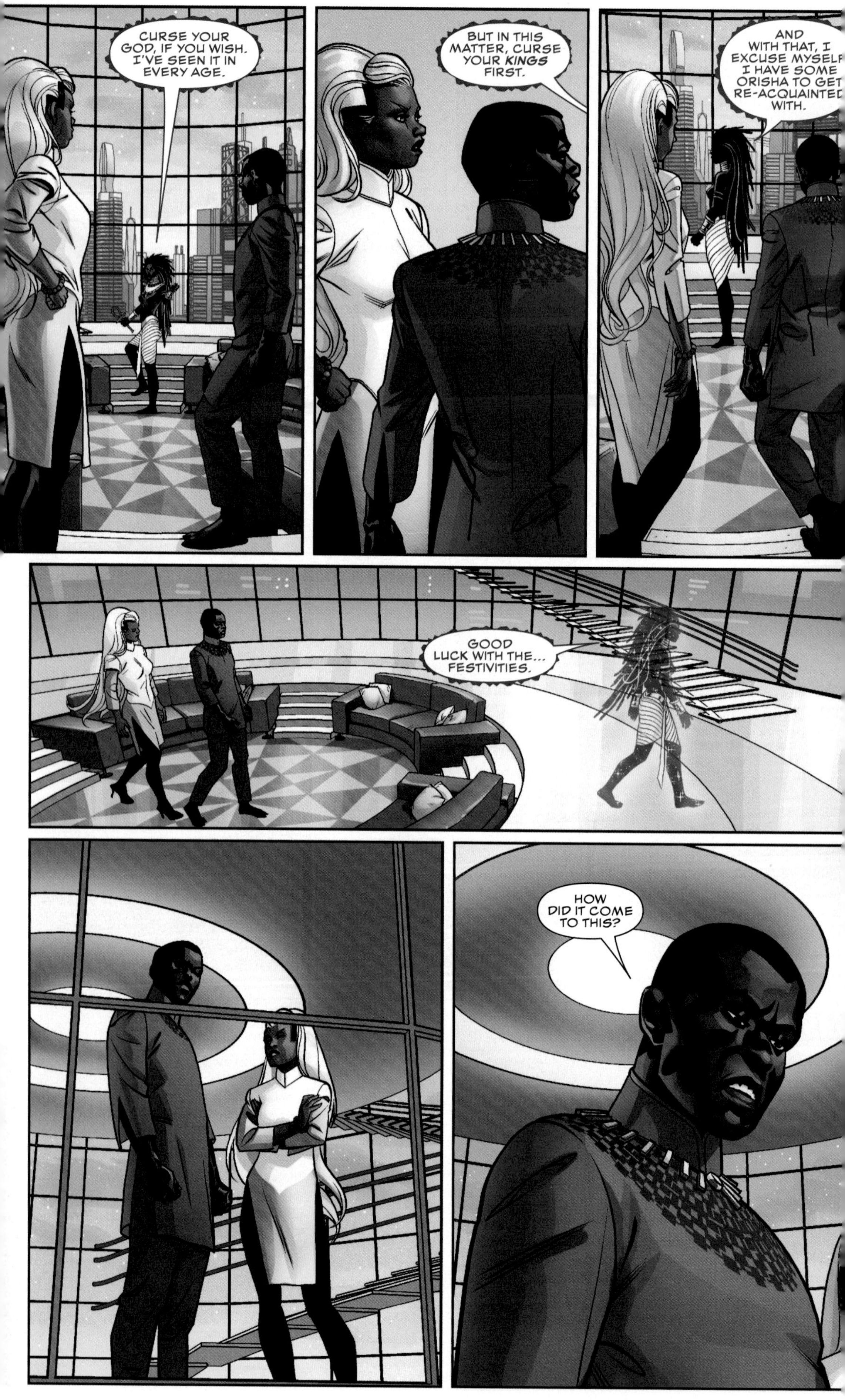
CURSE YOUR GOD, IF YOU WISH. I'VE SEEN IT IN EVERY AGE.
BUT IN THIS MATTER, CURSE YOUR *KINGS* FIRST.
AND WITH THAT, I EXCUSE MYSELF. I HAVE SOME ORISHA TO GET RE-ACQUAINTED WITH.
GOOD LUCK WITH THE... FESTIVITIES.
HOW DID IT COME TO THIS?

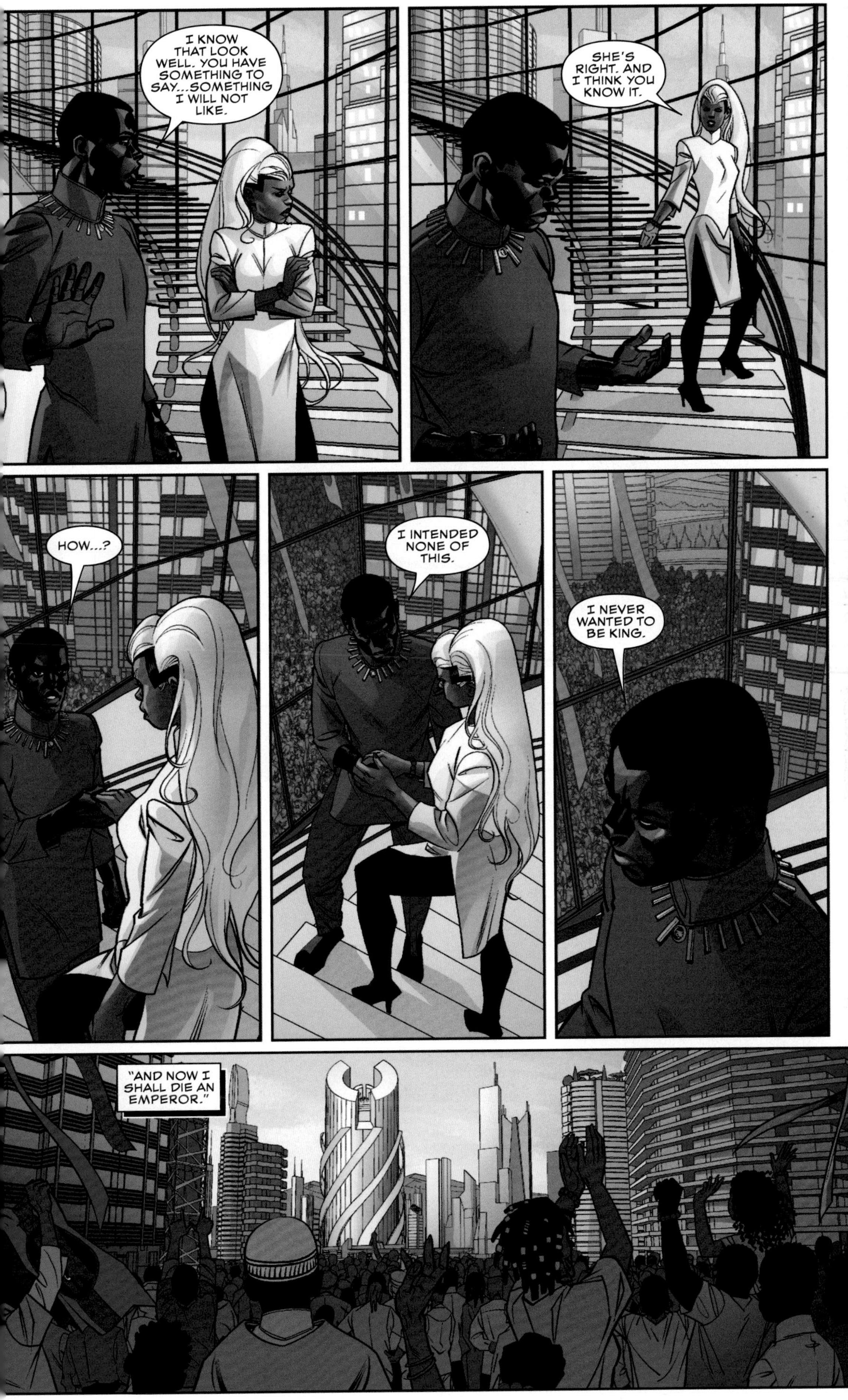
I KNOW THAT LOOK WELL. YOU HAVE SOMETHING TO SAY...SOMETHING I WILL NOT LIKE.
SHE'S RIGHT. AND I THINK YOU KNOW IT.
HOW...?
I INTENDED NONE OF THIS.
I NEVER WANTED TO BE KING.
"AND NOW I SHALL DIE AN EMPEROR."

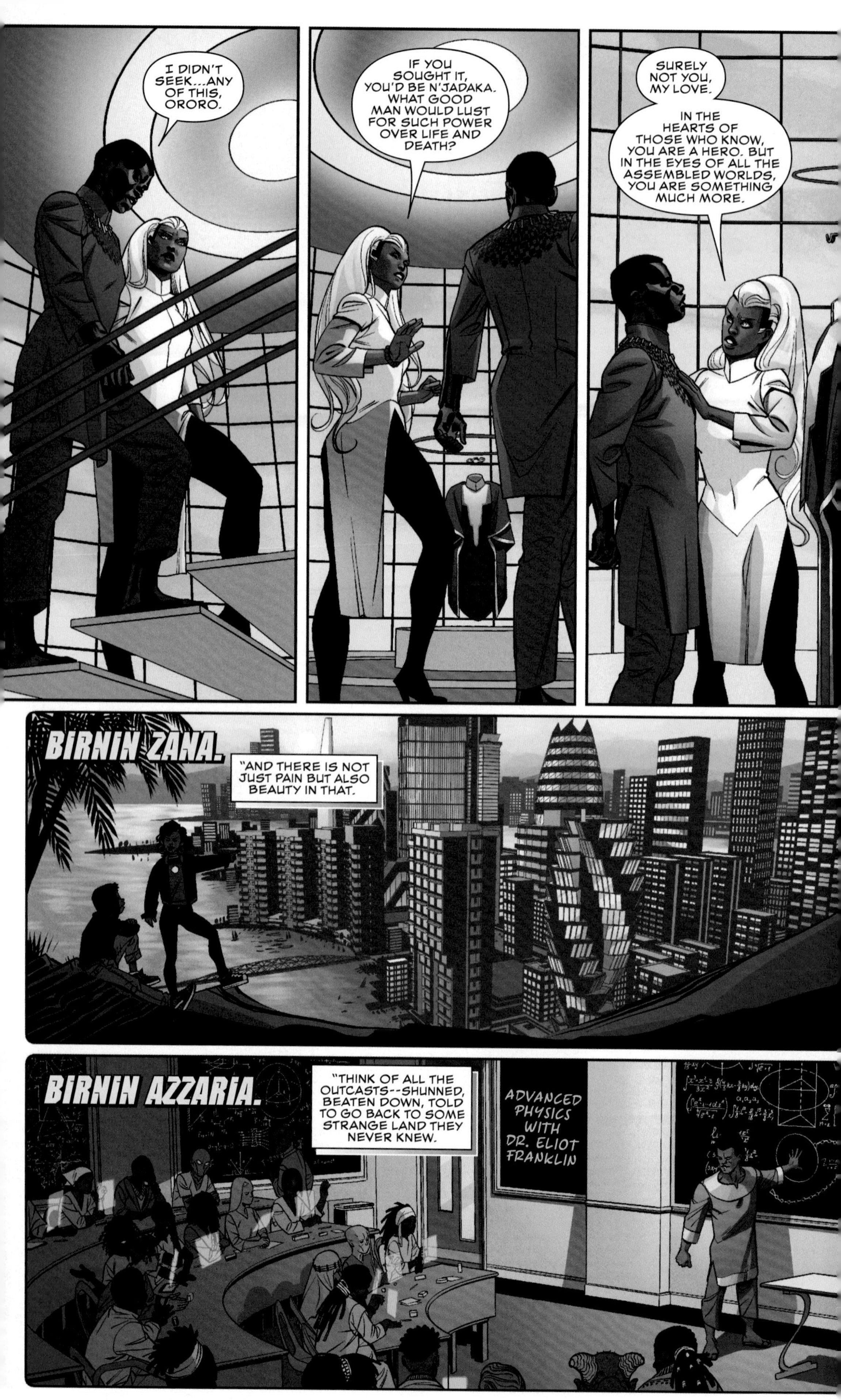
I DIDN'T SEEK...ANY OF THIS, ORORO.
IF YOU SOUGHT IT, YOU'D BE N'JADAKA. WHAT GOOD MAN WOULD LUST FOR SUCH POWER OVER LIFE AND DEATH?
SURELY NOT YOU, MY LOVE.
IN THE HEARTS OF THOSE WHO KNOW, YOU ARE A HERO. BUT IN THE EYES OF ALL THE ASSEMBLED WORLDS, YOU ARE SOMETHING MUCH MORE.
BIRNIN ZANA.
"AND THERE IS NOT JUST PAIN BUT ALSO BEAUTY IN THAT.
BIRNIN AZZARIA.
"THINK OF ALL THE OUTCASTS--SHUNNED, BEATEN DOWN, TOLD TO GO BACK TO SOME STRANGE LAND THEY NEVER KNEW.
ADVANCED PHYSICS WITH DR. ELIOT FRANKLIN

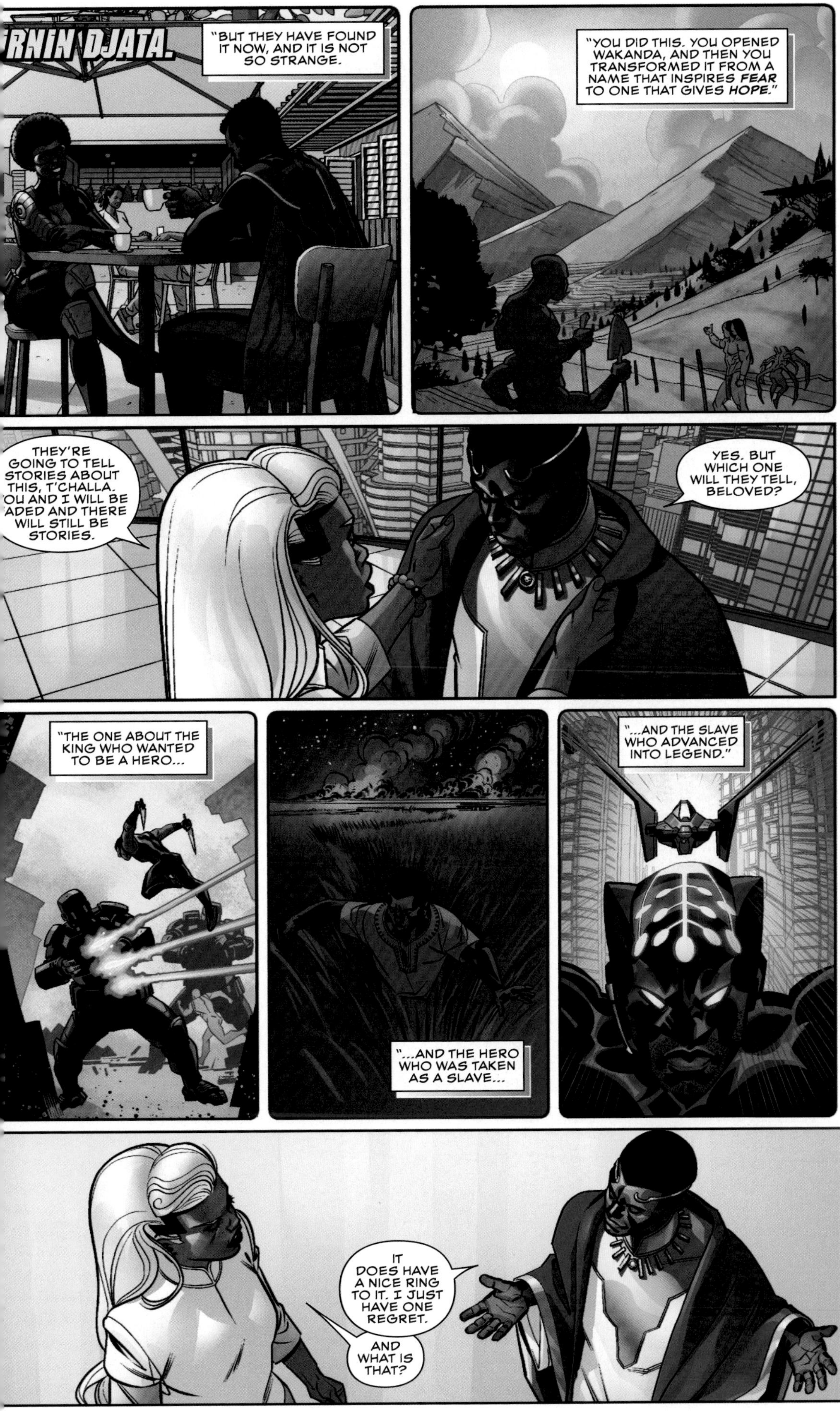
RNIN DJATA.
"BUT THEY HAVE FOUND IT NOW, AND IT IS NOT SO STRANGE.
"YOU DID THIS. YOU OPENED WAKANDA, AND THEN YOU TRANSFORMED IT FROM A NAME THAT INSPIRES FEAR TO ONE THAT GIVES HOPE."
THEY'RE GOING TO TELL STORIES ABOUT THIS, T'CHALLA. OU AND I WILL BE ADED AND THERE WILL STILL BE STORIES.
YES. BUT WHICH ONE WILL THEY TELL, BELOVED?
"THE ONE ABOUT THE KING WHO WANTED TO BE A HERO...
"...AND THE HERO WHO WAS TAKEN AS A SLAVE...
"...AND THE SLAVE WHO ADVANCED INTO LEGEND."
IT DOES HAVE A NICE RING TO IT. I JUST HAVE ONE REGRET.
AND WHAT IS THAT?

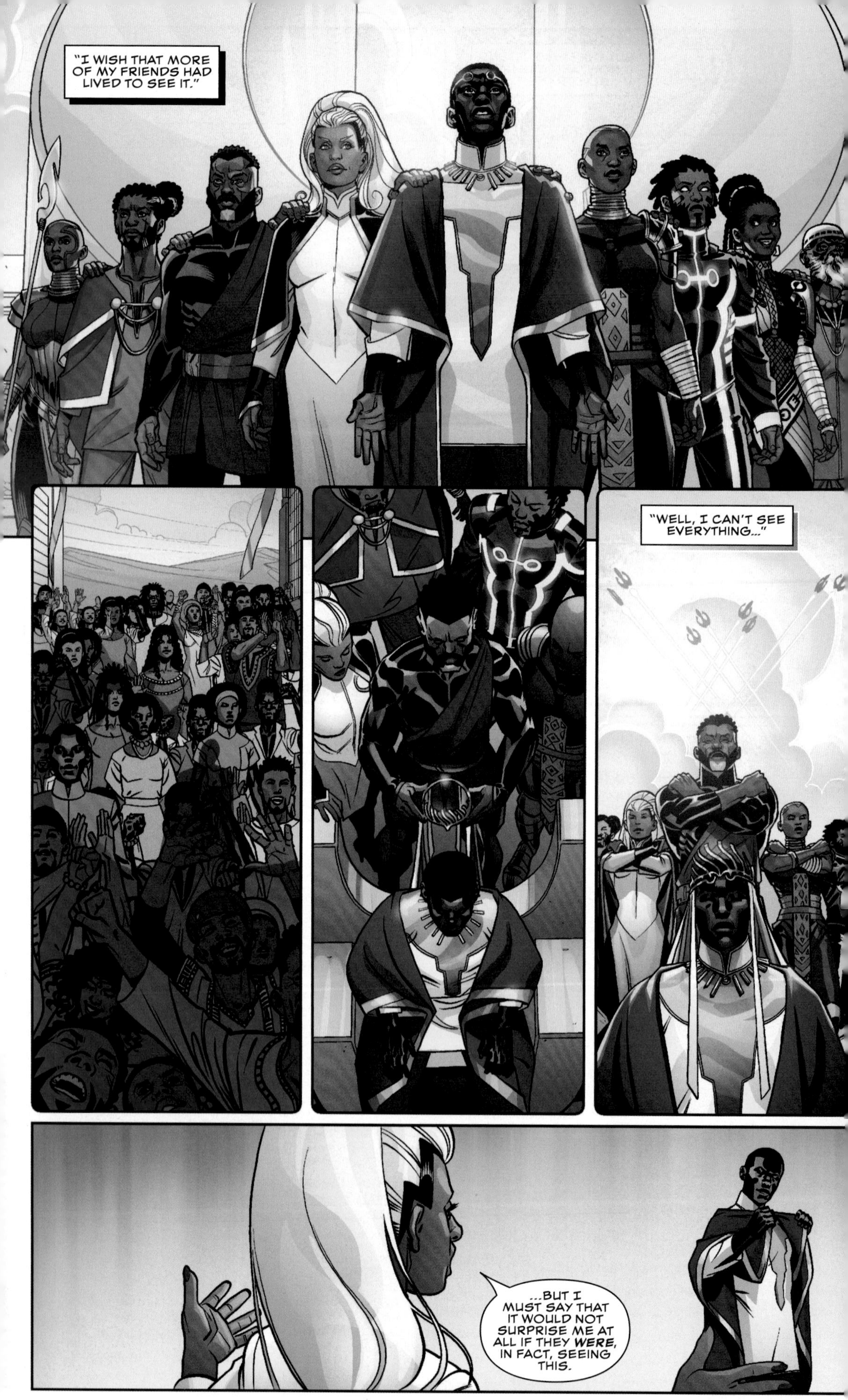
"I WISH THAT MORE OF MY FRIENDS HAD LIVED TO SEE IT."
"WELL, I CAN'T SEE EVERYTHING..."
...BUT I MUST SAY THAT IT WOULD NOT SURPRISE ME AT ALL IF THEY *WERE*, IN FACT, SEEING THIS.

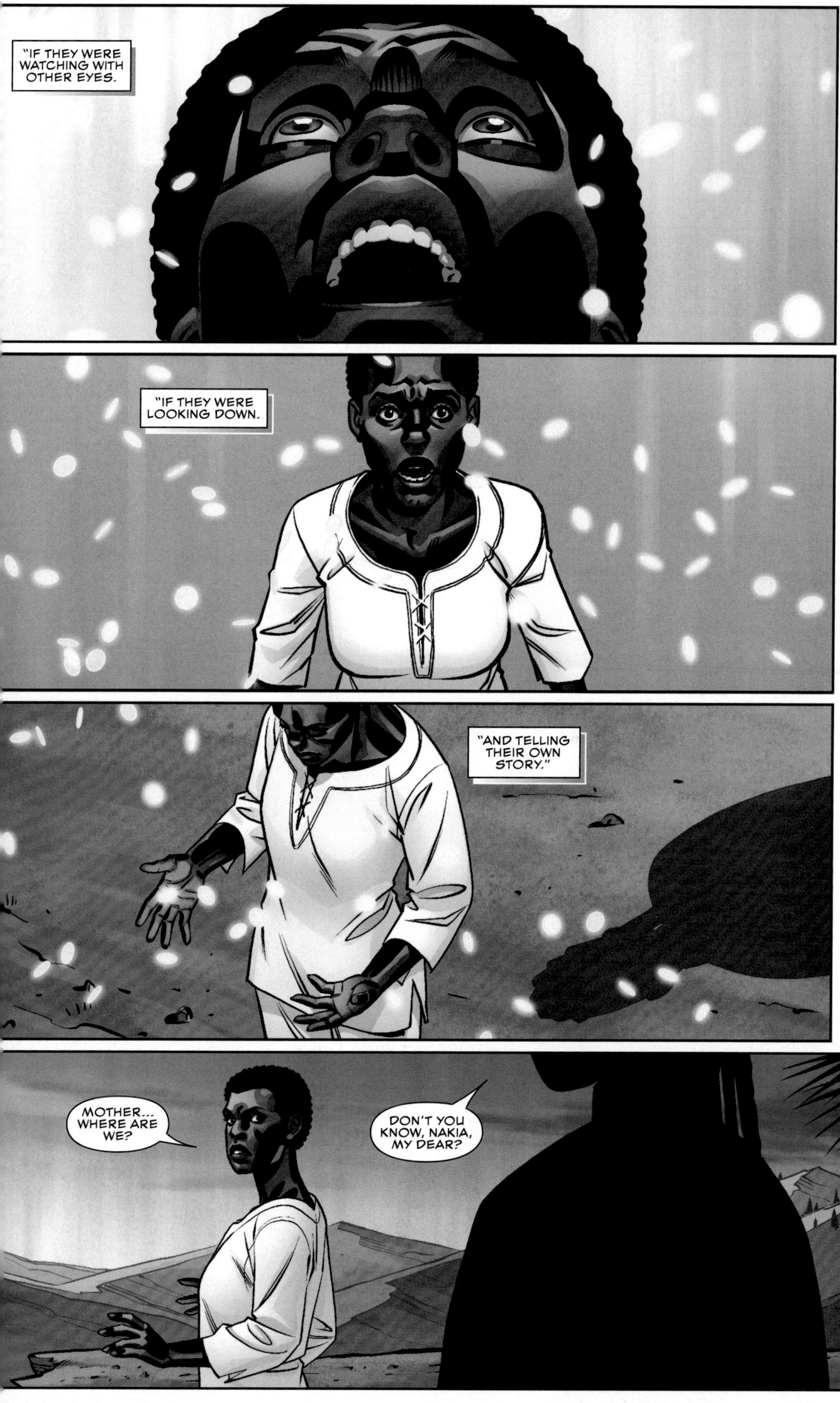

"IF THEY WERE WATCHING WITH OTHER EYES.
"IF THEY WERE LOOKING DOWN.
"AND TELLING THEIR OWN STORY."
MOTHER... WHERE ARE WE?
DON'T YOU KNOW, NAKIA, MY DEAR?

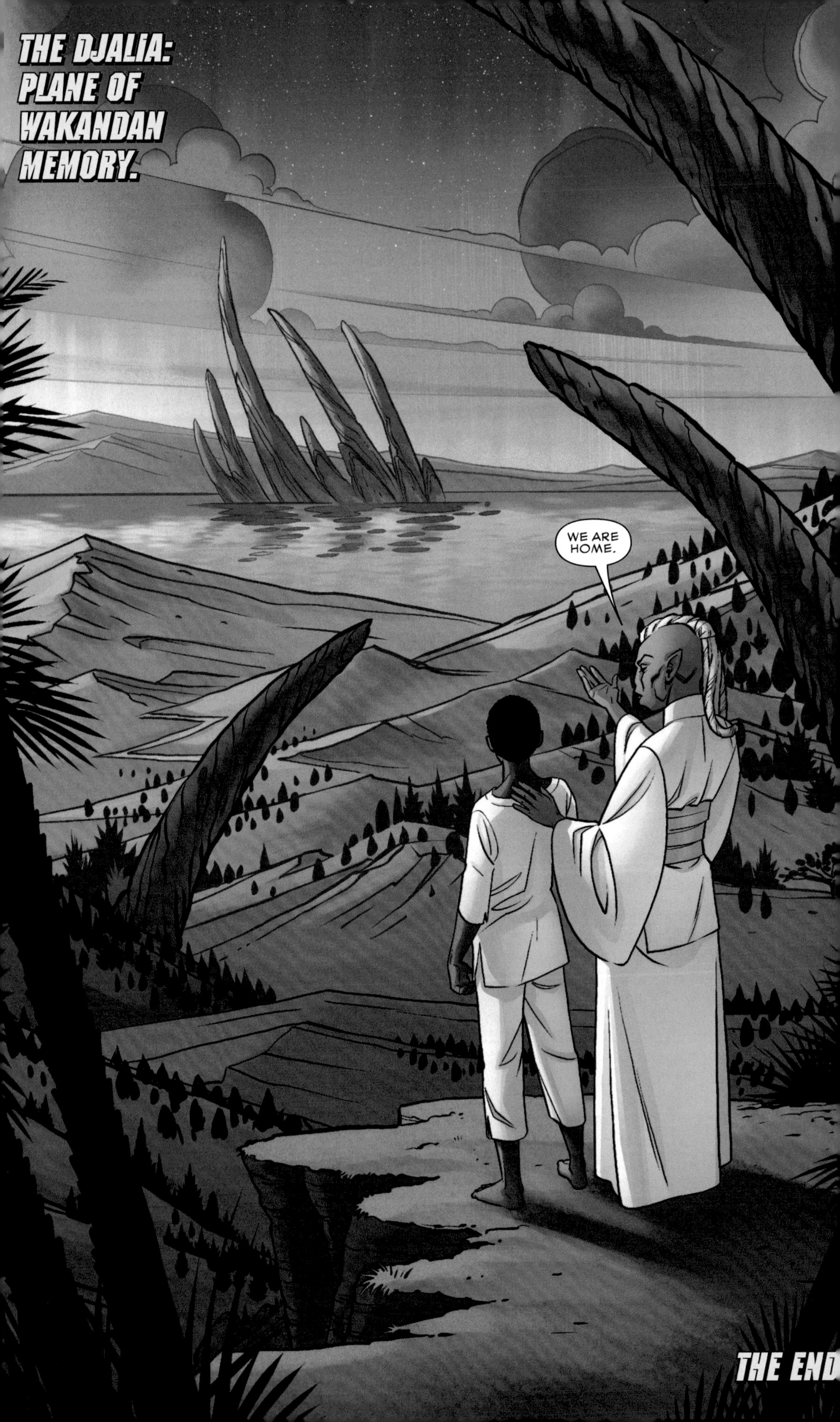
THE DJALIA: PLANE OF WAKANDAN MEMORY.
WE ARE HOME.
THE END

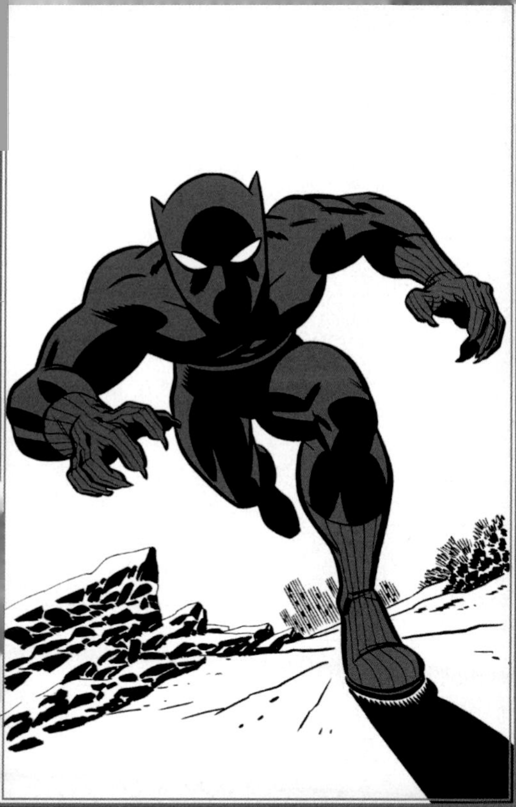

Michael Cho
24 TWO-TONE VARIANT

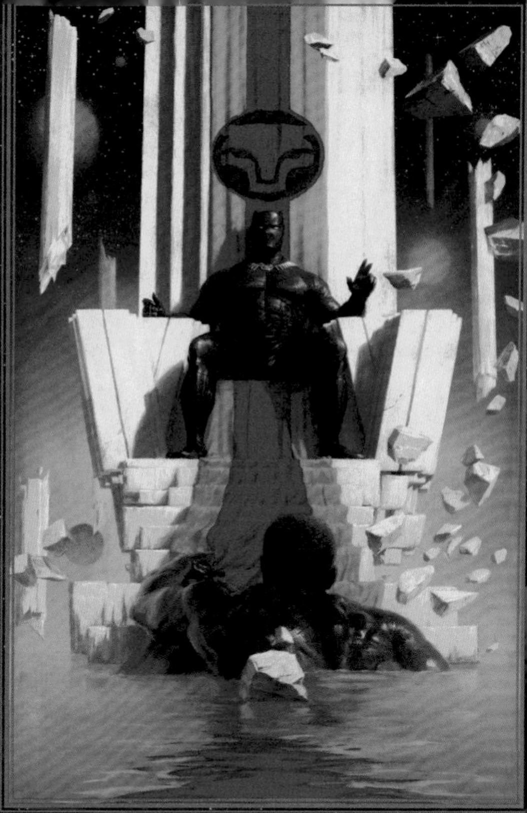

Sam Spratt
25 VARIANT

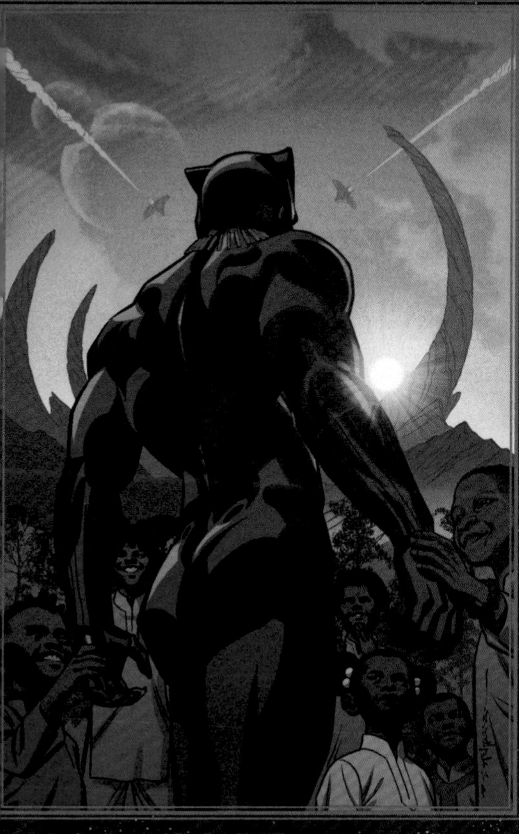

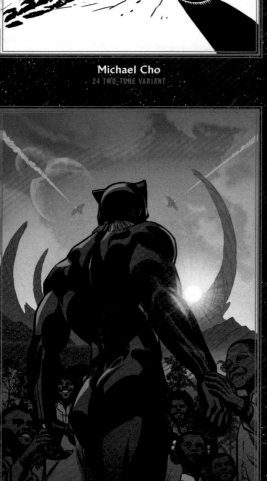

Brian Stelfreeze

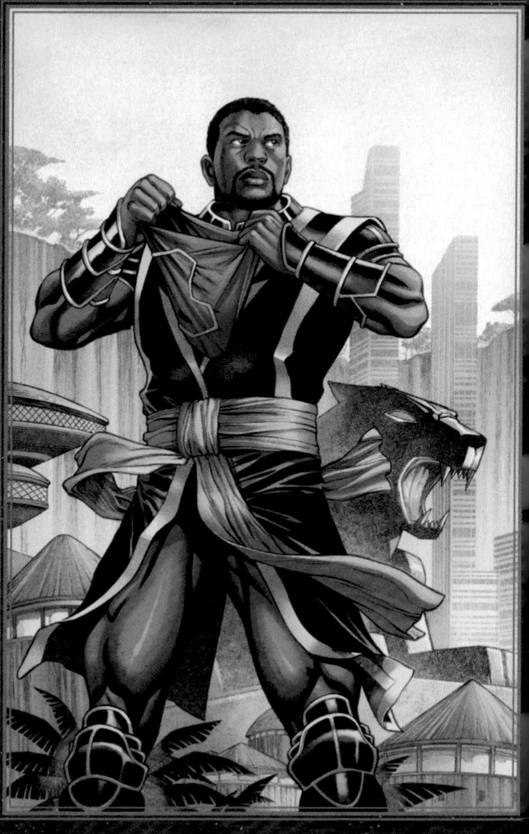

Carlos Pacheco, Rafael Fonteriz & Rachelle Rosenberg

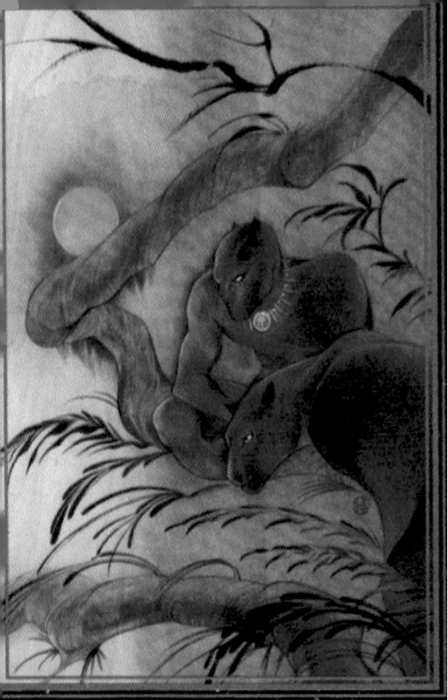

Peach Momoko
25 NIHONGA FINE ART VARIANT

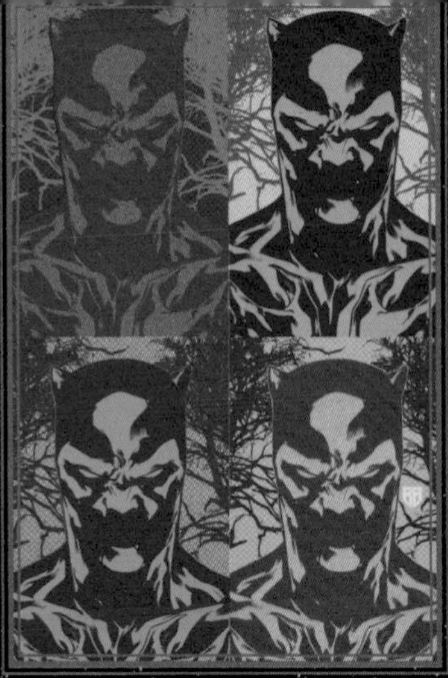

R.B. Silva
25 POP ART FINE ART VARIANT

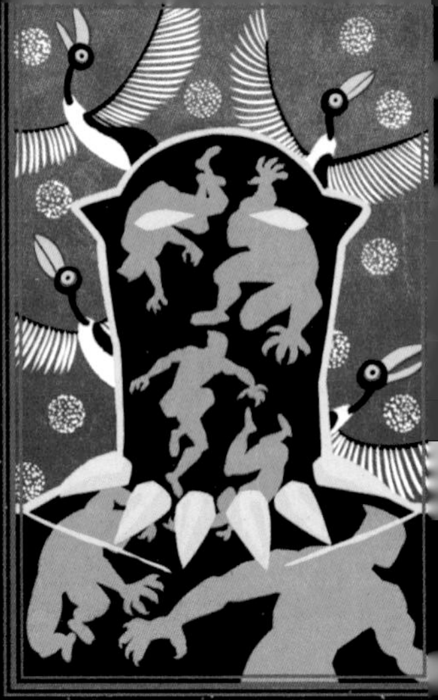

Natacha Bustos
25 ART BRUT-AFRICAN FINE ART VARIANT

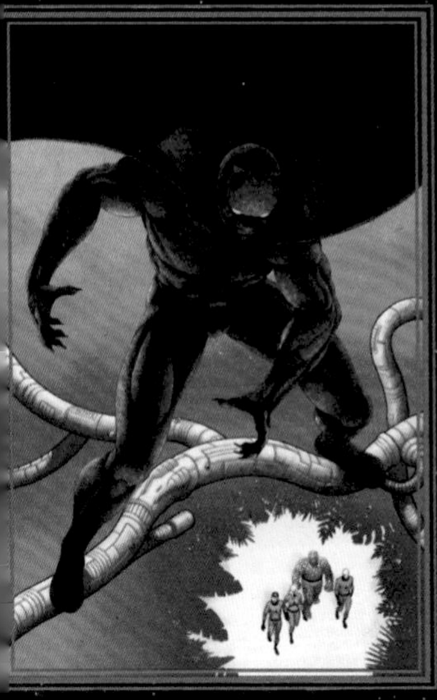

Juann Cabal & Richard Isanove
25 FLEMISH RENAISSANCE FINE ART VARIANT

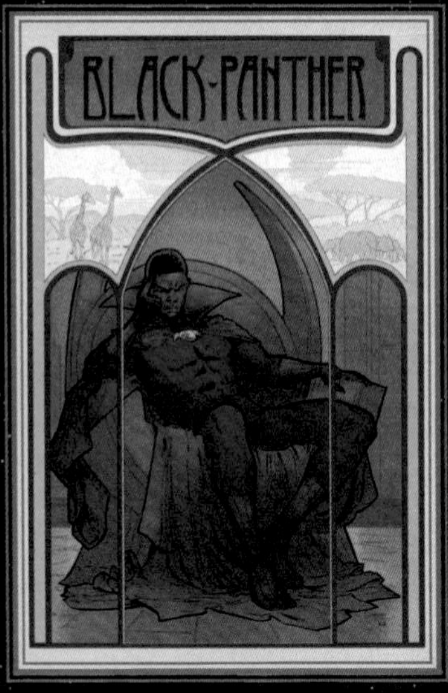
BLACK PANTHER

Carmen Carnero & Matthew Wilson
25 ART NOUVEAU FINE ART VARIANT

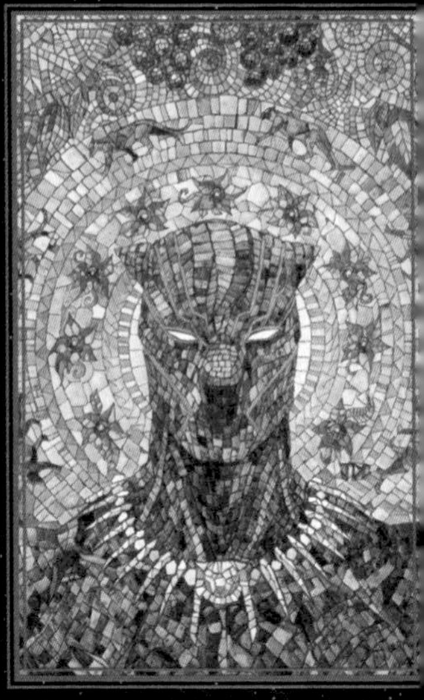

Joshua Cassara
25 BYZANTINE FINE ART VARIANT

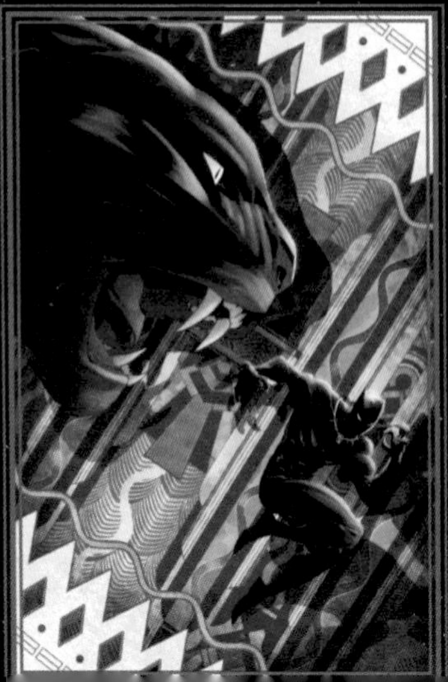

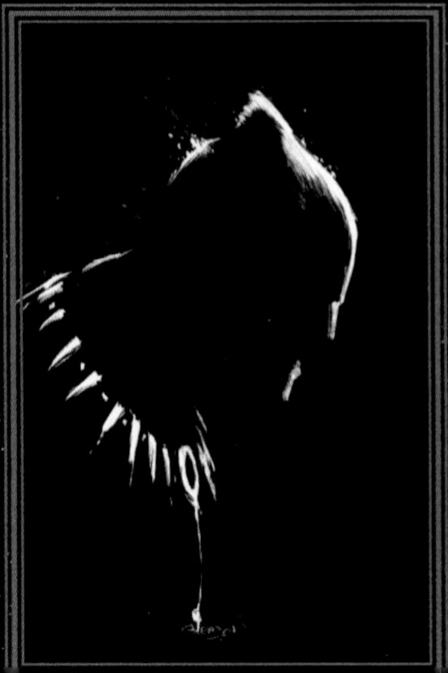